FLAMES OF WAR®

THE COMPLETE INTELLIGENCE HANDBOOK FOR FORCES IN

AFRIKA

AND THE MEDITERRANEAN 1942-1943

MID-1942-1943

Written By: Phil Yates, Jason Moffatt
Editors: Peter Simunovich, John-Paul Brisigotti
Photography: Battlefront Studio
Photographs: National Library of New Zealand, Imperial War Museum, Bovington Tank Museum, Australian War Memorial, Roger Key Private Collection, NARA, National Archives Of Canada, www.ww2modelmaker.com
Stories: David Billinghurst, Jon Cleaves, Fabio Degli Esposti, Steven Ross, Paul Beach
Assistant Writers: Jason Farley, Jonathon Forsey, Alun Gallie, Paul Goldstone, Mark Hazell, Tom Robertson, Richard Steer
Proof Readers: Paul Beach, Greg Spyridis

Graphic Design: Dion Holswich, Casey Davies
Miniatures Design: Evan Allen, Karl Cederman
Cover Art: Vincent Wai
Internal Art: Randy Elliott, Warren Mahy, David Pentland, Adrian Smith
Terrain Modelling: Richard Carlisle, Andrew Hunter, Dale Pepperell
Miniatures Painting: Evan Allen, Karl Cederman, Dion Holswich, Sam Knowles, Jeremy Painter, Andrew Salisbury, Glen Tibbles, Wayne Turner
And thanks to all the playtesters!

CONTENTS

This is a supplement for *Flames Of War, the World War II miniatures game*.
A copy of the rulebook for *Flames Of War* is necessary to fully use the contents of this book.

 ISBN: 0-9582536-6-8

THE WAR IN THE MEDITERRANEAN

The Opening Moves

On 10 June 1940 Italy joined World War II. The Italian dictator Mussolini, 'Il Duce' declared war on Great Britain and France—his aim a new 'Roman Empire' on the Mediterranean. The declaration of war caught the large but obsolescent Italian Army by surprise, and the hastily-assembled force that invaded France failed to make any headway before the French surrender.

In the Italian colony of Libya, Il Duce exhorted his reluctant commander Marshal Graziani to attack the British in Egypt. Finally in September, the Italians launched their ponderous assault, driving the outnumbered defenders back over the Libyan-Egyptian border, only to abruptly pull up at Sidi Barrani to dig in, handing the initiative back to the British.

General Wavell, British Commander in the Middle East, wasted no time, launching Operation Compass on 9 December 1940. Wavell used his more mobile forces to roll up the increasingly despondent Italians, who were dispersed in fortified positions that could be picked off one by one. The outnumbered British took Bardia and Tobruk before completing an ambitious sweep that caught the retreating Italians at Beda Fomm. The Italians suffered disastrous losses. Italy had lost over 130,000 men killed or captured in a campaign lasting two months.

Balkan Adventures

Italy also fared badly in an assault on Greece which was repulsed with heavy losses. British Prime Minister Churchill ordered an Expeditionary force to Greece to assist the Greek Army.

Tanks and Australian and New Zealand Troops were diverted from Egypt for this ill-fated campaign. In Egypt, the experienced 7th Armoured Division was replaced by the under strength 2nd Armoured and the 4th Indian Division went to Ethiopia to take part in the struggle to knock out Mussolini's isolated East African Empire. This dispersal of forces prevented any hope of a drive to knock the Italians out of Libya entirely, setting the stage for the entry of Germany's *Afrikakorps*, a small force which was to have a dramatic effect on the war in the desert.

The small British contribution to the war in Greece could do little to stem the Blitzkrieg in the Balkans. German forces fell on Yugoslavia in Operation 25 and then the over-extended Greeks Operation *Marita*, driving the mainly New Zealand and Australian forces from mainland Greece in a lightning campaign.

Those who took refuge on the island of Crete only had temporary respite, with German airborne forces launching an unprecedented assault in May 1941 with Operation *Merkur* which succeeded in capturing the island at heavy cost to the assaulting paratroopers.

Enter Rommel

Following Italy's belated acceptance of an offer of German assistance, *Generalleutenant* Erwin Rommel, a brilliant commander who had led the 7th Panzer Division to good effect in France during 1940, was dispatched to Tripoli with a small but powerful force. Consisting of the 5th Light Division and 15th Panzer Division, and support troops, the *Deutsches Afrikakorps (DAK)* officially came into being on 19 February 1941.

Rommel wasted no time in catching the weakened and dispersed British off their guard. Ignoring his orders Rommel struck towards Tobruk, smashing the British forces at El Agheila and driving them back in disarray toward Mersa Brega. The German forces swept onward, destroying the 2nd Armoured Division and capturing first Benghazi and then El Mechili on 7 April 1941.

Rommel pressed on to secure Fort Capuzzo, Halfaya pass and Sollum, concluding a sweeping campaign that had driven the British out of Cyrenaica in only twelve days. The thorn in his side remained the port of Tobruk, where the superbly led 9th Australian Division and other troops succeeded in holding out against everything the Italians and Germans could throw at them, secure in the knowledge of their resupply by the Royal Navy. But 'The Desert Fox', as Rommel had reversed the whole course of the campaign in North Africa.

Brevity and Battleaxe

General Wavell struck back, launching Operation Brevity in mid-May to recapture Halfya, Sollum and Capuzzo. His troops succeeded, only to be thrown out a mere ten days later. Undeterred, the British built up their strength, including new Crusader tanks specially shipped for the purpose. Wavell launched Operation Battleaxe on 15 June—attempting to encircle the Germans and attack Halfya from the rear. Strong German defence, centred on the dual role 88mm gun, took a heavy toll on the British armour and the offensive stalled after three days. Rommel counterattacked on 16 June, rolling the British back into Egypt and removing the pressure on the Halfya garrison.

The failure of these operations saw General Wavell replaced by General Auchinleck and a pause while both sides rebuilt. Rommel's troops were already feeling the effects of the interception of their supplies by the Royal Navy, something that was to plague them throughout the African campaign.

Crusader

Rommel planned to launch a massive attack on the stubborn defenders of Tobruk on 20 November 1941. The British were aware of his plans due to radio interceptions and launched Operation Crusader on 18 November, taking the Germans by surprise. This was the most ambitious operation to date by the newly designated Eighth Army, under Lieutenant General Cunningham.

The battle see-sawed back and forth, but the British fought grimly on and the Tobruk garrison broke out, joining up with advancing New Zealand troops at El Duda. Rommel was forced to withdraw along his extended supply lines, abandoning Cyrenaica and forming a new front line at El Aghiela in January 1942. Crusader had cost the British 18,000 casualties and 287 tanks, against Axis losses of 30,000 men and over 300 tanks.

Rommel Strikes Back

Rommel consolidated and immediately struck back at the over-extended British forces with Operation *Theseus*. By 21 January 1942, Italian troops pushed toward Benghazi, whilst mobile German forces forced the British back to Mechili and then to a point south of Gazala.

There both sides built up their strength. British forces at this time adopted the defensive tactic of isolated brigade-strength 'boxes' and were to learn, as the Italians had before them, that such tactics did not suit the fluidity of war in the desert.

Rommel's plan involved sweeping around the desert flank of the defensive line and his mobile forces did so in late May 1942, only to be frustrated by the stubborn defence of General Koenig's Free French Brigade at Bir Hachiem, the southern-most defensive box. This hampered the flow of supplies to the front and caused Rommel's supplies to run dangerously low, so that while several boxes were overrun after hard fighting, he could not press the advantage and had to divert the Italian *Ariete* and German 90th Light Divisions to take Bir Hacheim, which they did on 11 June.

Rommel then struck at Tobruk, where the defences had fallen into disrepair. The surrender of the garrison (2nd South African Division) on 21 June demoralised the British and saw Rommel promoted to the rank of Field Marshal, the youngest in the German Army. Rommel pressed on from Tobruk, wanting to capitalise on his success.

Auchinleck sought to halt the Germans at Mersa Matruh, but these positions became encircled. Only three divisions broke out. The British fell back to a strong natural defensive position at El Alamein. The first German units reached the Alamein line on 30 June 1942 where they were halted in fierce fighting.

Alam Halfa and Alamein

Disappointed, Churchill replaced General Alexander with General Auchinleck as C-in-C Middle East and General Montgomery took command of Eighth Army. The British received warning of Rommel's planned assault on their line on 30 August, allowing a trap to be laid. Artillery and powerful new Grant tanks deployed along the Alam Halfa ridge caught the advancing Germans and inflicted heavy losses forcing them back once again.

Montgomery then went onto the offensive on 23 October, pummelling the Axis positions with artillery and air strikes, commencing a ferocious battle that saw the British suffer heavy losses but cost the Axis many of its formations, particularly the static Italian infantry divisions who had held the front lines. The Axis forces were forced to abandon the Alamein line on 4 November, facilitated by the sacrifice of the Italian *Ariete* Division in a rearguard action. The victorious Eighth Army regrouped and followed up the retreating Axis forces.

Tunisia

Meanwhile, a thousand miles west of Alamein, British and American Forces landed in Morocco and Algeria, on 7 November 1942 in Operation Torch. Uneven resistance from the occupying Vichy French forces was quickly overcome, but the Allies were beaten to the crucial port of Tunis by an unexpectedly rapid build-up of Axis forces. Whilst the advancing allies were coping with poor weather, terrain and supply problems, as well as a chaotic command structure, the Axis moved over 100,000 men into the Tunisian bridgehead by the end of December 1942.

These troops blunted the Allied advance and faced off against the combined American, French and British forces in the rough Tunisian terrain. At the same time *DAK* forces withdrew toward the Tunisian perimeter.

Characteristically, Rommel counter-attacked, striking westward in a surprise attack on the inexperienced US troops in the Kasserine Pass. US resistance quickly stiffened after initial retreats, halting Rommel's advance.

Swinging eastward Rommel struck the Eighth Army at Medenine only to be stopped cold for the first time in his career. Over the next month Allied troops drove the retreating Axis forces back into Tunis capturing over 250,000 men. The Axis surrender came on 12 May 1943. After three years of bitter struggle across blazing desert sands and muddy hillsides the war in North Africa was finally over.

Sicily

The next stepping stone for the Allies was Operation Husky, the invasion of Sicily on 10 July 1943. With Italian resistance crumbling German troops fought a skilful rearguard action across the island as the British Eighth Army under Montgomery and the US II Corps under firebrand George S Patton raced for Messina in a costly campaign lasting 38 days.

Italy Invaded

Failure to protect his country led to Mussolini's overthrow two weeks after the landings, and Italy's surrender days after the Eighth Army attacked across the straits of Messina onto the Italian mainland in Operation Baytown on 3 September. These landings were followed up by Operation Avalanche, the landing of the new US Fifth Army

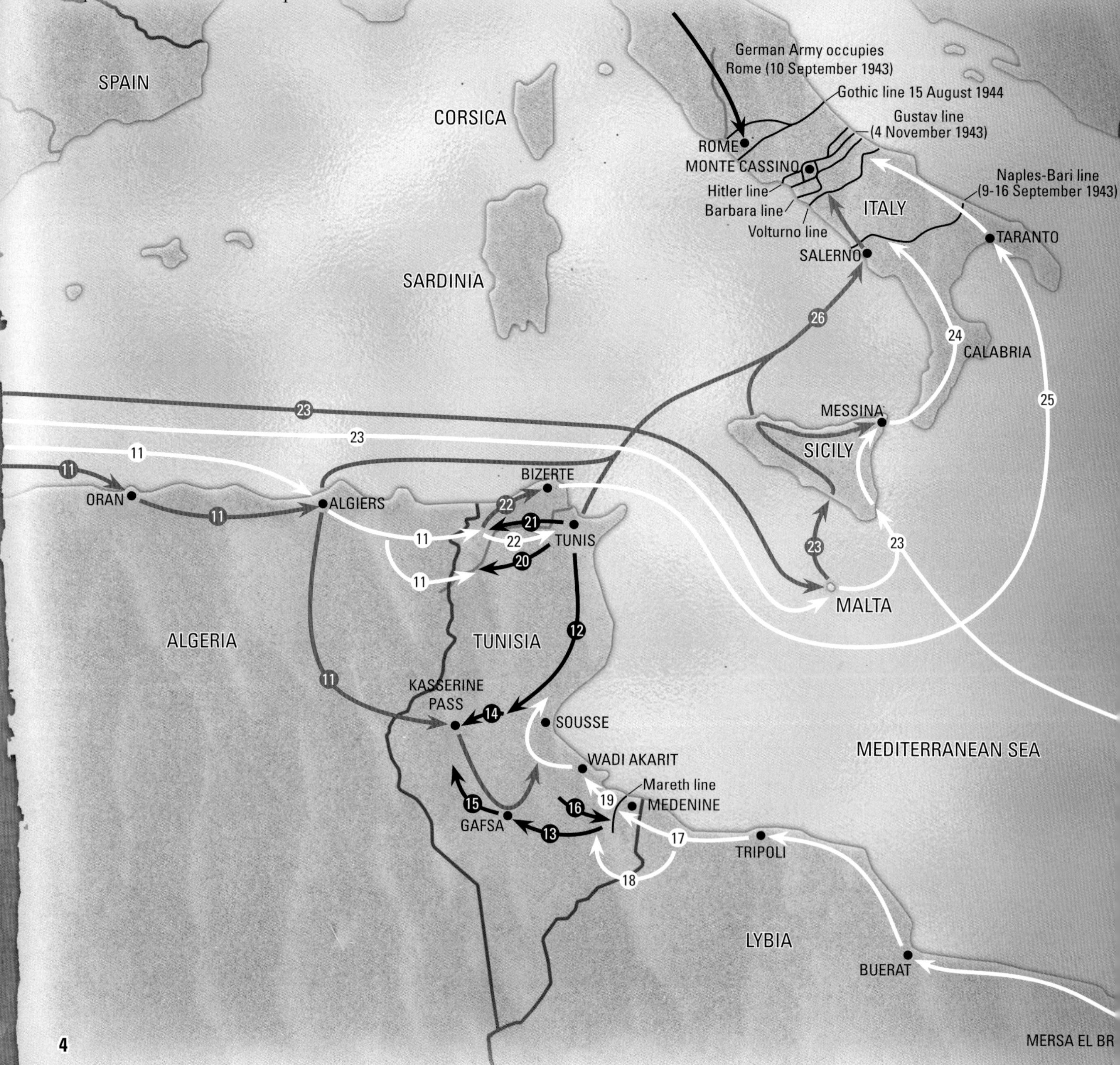

under Lieutenant General Mark W Clark at Salerno. Clark's men ran into problems from stiffening German resistance and secured their beachhead only with the assistance of powerful naval gunfire.

The invading Allies linked up and pushed slowly through Southern Italy, delayed by the rough terrain as much as by German rearguards. The German Tenth Army under Field Marshal Albert Kesselring finally halted the Allied advance on the Gustav Line, holding a key position at Monte Cassino. Bloody fighting by US, French, Polish, Indian and New Zealand troops sought to break the deadlock.

Anzio

The Allies gambled on an amphibious landing on the Italian west coast in an effort to outflank the defences. The US VI Corps landed almost without opposition at Anzio in Operation Shingle. However, failure to act aggressively and a rapid build-up of German defenders turned the outflanking manoeuvre into another deadlock. Heavy German counterattacks soon threatened to wipe this beachhead out. The failure of Operation Shingle only increased the need to capture the Cassino position, which finally fell in May 1944 after bitter fighting. After its fall, the Allies took the offensive once more capturing Rome on 5 June 1944.

Final Phase

The Allies, by this stage including US, British, Polish, Canadian, Indian, New Zealand, South African, Brazilian, Greek and Italian units, were then confronted by the defences of the 'Gothic Line' in the north of Italy. Months of hard fighting followed, with the defences holding until massive assaults in April 1945 punched through this last line of defence forcing the German surrender on May 2 1945.

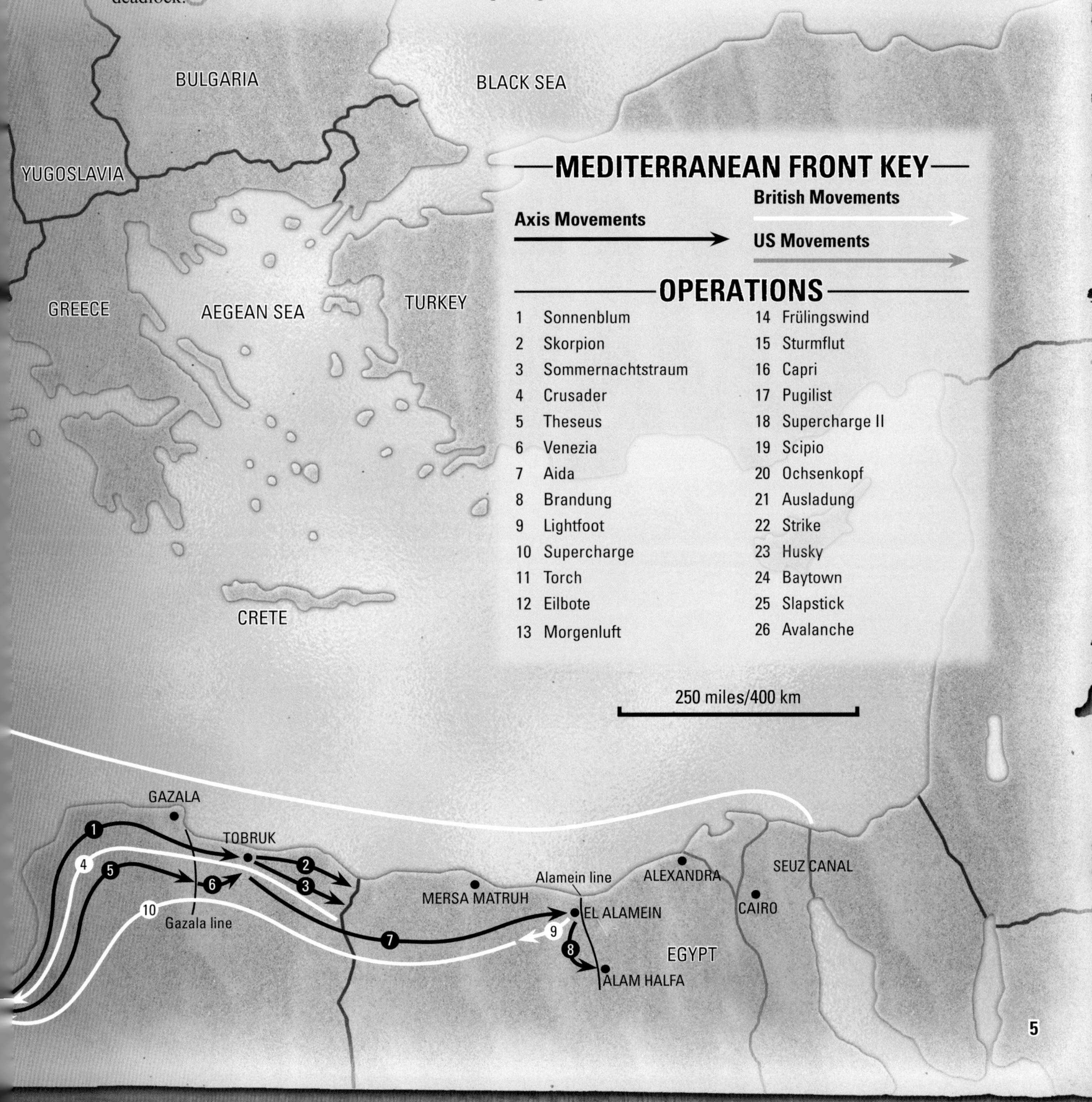

HOW TO USE THIS BOOK

The information contained within this book will enable you to create *Flames Of War* forces that accurately represent the armies that fought in the Mediterranean in 1942 and 1943.

To make the information more accessible we've split the book into a number of sections.

Choosing a Force page 7

This section gives you all the information that you will need to select your force. It provides an outline of how each countries army fits into the *Flames Of War* game and how they perform on the battlefield.

Intelligence Briefings page 13

Having decided on what army appeals most, its time to plan your force!

The main part of this book is dedicated to the Intelligence Briefings of each country involved in the conflict, Germany, Italy, Britain and the US.

At the beginning of each country's Intelligence Briefing you'll find a brief history of their greatest victories and defeats in the Mediterranean theatre of war. Also included in the introduction of each country is a list of divisions that fought in the campaign, making it easy to base your force upon an actual historical unit.

Painting Guides page 180

When you've planned the composition of your force, you'll know what miniatures you need to fight your tabletop battles. Once you've acquired these your next stop is the painting guides.

Here you'll find a paint colour chart for each country detailing authentic WWII colour schemes for your uniforms and vehicles, along with a step-by-step guide showing you how to paint your miniatures. A few expert tips then help you make them really stand out on the battlefield.

This section also shows the various markings used by armies to identify their vehicles. Give your force a unique look by adding decals using our easy to follow guide.

Airborne Assault Rules page 195

Both the Germans and the Americans have paratroops that can strike from the air! The special rules for airborne assaults presented here cover parachute landings and glider assaults, allowing you to bring your paratroops into the battle in a unique Death From Above airborne mission.

Arsenals page 202

The last section of this book contains the arsenals for each country. The game ratings for every weapon and vehicle in this book are listed here for ease of reference during your *Flames Of War* battles. Use this handy reference to keep track of your weapons' performance as well as those your opponent is fielding.

CHOOSING A FORCE

Your first step when building a ***Flames Of War*** army is deciding what country your troops will be from. You have four choices: Germany, Italy, Great Britain and the United States. Each has their own unique equipment and tactical style of play. Next choose the type of company you want to lead. Each country has one or more types of tank companies, mechanised companies and infantry companies. Having picked your company select the individual platoons that will make up your company from the appropriate section, until you have reached your points limit, then wage war!

Before fighting a battle, you need to choose your force. To make sure that you and your opponent choose forces that will give a fair fight and an interesting game, every unit has a points value. Agree with your opponent on the maximum points value that you may spend on your armies. The limit for a typical game is 1500 points.

CHOOSE A COUNTRY

Germany

The war in the west is over, France was decisively beaten, and Britain's army pushed into the sea at Dunkirk. Seizing what he considered to be a good opportunity, the Italian leader, Benito Mussolini, ordered the invasion of British-controlled Egypt, and in turn watched as his army was beaten back from Egypt and Italian Libya. Hitler answered his ally's call for help and sent a small force of tanks to counter the British. They were commanded by *Generalleutnant* Erwin Rommel, a brilliant tactician whose exploits in the deserts of North Africa earned him a new nickname, the 'Desert Fox'.

Your tough Afrikaners will face far more numerous foes, possessing immense resources of tanks, infantry, and artillery, but none with the training and skill to outfight you. If you take advantage of your superbly trained soldiers, your excellent tanks, your deadly anti-tank guns, and your mighty dual purpose '*acht-acht*' eighty-eight millimetre anti-aircraft guns, you will defeat any enemy that you face.

Italy

It was the bravery and dedication of the *Carristi* and *Bersaglieri*, the Italian tank crews and light infantry, that made many of Rommel's desert victories possible. It was the steadfast defiance of the *Artiglieri* and *Paracadutisti*, the Italian artillery men and parachutists, that saved Rommel from defeat time and again. It was the endurance of the *Fucilieri*, the Italian riflemen, that held the line for the Germans in the desert and in Africa when their own resources proved insufficient.

While the tank crews must rely on bravery, Italian infantry need not. With proper artillery support, they are capable to taking on any enemy on even terms. For the *bersaglieri* and *paracadutisti*, their courage does not even the odds, it gives them an edge over their foes.

Fielding an Italian force is not for the faint hearted. You can't hide behind thick armour and big guns. But if you have the guts to go for glory, your men will follow you anywhere.

Britain

The thin red lines of professional soldiers that created the British Empire has given way to a modern khaki-clad army, but despite all changes the infantry remain the Queen of the Battlefield. Soldiers from throughout the Empire, Australia, Canada, India, New Zealand, and South Africa, fight side-by-side to bring Hitler to his knees. British infantry fight with stubborn pride and, properly supported with tanks and artillery, they are well nigh unbeatable.

British armour leads the way with sheer dash and elan! Because the Desert Rats originally comprised regiments of Hussars, the Rifle Corps, and Royal Horse Artillery, it has a special kind of flamboyant cavalry style.

However, the bulk of the fighting of the British army falls on the shoulders of the infantry. Their work may not be glamorous, but it is essential. The tanks may be able to take ground, but only the infantry can hold it.

United States

Three years of war have exhausted Britain and the Soviet Union. If the Nazis are going to be stopped, the United States will have to do it. In 1941 and 1942 the United states, backed by the immense might of American industry, has not only re-equipped the tank forces of the British Army and sent thousands of tanks to the Soviet Union, but has formed the best-equipped divisions in the world. While the troops may be fresh from training, they learn fast.

Coming from the most industrialised nation on the planet, they have an abundance of equipment and ammunition other armies can only dream of. With such backing, US forces are invariably supported by massed firepower. No other army can field as much artillery with such destructive power!

Man-for-man the soldiers of the US Army are the equal of any. As yet they lack the experience of troops fighting since the start of the war, but they are learning fast.

CHOOSE A COMPANY

Tank Company

Tank companies are the armoured fist of any nations army. They combine mobility, firepower and protection in a way that allows them to penetrate deep into enemy territory, encircle them, and destroy them.

A tank force is aggressive, in most situations tanks will be going forward and attack, so it takes a brave person to command them in battle.

Mechanised Company

For those people who don't want to tackle the enemy head on, but prefer the indirect approach, the Reconnaissance and Armoured infantry give you a light armoured, hard hitting force. Moving swiftly, they rely on speed and shock to catch the enemy before they have deployed for battle. Their speed and armour allows them to move quickly into position before dismounting to attack.

Infantry Company

Infantry companies contain the brave soldiers that fight without the benefit of armour. Although some infantry drive to the battlefield in trucks, they always fight on foot. Their usual role is to attack fortified defences to create a breakthrough for tanks, and to dig in and hold their ground against enemy attacks.

A typical Afrikakorps Panzergrenadierkompanie (Infantry Company), made up of a number of platoons.

CHOOSE PLATOONS

The organisation charts describe each platoon in the following parts:

Unit Name: The title of the platoon and the number you can have in each company.

Organisation Diagram: Showing the composition and internal organisation of the platoon.

Platoon: A list of the basic platoon choices available and the points cost of each.

Options: Some platoons are shown with part of the diagram in grey indicating additional options. These are not part of the basic price for the platoon, but must be paid for separately if you wish to include them in your platoon.

Restrictions: In some cases there are additional restrictions on the availability of weapons and how many platoons of the same type your force may have.

The core of an army is usually two combat platoons and a company command.

The German Army

The German military—the Wehrmacht—is the most powerful war machine in existence. The proof is plain for all to see. Since the start of this war the Wehrmacht has ruthlessly crushed all those who have dared stand before it. Europe has already been conquered by German military power.

Panzerkompanie **Page 27**

Images of German Panzers (as they call their tanks) moving across the barren desert, sand streaming from their tracks scream 'Afrika Korps'. It is perhaps the most enduring image of the desert war. Every one of your Panzers carries a better gun than its Allied equivalent. Combine this with good armour, mobility, and first-class crews, and you have a force that will beat any foe one-on-one.

Panzergrenadierkompanie **Page 31**

The brave soldiers of the Panzergrenadierkompanie, or Panzergrenadier company, fight without the benefit of armour. Although they drive to the battlefield in their trucks, they fight on foot. Their usual role is to attack fortified defences to create a breakthrough for the Panzers, and to hold the ground they take with the Panzers as a counterattack reserve.

Gepanzerte Panzergrenadierkompanie **Page 36**

10. Panzerdivision was extremely fortunate in having an entire battalion of infantry in armoured half-tracks. An elite gepanzerte Panzergrenadierkompanie or armoured Panzergrenadier company from this battalion is equipped with armoured Sd Kfz 251 half-tracks giving it the speed and armour to accompany the tanks into the thickest fighting.

Panzerpionierkompanie **Page 38**

The Panzerpionierkompanie is an outstanding assault force. These combat engineers are heavily-armed assault specialists. They have more firepower per man than any other infantry force.

Aufklärungsschwadron **Page 39**

For those who don't want to tackle the enemy head on, but prefer the indirect approach, the Aufklärungsschwadron, or reconnaissance company, gives you armoured cars for scouting and a strong infantry component for fighting.

Grenadierkompanie **Page 41**

A Grenadierkompanie is the finest infantry force you can command. The troops are all experienced veterans and their equipment is as good as it gets. Of course, you'll always be outnumbered, but there's nothing like the satisfaction of facing an overwhelming horde... and winning!

Many a Grenadierkompanie was sent to hold the last bastion of Afrika, Tunisia, against the Allied invasion. They have the backing of the best weapons that the German army can provide, from the heavy sIG 33 and StuG assault guns, to the feared Tiger. Your Grenadierkompanie will never be under-gunned.

Fallschirmjägerkompanie (Airborne) **Page 47**

The Fallschirmjäger are parachute infantry. These are tough, highly-trained troops used wherever the fighting is the hardest.

The Diving Eagles are famous for their daring air assaults, such as capturing the vital fortress of Eben Emael and the island of Crete from the air. Any force selected from this list is capable of airborne assaults like these when playing Death From Above, the airborne assault mission on page 201.

Platoons that show a parachute symbol next to them are able to use the *Parachute Landings* rules on page 195.

Platoons that show a glider symbol next to them are able to use the *Glider Assaults* rules on page 199.

Fallschirmjägerkompanie (Ground Operations) **Page 52**

After the losses of the Battle of Crete, Hitler forbade large-scale airborne operations, although the *Fallschirmtruppen* continued to expand, fighting as elite infantry on every front and conducting smaller-scale airborne assaults.

If you add troops and equipment to your Fallschirmjägerkompanie from the additional organisation charts for ground operations, your force is no longer capable of airborne operations. However, you have much greater striking power with there heavier equipment available for ground operations.

THE ITALIAN ARMY

The Regio Esercito, the Royal Army, has never lost a war. Today, under the leadership of Il Duce, Benito Mussolini, and some small assistance from our German Allies, the Regio Esercito is bringing back the power and the glory of the ancient Roman Empire.

Compagnia Carri **Page 73**

The *carristi*, or tankers, of the Compagnia Carri, the tank company, are undoubtedly the most dashing Italian troops. With their small tanks, they have little choice but to close with the enemy and destroy them at short range. Fortunately they are backed by heavy guns to cover their advance.

Compagnia Bersaglieri **Page 75**

The *bersaglieri* are Italy's equivalent of Britain's Rifle Brigade. They are superbly trained light infantrymen. Although they have fewer trucks than they would like, a Compagnia Bersaglieri is the closest thing Italy has to motorised infantry—every heavy weapon has motorised transport. Organised with 'few men, many weapons', they have the firepower to see off any attack and the skill to finish off the enemy with a counterattack.

Compagnia Motociclisti **Page 78**

The Compagnia Motociclisti, or motorcycle company, provides petrol heads with a fully motorised variant on the Compagnia Bersaglieri. Every rifleman rides his own motorcycle for maximum mobility!

Compagnia Fucilieri **Page 81**

While the *carristi* and *bersaglieri* are the glamour boys, it is the *fucilieri*, the riflemen, who spend their days in the frontline trenches, boiling in the desert heat and freezing in Russian snow. A Compagnia Fucilieri, a rifle company, may not be glamorous, but it can still fight. Dig these boys in and they are hard to move. Meanwhile their artillery is pounding away at the enemy, whittling them down for a massed counterattack.

Compagnia Paracadutisti **Page 85**

If you want to lead the best of the best, then a Compagnia Paracadutisti, a parachute company, is for you. Every one of these soldiers is the fearless survivor of at least three low-level parachute jumps. The *paracadutisti* don't have a lot of heavy equipment, but their skill and bravery more than make up for it.

THE BRITISH ARMY

It has been said of the British Army that they always start a war by losing battles. However, they are nothing if not stubborn and persistent, and it can also be said that they always end a war by winning battles.

Armoured Squadron Page 105

The core of the force are tanks—not slow, lumbering infantry tanks, but high-speed cruiser tanks and hard-hitting heavy tanks. In the hands of a daring player, a squadron of Crusader cruiser tank will run rings around slower opponents. A more cautious player will field the big American Grant and Sherman heavy tanks, either on their own, or backing up the cruisers, to blow the opposition away with sheer firepower.

Motor Company Page 108

The riflemen of the motor companies support the armoured squadrons admirably. They are just the chaps for swanning around the desert shooting up enemy transport, or defending a safe base for the armour to attack from, and when the desert is far behind, in Tunisia, Sicily and Italy, and the terrain becomes too close for tanks, they lead the way.

Armoured Car Squadron Page 111

Armoured car squadrons replace the light cavalry of the past. Ranging far across the desert, they keep a watch on Rommel making sure he doesn't get up to any tricks. The squadrons are almost entirely equipped with armoured cars making them mobile and hard-hitting if they have to fight.

Rifle Company Page 115

Commanding an infantry company may not sound glamorous, but the infantry aren't called the 'Queen of Battle' for nothing. No battle has ever been won without the infantry doing their bit. Solid and enduring in defence and implacable in the attack, the infantry are the foundation for all other arms. Not that they can win battles on their own. No, the gunners of the Royal Artillery are indispensable, and good infantry tanks invaluable, but it is the infantryman getting out of his trench and walking across no-man's land to get the enemy out of his at the point of a bayonet that wins us victories.

Recce Squadron Page 120

On the other hand, if you prefer sneaking around to head-to-head conflict, the Recce Squadron's light armoured cars and scout carriers may be just the thing. The Recce Corps is the eyes and ears of the infantry. They scout ahead in advances and screen retreats. They cover the flanks and probe the enemy lines for weaknesses. They also fight, and fight hard, when they have to with their own infantry and anti-tank guns, and heavier support from divisional resources.

Commando Troop Page 122

The legendary Commandos are superb infantry The lightly-equipped raiders of a Commando Troop are some of the nastiest and toughest infantry around. They are deadly at close quarters where their extensive training in killing quickly and quietly pays off. They can go anywhere, climbing impossible cliffs and swimming unfordable rivers. At heart though, they are still infantry. They still take their place in the line of battle and beat the foe toe-to-toe.

British Empire Page 129

The British Empire is the largest the world has ever seen. It occupies a quarter of all the lands of the Earth and includes a quarter of the planet's population. The sun never sets on the British Empire.

When war broke out volunteers from throughout the Empire flocked to the flag ready to fight. Australians, Burmese, Canadians, Englishmen, Indians, Irishmen, New Foundlanders, New Zealanders, Nigerians, Rhodesians, Scotsmen, South Africans, Ugandans, and Welshmen fought side by side against Hitler's unfounded aggression.

You can bring this diverse character to the battlefields of *Flames Of War* by using these rules to customise your force into one of the various armies making up the Empire's armed forces.

THE UNITED STATES ARMY

When the German army ripped through France in six weeks, the American press coined a new word, 'Blitzkrieg' or Lightening War. It wasn't just the press that were impressed with the performance of the German Panzers, the US army realised that they needed a countermeasure, and fast.

Tank Company Page 157

Tank companies represent the mobile component of the US Army. Their task is turning a breakthrough into a total defeat for the enemy. Striking with the full power of their guns and armor, the tanks smash through the enemy lines before wreaking havoc in the enemy's vulnerable rear areas, destroying artillery and command centres.

Armored Rifle Company Page 160

The doughs of the Armored Rifle Company are some of the best-equipped infantry in the world. They have machine-guns, mortars, anti-tank guns, and bazookas aplenty. Everything they need to see off any foe. Combined with the unmatched mobility of their half-tracks they are outstanding both in attack and defence.

Armored Recon Company Page 163

If tanks or infantry aren't your thing, you can always take the cavalry! The Armored Recon Company allows you to field part of a Cavalry or Armored Reconnaissance Battalion. These are the eyes and ears of the army, although they are often called upon to fight for information or simply to hold a vulnerable flank.

Rifle Company Page 165

The humble GI is the foundation of the US Army. Without the Rifle Companies slogging their way forward step by step all the way to Berlin, the war could never have been won. They lack the glamour of the tankers and special forces, but they more than make up for it in their contribution to victory. A Rifle Company can mass the greatest concentration of firepower of almost any force anywhere. Their artillery is plentiful and effective and they have no shortage of support from tanks as good as any in their class anywhere

Ranger Company Page 169

Rangers are light infantry raiders. They are all volunteers eager to take the fight to the enemy anywhere, any time. As lightly-equipped raiders, they are used to taking on the enemy with only what they can carry on their backs. Their aggression combined with speed and mobility in the worst of terrain make them outstanding infantry capable of beating any force when properly employed.

Parachute Rifle Company Page 171

The paratroopers of the Parachute Rifle Company are some of the bravest (or most foolhardy) soldiers you'll ever find. Their chosen path to battle involves jumping out of a perfectly good airplane behind enemy lines! They are limited in armament by what they can drop from an aircraft, but are usually quickly reinforced by the land-based forces giving them artillery and armored support.

A Parachute Rifle Company can make airborne assaults and can play Death From Above, the airborne assault mission on page 201.

DESERT FOX

GERMAN FORCES IN THE MEDITERRANEAN

"In view of the tenseness of the situation, and the sluggishness of the Italian command, I decided to ignore my orders and to take command of the front with my own hands as soon as possible—at the very latest after the arrival of the very first German units"
—Generalleutnant Erwin Rommel, The Rommel Papers.

Born in 1891 into a middle-class Swabian family, Erwin Rommel joined the German Army in 1910. When the First World War began in 1914, Rommel served on the Western and Romanian fronts, earning a reputation as a fearless and brilliant infantry commander. In 1917, when on the Italian front, his alpine battalion of less than 500 men launched a daring attack, taking more than 9,000 prisoners and capturing 81 guns while breaking right through the Italian front line. For this he was awarded Germany's highest honour for gallantry, the Pour le Merite.

Peacetime Soldier

Rommel stayed with the army after the war. During this time he wrote *Infanterie Greift An* (Infantry Attacks!), a book on infantry tactics that became an instant bestseller. When war broke out Rommel was commanding Hitler's headquarters guard. Rommel was not a Nazi, but he and Hitler formed a friendly relationship. So when Rommel asked for command of *7. Panzerdivision* for the invasion of France, he got it.

Ghost Division

In May 1940 the Germans attacked France and Belgium in a surprise attack through the Ardennes forest and across the Meuse river with *7. Panzerdivision* leading the way. The sudden assault ruptured the French line. *7. Panzerdivision* raced deep into the French rear, sowing confusion and panic.

Under Rommel's leadership, *7. Panzerdivision* quickly earned the nickname the *Gespensterdivision*—the Ghost Division—as neither friend nor foe were ever sure where it was. In six weeks of fighting, the Ghost Division took 100,000 prisoners and Rommel

IWM MH5852

became one of the most famous generals in the German army.

Sonnenblume

In February 1941 Hitler summoned Rommel again. The Italians had been defeated by the British in North Africa, losing Libya, and needed help. Rommel was given command of the *Deutsches Afrikakorps* (*DAK*), the German Africa Corps. The name was a play on *Deutsches Alpenkorps*, the German Alpine Corps that Rommel had served in when he defeated the Italians 24 years earlier.

The force, consisting of *15. Panzerdivision* and *5. leichte Division*, was placed under Italian command, with orders to stay on the defence at Mersa El Brega. But Rommel characteristically disregarded his orders, and launched an attack under the codename *Sonnenblume*, routing British forces from Libya in a whirlwind advance.

His tactical cunning quickly earned him the nickname 'the Desert Fox'.

Tobruk

The speed of the advance was such that the 6th Australian Division was cut off and surrounded in the Libyan port of Tobruk. In a series of seesaw battles on the Egyptian border (Operations Brevity, *Skorpion*, Battle-axe, and *Sommernachtstraum*) the British and Germans attacked in turns. The British attacks to relieve Tobruk in May and June 1941 foundered on the dug-in 8.8cm guns of the *Afrikakorps*, while the German attacks only served to consolidate their hold on the frontier. Exhausted, both sides prepared for the next round.

Rommel's *Afrikakorps* received fresh tanks and anti-tank guns. This allowed *5. leichte Division* to be strengthened and re-titled *21. Panzerdivision.* Various independent units were organised into a new *Division Afrika zbV* (soon renamed *90. leichte Afrikadivision*) at the same time. These prepared for a renewed assault on Tobruk. On the other side of the frontier, the British were reinforced and reorganised, their forces being renamed the Eighth Army.

Totensontag

On 19 November 1941, just days before Rommel's planned attack on Tobruk, the Eighth Army launched a surprise offensive codenamed Crusader. A confusing series of tank battles took place east of Tobruk with Rommel often taking direct command of units to stop British attacks. On 23 November—*Totensonntag*, the Holy Sunday of the Dead—the *Afrikakorps* and their Italian allies scattered the remnants of the British armour.

The Desert Fox now made a rash decision. He ordered his two Panzer divisions to race to the Egyptian frontier, to cut off what he thought were the beaten remnants of the British army. It was a big mistake. The Eighth Army was still fighting on. Rommel's 'race to the wire' wore down his Panzers on a fruitless chase across the Libyan desert before returning to the Tobruk front, where fighting continued to rage. The *Afrikakorps* was now very weak while the British were getting more reinforcements daily. Reluctantly, Rommel ordered the retreat back to Gazala, and then Mersa El Brega.

Once again the British supply line was stretched thin while Rommel received reinforcements. Ignoring his Italian allies, the Desert Fox struck out in January 1942 with Operation *Theseus*. The inexperienced British 1st Armoured Division was caught by surprise and routed back to Gazala.

Venezia

On 26 May 1942 Rommel once again beat the British to the punch and commenced Operation *Venezia* to take Tobruk. In a daring manoeuvre the *Afrikakorps* swung south behind the fortified British line at Gazala. Uncoordinated but stubborn resistance by the British armoured regiments brought the *Afrikakorps* to a halt, trapped behind the British line, out of fuel and water, and outnumbered.

In his classic style, the Desert Fox appeared wherever the fighting was most desperate to inspire and take control. Rommel broke back through the British line to re-open his supply lines. Driving his men on, Rommel's forces then turned and routed the Eighth Army before storming Tobruk on 20 June, completing his greatest victory and taking 60,000 prisoners along with vast quantities of supplies. Complete victory in the Middle East beckoned.

'On To Cairo!'

Launching Operation *Aida*, Rommel pursued the fleeing British who turned to fight at El Alamein, barely 60 miles from the River Nile. The *Afrikakorps*, severely weakened by weeks of constant combat and thousands of miles of wear and tear across the harsh desert, constantly harried by the Royal Air Force, could not break through the hasty British line in this, the First Battle of Alamein. All of Rommel's energy and improvisation could not overcome lack of fuel and the exhaustion of his men. The daring offensive petered out.

Once again, both sides reinforced and, once again, it was Rommel who struck first. In late August the Desert Fox launched Operation *Brandung* and broke through the British line. But the new British commander, General Montgomery, was ready and repelled Rommel's attack at Alam Halfa ridge. Rommel's troops were outnumbered and low on supplies. They fell back to their starting position and dug deep minefields and waited for the inevitable British attack. Rommel, ill after 18 months in the desert, returned to Germany for a much needed rest.

El Alamein

On 23 October the British launched a massive offensive, the Second Battle of Alamein. Rommel quickly flew back to the front to take charge. The situation was dire. Rommel was outnumbered and British troops were already through the minefields and slowly chewing up his main defensive line. The fighting was hard. Counter-attacks by tanks to relieve his embattled German and Italian infantry were met by crushing British artillery and air attacks. Attempts by the British armour to breakthrough were met by lines of anti-tank guns.

After ten days of heavy fighting, Rommel's choices were to stay and get crushed by the relentless British attacks, or retreat—he ordered his army to prepare for an organised withdrawal.

Hitler immediately intervened, ordering Rommel to 'stand fast, yield not a yard of room and throw every gun and every man into the battle.... victory or death!'. Rommel knew the order was crazy. Defeat was certain, his army would be thrown away for nothing. For the first time Rommel began to doubt Hitler.

Another British attack smashed its way through the crumbling defences and Rommel, ignoring Hitler, ordered the remnants of the *Afrikakorps* to retreat west before they were overwhelmed.

Retreat To Tunisia

Pulling back from El Alamein, more bad news reached Rommel. A combined Anglo-American task force had landed in Morocco and Algeria far to his rear. Hitler was determined to hold onto North Africa and sent *10. Panzerdivision* and *Division General Göring* to Tunisia under General von Arnim who promptly attacked with Operation *Eilbote*, halting the Allied advance just short of Tunis.

Meanwhile, after retreating more than a thousand miles, standing at Mersa El Brega and Buerat, the *Afrikakorps* made it to the Mareth Line on the border of Tunisia and Libya and dug in. The Eighth Army, supply lines stretched to breaking, could only follow up slowly. The Desert Fox took the initiative once more.

Kasserine Pass

The *Afrikakorps* now struck west against the American forces. While von Arnim attacked from the north with his Operation *Frühlingswind*, Rommel launched Operation *Morgenluft* taking Gafsa and threatening the vital Kasserine Pass. Just as in 1941 and early 1942, the veteran *Afrikaneers* scattered their inexperienced opponents taking the pass in the follow-up Operation *Sturmflut*. The Americans quickly recovered and ultimately it was Rommel who had to retreat.

The *Afrikakorps* then turned and struck east launching Operation *Capri* against the Eighth Army at Medenine. Once again Montgomery was ready and waiting and the attack was easily stopped. The Eighth Army then attacked the Mareth Line. The *Afrikakorps* inflicted heavy losses on the initial British attack, but outflanked, were forced to retreat. On 9 March 1943 Rommel, still not recovered from his earlier illness, departed from Africa, never to return.

The rugged Tunisian terrain was well suited for defence, but the combined US, British and French forces were overwhelmingly superior. Von Arnim made one last attack, the twin Operations *Ochsenkopf* and *Ausladung*.

Finally, on 12 May the proud *Afrikakorps* sent its last message:

'Ammunition shot off. Arms and equipment destroyed. In accordance with orders received the *Afrikakorps* has fought itself into the condition where it can fight no more. The *Afrikakorps* must rise again. *Heia Safari*!'

Resurrection

Both 15. and 21. Panzer divisions were rebuilt to fight again. *15. Panzerdivision* fought on in Sicily and Italy as *15. Panzergrenadierdivision*, while *21. Panzerdivision* met their old adversaries the Desert Rats again in Normandy, France after the D-Day landings in June 1944.

And Death

Rommel was assigned to take command of the defence of the French coast against the expected D-Day invasion. However, even his formidable energy and gift for improvisation could not stop the landings. On 20 July 1944, a number of German officers, seeing no hope of winning the war, conspired to assassinate Hitler. The attempt failed, and the conspirators were killed. However, Rommel was implicated in the plot. Gestapo agents were sent to Rommel's home, demanding he take poison or they would murder him and his family. To save his beloved wife and son, Rommel took poison, still proclaiming his loyalty to Hitler.

IWM MH5828

Nord afrika 1942

1942 saw two of the Afrikakorps biggest battles against the British at Gazala and El Alamein with advances and retreats over thousands of miles of desert waste.

In the wide-open spaces of the desert, armoured cars raid a British outpost.

Generalfeldmarschal Rommel and 'Max'

The Panzer IV carried a powerful 7.5cm gun.

The fearsome 'acht-acht' or '88' can destroy any tank it can see.

An armoured Aufklärungs platoon reconnoitres ahead of the Afrikakorps.

The Panzer III is a match for any British tank.

Panzergrenadiers assault a 25 pdr battery

Tuneser 1943

By 1943, everything had changed. Now Rommel was fighting to hold Tunisia, the last bridgehead in North Africa, against the combined American and British forces.

Marder III tank hunters engage unsuspecting American half-tracks from afar.

Panzergrenadiers react quickly to a US attack.

Light infantry guns engage over open sights.

The gunners of the artillery battery quickly deploy to engage the enemy.

Heavy machine-guns prepare to repulse an American assault.

Anti-tank guns ambush careless Stuarts.

Panzergrenadiers launch a counterattack

Rettemeier leads his company into battle against American Sherman tanks.

Heavy armoured cars lead the advance.

Rommel controls the battle.

Gigantic Tiger I E heavy tanks are almost unbeatable!

German Divisions in North Africa

This table lists the German divisions that fought in North Africa in 1942 and 1943 covering the three Panzer divisions and the two leichte Afrika divisions in detail. Each of these divisions was unique in its equipment and organisation. To reflect this, the Intelligence Briefings that follow indicate which divisions each platoon and option applies to. All other divisions listed here are covered by the Tunisia, Sicily and Italy Symbol.

- – used by 10. Panzerdivision
- – used by 15. Panzerdivision
- – used by 21. Panzerdivision
- – used by 90. leichte Afrikadivision
- – used by 164. leichte Afrikadivision
- – used by divisions in Tunisia, Sicily and Italy

Division	Regiments	Arrived	Battles
Gazala and First Alamein			
21. Panzerdivision	5 Pz, 104	Feb 1941	*Sonnenblume*, Brevity, *Skorpion*, Battleaxe, *Sommernachtstraum*, Crusader, *Theseus*, *Venezia*, *Aida*, *Brandung*, Second Alamein, Mersa El Brega, Buerat, *Morgenluft*, *Sturmflut*, *Capri*, El Hamma.
15. Panzerdivision	8 Pz, 115	Mar 1941	*Sonnenblume*, Brevity, *Skorpion*, Battleaxe, *Sommernachtstraum*, Crusader, *Theseus*, *Venezia*, *Aida*, *Brandung*, Second Alamein, Mersa El Brega, Buerat, *Morgenluft*, *Sturmflut*, *Capri*, Mareth Line, Wadi Akrit, Enfidaville, Medjerda.
90. leichte Afrikadivision	155, 200, 361 Afrika, 288 zbV	Aug 1941	Crusader, *Theseus*, *Venezia*, *Aida*, *Brandung*, Second Alamein, Mersa El Brega, Buerat, *Capri*, Mareth Line, Wadi Akrit, Enfidaville.
Second Alamein (as above plus the following)			
164. leichte Afrikadivision	125, 382, 433	Aug 1942	*Aida*, Second Alamein, *Capri*, Mareth Line, El Hamma, Enfidaville.
Fallschirmbrigade Ramcke		Aug 1942	Second Alamein, *Sturmflut*, Enfidaville.
Tunisia (as above plus the following)			
Division von Broich (later von Manteuffel)	Barenthin FJ, 160, 10 Bersaglieri (Italian)	Nov 1942	Teboura, *Eilbote*, *Ochsenkopf*, Medjerda.
10. Panzerdivision	7 Pz, 190 Pz Bn, 69, 86	Nov 1942	Teboura, *Eilbote*, *Frühlingswind*, *Sturmflut*, *Ochsenkopf*, Medenine, El Guettar.
Division General Göring (part)	1 HG, Jäger HG	Nov 1942	Teboura, *Eilbote*, *Ochsenkopf*, Medjerda.
501. schwere Panzerabteilung	(later with 10. Panzer)	Dec 1942	Teboura, *Eilbote*, *Frühlingswind*, *Ochsenkopf*, Medjerda.
334. Infanteriedivision	754, 755, 756 Gebirgs, Phalange Africaine	Jan 1943	Eilbote, *Ausladung*, Bizerte.
999. Afrika Division	961 Afrika, 962 Afrika	April 1943	Fondouk, Medjerda.
504. schwere Panzerabteilung	(with 15. Panzer)	Mar 1943	Maknassy, Medjerda.

German Divisions in Sicily & Italy

Division	Regiments	Arrived	Battles
Sicily			
Fallschirmpanzerdivision Hermann Göring	Pz HG, 1 HG, 2 HG	July 1943	Sicily, Calabria, Volturno, Anzio.
15. Panzergrenadierdivision	215 Pz Bn, 104, 105, 129, Reggio Bn	July 1943	Sicily, Calabria, Cassino, Anzio.
29. Panzergrenadierdivision	129 Pz Bn, 15, 71	July 1943	Sicily, Calabria, Cassino, Anzio.
1. Fallschirmjägerdivision	1 FJ, 3 FJ, 4 FJ	July 1943	Sicily, Cassino.
Italy (as above plus the following)			
16. 'Stalingrad' Panzerdivision	2 Pz, 64, 69	Sep 1943	Salerno.
26. Panzerdivision	26 Pz, 9, 67	Sep 1943	Salerno, Volturno, Anzio.
3. Panzergrenadierdivision	103 Pz Bn, 8, 29	Sep 1943	Salerno, Cassino, Anzio.
5. Gebirgsdivision	85 GbJ, 100 GbJ	Dec 1943	Cassino.

German Terminology

Aufklärungs (owt-klairr-oongs): Reconnaissance.
Aufklärungsschwadron (owt-klairr-oongs shvad-rone): Reconnaissance squadron or company
Ausf, Ausführung (owss-few-roong): Version, e.g. Panzer III Ausf J = Tank mark III, version J.
Afrika (af-ri-ka): Africa.
Afrikaner (af-ri-ka-nerr): African. Nickname for soldiers in the Afrikakorps.
Aida (ai-dah): Girl's name. Codename for attack into Egypt.
AM, Alter Mann (al-terr man): Old Man. Nickname for Italian canned beef, staple diet of an Afrikaner. Also known as Asinus Mussolini, Mussolini's backside. AM stood for Amministrazione Militare.
Ausladung (owss-lah-doong): Unloading. Codename for northern supporting attack for Ochsenkopf.
Bison (bi-zon): Bison. Nickname for self-propelled infantry gun on Panzer II chassis.
Brandung (bran-doong): Breakers, waves. Codename for attack at Alam Halfa.
Capri (ka-pree): Capri. Codename for attack at Medenine.
DAK, Deutsches Afrikakorps (doitsh-ess af-ri-ka korps): German Africa Corps.
Diana (di-ah-nah): Girl's name. Nickname for self-propelled anti-tank gun on half-track chassis.
Eilbote (ile-boh-ter): Courier. Codename for von Arnim's attack on Pont du Fahs.
Fallschirmbrigade (fal-shirrm bri-gah-der): Parachute brigade.
Fallschirmjäger (fal-shirrm-yai-gerr): Parachute rifleman.
Fallschirmjägerdivision (fal-shirrm-yai-gerr di-vis-yon): Parachute rifle division.
Fallschirmjägerkompanie (fal-shirrm-yai-gerr kom-pan-ee): Parachute rifle company.
Fallschirmpanzerdivision (fal-shirrm-pant-serr di-vis-yon): Air Force armoured division.
Fallschirmpionier (fal-shirrm pi-o-neerr): Parachute combat engineer.
Fallschirmtruppen (fal-shirrm troop-en): Parachute troops.
FK, Feldkanone (felt ka-noh-ner): Field gun.
FlaK (flak), Flugabwehrkanone (flook ap-vairr ka-noh-ner): Anti-aircraft gun.
Flammpanzer (flam-pant-serr): Flame-thrower tank.
Freiherr (fri-hairr): Baron.
Frühlingswind (fryoo-lings vint): Spring wind. Codename for von Arnim's attack on Faid and Fondouk Passes.
GebG, Gebirgsgeschütz (ger-beerrg ger-shyoots): Mountain gun.
Generalfeldmarschall (gen-er-rahl felt marr-shal): Field Marshal.
Gepanzert, gep (ger-pant-serrt): Armoured.
Greif (grife): Griffin or attack. Rommel's half-track.
Grille (gril-er): cricket (SP Infantry gun).
GW, Granatwerfer (gra-naht verr-ferr): Grenade-launcher, mortar.
Hauptmann (howpt-man): Captain.
Heer (hairr): Army.
Heia Safari (hi-a za-farr-ee): Safari bed, sleeping rough. Name of a popular song and battle cry of the Afrikaners.
Herakles (hair-ah-klez): Codename for proposed invasion of Malta.
Hexenkessel (hex-en kesl): Witches cauldron.
Infanteriedivision (in-fan-ter-ree di-vis-yon): Infantry division.
Jäger (yai-gerr): Rifleman, private.
Kampfgruppe (kampf-groop-er): Improvised battle group.
Kettenkrad (ketn-kraht), Kettenkraftrad (ketn-kraft-raht): Tracked motorcycle.
Kfz, Kraftfahrzeug (kraft-fah-tsoik): Car or truck.
Kradschützen (kraht shyoot-sen): Motorcycle troops.
Leichte Afrikadivision (lish-ter af-ri-ka di-vis-yon): Light African-pattern motorised infantry division.
Leopard (lep-uhd): Codename for invasion of the island of Leros.
Leutnant (loit-nant): Lieutenant.
LG, leichte Geschütz (lish-ter ger-shyoots): Light gun, recoilless gun.
Lili Marlene (leel-ee marr-lay-ner): Name of a popular and sentimental song sung by Marlene Dietrich.
Luftlandesturmkompanie (looft lan-der shtoorrm kom-pan-ee): Airlanding assault company.
Luftwaffe (looft-vaf-er): Air Force.
Major (ma-yore): Major.
Merkur (merr-koorr): Mercury, code name for attack on Crete.
Morgenluft (morr-gen looft): Morning air. Codename for attack on Gafsa.
NbW, NW, Nebelwerfer (nay-bel verr-ferr): Gas launcher, chemical mortar, rocket launcher.
Nordafrika (norrt af-ri-ka): North Africa.
Oberjäger (oh-berr-yai-gerr): Squad leader
Oberstleutnant (oh-berrst-loit-nant): Lieutenant colonel.
Ochsenkopf (ox-sen kopf): Ox head. Codename for von Arnim's attack in northern Tunisia.
PaK, Panzerabwehrkanone (pant-serr ap-vairr ka-noh-ner): Anti-tank gun.
Panzer (pant-serr): Tank.
Panzerarmee Afrika (pant-serr arr-may af-ri-ka): Armoured Army of Africa.
Panzerdivision (pant-serr di-vis-yon): Tank division.
Panzergrenadierkompanie (pant-serr gre-nah-deerr kom-pan-ee): Mechanised infantry company.
Panzerknacker (pant-serr-k-na-ker): Tank buster.
Panzerkompanie (pant-serr kom-pan-ee): Tank company.
Panzerspahwagen (pant-serr-shpay vah-gen): Armoured car
Pionier (pi-o-neerr): Pioneer, combat engineer.
PJK, Panzerjägerkanone (pant-serr yai-gerr ka-noh-ner): Tank-hunter gun, anti-tank gun.
Püppchen (poop-shen): Little doll, dolly. 8.8cm RW43 anti-tank rocket launcher.
RW, Raketenwerfer (ra-kay-ten-verr-ferr): Rocket-launcher.
sPzB, schwere Panzerbüchse (schvair-rer pant-serr bewx-er): Heavy anti-tank rifle.
Schürzen (shyoot-sen): Protection, skirting to protect tanks from infantry anti-tank weapons.
Sd Kfz, Sonderkraftfahrzeug (zon-derr kraft-fah-tsoik): Special motor vehicle.
Skorpion (skorr-pi-one): Scorpion. Codename for recapture of Halfaya Pass.
Sommernachtstraum (zom-err nachts trowm): Midsummer's night dream. Codename for raid on Egypt.
Sonnenblume (zon-en bloo-mer): Sunflower. Codename for first attack from Lybia.
Stielgranate (shteel gra-nah-ter): muzzle-loading anti-tank grenade for an anti-tank gun.
Stummelwerfer (shtoo-mel vairr-ferr): Stump mortar, a cut-down mortar.
Sturmabteilung Koch (shtoorrm ap-tile-oong koch): Major Koch's glider assault detachment.
Sturmflut (shtoorrm floot): Storm flood. Codename for attack on Kasserine Pass.
'Tante Ju' (tan-ter yoo): 'Aunt Ju'. Nickname for Junkers Ju52 transport aircraft.
Theseus (tay-see-oos): Codename for second attack from Lybia.
Tiger (tee-gerr): Tiger. Name of German heavy tank.
Tuneser (too-neh-serr): Tunisia.
Venezia (ve-ne-tsee-a): Venice. Codename for attack at Gazala.
Wehrmacht (vairr-macht) Defence Force, Army.
Wüste (vyoost-er): Wasteland, desert.
Wüstefuchs (vyoost-er foox): Desert fox.
zbV, Zur besonderen Verwendung (tsoor be-zon-derr-en fer-ven-doong): For special use.

Oberstleutnant Walter Koch

Born in Bonn, Walter Koch was 28 when given the task of forming a parachute assault detachment.

Koch's group was responsible for spearheading the assault into Belgium to capture three bridges and the fortress of Eben Emael. The operation was a success and Koch was awarded the Knight's Cross.

His next assignment would be another airborne mission, Operation *Merkur,* the invasion of Crete. Within minutes of landing Koch received a serious head wound and had to be evacuated to Greece. He spent several months recovering before rejoining his battalion as they deployed to the Eastern front. Koch and his men would be involved in bitterly fought actions around Vyazma, Mius and Leningrad.

In early 1942 the newly promoted *Oberstleutnant* Koch returned to France to assume command of *5. Fallschirmjägerregiment*. By November the regiment was being airlanded in Tunis and scrambling to hold off the Allied invasion of Tunisia. In fighting near Depienne, the *Fallschirmjäger* captured a number of British paratroopers. These prisoners, many of whom were wounded, were put into the custody of a *Wehrmacht* unit. When Koch learned of the *Wehrmacht* intentions to execute the paratroopers in accordance with Hitler's order regarding allied commandos he returned and secured their safety.

Koch was again wounded at the beginning of 1943 and returned to Germany for treatment and recuperation. He died in Berlin on 27th October 1943 as a result of serious injuries sustained in a motor vehicle accident.

Characteristics

Koch is a Warrior and Higher Command team rated as **Fearless Veteran**. .

He is armed with an MP40 SMG with the following ratings:

Range: 4"/10cm, ROF: 3, Anti-tank: 1, and Firepower: 6.

Koch carries his weapon with him during airborne assaults so is always rated as above. Like an SMG team, Koch fires at full ROF when moving.

Koch can command any Fallschirmjägerkompanie for +25 points. Koch may pilot any glider in an airborne assault without affecting its carrying capacity.

Special Rules

Superb Glider Pilot: The intensive training Koch received has honed his flying skills, allowing Koch to land his glider on a dime. When making the landing run roll for Koch's glider, you may adjust the length of the landing run by 2"/5cm forward or back. If you roll a 1, ignore the crash landing result, the glider lands safely.

Schnell!: Koch and any platoon that he is currently leading may make Stormtrooper moves on a roll of 2+.

Fight on: Koch and any platoon he is currently leading always pass Motivation tests on a roll of 2+.

Oberst Josef-Willhelm Rettemeier

As a *Hauptmann*, Rettemeier won the Knight's Cross commanding the *2. Kompanie I/5. Panzerregiment* in Africa. Later, in 1944, he won the Oakleaves as a Major commanding *5. Panzerbataillon* of *25. Panzergrenadier-division* on the Eastern Front. After the war Oberst Rettemeier commanded a *Panzergrenadier* brigade in the new German Army.

Characteristics

Rettemeier is a Warrior and a Company Command team rated as **Confident Veteran**.

Rettemeier can join any Panzerkompanie for +50 points. He becomes the Company Command team retaining the previous commander's tank.

Special Rules

Ace Gunner: Re-roll any failed to hit rolls when firing Rettemeier's tank. This does not apply if his tank fires an artillery bombardment

Schnell!: Rettemeier's tank and any Panzer Platoon he commands may make a Stormtrooper move on a roll of 2+.

Panzers March: Each turn Rettemeier may re-roll one die rolled to receive reserves for his company.

..Gazala, 1942...

'Stand to! Close hatches!' comes across the radio. As the rest of the crew of 'Zitrone' pull their hatches closed, turning the tank into an oven, Feldwebel Ritgens continues to follow the movements of the advancing British cruisers through his binoculars.

'They are approaching very fast, Feldwebel,' the gunner Stöhr's nervous voice drifts up from the bowels of the tank.

'Keep your eyes on the sights, kid,' advises 'Papa' Philipps, the loader, at 32 the old man of the crew.

'Zitrone, this is Kirsche, take position to the right.' The platoon leader's voice sounds calm in their radio headphones.

Ritgens orders 'Driver, right, advance,' then 'Driver, halt.' The British are getting a lot closer, moving around the right flank. Unless help arrives soon, it'll be too late.

'Shouldn't we be shooting now, Feldwebel?' Stöhr's nervous whine continues.

'Relax kid, he knows what he's doing,' Papa replies. 'Just keep your eyes on the sights.'

'Will Rettemeier get here in time?' worries Stöhr. 'We'll be cut off if he doesn't.'

'Range 800, lead Panzer,' interrupts Ritgens. 'Don't worry, Hauptmann Rettemeier will make it, he always does.'

He pauses until his young gunner is on target, 'Feuer!'

Generalfeldmarschall Erwin Rommel

Characteristics

Rommel is a Warrior and a Higher Command team rated as **Fearless Veteran**.

Rommel is mounted in Greif (meaning both Griffin and Attack), his Sd Kfz 250/5 half-track, and can join any Panzerkompanie, Panzergrenadierkompanie, or Panzerpionierkompanie for +50 points.

A force led by Rommel may include an Escort Platoon equipped with captured Honey Stuart tanks (rated as **Confident Veteran**) for the following costs.

5 captured Honey Stuart	**320**	**points**
4 captured Honey Stuart	**255**	**points**
3 captured Honey Stuart	**190**	**points**

Special Rules

Fingertip Feeling: Rommel was said to have *Fingerspitzegefuhl*, a fingertip feeling for battle. One German platoon in Line of Sight of Rommel may make a normal move within its deployment area after both sides have deployed but before any Reconnaissance Deployment moves.

Rommel at the Point: '*Rommel an der Spitze*' was a common cry in the *Afrikakorps* where Rommel led from the front. Any German platoon in Line of Sight of Rommel may re-roll any failed Motivation Tests and failed Skill Tests to make Stormtrooper moves.

Herr General: If Rommel's Command team is Destroyed during a game the German war effort has suffered a severe blow, despite any other gains. The German player loses one Victory Point and their opponent gains one Victory Point at the end of the battle.

Mammut: As well as Greif, Rommel also travelled in a *Mammut* (Mammoth), a captured Dorchester Armoured Command Vehicle, named Max. Feel free to model him with Max rather than Greif, but keep the vehicle characteristics the same as for Greif.

Oberstleutnant Von der Heydte

Von der Heydte volunteered for the *Fallschirmtruppen* after winning the Iron Cross First Class in the Battle Of France in 1940. As a *Hauptmann* in Crete, he commanded *1. Bataillon* of 3. *Fallschirmjägerregiment* in the fighting for Prison Valley, Galatas, and Canea for which he was presented the Knight's Cross by Hitler.

Promoted to *Major*, he led his battalion in heavy fighting around Leningrad where he was wounded late in 1941. The battalion was withdrawn from Russia at the end of the year, rebuilt and renamed the *Lehr* (demonstration) battalion, before joining the Ramcke Brigade in the Battle of El Alamein.

After taking part in the fighting around Rome to disarm the Italian Army, Von der Heydte was given command of 6. *Fallschirmjägerregiment* in Normandy. After heavy fighting against US Airborne and Army forces in Carentan and around St. Lô, the regiment was back in action in September fighting the US paratroopers again as part of Operation Market Garden in Holland for which he was awarded the Oakleaves to his Knight's Cross.

Von der Heydte's war ended with the last German airborne assault during the Battle of the Bulge. He parachuted with one arm in a sling and injured the other on landing. With the failure of this operation, Von der Heydte was captured by the US Army.

Characteristics

Von der Heydte is a Warrior and a Higher Command team rated as **Fearless Veteran**.

He is armed with a pistol with the following ratings:

Range: 4"/10cm, ROF: 1, Anti-tank: 1, Firepower: 6.

Von der Heydte can command any Fallschirmjäger-kompanie for +50 points.

Special Rules

Never Surrender: Von der Heydte, and any platoon he is currently leading, always passes Motivation Tests on a roll of 2+.

Rally Once More: When teams from Fallschirmjäger Platoons (just the Combat Platoon on page 48) are Destroyed, remove them from the table, but keep them aside. At the start of any turn while Rallying Pinned Down platoons, Von der Heydte may attempt to regroup the survivors of one Fallschirmjäger Platoon within 6"/15cm. Roll a dice for each destroyed team from that platoon kept aside.

- On a roll of 5 or 6, the team is returned to play adjacent to Von der Heydte. It no longer counts as having been Destroyed.
- Otherwise, the team is permanently Destroyed and removed from play.

Panzerkompanie

(TANK COMPANY)

Tank combat in the desert is no picnic. Up before dawn to eat a bite of Alter Mann in the freezing cold. Then once the sun rises you fight in an oven. The tank gets so hot you can fry an egg on it! You fight all day in the heat and the stink, then, after dark, you try and find fuel and ammunition before standing watch and grabbing an hour or two of sleep.

—Gefreiter Albert Meyer

A force based around a Panzerkompanie must contain:

- a Company HQ, and
- two to four Panzer Platoons.

Weapons Platoons available to a Panzerkompanie are:

- a Light Panzer Platoon,
- a Scout Platoon,
- an Anti-aircraft Platoon.
- a Flame-tank Platoon, and,
- a Pioneer Platoon

Support Platoons for a Panzerkompanie can be:

- Panzergrenadier Platoons,
- Aufklärungs Platoons,
- Armoured Car Patrols,
- Panzerpionier Platoons, and,
- Divisional Support Platoons.

You may have up to **one** Support Platoon attached to your company for each Panzer Platoon you are fielding.

Motivation and Skill

The Panzertruppen have years of combat behind them and are confident of their ability to utilise their superior tactics and equipment to defeat their enemies. A Panzerkompanie is rated as **Confident Veteran**.

– used by 10. Panzerdivision

– used by 15. Panzerdivision

– used by 21. Panzerdivision

– used by divisions in Tunisia, Sicily and Italy

HEADQUARTERS

1 Company HQ

Headquarters

Company HQ with

2 Panzer III G, H, or J (early) 180 points

- Upgrade any or all Panzer III G to:
  Panzer III J (late) for +15 points per tank,
  Panzer III L or M for +25 points per tank,
  Panzer III N for +15 points per tank,
  Panzer IV E or F_1 for +15 points per tank,
  Panzer IV F_2 or G for +60 points per tank.
  Panzer IV G (late) or H for +75 points per tank.

Option

- Add Schürzen sideskirts to any Panzer III L, M or N, Panzer IV G (late) or H for +5 points per tank.
- Add an Sd Kfz 9 (18t) recovery half-track for +5 points.

Platoons from 10. Panzerdivision, Tunisia, Sicily and Italy must upgrade all Panzer III G, H, or J (early) to Panzer III L or M or Panzer IV F_1, F_2 or G.

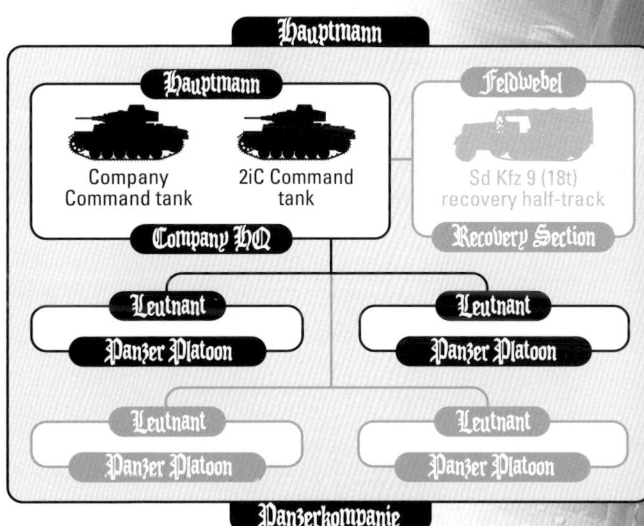

The Panzer company HQ coordinates the actions of the entire company, issuing orders and bolstering combat platoons at critical moments. The effect the company HQ can have on the outcome of the battle is enormous.

Recovery vehicles like the *Famo Sd Kfz 9* use the vehicle recovery rules to get stuck vehicles moving again.

COMBAT PLATOONS

2 to 4 Panzer Platoons

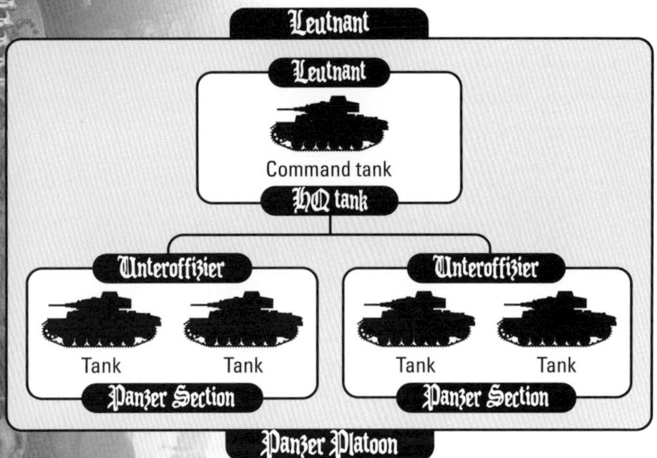

Platoon	
5 Panzer III G, H, or J (early)	450 points
4 Panzer III G, H, or J (early)	360 points
3 Panzer III G, H, or J (early)	270 points

- Upgrade any or all Panzer III G to:
  Panzer III J (late) for +15 points per tank,
  Panzer III L or M for +25 points per tank,
  Panzer III N for +15 points per tank,
  Panzer IV E or F_1 for +15 points per tank,
  Panzer IV F_2 or G for +60 points per tank.
  Panzer IV G (late) or H for +75 points per tank.

Option

- Add Schürzen sideskirts to any Panzer III L, M or N, Panzer IV G (late) or H for +5 points per tank.

Each tank in a Panzer Platoon may have different upgrades.

Panzer platoons are a powerful strike force. Use them to strike hard and fast, destroying the enemy before they can organise themselves.

As *DAK* entered its second year in the desert its tanks were a mix of old Panzer III G & H and Panzer IV E tanks with newer Panzer III J and Panzer IV F_1 types to replace earlier losses.

The new long-barrelled Panzer III J (late), known as the Mark III Special to the British, appeared in very small numbers in Operation *Venezia* at Gazala in May 1942 with more appearing during the Operation *Aida* in the First Battle of Alamein. The Panzer III L with spaced armour on the hull and turret front arrived in greater numbers in August and September, making up half the Panzer III numbers by the Second Battle of Alamein in October. These were joined by the similar Panzer III M and the 7.5cm-armed Panzer III N in Tunisia. Both of these marks fought on in Sicily and Italy

The long-barrelled Panzer IV F_2, Mark IV Special to the British, first appeared in the First Battle of Alamein in July 1942 and outnumbered the older types of Panzer IV two to one by October. In the later stages of the Tunisia campaign, the latest Panzer IV G was found in considerable numbers as all replacements sent were of this type since production of the Panzer III had ceased.

The Panzer IV G (late) and H appeared in Sicily and Italy with the newly-equipped divisions fighting there.

WEAPONS PLATOONS

0 to 1 Light Panzer Platoon

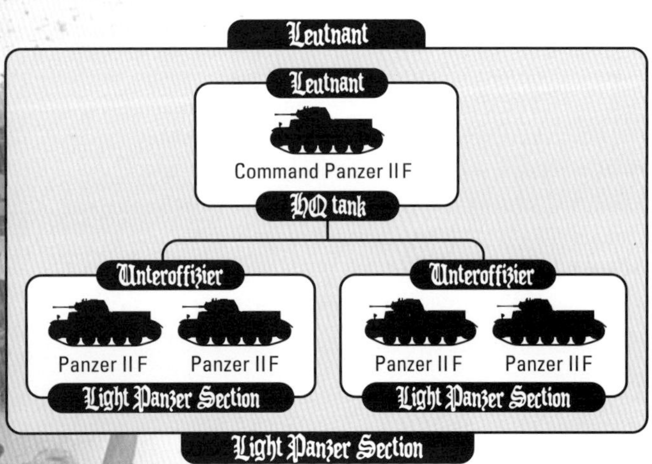

Platoon	
5 Panzer II F	250 points
4 Panzer II F	200 points
3 Panzer II F	150 points

The light Panzer II was no longer suitable for front-line combat by 1942, but was still useful for scouting and flank security work.

Light Panzer Platoons are Reconnaissance Platoons.

0 to 1 Scout Platoon

Platoon	
HQ Section with:	
3 Scout Squads	165 points
2 Scout Squads	125 points
1 Scout Squad	85 points

Options

- Replace any or all motorcycles and sidecars with two solo motorcycles based together, or a Kübelwagen jeep per motorcycle and sidecar at no cost.

The battalion scout platoon has many roles, from scouting potential ambush sites to checking whether roads and tracks are usable.

Scout Platoons are Reconnaissance Platoons

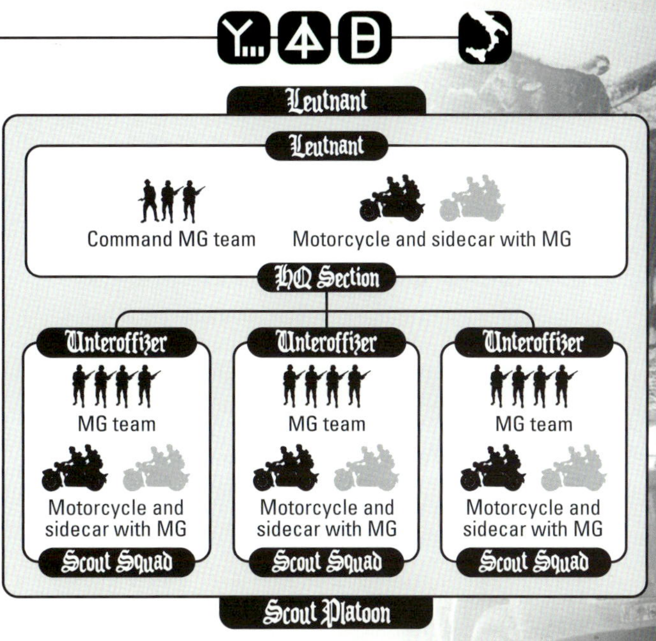

0 to 1 Anti-aircraft Platoon

Platoon	
3 Sd Kfz 7/1 (Quad 2cm)	165 points
2 Sd Kfz 7/1 (Quad 2cm)	110 points

All ground troops are responsible for their own anti-aircraft protection. Anti-aircraft platoons provide the *Panzertruppen* with mobile anti-aircraft weapons that can keep up with the speed of their advance.

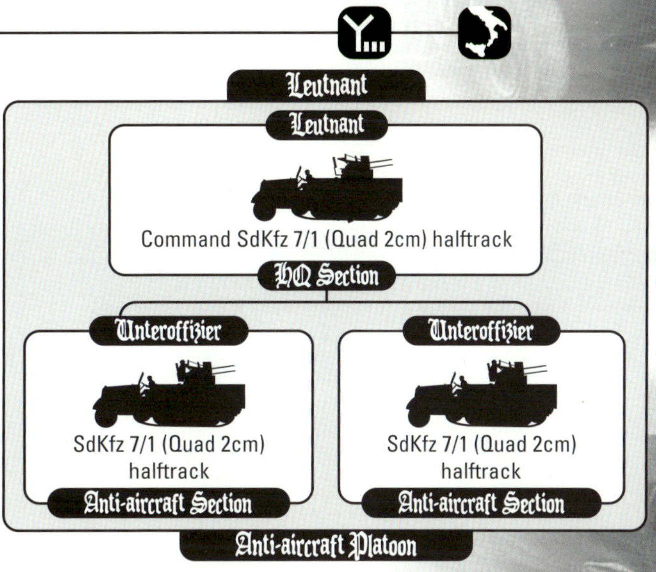

0 to 1 Flame-tank Platoon

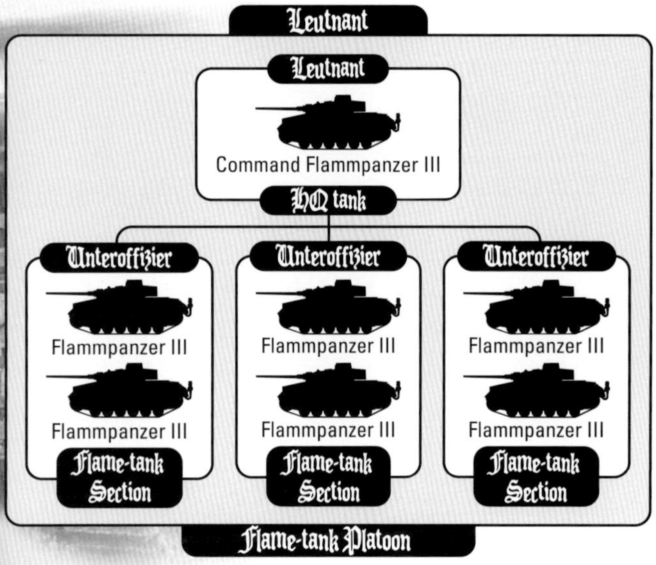

Platoon	
7 Flammpanzer III	580 points
6 Flammpanzer III	500 points
5 Flammpanzer III	420 points
4 Flammpanzer III	340 points
3 Flammpanzer III	260 points

16. and *26. Panzerdivision* were fully equipped for their return to the Eastern Front when they were rushed to defend the beaches at Salerno, where their flame-tank platoons counterattacked the beaches with their *Flammpanzer III* flame-tanks

0 to 1 Pioneer Platoon

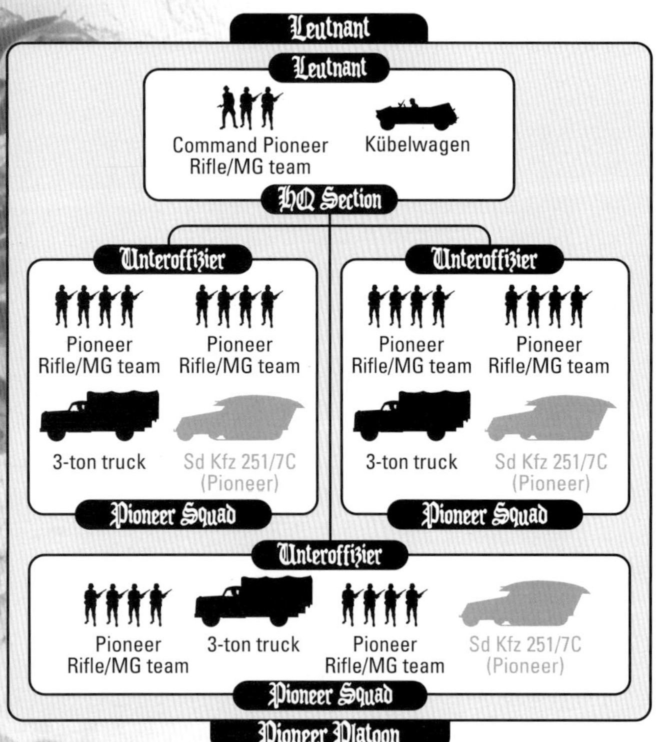

Platoon

HQ Section with:

3 Pioneer Squads	225 points
2 Pioneer Squads	160 points
1 Pioneer Squad	95 points

Options

- Replace all 3-ton trucks with Maultier half-tracks for +5 points for the platoon.
- Add an Sd Kfz 251/7C (Pioneer) half-track to each squad for +20 points per half-track.

The battlefield is full of obstacles, be they simply blown bridges or cratered roads, or more malicious hazards like minefields and anti-tank ditches. The pioneer platoon quickly overcomes these obstacles allowing the Panzers to roll on once more.

Captured Equipment

The *Deutsches Afrikakorps* was always desperately short of trucks. The desert was hard on vehicles and the *Afrikakorps* had a supply line extending a thousand miles back to Tripoli. To make up numbers, the *Afrikakorps* pressed into service huge numbers of captured British trucks (and a not inconsiderable number of Italian trucks that they recaptured from the British). To recreate this effect, replace any model of a German truck with its British equivalent, treating it as the original model in game terms. For example, you could replace a Kfz 70 truck with a CMP 15 cwt truck, but keep the characteristics of a Kfz 70 truck.

In Tunisia, the *Afrikakorps* found a new source of vehicles—the US Army! They used captured American vehicles in the same way as they did British ones. Even an armoured Panzergrenadier unit that lost a half-track played this game, they simply replaced it with an abandoned American one!

Panzergrenadierkompanie

(INFANTRY COMPANY)

I've always loved motor vehicles, right from when I went to watch cars race with my father. When I joined the army, I joined the Panzergrenadiere, the motor infantry. We lead the way in advances and cover the rear in retreats. We live from our trucks. They carry everything we own, our machine-guns, our fuel, our food, everything.
—Panzergrenadier Urs Zehnpfennig

A force based around a Panzergrenadierkompanie must contain:

- a Company HQ, and
- two or three Panzergrenadier Platoons.

Weapons Platoons available to a Panzergrenadier-kompanie are:

- a Heavy Platoon,
- a Motorised Machine-gun Platoon,
- a Motorised Mortar Platoon,
- two Light Anti-tank Gun Platoons, and
- a Panzer Pioneer Platoon.

Support Platoons for a Panzergrenadierkompanie can be:

- a Scout Platoon,
- a Light Infantry Gun Platoon,
- a Heavy Infantry Gun Platoon,
- Panzer Platoons,
- Panzer Pioneer Platoons,
- Armoured Car Patrols, and
- Divisional Support Platoons.

You may have up to **two** Support Platoons attached to your company for each Panzergrenadier Platoon you field.

Motivation and Skill

The Panzergrenadiers have fought and won for years. A Panzergrenadierkompanie is rated as **Confident Veteran**.

– used by 10. Panzerdivision

– used by 15. Panzerdivision

– used by 21. Panzerdivision

– used by 90. leichte Afrikadivision

– used by 164. leichte Afrikadivision

– used by divisions in Tunisia, Sicily and Italy

HEADQUARTERS

1 Company HQ

Headquarters

Company HQ	45 points

Options

- Replace either or both Command SMG teams with Command Panzerknacker SMG teams for +5 points per team.
- Add an Anti-tank Rifle Section with: an Anti-tank Rifle team for +30 points, a 2.8cm sPzB41 gun for +35 points, or both teams for +60 points.
  All Anti-tank Rifle Sections have one Kfz 70 truck at no cost.

Options (10. Panzerdivision only)

- Replace 2.8cm sPzB41 gun with an 8.8cm RW43 (Püppchen) launcher for +5 points.

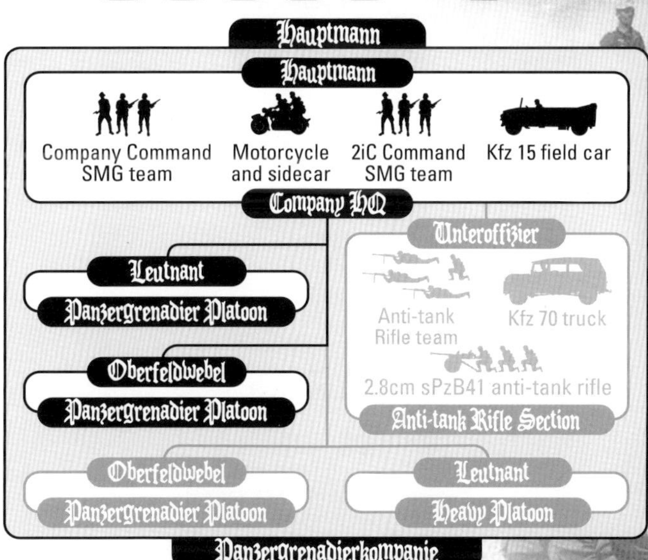

The Panzergrenadier platoons of the *Deutsches Afrikakorps* were all mounted in trucks allowing them to keep up with the tanks in battle.

The Panzergrenadier companies are organised on a basis called 'Few men, many weapons'. Each battalion formed four identical companies rather than three infantry companies and a heavy weapons company. Each company had two or three Panzergrenadier platoons and a mix of heavy and anti-tank platoons.

COMBAT PLATOONS

2 or 3 Panzergrenadier Platoons

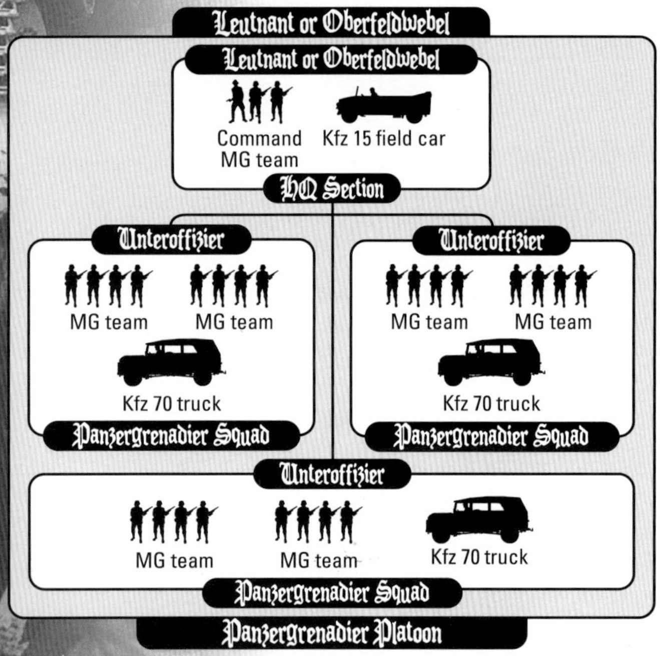

Platoon

HQ Section with

3 Panzergrenadier Squads	**220 points**
2 Panzergrenadier Squads	**160 points**

Options

- Replace the Command MG team with a Command Panzerknacker SMG team for +5 points.

Option (90. & 164. Afrikadivision only)

- Replace the Kfz 15 field car and all Kfz 70 trucks with one 3-ton truck per Panzergrenadier Squad at no cost. The HQ Section ride with the Panzergrenadier Squads.

Panzer divisions in Africa were always short of soldiers and vehicles, so they adopted an organisation with each small section carried in one Kfz 70 truck. The light Africa divisions generally had a lower allocation of vehicles and were issued a 3-ton truck for each squad rather than individual Kfz 70 trucks.

WEAPONS PLATOONS

0 to 1 Heavy Platoon

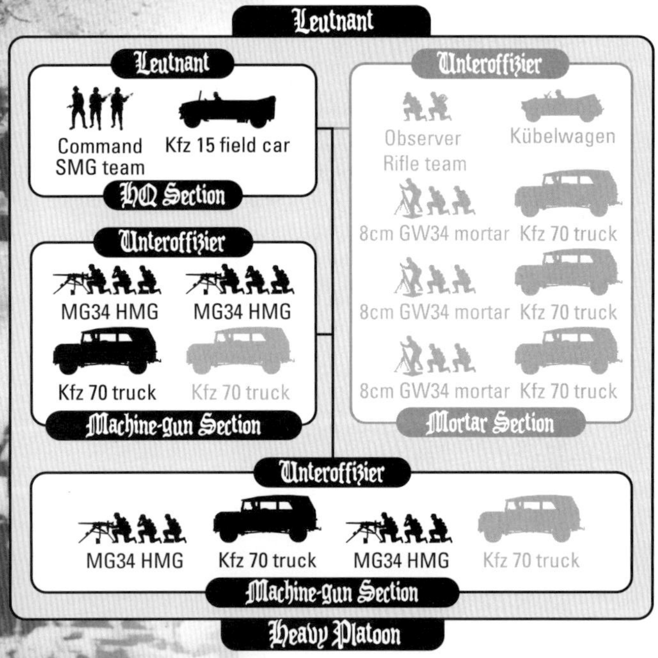

Platoon

HQ Section with:

2 Machine-gun Sections	**165 points**
1 Machine-gun Sections	**95 points**
No Machine-gun Sections	**25 points**

Options

- Add a Mortar Section with two 8cm GW34 mortars for +65 points.
- Add a third 8cm GW34 mortar to the Mortar Section for +30 points.
- Add a second Kfz 70 truck per Machine-gun Section at no cost.

A Heavy Platoon must have a Mortar Section if it has no Machine-gun Sections.

In the free-flowing desert battles it was useful to allocate heavy weapons out to each company. The company's heavy platoon forms a base of fire for the Panzergrenadier's attacks and a strongpoint in their defence.

Heavy Platoons may make Combat Attachments to Combat Platoons.

0 to 2 Light Anti-tank Gun Platoon

Platoon

HQ Section with:

3 2.8cm sPzB41	105 points
2 2.8cm sPzB41	80 points

HQ Section with:

3 3.7cm PaK36	105 points
2 3.7cm PaK36	80 points

Option (90. Afrikadivision only)

- Replace all 3.7cm PaK36 guns with 4.2cm PJK41 guns for +10 points per gun.

HQ Section with:

3 5cm PaK38	145 points
2 5cm PaK38	105 points

- Replace all Kfz 70 trucks with Sd Kfz 10 half-tracks for +5 points for the platoon.

Options

- Replace all 5cm PaK38 guns with captured 6 pdr guns for +5 points for the platoon.
- Replace all 5cm PaK38 guns and Kfz 70 trucks with 7.62cm PaK36(r) guns and 3-ton trucks for +25 points per Anti-tank Gun Section.
- Replace all 3-ton trucks with Sd Kfz 11 half-tracks for +5 points for the platoon.

Your force may not contain more than one Anti-tank Gun Platoon armed with 2.8cm sPzB41, 3.7cm PaK36, or 4.2cm PJK41 guns.

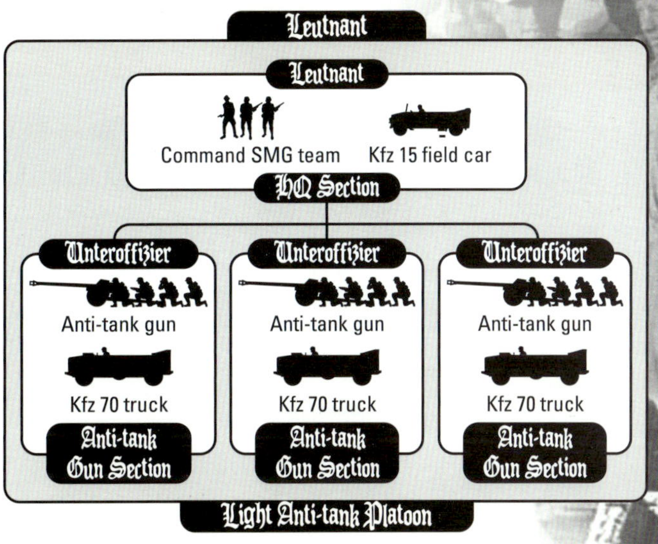

In the open desert anti-tank guns are vital for the infantry's survival. DAK was equipped with more and better anti-tank guns than any comparable formation in the world.

Every infantry battalion was supposed to have between three and twelve 5cm anti-tank guns as well as its lighter 2.8cm heavy anti-tank rifles. In practice, the number of guns varied almost as widely as their types with captured British and Soviet guns sometimes outnumbering the German ones. *288. Regiment zbV* of *90. leichte Afrikadivision* even fielded the 4.2cm PJK41 normally issued to parachute units!

Light Anti-tank Gun Platoons may make Combat Attachments to Combat Platoons.

0 to 1 Panzer Pioneer Platoon

The battalion Panzer Pioneer Platoons are organised the same as the Pioneer platoons shown on page 38.

0 to 2 Motorised Machine-gun Platoons

Platoon

HQ Section with:

2 Machine-gun Sections	155 points
1 Machine-gun Section	90 points

Panzergrenadier divisions consolidated their heavy weapons in one heavy company per battalion. These were allocated out as needed.

Motorised Machine-gun Platoons may make Combat Attachments to Combat Platoons.

0 to 1 Motorised Mortar Platoon

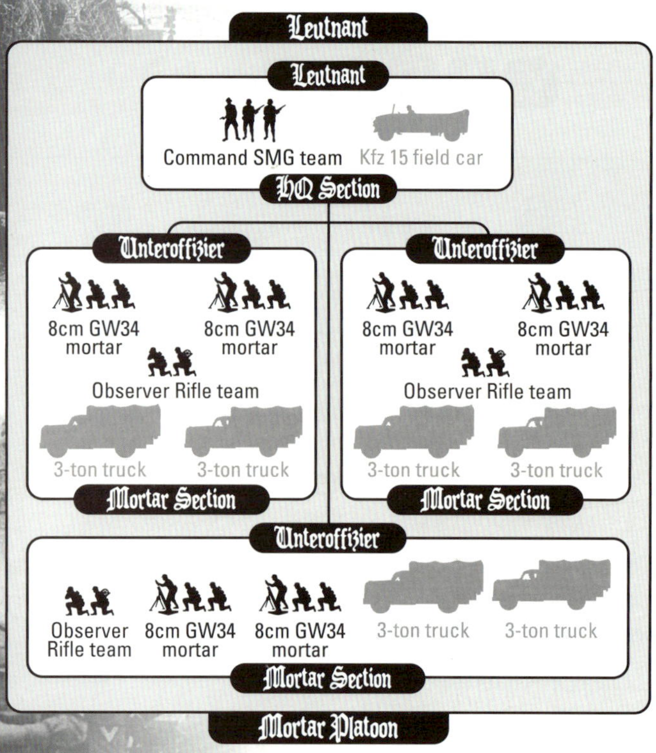

Platoon

HQ Section with:

3 Mortar Sections	215 points
2 Mortar Sections	150 points
1 Mortar Section	85 points

Options

- Add Kfz 15 field car and 3-ton trucks to the platoon at no cost.

The heavy company's mortar platoon gives the battalion's Panzergrenadier platoons instant firepower when they need it. With up to six tubes, the platoon rains devastation on any target in range.

SUPPORT PLATOONS

0 to 1 Scout Platoon

Scout Platoons are organised in the same way for both Panzer and Panzergrenadier forces. The organisation is shown on page 29.

0 to 1 Light Infantry Gun Platoon

Platoon

HQ Section with:

2 Gun Sections	95 points

Options

- Add Kfz 15 field car and Kfz 70 trucks to the platoon at no cost.
- Replace all Kfz 70 trucks with Sd Kfz 10 half-tracks for +5 points for the platoon.

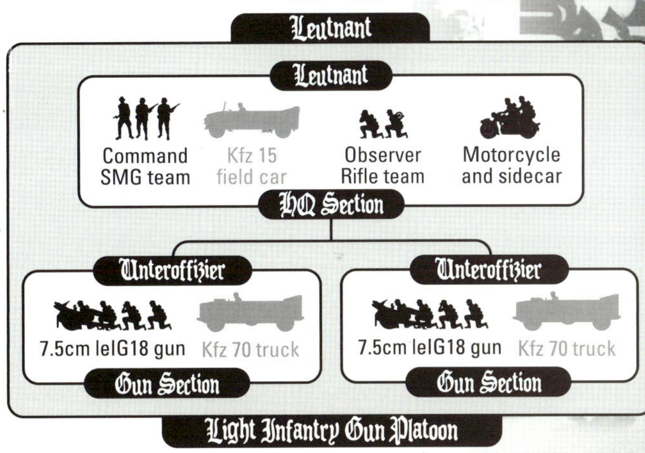

Light infantry guns were not particularly useful in the open desert, however the Panzer-grenadiers of *10. Panzerdivision* found them invaluable in the rough terrain of Tunisia. They were more common in the closer country of Italy however.

0 to 1 Heavy Infantry Gun Platoon

Platoon

HQ Section with:

2 Gun Sections	155 points

Options

- Replace each Bison (15cm sIG) with a 15cm sIG33 gun and Sd Kfz 11 half-track for -5 points for the platoon.
- Replace all Bison (15cm sIG) with Grille (15cm sIG) H self-propelled guns for +30 points for the platoon.

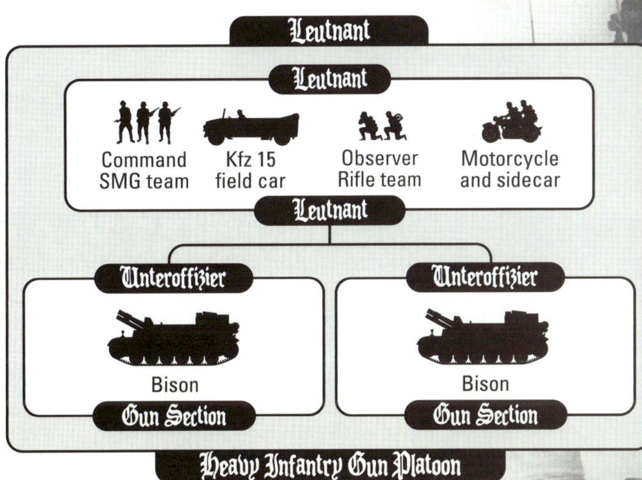

In 1942 the Afrikakorps received self-propelled infantry guns in the form of *707.* and *708. sIG Kompanie (mot S)*. Later in Italy, the mobile divisions received newer *Grille* self-propelled guns instead.

Gepanzerte Panzergrenadierkompanie

(MECHANISED COMPANY)

10. Panzerdivision *was the only Panzer division that served in Africa to have a gepanzerte* Panzergrenadierbataillon *(armoured Panzergrenadier Battalion),* I/ 69. Panzergrenadierregiment. *The infantry of this battalion had armoured half-tracks giving them greater mobility and firepower.*

You may field a gepanzerte Panzergrenadierkompanie, or armoured Panzergrenadier Company, containing:

- a Company HQ, and
- two or three Panzergrenadier Platoons.

Weapons Platoons for a gepanzerte Panzergrenadierkompanie are:

- an Armoured Heavy Platoon,
- a Light Infantry Gun Platoon,
- a Light Anti-tank Gun Platoon,
- and a Panzer Pioneer Platoon.

Support Platoons for an gepanzerte Panzergrenadierkompanie can be:

- a Scout Platoon,
- an Armoured Flame-thrower Platoon,
- Panzer Platoons,
- Armoured Panzer Pioneer Platoons,
- Armoured Car Patrols, and
- Divisional Support Platoons.

You may have up to two Support Platoons attached to your company for each Armoured Panzergrenadier Platoon you field.

Motivation and Skill

A Gepanzerte Panzergrenadierkompanie is well trained with plenty of combat veterans from the Eastern Front. The company is rated as **Confident Veteran**.

HEADQUARTERS

1 Company HQ

The Company HQ is organised like that of the Panzergrenadierkompanie on page 31. You must replace the Kfz 15 field car and may replace any Kfz 70 trucks or motorcycles, with Sd Kfz 251/1C half-tracks for +15 points per half-track.

COMBAT PLATOONS

2 or 3 Panzergrenadier Platoons

The Panzergrenadier Platoons are organised like the Panzergrenadier Platoon on page 32. In at least half of your Panzergrenadier Platoons you must replace the Kfz 15 field car with an Sd Kfz 251/10C (3.7cm) half-track for +20 points and each Kfz 70 truck with an Sd Kfz 251/1C half-track for +15 points per Panzergrenadier Squad.

Armoured Panzergrenadier Platoons have the Mounted Assault special rule

WEAPONS PLATOON

0 to 1 Armoured Heavy Platoon

Platoon

HQ Section with:

2 Machine-gun Sections	**200 points**
1 Machine-gun Sections	**120 points**
No Machine-gun Sections	**35 points**

Options

- Add a Mortar Section for +110 points.

An Armoured Heavy Platoon must have a Mortar Section if it has no Machine-gun Sections.

Armoured Heavy Platoons may make Combat Attachments to Combat Platoons.

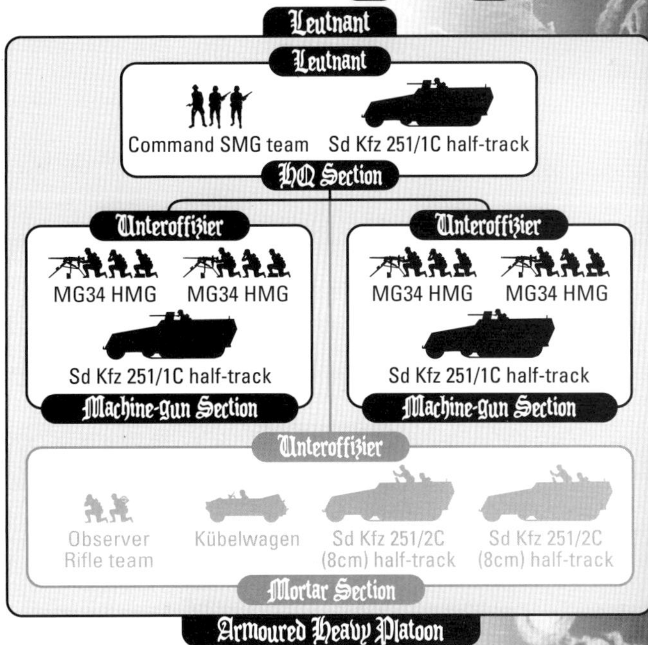

0 to 1 Light Anti-tank Gun Platoon

A light anti-tank gun platoon is organised like the motorised version on page 33. You may replace all Kfz 15 field cars and Kfz 70 trucks with Sd Kfz 251/1C half-tracks for +15 points per half-track.

0 to 1 Light Infantry Gun Platoon

A light infantry gun platoon is organised like the motorised version on page 35. You may replace all Kfz 15 field cars and Kfz 70 trucks with Sd Kfz 251/1C half-tracks for +15 points per half-track.

SUPPORT PLATOONS

0 to 1 Armoured Flame-thrower Platoon

Platoon

HQ Section with:

3 Flame Sections	**485 points**
2 Flame Sections	**330 points**
1 Flame Section	**175 points**

The *Sd Kfz 251/16 Flammpanzerwagen* armoured flame-thrower half-track is a terrifying weapon. Few troops are willing to stand as these half-tracks rush forward with flame gushing from each side. Be careful to keep them out of sight until the last moment though, they tend to explode when hit!

The Command Sd Kfz 251/1C half-track counts as a Tank team in an Armoured Flame-thrower Platoon.

The Command Sd Kfz 251/1C half-track in this platoon always counts as having its rear AA MG fitted, even though it doesn't carry any passengers.

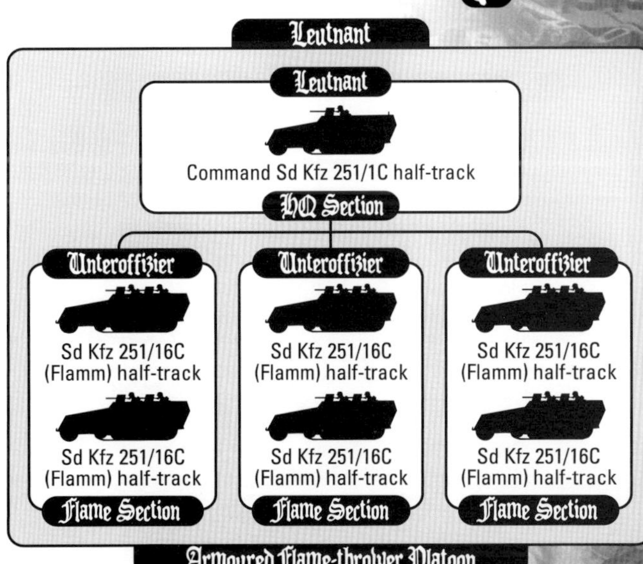

The Sd Kfz 251/16 mounts one flame-thrower on each side of the body. These can both fire at the same time, but must fire at the same enemy platoon. Each flame-thrower can fire at any target on its side of the half-track, from straight ahead to straight behind.

Panzerpionierkompanie

(INFANTRY COMPANY)

A division's Panzerpionierabteilung or armoured pioneer battalion is both a combat engineering unit, and its premier assault force armed with flame-throwers and demolition charges.

You may field a Panzerpionierkompanie containing:

- a Company HQ, and
- two or three Panzer Pioneer Platoons.

Weapons Platoons available to a Panzerpionierkompanie are:

- two Light Anti-tank Gun Platoons.

Support Platoons for a Panzerpionierkompanie can be:

- Heavy Infantry Gun Platoons,
- Panzer Platoons, and
- any Divisional Support Platoons.

A Panzerpionierkompanie may have up to **two** support platoons for each Panzer Pioneer Platoon in the force.

Motivation and Skill

The Panzerpionierkompanie is extremely well trained and confident of its abilities. It is rated as **Confident Veteran**.

HEADQUARTERS

1 Company HQ

The Company HQ is organised like that of the Panzergrenadierkompanie on page 31, but without an Anti-tank Rifle Section. You may add one Machine-gun Section from the Heavy Platoon on page 32 to the Company HQ platoon for +65 points.

COMBAT PLATOONS

2 or 3 Panzer Pioneer Platoons

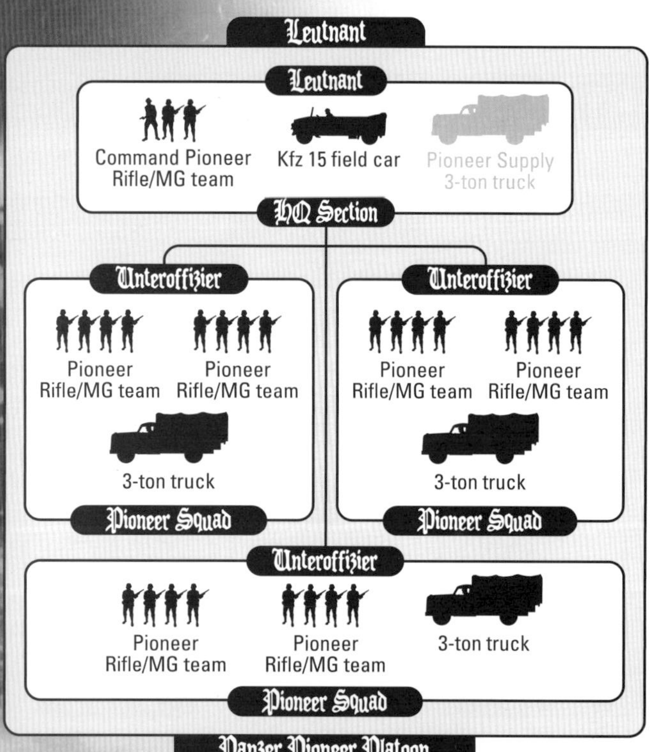

You may replace one Pioneer Rifle/MG team per Pioneer Squad with a Flame-thrower team at the start of the game before deployment.

Platoon

HQ Section with:

3 Pioneer Squads	225 points
2 Pioneer Squads	160 points
1 Pioneer Squad	95 points

Options

- Add Pioneer Supply 3-ton truck for +25 points.

Armoured Panzer Pioneer Platoon

Your company may upgrade one Panzer Pioneer Platoon to an Armoured Panzer Pioneer Platoon. To do so replace the Kfz 15 field car with an Sd Kfz 251/7C half-track for + 15 points and replace each 3-ton truck with two Sd Kfz 251/7C (Pioneer) half-tracks for +30 points per Pioneer Squad. You may arm the platoon commander's Sd Kfz 251/7C half-track with a 2.8cm anti-tank rifle in place of its hull MG for +5 points.

If you do so, the company becomes a Mechanised Company instead of an Infantry Company.

Armoured Panzergrenadier Platoons mounted in Sd Kfz 251/7C half-tracks have the Mounted Assault special rule

Aufklärungsschwadron

(RECONNAISSANCE MECHANISED COMPANY)

Every division in Africa has a Panzeraufklärungsabteilung, *an armoured reconnaissance battalion, with one or two scout companies (*Aufklärungsschwadron *pronounced owf-klairr-oongs shvad-rone) to back up the actual reconnaissance element of half a dozen armoured car patrols.*

You may field an Aufklärungsschwadron, or Scout Squadron, containing:

- a Company HQ, and
- one to three Aufklärungs Platoons.

Weapons Platoons for an Aufklärungsschwadron are:

- a Heavy Platoon,
- up to six Armoured Car Patrols,
- a Heavy Armoured Car Platoon,
- a Light Infantry Gun Platoon,
- two Light Anti-tank Gun Platoons,
- a Pioneer Platoon, and
- an Artillery Battery equipped with captured 25 pdr guns.

Support Platoons for an Aufklärungsschwadron can be:

- Panzer Platoons,
- Panzer Pioneer Platoons, and
- Divisional Support Platoons.

You may have up to **two** Support Platoons attached to your company for each Aufklärungs Platoon you field.

Motivation and Skill

An Aufklärungsschwadron is rated as **Confident Veteran**.

HEADQUARTERS

1 Company HQ

The Company HQ is organised like that of the Panzergrenadierkompanie on page 31.

You may replace the Kfz 15 field car and any Kfz 70 trucks or motorcycles with Sd Kfz 250 half-tracks for +15 points per half-track.

COMBAT PLATOONS

1 to 3 Aufklärungs Platoons

Aufklärungs Platoons are organised like the Panzergrenadier Platoon on page 32.

Aufklärungs Platoons must replace each Kfz 70 truck with two teams of one or two motorcycles and sidecars, or Kübelwagen jeeps, armed with a passenger-fired MG and mounted on the same base, for +5 points per platoon. They retain their Kfz 15 field car in the HQ Section.

If your Company HQ contains half-tracks, you must upgrade at least one platoon to an Armoured Aufklärungs Platoon instead. Replace the Kfz 15 field car with an Sd Kfz 250/10 (3.7cm), 250/11 (2.8cm), or 251/10C (3.7cm) half-track for +20 points and each Kfz 70 truck with either one Sd Kfz 251/1C half-track for +15 points or two Sd Kfz 250 half-tracks for +25 points per Panzergrenadier Squad.

Armoured Aufklärungs Platoons have the Mounted Assault special rule

If you only have one Aufklärungs Platoon in your company, you must also have at least one Weapons Platoon.

WEAPONS PLATOONS

0 to 1 Heavy Platoon

Heavy Platoons are organised like the Heavy Platoon shown on page 32.

Heavy Platoons must mount their Machine-gun Sections on motorcycles. Replace each Kfz 70 truck with two teams of one or two motorcycles and sidecars or Kübelwagen jeeps, armed with a passenger-fired MG and mounted on the same base for +5 points for the platoon. They retain their Kfz 15 car for the HQ Section and the Kfz 70 trucks for the Mortar Section.

If your Company HQ contains armoured half-tracks, you may upgrade the platoon to an Armoured Heavy Platoon instead as follows:

- Replace the Kfz 15 car in the HQ Section with an Sd Kfz 250 half-track for +10 points,
- Replace the Kfz 70 in each Machine-gun Section with two Sd Kfz 250 half-tracks for +40 points per Machine-gun Section, and,
- In the Mortar Section, replace the Kübelwagen with an Sd Kfz 250 half-track and the 8cm GW34 mortars and Kfz 70 trucks with Sd Kfz 250/7 (8cm) half-tracks for +30 points for the section. You may not add a third mortar to the section.

Note: The above platoons are not reconnaissance platoons. Their role is to clear the way for the armoured car platoons which are reconnaissance platoons.

0 to 6 Armoured Car Patrols

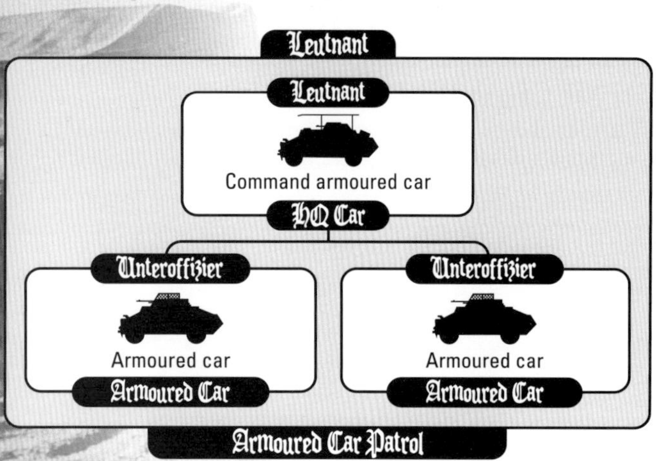

Platoon	
2 Sd Kfz 231 (8-rad)	**90 points**
Sd Kfz 223 (radio) with:	
2 Sd Kfz 222 (2cm)	**115 points**
1 Sd Kfz 222 (2cm)	**75 points**

- Replace any or all Sd Kfz 222 (2cm) with Sd Kfz 221 (2.8cm) at no cost.

Armoured cars and scout tanks perform an essential role as the eyes and ears of the *Panzertruppen*. Moving ahead of the advancing army, they stealthily seek out the enemy and report their activities.

Armoured Car Platoons are Reconnaissance Platoons.

0 to 1 Heavy Armoured Car Platoon

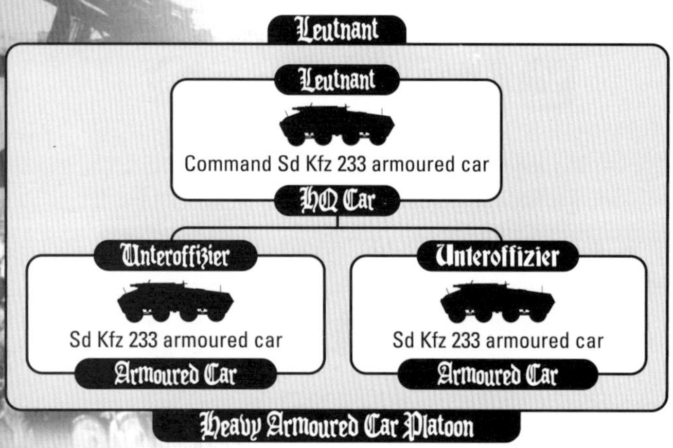

Platoon	
3 Sd Kfz 233 (7.5cm)	**185 points**
2 Sd Kfz 233 (7.5cm)	**125 points**

Schwere Panzerspähwagen (7.5cm) Sd Kfz 233 heavy armoured cars give their lighter brethren support against enemy road blocks. Their 7.5cm StuK37 (L/24) guns are excellent against entrenched infantry and useful against tanks

Heavy Armoured Car Platoons are* not *reconnaissance platoons.

0 to 2 Light Anti-tank Gun Platoons

Light Anti-tank Gun Platoons are organised like those of a Panzergrenadierkompanie, see page 33.

You may not upgrade these platoons with 7.62cm PaK36(r) guns.

0 to 1 Light Infantry Gun Platoon

The Light Infantry Gun Platoon is organised like that of a Panzergrenadierkompanie, see page 35.

If your Company HQ has armoured half-tracks, you may replace all Kfz 15 field cars and Kfz 70 trucks with Sd Kfz 251/1C half-tracks for +15 points per half-track.

0 to 1 Panzer Pioneer Platoon

The Panzer Pioneer Platoon is organised like that of a Panzerpionierkompanie, see page 38.

If your Company HQ has armoured half-tracks, you may make the Panzer Pioneer Platoon into an Armoured Panzer Pioneer Platoon.

0 to 1 Artillery Battery

This Artillery Battery is organised like the divisional support Artillery Battery on page 57.

The battery must be armed with captured 25 pdr guns.

Grenadierkompanie

(INFANTRY COMPANY)

'The foot-slogging Grenadierkompanie are tough, self-reliant warriors. German Grenadiers have fought and gained great victories for the Fatherland, bringing more land under the rule of the Third Reich, now they must hold this last bastion in Afrika, Tunisia.'
—Hauptmann Arndt Strauss

A force based around a Grenadierkompanie must contain:

- A Company HQ, and
- two or three Grenadier Platoons.

Weapons Platoons available to a Grenadierkompanie are:

- two Machine-gun Platoons, and
- a Mortar Platoon.

Support Platoons available to a Grenadierkompanie are:

- an Infantry Gun Platoon,
- a Scout Platoon,
- a Pioneer Platoon, and
- any Divisional Support Platoons.

You may have **two** Support Platoons for each Grenadier Platoon you field.

Motivation and Skill

The German Army is well trained and has many victorious campaigns behind it. The soldiers are confident that victory lies in the near future. A Grenadierkompanie is rated as **Confident Veteran**.

– used by divisions in Tunisia, Sicily and Italy.

HEADQUARTERS

1 Company HQ

Headquarters

Company HQ	40 points

Options

- Replace either or both Command SMG teams with Command Panzerknacker SMG teams for +5 points per team.
- Add an 8.8cm RW43 (Püppchen) launcher for +30 points.
- Add Mortar Section for +70 points.

The *Grenadierkompanie* may not be as glamorous as the motorised troops, but its role is every bit as important.

As the *Hauptmann*, you must lead your troops through assaults and defend your gains against the enemy using the resilience and courage of your Grenadiers as much as the power of their weapons.

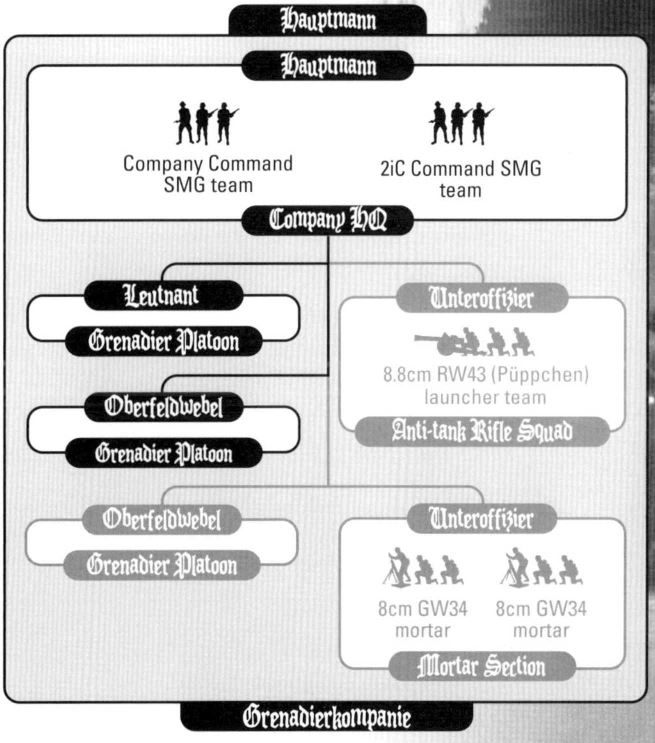

COMBAT PLATOONS

2 or 3 Grenadier Platoons

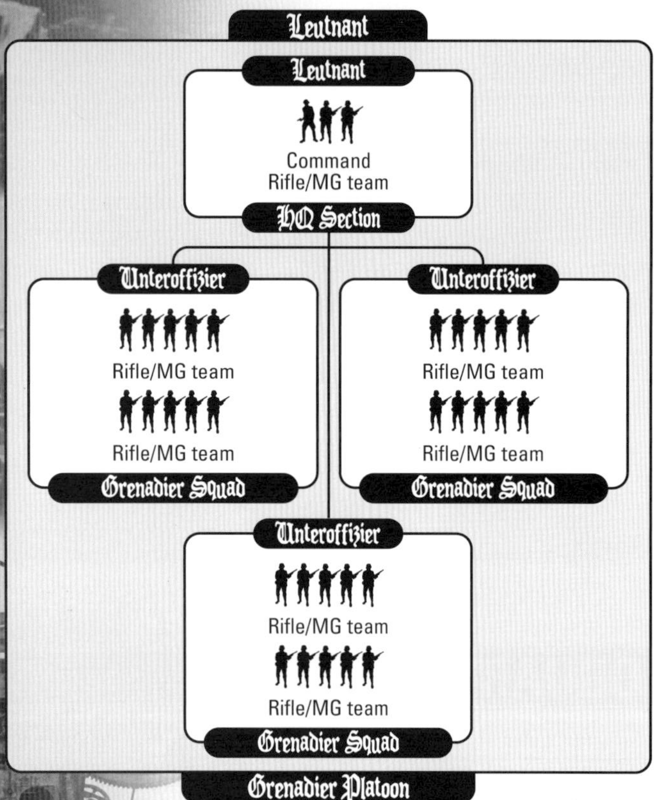

Platoon

HQ Section with:

3 Grenadier Squads	**155 points**
2 Grenadier Squads	**110 points**

Option

- Replace Command Rifle/MG team with a Command Panzerknacker SMG team for +5 points.

Grenadiers are the core components of the German war machine, performing brave and heroic deeds for the Fatherland.

German Grenadiers are better trained than any other army's soldiers. With their superior training, self-reliant Grenadiers perform the real work of the German Army, assaulting and capturing enemy positions, and holding these against counterattacks.

The *Infanterieregiment* has considerable engineering capability of its own and each battalion forms a pioneer platoon from its Grenadiers as needed. These infantry pioneers are called 'white' pioneers because they wear the white piping of infantry rather than the black piping of engineers.

If your Grenadierkompanie has three Grenadier Platoons, you may upgrade the smallest Grenadier Platoon to a Grenadier Pioneer Platoon for +15 points per Grenadier Squad. This converts the Command team and every Rifle/MG team into Pioneer teams with the same armament. The Grenadier Pioneer Platoon may have a horse-drawn Pioneer Supply truck for an additional +25 points.

Marschkompanie

When the Allies invaded French North Africa in Operation Torch, the German High Command responded by rounding up any available troops into *Marschbataillonen*, or March Battalions, and rushing them to Tunisia.

March battalions are normally formed to group together replacements from several units while they march to the front where they rejoin their own units. While the march battalions sent to Tunisia lacked the cohesion of permanent battalions, they still performed moderately well in combat considering their rushed creation.

You can field your Grenadierkompanie as a *Marschkompanie*, or March Company, making the Training rating of the entire company and its supporting troops Trained rather than Veteran. If you do this the number of points you have available to spend on your force increases as follows:

Normal Force	Marschkompanie force
1000 points	1300 points
1500 points	1950 points
2000 points	2600 points

- Your force cannot contain Infantry Gun Platoons.
- You may only have one Anti-tank Gun Platoon.

All Divisional Support Platoons remain Veteran, however their cost increases by +15 points for every 50 points or part thereof spent on them.

GERMAN

WEAPONS PLATOONS

0 to 1 Machine-gun Platoon

Platoon

HQ Section with:

2 MG Sections	145 points
1 MG Section	85 points

Option

- Replace Command SMG team with a Command Panzerknacker SMG team for +5 points.

Machine-gun platoons provide a *Schwerpunkt*, a concentration of intense firepower, to support the Grenadiers advance. Their devastating fire keeps the enemy's heads down as the infantry attack.

The machine-gun platoons also provide the main defensive fire against enemy counterattacks. As soon as an important objective is taken they dig in to hold them against all-comers.

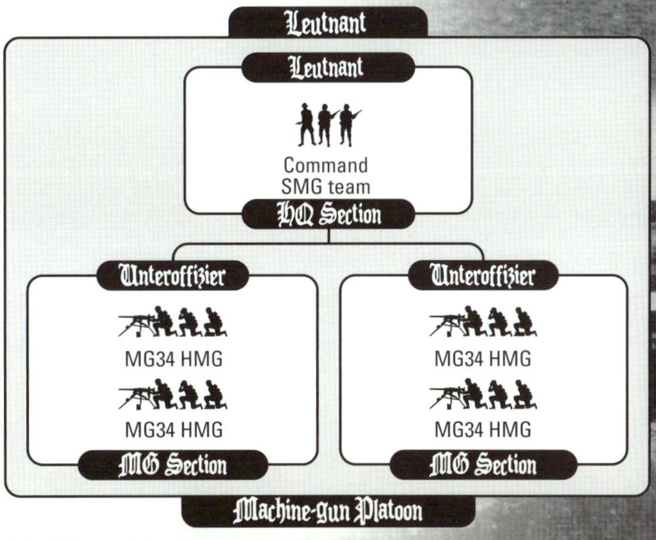

Machine-gun Platoons may make Combat Attachments to Combat Platoons.

0 to 1 Mortar Platoon

Platoon

HQ Section with:

3 Mortar Sections	205 points
2 Mortar Sections	145 points
1 Mortar Section	85 points

Option

- Replace Command SMG team with a Command Panzerknacker SMG team for +5 points.

Mortar platoons provide the Grenadierkompanie with their own artillery to bombard the enemy lines prior to an attack. While the enemy is looking heavenward the Grenadierkompanie will crush them from the front.

The mortar platoon is equally useful screening enemy strong points with smoke to neutralise them while the Grenadiers attack.

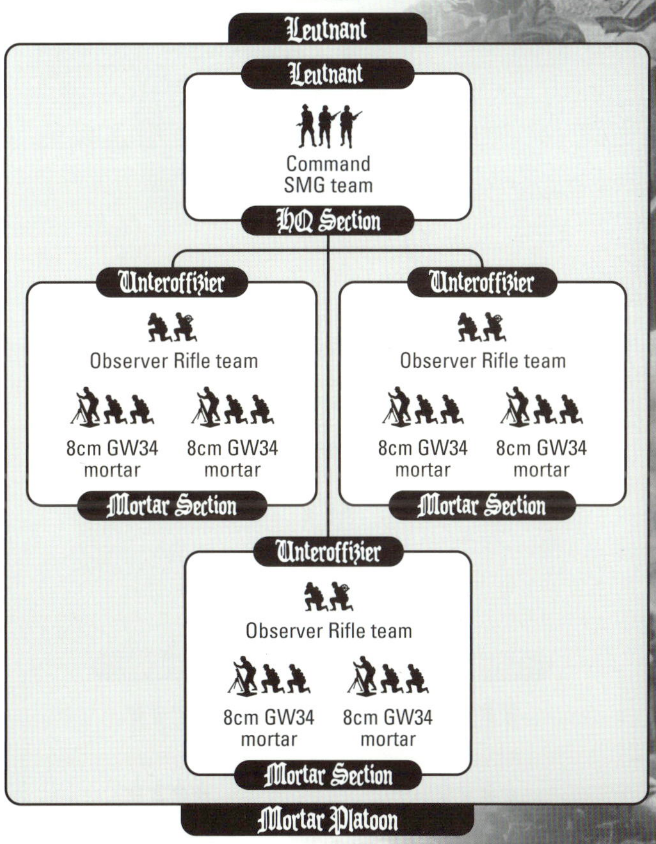

SUPPORT PLATOONS

0 to 1 Infantry Gun Platoon

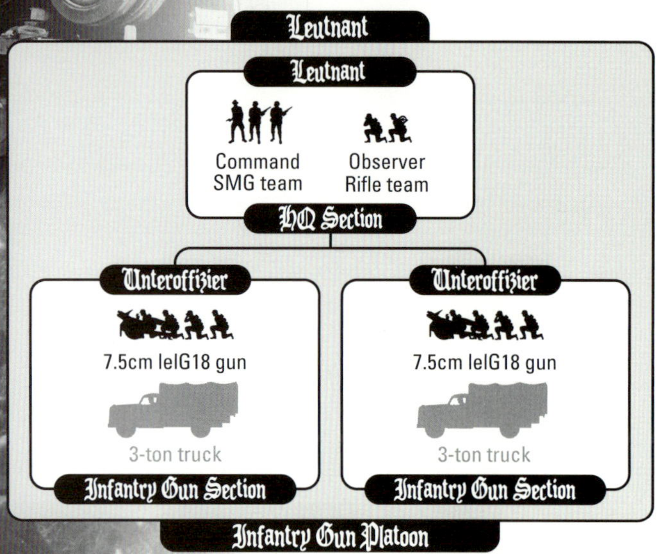

Platoon

HQ Section with:

2 Infantry Gun Sections	**90 points**

Options

- Add 3-ton trucks to the platoon at no cost.
- Replace Command SMG team with a Command Panzerknacker SMG team for +5 points.
- Replace all 7.5cm leIG18 guns with 15cm sIG33 guns for +55 points for the platoon.

Infantry Gun Platoons provide the Grenadierkompanie with close-support artillery, taking out targets such as gun positions, bunkers and machine-gun nests with direct fire.

The 7.5cm leIG18 guns are also effective at destroying enemy tanks should any stray towards the German lines.

The heavy 15cm sIG33 is not as handy or as versatile, but nothing beats it for sheer destructive power. Defences in buildings and bunker positions crumble before its heavy shells.

0 to 1 Scout Platoon

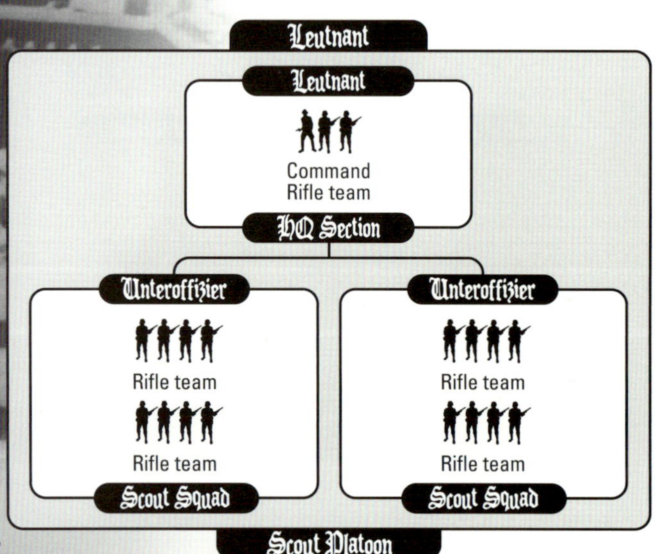

Platoon

HQ Section with:

2 Scout Squads	**110 points**
1 Scout Squad	**65 points**

Options

- Replace Command Rifle team with Command Panzerknacker SMG team for +15 points.

The scout platoons are the eyes of the German army, reconnoitring in front of the Grenadiers' advance, protecting the army from unpleasant surprises. The scouts can also operate as an advance force, taking important objectives by stealth and holding the enemy back until reinforcements arrive.

Scout Platoons are Reconnaissance Platoons

0 to 1 Pioneer Platoon

Platoon

HQ Section with:

3 Pioneer Sections	**220 points**
2 Pioneer Sections	**155 points**
1 Pioneer Section	**90 points**

Options

- Replace Command Pioneer Rifle team with Command Pioneer Panzerknacker SMG team for +5 points.
- Add Pioneer Supply 3-ton truck for +25 points.
- Add 3-ton trucks for +5 points per section.

'Black' pioneers perform all the specialist tasks that are required to get the army to the front. The divisional pioneers clear minefields, dig ditches and build roads and bridges. They also lead assaults against particularly tough enemy strong-points.

You may replace up to two Pioneer Rifle teams with Flame-thrower teams at the start of the game before deployment.

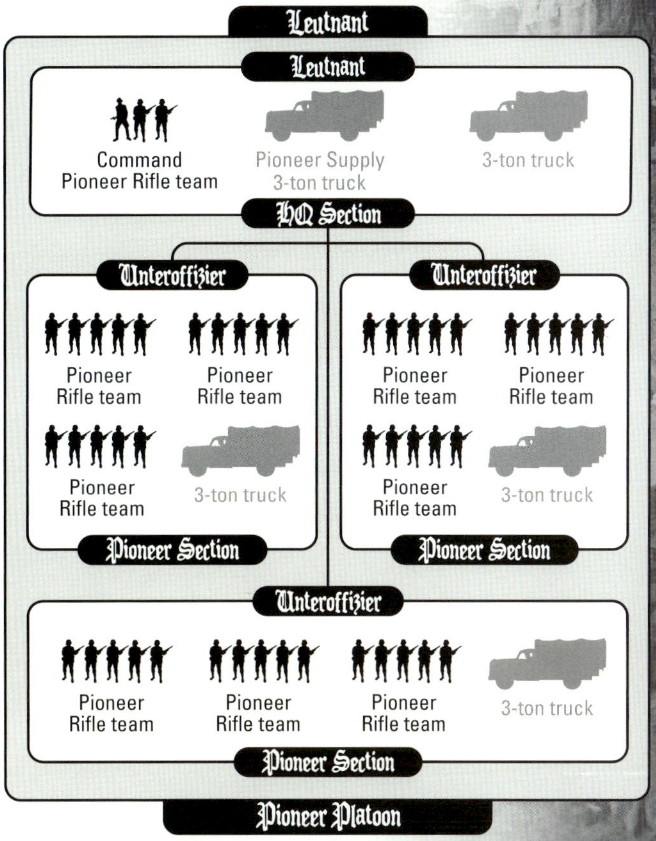

Operation Aida

Wehrmacht Communique
27 June 1942

MERSA MATRUH CAPTURED!

The English fortress of Mersa Matruh fell to the Afrikakorps in heavy fighting today. The entire 50. and 10. Indian Division was captured. The New Zealand Division is surrounded at Minqar Quiam outside the fortress and faces imminent destruction. Little now stands between our forces in Africa and total victory.

Wehrmacht Communique
28 June 1942

Last night the butchers of the New Zealand Division using gangster methods, including the slaughter of wounded soldiers, broke through the surrounding German troops. However few of the enemy escaped and many prisoners were taken.

Wehrmacht Communique
2 July 1942

VICTORY IN EGYPT!

For the last two days the Afrikakorps has launched heavy attacks on the final English position in front of Cairo at El Alamein. 21. Panzerdivision overran an Indian Brigade while 90. leichte Division attacked the South African Division making headway against intense artillery fire. The next few days may see the end of English resistance in Egypt.

Wehrmacht Communique
11 July 1942

21. Panzerdivision has captured several New Zealand positions south of the El Alamein position, despite a furious counterattack by the Australian Division against Italian troops at Tel El Eisa on the coast. The Australian attack has been stopped with heavy losses to the enemy.

Wehrmacht Communique
15 July 1942

Heavy fighting saw the virtual destruction of 5. Indian Division and the New Zealand Division on Ruweisat Ridge. The English divisions attacked at night capturing some of the ridge from the Italian defenders, but were quickly overwhelmed at first light by concentrated attacks made by the Afrikakorps. The enemy continues to batter themselves against our strong positions in front of El Alamein.

Wehrmacht Communique
22 July 1942

ALAMEIN LINE HOLDS!

Today the Afrikakorps repulsed further heavy attacks by English forces around Ruweisat Ridge. Over one hundred English tanks were destroyed and a New Zealand and an Indian Brigade overrun and taken prisoner. Anti-tank gunner Günter Halm of 104. Panzergrenadierregiment has been nominated for the Knight's Cross for destroying sixteen enemy tanks in this action. The Afrikakorps is heavily engaged all along the line, but continues to hold its positions and make local gains.

Wehrmacht Communique
30 July 1942

The crisis in North Africa is over. The English counterattacks by the Australian, Indian, and New Zealand Divisions of the last weeks have been beaten back with heavy losses to the enemy.

The Afrikakorps under Feldmarschall Rommel is preparing for a major offensive in August to destroy the exhausted remnants of the English Army, drive to the Nile, and complete the capture of Egypt. New tanks arrive daily and Mussolini has promised increased supplies of fuel.

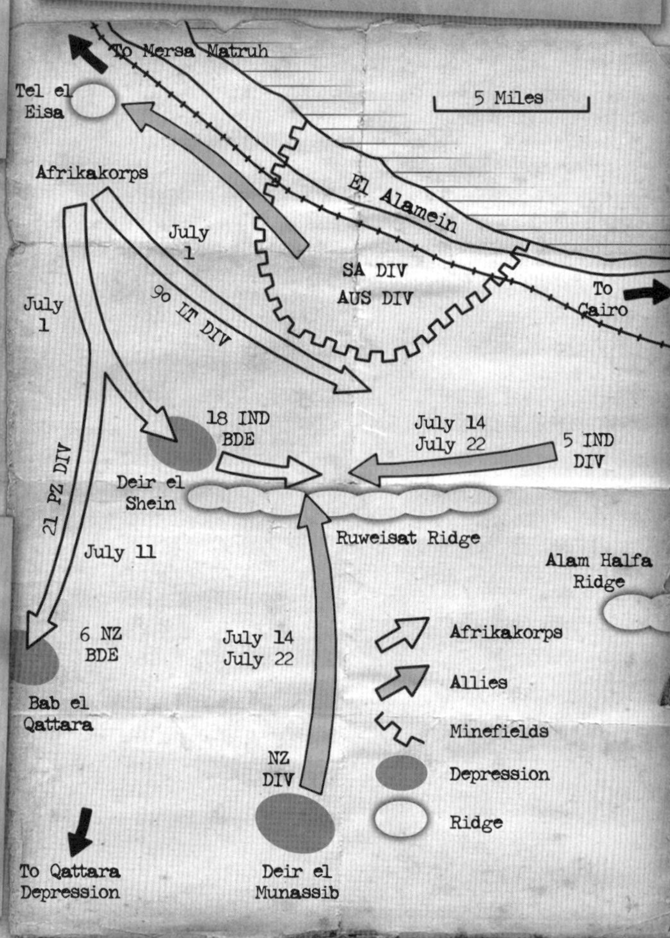

Fallschirmjägerkompanie

(INFANTRY COMPANY)

"The Diving Eagle badge says everything that one needs to know about the Fallschirmjäger, the parachute troops. The eagle symbolises the German soldier, brave, strong, and alert. It flies like the eagle of the Luftwaffe, the air force of which they are part. Diving towards the earth, it represents the swift and ferocious descent of the parachutist on his land-bound foe. The wreath speaks of valour and deeds of courage. Only a veteran of six parachute jumps may wear that badge on their breast. Only the bravest and the best."
—Hauptmann Hugo Sydow

A Fallschirmjägerkompanie force suitable for air assault operations must contain:

a Company HQ, and
two or three Fallschirmjäger Platoons.

Weapons Platoons available to a Fallschirmjägerkompanie are:

- two Parachute Machine-gun Platoons,
- a Parachute Mortar Platoon, and
- a Light Gun Platoon.

Support Platoons for a Fallschirmjägerkompanie can be:

- a Parachute Heavy Mortar Platoon,
- a Parachute Anti-tank Gun Platoon,
- a Parachute Anti-aircraft Platoon,
- a Glider Light Artillery Battery, or
- a Parachute Pioneer Platoon.

A Fallschirmjägerkompanie may not take any support platoons from the Divisional Support section for airborne operations except air support.

You may have up to **two** Support Platoons attached to your company for each Fallschirmjäger Platoon in it.

Motivation and Skill

All Fallschirmjäger are volunteers. They are put through rigorous selection examinations and hard training before they win their wings. A Fallschirmjägerkompanie is rated as **Fearless Veteran**.

HEADQUARTERS

1 Company HQ

Headquarters

Company HQ	55 points

Options

- Replace either or both Command SMG teams with Command Panzerknacker SMG teams for +5 points per team.
- Add an Anti-tank Rifle Squad with: an Anti-tank Rifle team for +30 points, a 2.8cm sPzB41 anti-tank rifle for +45 points or an 8.8cm RW43 (Püppchen) launcher for +50 points.
- Add a Mortar Section of up to three Light Mortar teams for +20 points per team, or up to three 8cm GW42 (Stummelwerfer) mortars for +30 points per mortar.

Fallschirmjäger used 5cm leGW36 light mortars and 7.92mm PzB39 anti-tank rifles in the Crete landings. Later the paratroops replaced their light mortars with more effective *Stummelwerfer* and adopted the heavy 2.8cm sPzB41 anti-tank rifle, and then, in Tunisia, the *Püppchen* rocket launcher.

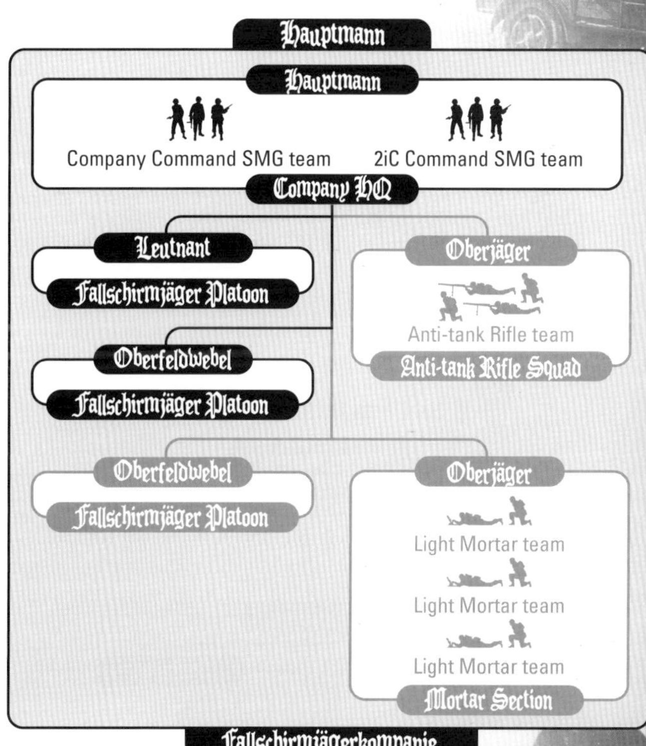

COMBAT PLATOONS

2 or 3 Fallschirmjäger Platoons

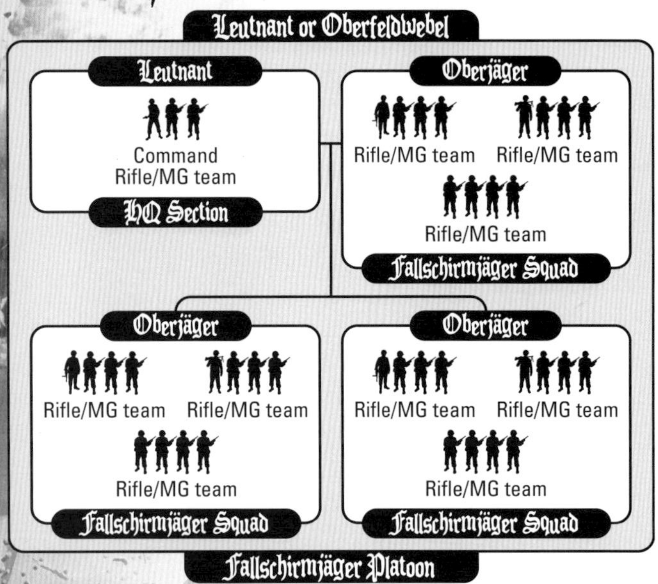

Platoon

HQ Section with

3 Fallschirmjäger Squads	**280 points**
2 Fallschirmjäger Squads	**195 points**

Option

- Replace Command Rifle/MG team with a Command Panzerknacker SMG team for +5 points.

The versatility of the Fallschirmjäger platoon makes it the core of the Fallschirmjägerkompanie. Six MG34 machine-guns make them deadly in a firefight, but determination and hard training make them even more dangerous in an assault.

WEAPONS PLATOONS

0 to 2 Parachute Machine-gun Platoons

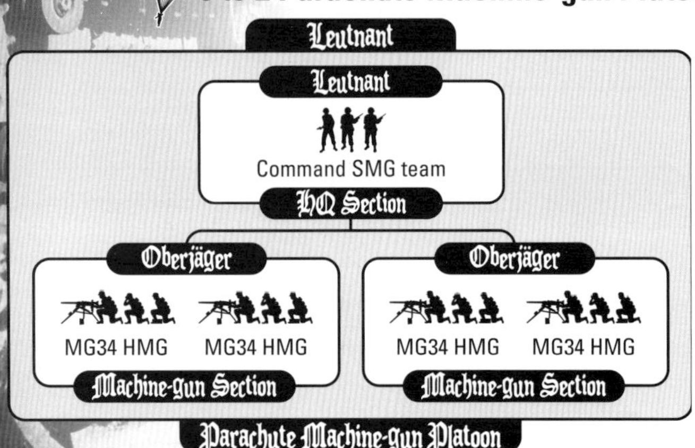

Platoon

HQ Section with

2 Machine-gun sections	**175 points**
1 Machine-gun section	**105 points**

Option

- Replace Command SMG team with a Command Panzerknacker SMG team for +5 points.

The massed long-range firepower of the machine-gun platoon is invaluable in both attack and defence.

Parachute Machine-gun Platoons may make Combat Attachments to Combat Platoons.

0 to 1 Parachute Mortar Platoon

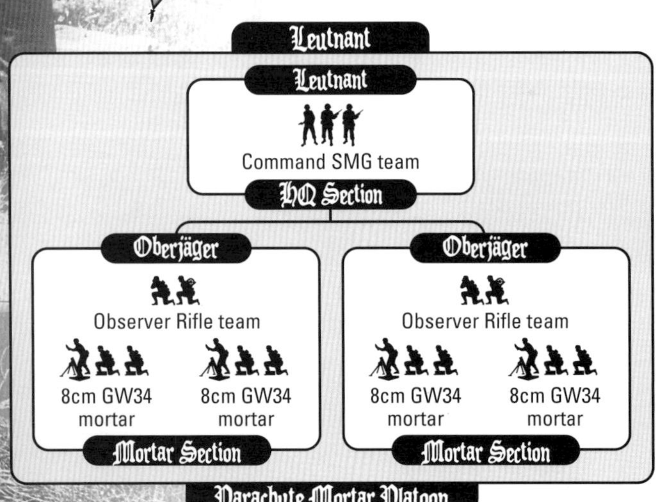

Platoon

HQ Section with

2 Mortar Sections	**175 points**
1 Mortar Section	**100 points**

Options

- Replace Command SMG team with a Command Panzerknacker SMG team for +5 points.
- Replace all 8cm GW34 mortars with 8cm GW42 (Stummelwerfer) mortars for -5 points per mortar section.

Mortars give the Fallschirmjägerkompanie its own artillery, able to deliver concentrated firepower anywhere along the company front.

0 to 1 Light Gun Platoon

Platoon

HQ Section with

2 Gun Sections	**90 points**
1 Gun Section	**60 points**

Option

- Replace Command SMG team with a Command Panzerknacker SMG team for +5 points.

The recoilless 7.5cm LG40 light gun entered service just in time for four of them to be used in the battles on Crete. Since then, they have been issued throughout the airborne forces as regimental anti-tank weapons.

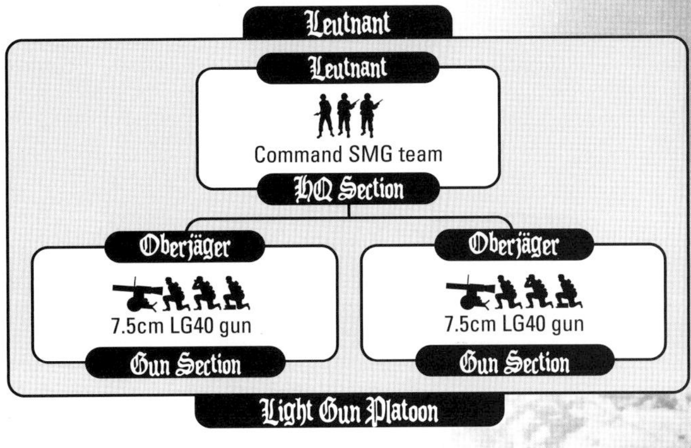

SUPPORT PLATOONS

0 to 1 Parachute Heavy Mortar Platoon

Platoon

HQ Section with

2 Mortar Sections	**200 points**
1 Mortar Section	**115 points**

Heavy mortars give the Fallschirmjägerkompanie the ability to blast enemy infantry out of buildings and trenches, as well as using their range to break up enemy counterattacks at a distance.

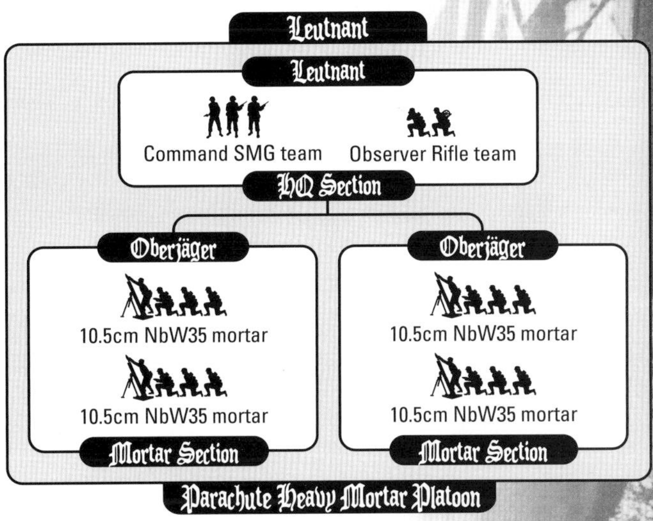

0 to 1 Parachute Anti-tank Gun Platoon

Platoon

HQ Section with

4 Anti-tank Gun Sections	**150 points**
3 Anti-tank Gun Sections	**120 points**
2 Anti-tank Gun Sections	**90 points**

Lightly equipped paratroops will always be vulnerable to armoured counterattacks. Air-droppable light 3.7cm PaK36 anti-tank guns protect against this serious threat.

In the early campaigns the anti-tank guns could only be airlifted in after an airfield was captured, but by the time of Crete, a new quadruple parachute allowed the guns to be dropped with the assault troops.

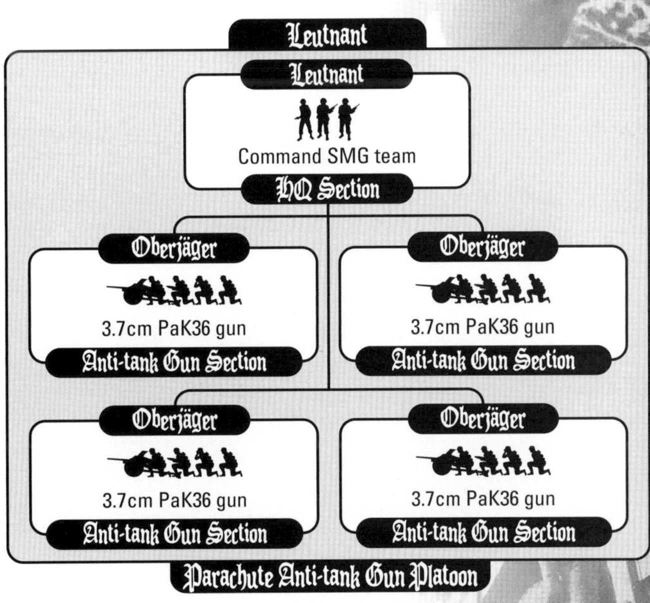

0 to 1 Parachute Anti-aircraft Gun Platoon

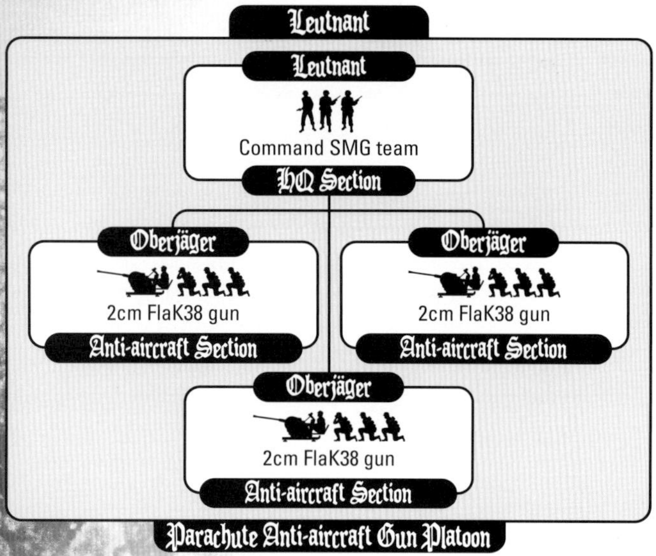

Platoon	
HQ Section with	
3 Anti-aircraft Sections	90 points
2 Anti-aircraft Sections	70 points

Tanks are not the only problem for lightly-equipped airborne troops. Although the *Luftwaffe* always provides maximum air support for airborne landings, they can't be everywhere all the time. That's where the anti-aircraft gun platoon comes in, keeping any enemy aircraft that break through the *Luftwaffe* fighters at bay. In the absence of enemy aircraft, the anti-aircraft guns are deadly against infantry.

0 to 1 Glider Light Artillery Battery

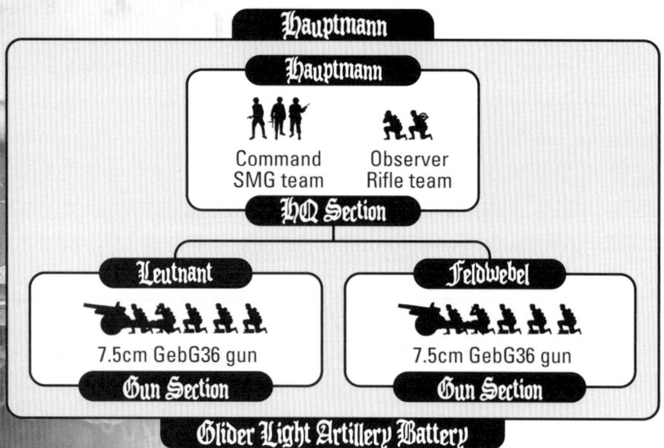

Platoon	
HQ Section with	
2 Gun Sections	155 points
1 Gun Section	100 points

Due to the scale of German airborne operations in the mid-war period, the deployment of light artillery by air was relatively rare. The 10.5cm LG40 recoilless gun and the 7.5cm GebG36 mountain gun are by far the heaviest equipment available in an air assault. These guns could only be delivered to the battlefield by gliders.

You may replace all 7.5cm GebG36 guns with 10.5cm LG40 recoiless guns at the start of the game before deployment

...Crete, 1941...

"We were dug in overlooking Maleme Airfield. We got a pasting from Stukas and Ju88's and then the Ju52's came into view. We thought they were Heinkels at first. But then the paratroopers began to drop."

"They looked like thistledown, drifting on the wind. Then we realized there were men under those canopies. We hosed 'em with everything we had. Some we shot, some fell into the sea. And still they came on."

"And could those blighters fight! They'd land with a pistol and a couple of grenades. Then, they'd have to fight their way to their weapons canisters. A puff of wind could put 'em hundreds of yards from their mates, or from their weapons, but still they fought. We really didn't know what we were facing."

"We drove them out of Galatas three times. At bayonet point. By then, we were too tired, and too few, to hold the town. We fell back. They followed and attacked. We held 'em. Even counterattacked. But they worked their way around our positions. We were trapped, caught in a crossfire. We held on until nightfall, then fell back again."

"We had little food and no water. The paratroopers didn't have it any easier. One I talked to later said they'd nothing to eat for five days."

"At one stage we were sharing a stream with a group of paratroopers. Our water party would go down and fill our water bottles, and then theirs would do the same for them. This worked well until someone with more ammunition than sense decided to take a shot. Nobody got any water after that."

0 to 1 Parachute Pioneer Platoon

Platoon

HQ Section with

3 Pioneer Squads	**360 points**
2 Pioneer Squads	**250 points**
1 Pioneer Squad	**140 points**

Options

- Replace Command Pioneer Rifle/MG team with a Command Panzerknacker Pioneer SMG team for +5 points.

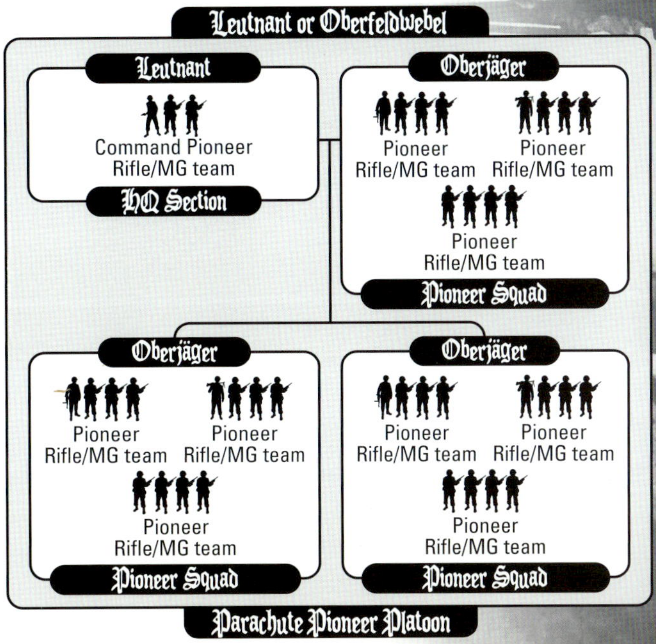

The Pioneer Platoons were true assault engineers. They are expected to be in the forefront of attacks on fortified positions where their flame-throwers and demolition charges give them an edge.

You may replace up to one Pioneer Rifle/MG team per Pioneer Squad with a Flame-thrower team at the start of the game before deployment.

Glider Assaults

Pioneers often land by glider in a surprise strike at the start of an airborne assault. The gliders are small and only carry eight men so the squad must pick its best soldiers for the operation.

You may land a Parachute Pioneer Platoon by glider instead of by parachute for an additional cost of +75 points for the platoon. This gives the platoon one glider per Pioneer Squad. The HQ Section travels with a Pioneer Squad in the lead glider.

A platoon that lands by glider reduces each Pioneer Squad to two Pioneer Rifle/MG teams instead of three. If you land by glider you may also replace one of the Pioneer Rifle/MG teams in each platoon with a Pioneer HMG team at no cost.

Fallschirmpionierkompanie

(PARACHUTE PIONEER INFANTRY COMPANY)

The *Fallschirmjäger* assault engineers were deployed in every theatre the *Fallschirmjäger* were present, from Crete to the Eastern Front. A particularly high proportion of the *Fallschirmjäger* defending Tunisia were pioneers, including the men of *Hauptmann* Witzig's *Fallschirmpionierbataillon* who fought with such skill and ferocity at Djebel Abiod and Jefna, and Barenthin's *Fallschirmjäger* battalion. To recreate their exploits you can form a Fallschirmpionierkompanie.

A force from a Fallschirmpionierkompanie contains:

- a Company HQ, and
- two to four Parachute Pioneer Platoons.

The Company HQ is organised like that of a Fallschirmjägerkompanie, but has no Mortar Section. Instead it may have a Machine-gun Section with one or two MG34 HMG teams for +35 points per team. The Company HQ may land by glider for free if all of the Parachute Pioneer Platoons do so.

The weapons and support platoons available to a Fallschirmpionierkompanie are identical to those of a Fallschirmjägerkompanie, with exception of heavy mortar platoons which are not available.

A Fallschirmpionierkompanie may take part in airborne or ground operations.

Fallschirmjäger Ground Operations

Although the Diving Eagles are specialists in airborne assaults, they often fight in ground operations. Even after a successful airborne assault there are always counter-attacks to fight off and pockets of resistance that must be reduced. For these operations the initial parachute force is reinforced with heavy weapons and transport vehicles airlifted into captured airfields.

As elite infantry, the Fallschirmjäger fight other battles entirely on the ground, playing a significant part in Germany's battles on every front including operations in Russia, the Desert, Tunisia, and Italy.

Regular army troops frequently support the Fallschirmjäger in both types of operation. In normal infantry operations the infantry, armour, and artillery of the army units they are supporting work closely with the paratroopers. Since they are the best, it is not unusual to see heavy Tiger tanks fighting alongside the paratroops.

As usual, you may have up to **two** Support Platoons attached to your company for each Fallschirmjäger Platoon you field.

Support Platoons for a Fallschirmjägerkompanie fighting a ground operation can be:

- a Heavy Mortar Platoon,
- up to two Towed Anti-tank Gun Platoons,
- a Parachute Tank-hunter Platoon,
- an Anti-aircraft Gun Platoon,
- a Light Artillery Battery, or
- a Parachute Pioneer Platoon.

As these are the normal Fallschirmjägerkompanie support platoons equipped for ground operations with heavier weapons and more vehicles, they remain rated as **Fearless Veteran.**

A Fallschirmjägerkompanie supported by any of these support platoons cannot take part in an airborne assault.

You may also support your Fallschirmjägerkompanie with regular army platoons for ground operations. See page 55 for a guide to which platoons are available in the various theatres of war. Troops fielded in this way count towards your force's total of allowable Support Platoons.

0 to 1 Heavy Mortar Battery

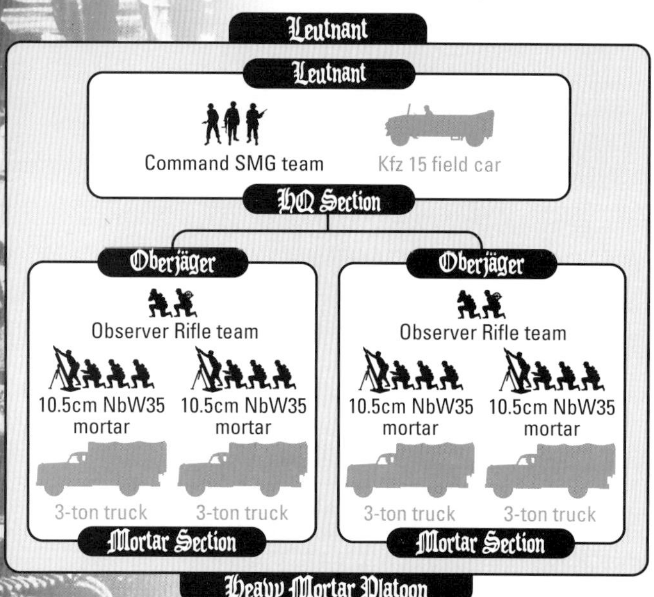

Platoon

HQ Section with

2 Mortar Sections	**215 points**
1 Mortar Section	**120 points**

Option

- Add Kfz 15 field car and 3-ton trucks at no cost.

For ground operations heavy mortar platoons are often equipped with trucks to carry their weapons and equipment. The extra mobility makes them much handier in attacks since they can move rapidly to wherever their support is most needed.

Motorcycles

In Tunisia and Italy some units formed motorcycle detachments to give them a mobile reserve. To reflect this, you may equip your Fallschirmjäger Platoons with motorcycles for ground operations.

Your Company HQ may be equipped with a motorcycle team with a passenger-fired MG for each of the two command teams for +10 points. Any or all Fallschirmjäger Platoons may be equipped with a motorcycle team with a passenger-fired MG for each Rifle/MG team for +5 points per team.

A company equipped with motorcycles is a Mechanised Company.

0 to 2 Towed Anti-tank Gun Platoons

Platoon

HQ Section with

3 Anti-tank Gun Sections	125 points
2 Anti-tank Gun Sections	95 points

Options

- Replace all motorcycles & sidecars with Kettenkrad tractors at no cost or Kfz 70 trucks for +5 points for the platoon.
- Equip all 3.7cm PaK36 guns with Stielgranate ammunition for +5 points per gun.
- Replace all 3.7cm PaK36 guns and motorcycles with 4.2cm PJK41 guns and Kfz 70 trucks for +10 points per section.
- Replace all 3.7cm PaK36 guns and motorcycles with 5cm PaK38 guns and Kfz 70 trucks for +15 points per section.
- Replace all 3.7cm PaK36 guns and motorcycles with 7.5cm PaK40 guns and 3-ton trucks for +60 points per section.
- You must add a Kfz 15 field car to any platoon equipped with Kfz 70 or 3-ton trucks for +5 points.

You may only have one Towed Anti-tank Gun Platoon equipped with 4.2cm PJK41, 5cm PaK38, or 7.5cm PaK40 anti-tank guns.

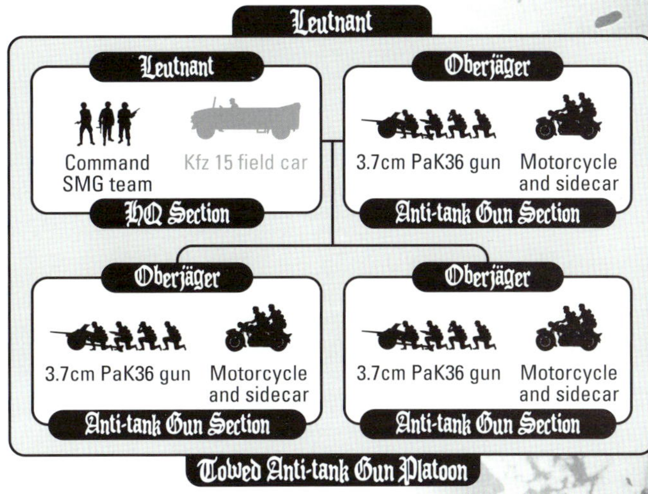

Once they have taken an airfield, the Diving Eagles quickly fly in more anti-tank guns complete with motorcycle or *Kettenkrad* tractors. These are replaced with Kfz 70 trucks for ground operations, making them a truly mobile force.

As air assault operations began to take a back seat to normal infantry operations, the necessity for weapons to be air-transportable lessened and the paratroops gained small numbers of heavier anti-tank guns like the 4.2cm PJK41, 5cm PaK38 and the 7.5cm PaK40.

0 to 1 Parachute Tank Hunter Platoon

Platoon

4 Marder II	520 points
3 Marder II	390 points
2 Marder II	260 points

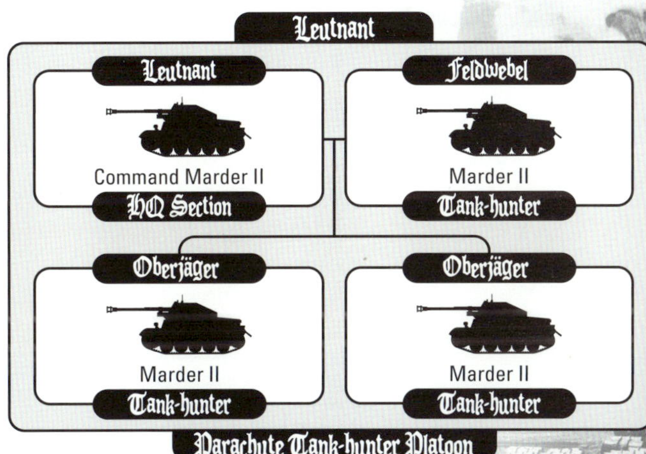

As ground operations became more common, the Fallschirmjäger were issued with more heavy weapons like self-propelled tank-hunters. These arrived in time for the Sicily and Italy campaigns.

The heavy guns of the Marder tank-hunters can destroy any tank the enemy cares to send against them, although their light armour and lack of overhead protection make them very vulnerable to enemy fire.

0 to 1 Anti-aircraft Platoon

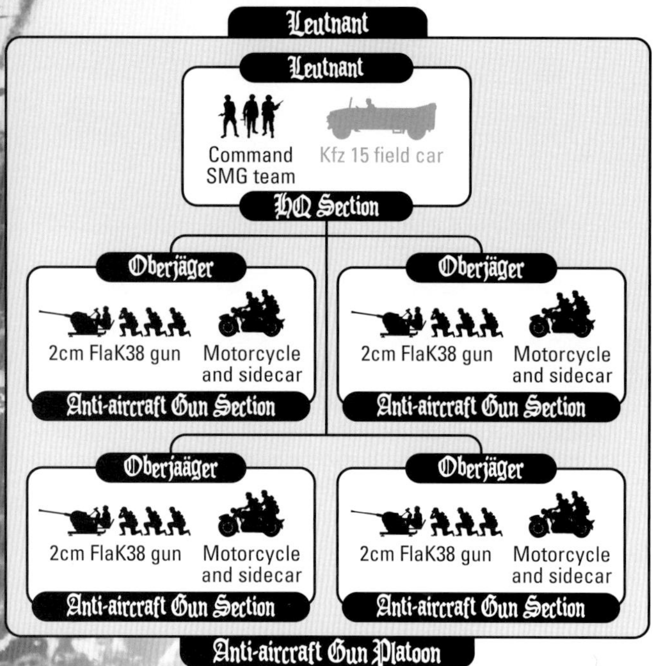

Platoon

HQ Section with

4 Anti-aircraft Sections	**135 points**
3 Anti-aircraft Sections	**110 points**
2 Anti-aircraft Sections	**85 points**

Options

- Remove gun shields from all 2cm Flak38 guns for -5 points per gun.
- Replace all motorcycles and sidecars with Kettenkrad tractors at no cost or Kfz 70 trucks for +5 points for the platoon.
- You must add a Kfz 15 car to any platoon equipped with Kfz 70 trucks for +5 points.

Anti-aircraft guns and their motorcycle tractors arrive as soon as an airfield is captured. Once the surprise of an air assault is gone, anti-aircraft guns are vital to protect ground forces.

0 to 1 Light Artillery Battery

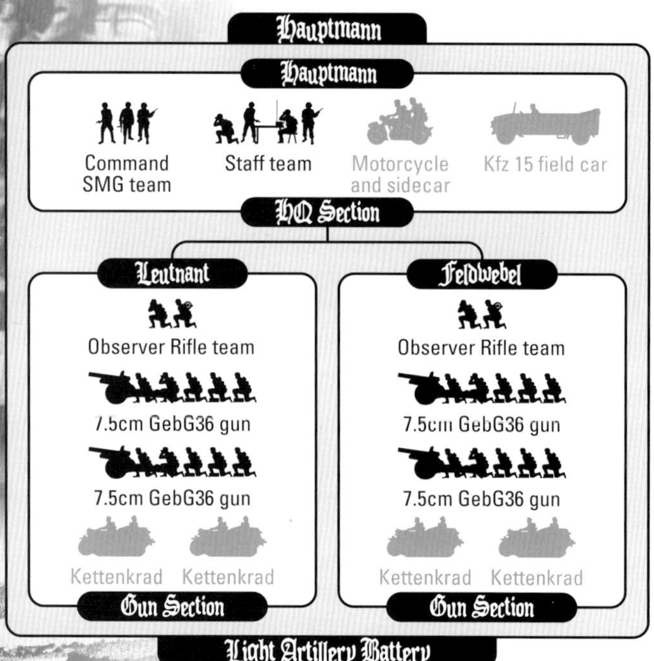

Platoon

HQ Section with

2 Gun Sections	**270 points**
1 Gun Section	**155 points**

Options

- Add Motorcycle and sidecar and Kettenkrad tractors at no cost.
- Replace motorcycle and sidecar with a Kfz 68 radio truck and add a Kfz 15 field car to HQ section for +5 points.
- Replace all Kettenkrad tractors with Kfz 70 trucks for +5 points per section.

Usually, the crews of the light artillery batteries are equipped with two different artillery pieces, the conventional 7.5cm mountain gun and the newly developed 10.5cm recoilless gun. Before an operation the *Fallschirmjäger* commander selects the most appropriate weapon for the mission.

You may replace all 7.5cm GebG36 guns with 10.5cm LG40 recoilless guns at the start of the game before deployment.

0 to 1 Parachute Pioneer Platoon

After the initial assault, the Pioneer Platoon eagerly awaits the '*Tante Ju*' transport aircraft carrying replacement demolition charges and other stores, readying themselves for ground operations.

See page 49 for the organisation of a Parachute Pioneer Platoon. You may add a Pioneer Supply 3-ton truck to the HQ Section for +25 points.

Army Support

The Desert

As *Fallschirmbrigade Ramcke* received its urgent call-up to El Alamein , the unit was in Italy preparing for Operation *Herakles*, the planned airborne invasion of Malta. Upon arrival in North Africa, the Brigade was still only equipped with light airborne weapons. They were positioned in the line between the infantry divisions and their Italian comrades, the *Folgore* Parachute Division. The *Fallschirmjäger* anti-tank company was equipped with light 3.7cm PaK36 and 4.2cm PJK41 guns. These along with attached *Luftwaffe* anti-aircraft guns and army artillery gave the Brigade enough firepower to hold an extended section of the line.

It was fortunate that the main battles bypassed them as the only Axis armoured vehicles present were an occasional platoon of Italian tanks and armoured car patrols. The paratroopers' own Marder tank-hunters were not yet available.

For ground operations in the Desert, you may field a total of **two** of the following platoons as Support Platoons:

- an Armoured Car Patrol,
- an Artillery Battery,
- a Heavy Anti-aircraft Gun Platoon,
- an allied Italian Carri Platoon or
- an allied Italian Paracadutisti Platoon.

Tunisia

Following the Allied invasion of French North Africa, ad-hoc groupings of *Fallschirmjäger* valiantly repelled the initial Allied advances into Tunisia. These hastily assembled units were part of the *General Göring* and *Von Broich* (later *Von Manteuffel*) Divisions. They could call upon support from many regular units throughout the campaign, both German and Italian, and were much better equipped for ground operations than previously. The additional anti-tank weapons including the 5cm PaK38 and 7.5cm PaK40 heavy anti-tank guns.

Fighting alongside the deadly new Tigers, the *Fallschirmjäger* led attacks that stalled and drove back the invaders. Even as the superior weight of Allied firepower pierced the Axis perimeter, the *Fallschirmjäger* fought on.

For ground operations in Tunisia, you may field up to **two** of the following platoons as Support Platoons:

- a Panzer Platoon,
- a Light Panzer Platoon,
- a Panzergrenadier Platoon,
- an Armoured Car Patrol,
- an Artillery Battery,
- a Tank-hunter platoon,
- a Heavy Anti-aircraft Gun Platoon,
- a Rocket Launcher Battery, or
- a Heavy Tank Platoon,
- an allied Italian Self-propelled 75/18 Platoon,
- an allied Italian Bersaglieri Platoon,
- an allied Italian Motorised Anti-tank Platoon, or
- an allied Italian Self-propelled 47/32 Platoon.

Sicily and Italy

The *Fallschirmjäger* units that landed on Sicily to counter the Allied invasion were fresh from reforming in France. Hastily formed into *Kampfgruppen* with elements of the *Hermann Göring* Panzer Division, they were in action almost immediately. The rugged nature of the terrain on Sicily, which had dictated Allied selection of landing beaches, also meant that bridges were to play a major strategic role in the campaign. In defence of these, as well as the airfield at Catania, the *Fallschirmjäger* were supported by their own Marder tank-hunters for the first time and Tiger heavy tanks and StuG assault guns from the *Hermann Göring* Division. They fought many delaying actions to allow Axis forces to evacuate to the Italian mainland.

Fallschirmjäger units were amongst the German troops that had been spirited into Italy prior to the Italian surrender, and were attached to a variety of Panzer and *Panzergrenadier* divisions in the subsequent campaign against the invading Allies. The *Fallschirmjäger* received a lot of heavy support as they offered fierce resistance from a succession of defensive lines that crossed the Italian peninsula.

For ground operations in Sicily, you may field up to **two** of the following platoons as Support Platoons:

- a Panzer Platoon
- a Panzergrenadier Platoon
- a Heavy Tank Platoon
- an Assault Gun Platoon
- a Heavy Anti-aircraft Gun Platoon, or
- an Artillery Battery.

When fighting ground operations in Italy, you may add the following platoons to the list:

- an Armoured Car Patrol and,
- a Rocket Launcher Battery.

...Koch, Medjez-el-Bab 1943...

The winter moon hung high above us, casting a strange light upon the town. We found ourselves hunkered down upon the banks of the river that flowed past Medjez, hidden amongst the outcrops of eucalyptus and cacti. Our uniforms were soaked with water from the river and sweat, the anticipation of battle. I wondered if the enemy knew we were coming. Oberstleutnant Koch was up ahead next to a rocky outcrop with Marke and Freytag. They were crouched around a map. I could see their breath clearly in the cold night air. Soon, the message was being passed down the line from man to man, check equipment and weapons; we were to move any minute. I checked the firing mechanism on my Maschinenpistole carefully as I had grown accustomed to, always thinking back to poor Heinz. Dreadful. Secured in my webbing belt sat two Steilhandgranaten and I had also been issued a satchel charge which I had secured against my left leg. Then the order came! It was time! Move, move! Keep low, move fast! Koch was the first to make his way up the rocky river bank and soon we were all on our feet and following.

The high-pitched staccato of the MG34 erupted furiously from behind us as we advanced upon the town. Tracer fire cut the air above us, roaring incessantly as we threaded between the rocks and cacti. My heart hammered, my breathing was ragged, yet on we moved keeping low until we could close with the enemy. Still the machine-guns spat fire and we could see the impacts as they struck the earthworks that the enemy lay behind. By this time, they had roused from their initial surprise and had begun to return fire. Our advance stalled somewhat. Kleiner and Brehme both fell in quick succession close to me. I could hear Koch urging us onwards, to keep advancing, to keep moving. My legs felt like leaden weights beneath me. Bullets flashed and cracked among us but soon we closed on the outer buildings of Medjez. We fell upon the enemy with such speed and ferocity that he knew not what to do. Confusion reigned. Chaos erupted about us as we stormed into the town. Everything was a target. I loosed off a quick burst of fire from my Maschinenpistole towards a doorway. The mangled and broken door swung drunkenly from its hinges. I tossed a grenade into the aperture. A dull explosion erupted from within the building, scattering wood and brick in every direction.

We advanced quickly through the streets of Medjez. The Oberstleutnant was everywhere, urging us on. Grenades and bullets were sent into every shadow. Every building, any place that the enemy could find to hide was destroyed. Soon the enemy resistance became sporadic and fleeting. They were slowly falling back under the strength of our assault. The order was passed around, dig in and await the counterattack.

Divisional Support Platoons

Your force may have the following support platoons:

- Artillery Batteries,
- Anti-tank Gun Platoons,
- Tank-hunter Platoons,
- a Heavy Anti-aircraft Gun Platoons,
- Rocket Launcher Batteries,
- Light Anti-aircraft Platoons,
- an Assault Gun Platoon
- a Heavy Tank Platoon
- an allied Italian Carri Platoon,
- an allied Italian Bersaglieri Platoon, and
- an allied Italian Self-propelled 75/18 Platoon

Motivation and Skill

Like the combat troops they support, the divisional support platoons are experienced troops that know their own worth. Divisional Support Platoons are rated as **Confident Veteran**.

Air Support

Aircraft	Priority Air Support	Limited Air support
Ju 87D Stuka	175 points	135 points
Ju 87G Stuka	175 points	135 points
Hs 129B	200 points	155 points
Bf 109E or FW 190F	165 points	130 points

Artillery Battery

Platoon

HQ Section with:

2 Gun Sections	220 points
1 Gun Section	125 points

Option

- Add Kfz 15 field car, Kfz 68 radio truck and 3-ton trucks at no cost.
- Replace Kübelwagen jeeps with Sd Kfz 250, 253, or 254 half-tracks for +10 points per half-track
- Replace any or all Observer Rifle teams and their Kübelwagen with Observer Panzer II tanks for +25 points per tank.
- Replace all 3-ton trucks with Sd Kfz 11 half-tracks for +5 points for the battery.
- Replace all 10.5cm leFH18 guns with captured 25 pdr guns at no cost.

Option (15. & 21. Panzerdivision only)

- Replace each 10.5cm leFH18 gun and its tractor with a 15cm (Sf) Lorraine Schlepper for +30 points per Gun Section.

Option (90. Afrikadivision only)

- Replace all 10.5cm leFH18 guns with 7.62cm FK36(r) guns for +20 points per Gun Section.

Option (164. Afrikadivision only)

- Replace all 10.5cm leFH18 guns with 7.5cm GebG36 guns for -25 points per Gun Section.
- Remove gun shields from 7.5cm GebG36 guns for -15 points per Gun Section. 7.5cm GebG36 guns without gun shields are Medium Gun teams.

DAK is always short of artillery, so every division uses the British 25 pdr guns they capture to make up the numbers. When *90. leichte Afrikadivision* formed, there were no German guns available, so its single artillery battalion has 25 pdr and Soviet 7.62cm guns.

The second artillery battalion of *164. leichte Afrikadivision* brought its mountain guns with it from Crete, the first has 10.5cm howitzers.

Both *15.* and *21. Panzerdivision* had two batteries of 15cm (Sf) Lorraine Schlepper self-propelled guns at El Alamein, but lost them all in the subsequent retreat.

Anti-tank Gun Platoon

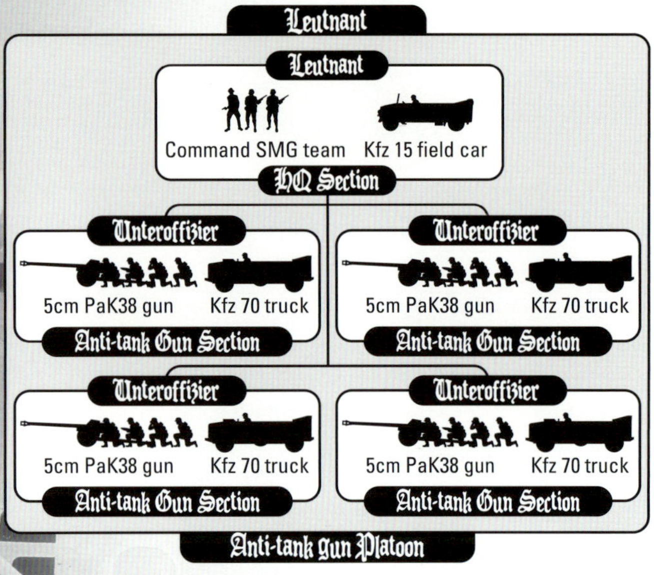

Platoon

HQ Section with:

4 Anti-tank Sections	**185 points**
3 Anti-tank Sections	**145 points**
2 Anti-tank Sections	**105 points**

Options

- Replace all Kfz 70 trucks with Sd Kfz 10 half-tracks for +5 points for the platoon.
- Replace all 5cm PaK38 guns and Kfz 70 trucks with 7.5cm PaK40 guns and Sd Kfz 11 half-tracks for +40 points per section.

Most of the anti-tank guns were issued to the Panzergrenadier battalions and replaced with self-propelled tank hunters. Only a small reserve of 5cm guns remained under divisional control.

Tank-hunter Platoon

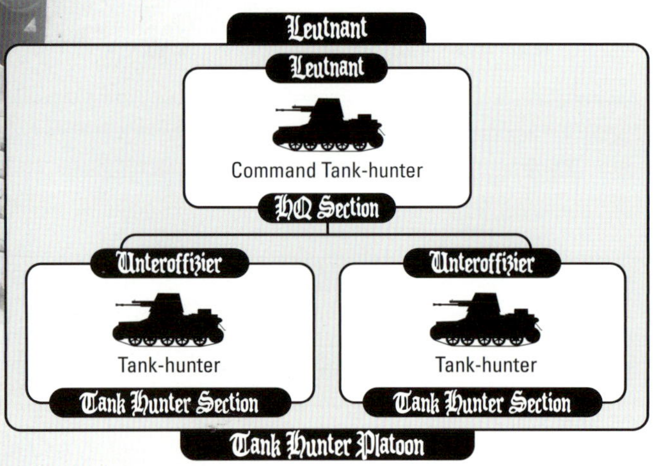

Platoon

HQ Section with:

3 Panzerjäger I	**130 points**
2 Panzerjäger I	**95 points**

Options

- Replace all Panzerjäger I tank-hunters with:

  Diana tank-hunters for +35 points per tank-hunter, or Marder III (7.62cm) tank-hunters for +60 points per tank-hunter.

Option (334 Infantriedivision only)

- Replace all Panzerjäger I tank-hunters with Marder I tank-hunters for +45 points per tank-hunter.

334 Infanteriedivision must upgrade to Marder I tank-hunters.

The wide-open spaces of the desert made towed guns difficult to conceal, so the *Afrikakorps* always contained a significant number of tank-hunters. The *Panzerjäger I* was rather light for the role, so the half-tracked Diana hastened into service to join it at Gazala. The more powerful Marder III arrived in time for the Alamein battles, and a few Marder I tank-hunters fought in Tunisia.

0 to 1 Heavy Anti-aircraft Gun Platoon

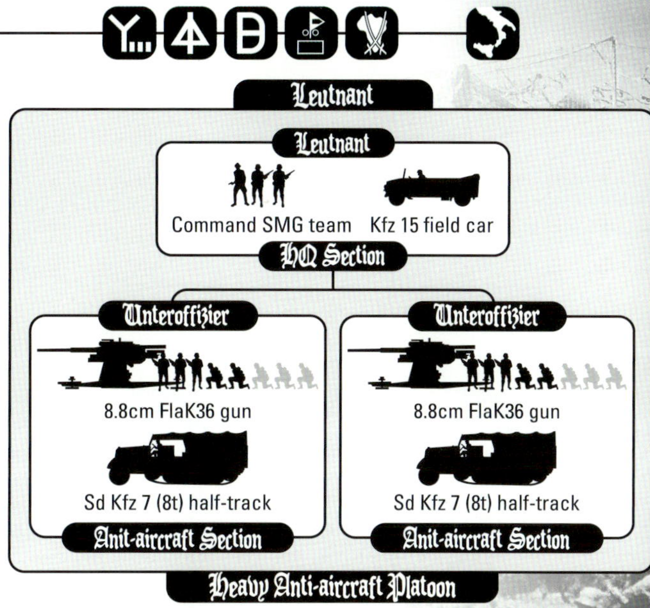

Platoon

HQ Section with:

2 Anti-aircraft Sections	280 points
1 Anti-aircraft Section	150 points

Option

- Model 8.8cm FlaK36 guns with eight or more crew and increase their ROF to 3 for +10 points per gun.

The 8.8cm FlaK36 will easily destroy any enemy tank at long range and is often called upon to defeat the heavily armoured British infantry tanks. However, the cost is high as Rommel's supply lines are constantly pounded by Allied bombers and the guns are also needed at the ports to protect shipping bringing vital fuel.

Rocket Launcher Battery

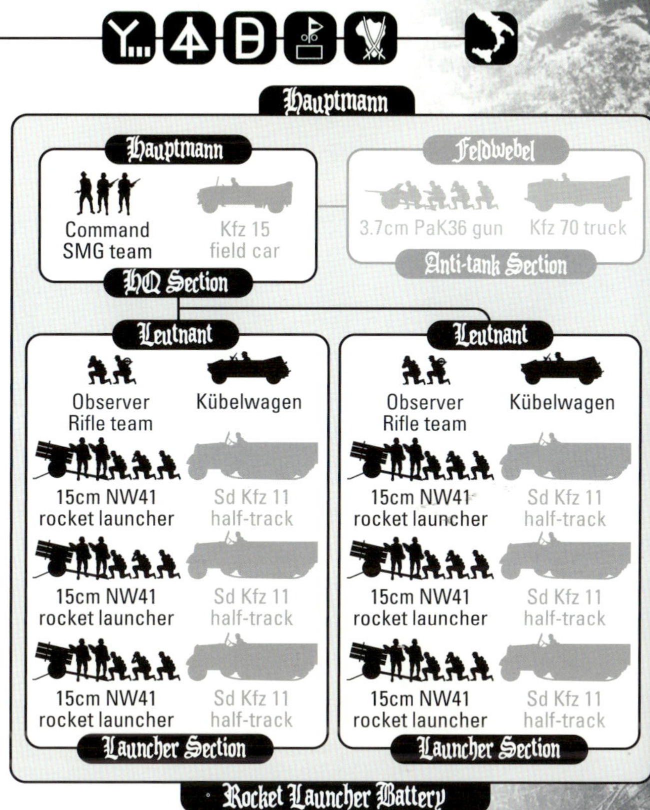

Platoon

HQ Section with:

2 Launcher Sections	280 points
1 Launcher Section	150 points

Options

- Add Kfz 15 field car and Sd Kfz 11 half-tracks to the platoon at no cost.
- Add Anti-tank Section for +25 points.
- Replace 3.7cm PaK36 gun with 5cm PaK38 gun for +15 points.
- Replace Kfz 70 truck with Sd Kfz 10 half-track for +5 points.

Light Anti-aircraft Platoons

Platoon	
3 Sd Kfz 10/5 (2cm)	90 points
2 Sd Kfz 10/5 (2cm)	60 points

Light anti-aircraft platoons are useful for keeping enemy aircraft at bay when the *Luftwaffe* is busy elsewhere. They are both essential and plentiful in all of the divisions in Africa.

0 to 1 Assault Gun Platoon

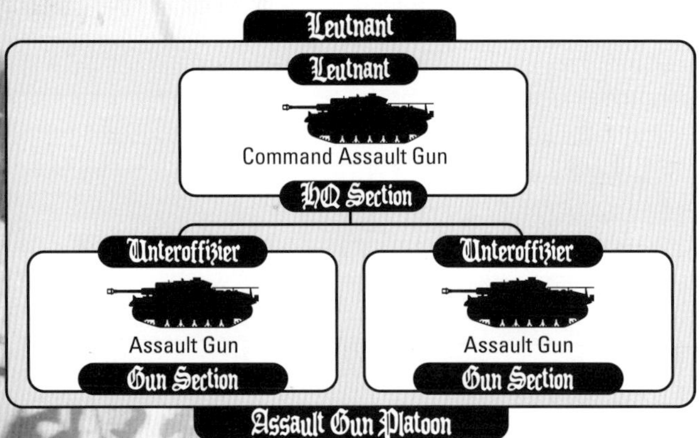

Platoon	
3 StuG F/8	535 points
2 StuG F/8	355 points
Platoon (90 Afrikadivision only)	
2 StuG D	200 points
1 StuG D	100 points

Your force may not contain more than one Assault Gun Platoon.

StuG assault guns were very rare in Africa. *288 zbV Regiment* of *90. leichte Afrikadivision* had two StuG D at Gazala, but lost one. The remaining one was lost at El Alamein.

0 to 1 Heavy Tank Platoon

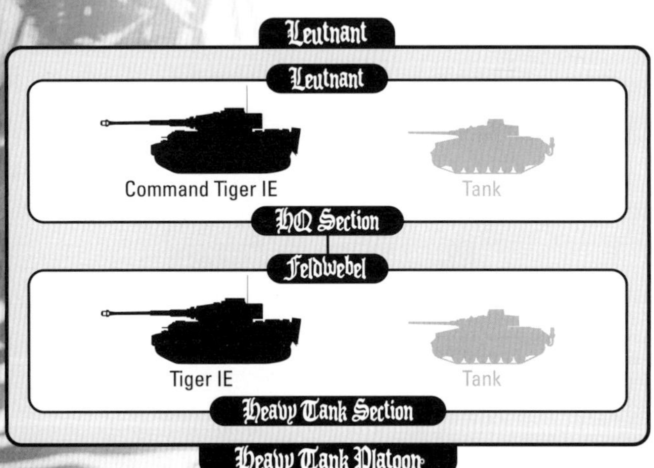

Platoon	
2 Tiger I E	770 points
1 Tiger I E	385 points

Options

- Add either: one or two Panzer III L or M tanks for +115 points per tank, or one or two Panzer III N tanks for +105 points per tank, or one or two Tiger I tanks for +385 points per tank.

Remember to roll for your Tiger Ace Skills before each game!

Parts of two heavy tank battalions reached Tunisia before the end. The first company from *501 schwere Panzerabteilung* (with Tiger I and Panzer III N tanks) arrived in late November and went into action on 1 December 1942. The second company followed later in December. At the end of February, the battalion became part of *10. Panzerdivision.*

The first and only company from *504. schwere Panzerabteilung* (with Tiger I and Panzer III M tanks) to reach Tunisia joined *15. Panzerdivision* in early April. The rest of the battalion fought in Sicily and Italy, having replaced their light Panzer III tanks with more Tiger tanks.

Tiger tanks are the deadliest killers on the battlefield—each Tiger tank is worth a platoon of lesser tanks. Their biggest limitation is simply the small numbers available.

AVANTI SAVOIA

ITALIAN FORCES IN THE MEDITERRANEAN

'The German soldier impressed the world, the Italian Bersaglieri impressed the German soldier!'
'The men of the Folgore are equal to our very best.'
—German General Rommel, 'The Desert Fox'

ORIGINS

132º divisione corazzata 'Ariete', the 132nd 'Ram' Armoured Division was formed in early 1939 as Italy's first armoured division. Its equipment at the time was limited to the tiny 3-ton L3/35 tankette, but it was soon equipped with Italy's first medium tank, the 11-ton M11/39.

WAR BREAKS OUT

When war broke out in 1939, Italy watched their German allies with interest. When the Germans attacked France in May 1940, the Italian dictator Benito Mussolini declared war as well, planning on piggy-backing on the German Army's stunning successes. Attacks against the French defending the Alpine border and British forces in Egypt resulted in few gains, although the French surrender to the Germans gave the Italians the opportunity to confiscate some French territory.

LIBYAN DISASTER

The Italian army that invaded Egypt was largely composed of marching infantry making it totally unsuitable for desert warfare. When the British counter-attacked with an armoured force in December 1940, they could pick and choose their battles and quickly threw the Italian invaders back into Libya. Even a special brigade of tanks detached from *Ariete* couldn't make a real difference. Despite winning a battle against the advancing British tanks at Mechili in mid-January, the Italian tanks were overwhelmed at Beda Fomm in early February 1941 and the entire Italian invasion force captured or destroyed.

TO TOBRUK

All that stood between the British and the loss of Libya was the newly arrived *Ariete* division (now equipped

with small numbers of the new 13-ton M13/40 tank) and *27° divisione fanteria 'Brescia'*, the 27th 'Brescia' Infantry Division. These were soon joined by a German force, the *Deutsches Afrikakorps* or *DAK* (German Africa Corps), under General Erwin Rommel.

With this meagre force, the 'Desert Fox', as Rommel quickly became known, swept the disorganised British before him. *Ariete* earned its first victory, beating the British 3 Indian Motor Brigade at Mechili on 8 April 1941, before sweeping on to surround the vital port of Tobruk.

Unable to break through the staunch defence of the 7th Australian Division, Rommel regrouped his forces and prepared to take the port in a new offensive planned for November 1941. *Ariete* took advantage of the lull to entirely re-equip with M13/40 medium tanks and complete its training. The Division was joined by *101° divisione motorizzata 'Trieste'*, the 101st 'Trieste' Motorised Division, to form the *Corpo d'Armata di Manovra (CAM)*, the Manoeuvre Corps.

OPERATION CRUSADER

In Rommel's plan to take Tobruk, *CAM* was tasked with protecting the rear of *DAK* against an anticipated British offensive. *Trieste* held the deep flank at Bir Hacheim, while *Ariete* was forward at Bir el Gubi.

The British attack, codenamed Operation Crusader, preempted Rommel's attack. Their 7th Armoured Division, the famous 'Desert Rats', were tasked with taking Bir el Gubi. 158 British Crusader tanks faced 146 Italian M13/40 tanks supported by the infantry and guns of *Ariete* who emerged victorious from the fierce fighting, putting the Desert Rats out of the battle for several days for the loss of less than 40 of its own tanks.

Ariete then joined *DAK* to destroy 5 South African Brigade and maul 2nd New Zealand Division, clashing repeatedly with British armoured brigades before taking part in Rommel's failed 'dash to the wire' aimed at cutting off the British forces. By this time however, the battle was lost. *Ariete* (down to just 30 tanks) covered the withdrawal in heavy fighting with 5 Indian Brigade around Alam Hamza.

As 1941 drew to a close, *Ariete* took stock. Despite its successes, the Division was badly depleted and withdrew with the rest of the Axis forces to El Agheila before returning to positions facing the British defensive line at Gazala.

GAZALA

Both sides spent the first five months of 1942 preparing for the next round. *CAM* was redesignated as *XX CAM* (20 Manoeuvre Corps). *Ariete* gained heavier artillery support in the form of *Semovente 75/18* self-propelled guns, heavy 88/56 anti-aircraft guns, and self-propelled *Lancia da 90/53* anti-aircraft guns, but still fielded its old M13/40 tanks, despite the arrival of 26-ton Grant tanks on the British side.

On 27 May 1942, Rommel attacked. While the Italian infantry divisions launched frontal assaults on the Gazala Line and *DAK* swung south to outflank the line, *XX CAM* was to go wider to protect their eastern flank. In the event, *Trieste* became separated from *Ariete* and collided with the Free French Brigade holding Bir Hacheim while *Ariete* found its way blocked by its old adversary, 3 Indian Motor Brigade at Point 171. *Ariete* pressed home its attack with great élan and broke the poorly positioned Indian Brigade, causing nearly 500 casualties and taking 600 prisoners.

Ariete then turned back to help Trieste at Bir Hacheim, but here the gallant attacks that had proved successful against the Indians foundered on the dense minefields and massed guns of the Free French position. *Colonnello* Prestisimone commanding *IX battaglione corazzato* (9th Armoured Battalion) had several 'mounts' shot from under him leading repeated attacks, but the well-fortified French position proved too tough. *Ariete* had lost 31 tanks, a *Semovente* self-propelled gun, and 124 men captured or killed by the time they were ordered to bypass the stubborn French.

The following two days saw scattered fighting between *Ariete* and the British 1 Army Tank and 2 Armoured Brigades, where the inferiority of the M13/40 tank to the new Grant was evident, though the latter were roughly handled by the 88/56 and 90/53 anti-aircraft guns and divisional artillery.

ASLAGH RIDGE

During this time *Ariete* occupied positions on Aslagh ridge facing westward to cover Rommel's attempts to break back through the Gazala Line to relieve his now surrounded force. It took the British five days to decide what to do before they finally attacked the Italo-German forces who by this time had opened their supply line again. Despite the delay, the attacks when they came were disjointed and *Ariete* had no difficulty in repulsing 9 and 10 Indian Brigades. They then combined with *DAK* to complete their destruction. Within days the British forces were in full retreat. Rommel noted that *Ariete* had played a vital role in holding the eastern face of the 'Cauldron'.

BACK TO TOBRUK

With the British on the run, *Ariete* found itself once again outside Tobruk. It was quickly brought up to strength at the expense of the latest arrival in *XX CAM, 133° divisione corazzata 'Littorio'*, the 133rd 'Executor' Armoured Division. Thus reinforced, *Ariete* took the left-flank position in the successful assault on Tobruk.

ON TO EGYPT

With Tobruk safely in the bag, Rommel had a choice. Stop and wait for the invasion of the British-held island of Malta to clear his supply lines across the Mediterranean, or press on into Egypt hoping to win before his supplies ran out. Ever the gambler and with large stocks captured at Tobruk, Rommel rolled into Egypt, striking for the Nile.

By late June *XX CAM* had advanced to Mersa Matruh where it played a key role in bouncing the British from their new defensive line. The British fell back to El Alamein. The Italo-German forces had been advancing and fighting non-stop for over a month, but despite their exhaustion, they pushed on with the Nile only 60 miles away.

July was occupied by confused fighting on the Alamein Line as first one side attacked, then the other. Rommel brought up the Italian infantry divisions to assist the mechanised corps, but to no avail. Both sides took heavy casualties and by the end of the month had worn themselves out and the fighting died down.

August was spent rebuilding their strength. Large numbers of new tanks arrived and those tanks damaged and broken down in the previous two months of fighting were repaired. The forces that were to have attacked Malta arrived to reinforce the desert push instead, amongst them *185º divisione paracadutisti 'Folgore'*, the 185th 'Folgore' Parachute Division.

ONE LAST PUSH

Having failed to take either Egypt or Malta, Rommel was now in trouble. His ammunition and petrol supplies were low with little prospect of improvement. Meanwhile the British were growing stronger at an alarming rate. To Rommel there was only one possible solution, to attack.

Once again *XX CAM* was assigned the role of protecting the flanks of the main push by *DAK* aimed at the Alam Halfa Ridge. Unfortunately British deception measures lead the Italo-German forces onto previously unsuspected minefields. A well-prepared British defensive position and continuous heavy air attacks quickly ended Rommel's last desert offensive and the Italo-German forces retired to their starting positions to await their fate.

EL ALAMEIN

Rommel now had to hold the forty-mile long Alamein Line against the coming British offensive. He reorganised his forces to intermingle Italian and German infantry divisions along the entire front to give the Italian forces the benefit of their heavier German armament. *XX CAM* swapped *Littorio* with *DAK* for the German *21. Panzerdivision* taking position behind *Folgore* at the south of the line. *DAK* was in reserve in the north.

The British attack finally came on the night of 23 October 1942 with attacks in both the north and the south. *Folgore* held the attacks in the south at bay, but the stronger attacks in the north broke through the front. Only strong counterattacks by the Italo-German armoured divisions prevented a complete rupture of the line.

Over the next week *Littorio* and *Trieste* were virtually wiped out in the face of almost continuous British attacks. Their sacrifice was to no avail. The stronger British forces eventually broke through the weakened front. By 3 November 1942, the Italo-German forces were retreating.

REARGUARD

The only force left to cover the Axis retreat was *Ariete*, hurriedly brought north to stem the British tide. Moving toward Tel el Aqqaqir on 4 November, Ariete became locked in an unequal struggle with the British 22 Armoured Brigade. The crews of its M14/41 tanks watching fatalistically as their projectiles bounced off the thick hulls of the heavier British Grant and Sherman tanks.

The Division managed a day-long stand against overwhelming odds, and fought again the next day to prevent the withdrawing Axis forces from being surrounded and cut off. Their gallant stand allowed the surviving Axis mobile units the chance to escape, although the Italian infantry divisions, left behind without transport, had little alternative but to surrender.

Ariete had been destroyed as a division. Rommel noted in his diary that 'In the *Ariete* we lost our oldest Italian comrades.' He was perhaps a little premature with his obituary as the remnants of *XX CAM* joined forces with the newly arrived *131º divisione corazzata 'Centauro'*, the 131st 'Centaur' Armoured Division to fight on as the rearguard during the long retreat to Tunisia until the eventual destruction of all Axis forces in Africa in May 1943.

GAZALA

Sweeping around the Gazala Line, tanks of the Ariete armoured division smash into the Allied defences.

The lighter Italian tanks falter facing the heavier British tanks, forcing them to rely on the heavier guns of the Semovente's.

Armoured support in the form of Autoblindo armoured cars reinforce the attack at Bir Hacheim.

Libya, North Africa.
May 27 ~ June 20, 1942

Elements of the ***Divisione Motorizzata 'Trieste'*** assault the stubborn Free French at Bir Hacheim.

The Italians push on to Tobruk, right on the heels of the retreating Allied forces.

EL ALAMEIN

The Italian forces try to break the tenacious attacks on their defensive lines.

Artillery breaks up infantry formations and blinds the enemy with smoke.

Light, fast vehicles get around the flanks of the enemy...

...pushing a gap through to the train station...

The Allied forces defend against a vicious counterattack from the Italians.

...where the Allies are prepared for the ensuing assault.

TUNISIA

Tunis, North Africa.
October 23 ~ November 04, 1942

Hitting the enemy in the flanks helps turn the favour towards the smaller and lighter M14/41 tanks.

The battle stagnates into stationary fire, the Italian tanks suffer...

...and the Allies push through to the dug-in defences.

Semovente 75's turn up just at the right time to surprise the Allied forces and push them back to regroup.

THE ITALIAN ARMY IN NORTH AFRICA 1942-1943

Italian divisions are usually named for their city of origin (Pistoia, Pavia, Trieste, etc). Specialist divisions like armoured or parachute divisions usually take a name suited to their role instead, like *Ariete* or Ram for the 132nd Armoured Division or *Folgore*, Thunderbolt, for the 185th Parachute Division.

Regiments are shown in Arabic numerals (1, 2, 3, etc). Battalions are shown in Roman numerals (I, II, III, etc). Unless noted a regiment bears the same name as its parent division. Most infantry regiments have two battalions (I and II) and a weapons battalion (III) unless otherwise noted.

battaglione = battalion, *reggimento* = regiment, *brigata* = brigade, *divisione* = division, *autotrasportabile* = truck transportable, *aviotrasportata* = air transportable, *bersaglieri* = light infantry, *corazzata* = armoured, *d'assalto* = assault, *fanteria* = infantry, *guastatori* = assault engineers, *motorizzata* = motorised, *paracadutisti* = parachute

Armata Italo-tedesca (Italian-German Army), 1942

Unit	Battalions and Regiments
16ª Divisione Fanteria 'Pistoia'[1]	35, 36, 3 'Fossalta' Artillery
X Corpo d'Armata (part of XXI CA until August 1942)	
XXXI Battaglione Guastatori	
9º Reggimento Bersaglieri	XXVIII, XXX
17ª Divisione Autotrasportabile 'Pavia'	27, 28, 26 'Rubicone' Artillery
27ª Divisione Autotrasportabile 'Brescia'	19, 20, 55 Artillery
185ª Divisione Paracadutisti 'Folgore'[2]	186 (V, VI, VII), 187 (II, IV, IX, X), 185 Artillery, VIII Guastatori
Fallschirmbrigade Ramcke (German)	
XX Corpo d'Armata di Manovra (CAM)	
XXXII Battaglione Guastatori[3]	
101ª Divisione Motorizzata 'Trieste'	XI Armoured, 65 & 66 'Valtellina', 21 'Po' Artillery, VIII Armoured Bersaglieri (AB41)
132ª Divisione Corazzata 'Ariete'	132 Armoured (IX, X, XIII), 8 Bersaglieri (V, XII), 132 Artillery, DLI Semovente, DLII Semovente, III Armoured Car 'Nizza Cavaleria' (AB41)
133ª Divisione Corazzata 'Littorio'[4,5]	133 Armoured (IV, XII, LI), 12 Bersaglieri (XXIII, XXXVI), 3 Artillery, DLIV Semovente, DLVI Semovente, III Armoured 'Lancieri di Novara' (L6/40)
164. leichte Afrikadivision (German)[2]	
XXI Corpo d'Armata	
7º Reggimento Bersaglieri	VIII, X
25ª Divisione Autotrasportabile 'Bologna'	39, 40, 205 Artillery
60ª Divisione Autotrasportabile 'Sabratha'[3,6]	85 & 86 'Verona', 42 Artillery
102ª Divisione Motorizzata 'Trento'	61, 62, 46 Artillery
Deutsches Afrikakorps (DAK)	
136ª Divisione Motorizzata 'GGFF'[1]	136, IX, 136 Artillery, III Armoured Car 'Cavalleggeri di Montferrato' (AB41)
15. & 21.[7] Panzerdivision (German)	

The situation in 1943 is quite confused as the Italians and their German allies threw together any battleworthy units to hand to stop each successive Allied thrust. Most Italian units fought under the 1st Italian-German Army in the south of Tunisia, but some units also operated as part of the German 5th Panzer Army in the north.

1ª Armata Italo-tedesca (1st Italian-German Army), 1943

Unit	Battalions and Regiments
184º Reggimento Paracadutisti 'Nembo'	X bis, XV, XVI
XX Corpo d'Armata	
16ª Divisione Autotrasportabile 'Pistoia'	as for 1942
80ª Divisione Aviotrasportata 'la Spezia'	125, 126, XXXIX Bersaglieri, 80 Artillery
101ª Divisione Motorizzata 'Trieste'	as for 1942 with a composite battalion from Folgore
90. leichte Afrikadivision (German)	
XXI Corpo d'Armata	
131ª Divisione Corazzata 'Centauro'	XVII Armoured, 5 Bersaglieri (XIV, XXIV), 131 Artillery, DLVIII Semovente, XV 'Cavalleggeri di Lodi' (L6/40)
136ª Divisione Motorizzata 'GGFF'	as for 1942 plus 8 Bersaglieri
164. leichte Afrikadivision (German)	

Panzerarmeeoberkomando 5. (German 5th Panzer Army)

Unit	Battalions and Regiments
XXX Corpo d'Armata	
50ª Brigata Speziale 'Imperiali'	XV Armoured, 6 Bersaglieri (VI, XIII), DLVII Semovente
1ª Divisione d'Assalto 'Superga'	91 'Basilicata', 92 'Basilicata', 5 Artillery
XC Armeekorps (German)	
Division von Broich (German)	included 10º Reggimento Bersaglieri (XVI, XXXIV)

1 From November 1942
2 From September 1942
3 Disbanded August 1942
4 Joined DAK in September 1942
5 From July 1942
6 With CAM until July 1942
7 With CAM from September 1942

ITALIAN ARMY TERMINOLOGY

AM, Asino Morto (ah-see-noh morr-toh): Dead ass. Nickname for Italian canned beef.
Alpini (ahl-pee-nee): Mountain troops.
Armata Italo-tedesca (ahrr-mah-tah ee-tah-loh teh-deh-skah): Italian-German Army. The combined Italian and German army in Libya and Tunisia.
ARMIR, Armata Italiana In Russia (ahrr-meerr): Italian Army in Russia, the Italian 8th Army.
Ariete (ah-ree-eht-eh): Ram. 132nd Armoured Division.
Artiglieria (ahr-tee-yearr-ee-ah): Artillery.
Artiglieria Celere (ahr-tee-yearr-ee-ah cheh-leh-reh): Fast artillery. Units of truck-mounted artillery.
AS, Africa Settentrionale (ahf-ree-kah sayt-tehn-tree-oh-nah-leh): North Africa.
Autoblindo (ow-toh-bleen-doh): Armoured car.
Autocannone (ow-toh-kahn-noh-neh): Truck-mounted gun.
Avanti Savoia (ah-vahn-tee sah-voi-ah): Forward Savoy! Savoy is the royal house of Italy.
Bare d'Acciaio (bahrr-eh dahk-chee-ai-oh): Steel coffin. Nickname for Italian tanks.
Battaglione (baht-tah-yee-oh-neh): Battalion.
Batteria (baht-teh-ree-ah): Battery.
Bersaglieri (bearr-sah-yearr-ee): Elite light infantry renowned for marching at the run.
Bombe Passaglia (bohm-beh pahs-sah-yee-ah): Anti-tank grenade designed by Passaglia, an engineer officer. Basically a minestrone tin full of explosives ignited by a hand grenade.
Buca (boo-kah): Hole. Slit trench.
CA, Corpo d'Armata (korr-poh dahrr-mah-tah): Army corps.
CAM, Corpo d'Armata di Manovra (korr-poh dahrr-mah-tee dee mahn-oh-vrah): Mobile corps. The corps containing the armoured divisions.
Camionetta (kah-mee-oh-neht-tah): Truck.
Cannone (kahn-noh-neh): Gun.
Caporale (kah-poh-rah-leh): Corporal.
Carabinieri (kah-rah-bee-nee-ehrr-ee): Military Police.
Carri (kar-ree): Tanks.
Carristi (kar-ree-stee): Tank crewmen.
ca, Contraerea (kohn-trah-eh-reh-ah): Anti-aircraft.
cc, Controcarro (kohn-troh karr-roh): Anti-tank.
CCNN, Camice Nere: (kah-mee-cheh neh-reh): Black Shirts, the armed forces of the Fascist Party.
Centauro (chen-tau-roh): Centaur. 131st Armoured Division.
Capitano (kah-pee-tah-noh): Captain.
Carro Comando (kar-roh koh-mahn-doh): Command tank.
Compagnia (kom-pan-yee-ah): Company.
Corazzato (koh-raht-tsah-toh): Armoured.
Crucchi (kroo-kee): Slang for Germans.
CSIR, Corpo Spedizione In Russia (chee-seerr): Expeditionary Corps In Russia in 1941.
Divisione d'Assalto (dee-vee-see-ohn-eh dahs-sahl-toh): Assault division.
Divisione Autotrasportabile (dee-vee-see-ohn-eh ow-toh-trahs-porr-tah-bee-leh): Infantry division ready for truck transport.
Divisione Aviotrasportata (dee-vee-see-ohn-eh ah-vee-oh-trahs-porr-tah-tah): Air transported division.
Divisione Celere (dee-vee-see-ohn-eh cheh-leh-reh): Fast or cavalry division.
Divisione Corazzata (dee-vee-see-ohn-eh koh-raht-tsah-tah): Armoured division.
Divisione Fanteria (dee-vee-see-ohn-eh fahn-teh-ree-ah): Infantry division.
Divisione da Montagna (dee-vee-see-ohn-eh dah mohn-tah-nyah): Mountain division.
Divisione Motorizzata (dee-vee-see-ohn-eh moh-toh-reet-tsah-tah): Motorised infantry division.
Divisione Paracadutisti (dee-vee-see-ohn-eh pah-rah-kah-doo-tee-stee): Parachute division.
Dovunque (doh-voon-kweh): Anywhere. All-terrain truck.
Elefantino (el-eh-fahn-tee-noh): Little elephant. Nickname for 47/32 gun.
EP, Effetto Pronto (ehf-feht-toh prohn-toh): Rapid effect. Italian name for High Explosive Anti-tank (HEAT) round.
Fantaccino (fahn-tah-chee-noh): Nickname for rifleman.
Fascio (fah-shoh): Fasces. Bundle of sticks and an axe. Symbol of Italian Fascist Party. Previously symbol of the power of a Roman senator carried by his lictor.
Ferrea Mole, Ferreo Cuore (fehr-reh-ah moh-leh fehr-reh-oh koo-ohrr-eh): Iron Hulls, Iron Hearts. Motto of Italian tankers.
Folgore (fohl-gorr-eh): Thunderbolt. 185th Parachute Division.
Fucile (foo-chee-leh): Rifle.
Fucilieri (foo-chee-lyearr-ee): Riflemen.
GGFF, Giovani Fascisti (jee-oh-vahn-nee fah-sheest-ee): Young Fascists. Fascist youth organisation.
Greche (greh-keh): Greeks. Nickname for generals from the Greek lace on their collars.
Guastatori (gwah-stah-torr-ee): Demolishers. Assault engineers.
I Mussolini (ee moos-soh-lee-nee): The Mussolinis. Disparaging name for CCNN 'M' battalions.
Il novantuno (eel noh-vahn-too-noh) The Ninety-one. Nickname for standard Carcano model 1891 rifle.
Inglesi (een-gleh-see): British.
Italia (Ee-tah-lee-ah): Italy.
Lancia (lahn-chee-ah): Spear. Italian vehicle manufacturer.
Lanciafiamme (lahn-chee-ah-fee-ahm-meh): Flame-thrower.
L'ottantotto (loht-tahn-toh-oht-toh): The eighty eight. Nickname of the British 25 pdr (an 88mm gun).
Littorio (lee-tor-ree-oh): Lictor. Official who holds a senator's fasces and executes sentences. 133rd Armoured Division.
Mitraglieri (mee-trah-yearr-ee): Machine-gun.
Modello (moh-dehl-loh): Model.
Mortaio (morr-tai-oh): Mortar.
Moto Guzzi (moh-toh goot-tsee): Italian motorcycle manufacturer.
Motocicletta (moh-toh-cheek-leht-tah): Motorcycle.
Motociclisti (moh-toh-cheek-leest-ee): Motorcyclists.
Motorizzati ai piè (moh-toh-reet-tsah-tee ah-ee pee-eh): Motorised on foot. A cynical reference to the actual state of most Italian 'motorised' divisions.
Multiplo di quattro (mool-tee-ploh dee kwaht-troh): Multiple of four. British bombardments as they arrived in fours.
Nastrini (nah-stree-nee): Ribbons. Nickname for senior officers.
Nembo (nehm-boh): Cloud. 184th Parachute Division.
Obice(oh-bee-cheh): Howitzer.
Paracadutisti (pah-rah-kah-doo-teest-ee): Parachutists.
Piumetto (pee-oo-meht-toh): Plumes. Black cockerel feathers worn by bersaglieri to celebrate their origin as 'hunters'.
Picchiatello (peek-kee-ah-tehl-loh): Nutter. Nickname for Ju87 dive bomber playing on the Italian word for diver.
Plotone (ploh-toh-neh): Platoon.
Radio Scarpa (rah-dee-oh skahrr-pah): Shoe Radio. Word of mouth.
RA, Regia Aeronautica (reh-jee-ah eh-roh-now-tee-kah): Royal Air Force
Raggruppamento (rahg-groop-pah-mehn-toh): Artillery group.
RE, Regio Esercito (reh-jee-oh eh-sehrr-chee-toh): Royal Army.
RECo, Raggruppamento Esplorante Corazzato (rahg-groop-pah-mehn-toh ehs-ploh-rahn-teh koh-raht-tsah-toh):Armoured reconnaissance battalion.
Reggimento (reh-jee-mehn-toh): Regiment.
Semovente (say-moh-ven-teh): Self-propelled gun.
Sergente (sehr-jehn-teh): Sergeant.
Solothurn (soh-loh-toornn): Maker of anti-tank rifle.
Tedeschi (teh-deh-skee): Germans.
Tenente (teh-nehn-teh): Lieutenant.
Trattore (traht-torr-eh): Tractor.

AVANTI SAVOIA SPECIAL RULES

The Regio Esercito, the Royal Army, was unprepared for war in 1940, despite Mussolini's call for an army of '8 million bayonets'. The resulting force is very uneven—some officers are excellent, while others are simply abysmal, and the training of their soldiers and these special rules reflect this.

Avanti!

The Italian Army learned many lessons from the First World War. From the Germans they took the concept of speed and mobility in breakthrough operations. From the French they gained the techniques of methodical destruction of the enemy defences. The resulting doctrine emphasised mobile warfare and demanded rapid movement into contact with the enemy before bringing massive firepower to bear to open a gap and allow manoeuvre once more.

Any Italian platoon with a Command team may attempt an Avanti move at the start of its Shooting step instead of shooting. If a platoon attempts to make an Avanti move, it may not shoot even if fails to make an Avanti move.

Roll a Skill test for each platoon:

- If the test is successful, the platoon may move another 4"/10cm,
- Otherwise the platoon cannot move this step.

All of the normal rules apply for this movement. Platoons cannot make Avanti moves if they are Pinned Down or moved At the Double. Bogged Down or Bailed Out vehicles cannot make Avanti moves.

8 Million Bayonets

Mussolini demanded an army eight million strong to create his new Roman Empire. The rapid expansion needed for this led to reservist officers being recalled to the colours with little extra training. After 20 years of civilian life, some were still good soldiers, however most were not!

To reflect the variable quality of Italian officers, Italian platoons are rated as Regular, Elite, or Artillery. After deployment, but before the first turn, roll a die for each platoon and its attached teams and consult the 8 Million Bayonets table to determine their Training and Motivation characteristics.

Heroism

The Italian Army's lack of modern equipment gave its officers plenty of opportunities to display extreme eroismo, heroism, usually in extremis. Because these great deeds were usually fatal to the hero, it was impossible to know in advance who the heroes were, though if their comrades survived, their deeds would be enshrined in heroic prose and a medal sent to their dearest.

When your company first has a Command team Destroyed by the enemy, roll a Motivation test for that Command team. This test can never be re-rolled for any reason.

- If they pass the Motivation test, the officer shrugs off his wounds, shouts encouragement to his men and a challenge to the enemy and fights on as an Unknown Hero.
- On any other roll, the Command team is Destroyed as normal and you roll again to discover your hero the next time a Command team is Destroyed.

Once you have found your Unknown Hero, stop rolling. There can only be one Unknown Hero in your company in each game.

If the Unknown Hero is an Infantry team, bring the team back into play. If the Unknown Hero was a Tank team, the hero transfers to any other tank in his platoon that is within Command Distance making that the Platoon Command team. If no suitable tank is within Command Distance, the Unknown Hero is out of the battle and removed from the game.

An Unknown Hero and any platoon led by him always passes all Motivation tests on a roll of 2+. If the Unknown Hero is Destroyed while leading a platoon, the platoon will continue to take Motivation tests as if led by the Unknown Hero, although all other penalties for being Out Of Command still apply.

8 Million Bayonets

Roll	Regular	Elite	Artillery	Parachutist
1	Reluctant Trained	Confident Trained	Confident Trained	Fearless Veteran
2	Reluctant Trained	Confident Trained	Confident Veteran	Fearless Veteran
3	Reluctant Trained	Confident Veteran	Confident Veteran	Fearless Veteran
4	Confident Trained	Confident Veteran	Confident Veteran	Fearless Veteran
5	Confident Trained	Confident Veteran	Confident Veteran	Fearless Veteran
6	Fearless Conscript	Fearless Veteran	Fearless Veteran	Fearless Veteran

TENENTE CAPO COMPAGNIA LUIGI PASCUCCI

Sottotenente (Second Lieutenant) Luigi Pascucci fought as a *Tenente Capo Compagnia* (Lieutenant in charge of a company) in the *132° reggimento fanteria carrista* of the famed *Ariete* Armoured Division, during the Second Battle of El Alamein. His company took part in the bitter fighting against the British 22 Armoured Brigade around Bir El Abd just west of El Alamein on 4 November, 1942.

The next day his company was assigned to hold the left flank of the Regiment against the British 8 Armoured Brigade during Ariete's fighting withdrawal to Fuka. Despite being outnumbered and outgunned by the superior allied armour, he succeeded in holding the flank long enough to allow the rest of the regiment to fall back in good order.

Knowing that he was cut off and the main body of the Italian force still needed time to regroup, Pascucci bravely ignored heavy enemy fire to lead the remaining eleven tanks of his company in a charge straight at the centre of the British armoured formation.

The unexpected ferocity of this attack buckled the British line, then broke it in disorder. Leading from the front he continued the pursuit of the fleeing British.

Pascucci was found after the battle lying in his burnt out tank. His supreme sacrifice a demonstration of his fighting spirit. In recognition of his heroic actions he was awarded the *Medaglia D'Oro Al Valore Militare*, the Gold Medal for Military Valor, Italy's highest award.

Characteristics

Tenente Pascucci is a Warrior and a Company Command team rated as **Fearless Veteran**.

Pascucci can join any Compagnia Carri for +50 points. He becomes the Company command team retaining the previous commander's tank.

Special Rules

Iron Heart: Pascucci and any platoon currently being led by Pascucci always pass Motivation tests on a roll of 3+ instead of their normal roll.

Aim For The Tracks: Pascucci makes excellent use of his tank's cannon, aiming for the weak spots of enemy tanks. When an enemy tank makes an Armour Save at a range of up to 16"/40cm and the save result is exactly 7, Pascucci may treat his 47mm gun as having an Anti-tank rating of 8.

Never Surrender: If Pascucci fails a Company Morale Check, he doesn't count as having failed it this turn, but automatically fails the Company Morale Check next turn. However, every platoon in the Italian force must take an immediate Platoon Morale Check. If they pass the Platoon Morale Check, they fight on, otherwise they are immediately removed from the game counting as Destroyed.

COMPAGNIA CARRI

(TANK COMPANY)

It looks like that German Rommel is a real ardito, a real fire eater! Well he'll find us carristi more than willing to fight, no matter what the odds. We'll never let him down. Not that he's that concerned about Italia mind you. He seems happy enough to run off and leave good Italian soldiers behind when it suits him! Still, we'll take him on to Alexandria and beyond—'Ferrea Mole, Ferreo Cuore', 'Iron Hulls, Iron Hearts', that's us.

—Capitano Ernesto Alberto

A force based around a Compagnia Carri must contain:

- a Company HQ, and
- two or three Carri Platoons.

There are no Weapons Platoons available to a Compagnia Carri.

Support Platoons for a Compagnia Carri can be:

- a Self-propelled 75/18 Platoon,
- Armoured Car Platoons,
- Bersaglieri Platoons,
- Light Tank Platoons,
- Motociclisti Platoons, and
- Divisional Support Platoons.

You may also field any of the following platoons from the German section as an allied Support Platoon.

- a Panzer Platoon equipped with Panzer III or Panzer IV,
- a Panzergrenadier Platoon
- an Anti-tank Gun Platoon, or
- an Artillery Battery.

You may have up to **two** Support Platoons attached to your company for each Carri Platoon you field.

Motivation and Skill

Italian tankers have been fighting the British in the desert for years. Their equipment may not be the best, but the soldiers are some of the best that Italy has to offer. The platoons of a Compagnia Carri are rated as **Elite**.

'Centauro' Division

ITALIAN

HEADQUARTERS

1 Company HQ

Headquarters

Company HQ	60 points

Option

- Arm Command tank with an AA MG for +5 points.
- Equip M14/41 tank with Improvised Armour for +5 points.

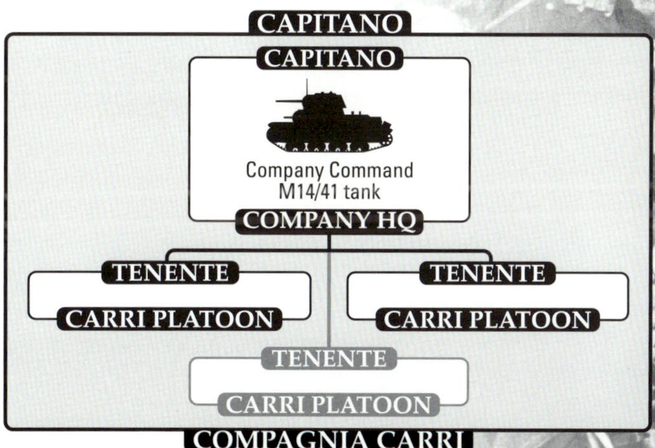

The *Capitano* leading the *carristi*, the tankers, of a Compagnia Carri is the bravest of the brave. Every day he leads his men into battle against overwhelming odds, and every day he must triumph.

COMBAT PLATOONS

2 or 3 Carri Platoons

Platoon

5 M14/41	**300 points**
4 M14/41	**240 points**
3 M14/41	**180 points**

Option

- Arm any or all tanks with an AA MG for +5 points per tank.
- Equip all M14/41 tanks with Improvised Armour for +5 points per tank.

The armoured divisions rely on the M14/41 tanks (and the older but visually identical M13/40) in the Carri Platoons. Although their armour is thin and their guns small, their crews are brave and overcome the odds to win fight after fight.

SUPPORT PLATOONS

0 to 1 Self-propelled 75/18 Platoon

Platoon

1 Carro Comando with:

4 Semovente 75/18	**310 points**
3 Semovente 75/18	**240 points**
2 Semovente 75/18	**170 points**

Option

- Arm any or all Carro Comando tanks and Semovente 75/18 assault guns with an AA MG for +5 points per vehicle.
- Equip all Semovente 75/18 assault guns with Improvised Armour for +5 points per gun.

Seeing the success of the German StuG assault guns, the Italian High Command decided to build a self-propelled gun along the same lines. Thus was born the *Semovente da 75/18*, based on the M14/41 hull and armed with a 75mm artillery piece.

Semoventi or self-propelled guns give the carri platoons support using their bigger guns to destroy the enemy Grant and Sherman heavy tanks allowing the carristi to destroy the enemy infantry and artillery.

THE TEN POINTS OF A BERSAGLIERE

In 1836 General Lamarmora, creator and mentor of the Bersaglieri, defined the core character of his men in the Decalogo del Bersagliere as follows:

1. Obbedienza	1. Obedience
2. Rispetto	2. Respect
3. Conoscenza assoluta della propria carabina	3. Absolute knowledge of one's weapon
4. Molto esercizio di tiro	4. Lots of target practice
5. Ginnastica di ogni genere fino alla frenesia	5. Fanatical devotion to physical fitness
6. Cameratismo	6. Camaraderie
7. Sentimento della famiglia	7. Family values
8. Amore al re	8. Devotion to the King
9. Amore alla patria	9. Love of one's country
10. Fiducia in se' fino alla presunzione	10. Self-esteem to the point of conceit

COMPAGNIA BERSAGLIERI

(INFANTRY COMPANY)

Up men up...to the front. Just as Il Duce was willing to give his blood for his country in the First World War, we shall do the same now. For we are the elite of the Italian Army, chosen by Comando Supremo as the best of the best. With the aid of our well-built motorcycles and trucks we are able to strike fast and hard wherever we are needed.
—Bersagliere Gianpaolo Brisigotti

A force based around a Compagnia Bersaglieri must contain:

- a Company HQ,
- one Bersaglieri Platoon, and
- one to three Bersaglieri, Bersaglieri Machine-gun, or Bersaglieri Anti-tank Platoons.

Weapons Platoons available to a Compagnia Bersaglieri are:

- a Bersaglieri Anti-aircraft Platoon.

Support Platoons for a Compagnia Bersaglieri can be:

- a Bersaglieri Mortar Platoon,
- Motociclisti Platoons,
- two Motorised Anti-tank Platoons,
- Carri Platoons,
- a Self-propelled 75/18 Platoon,
- Armoured Car Platoons,
- Light Tank Platoons, and
- Divisional Support Platoons.

You may also field any of the following platoons from the German section as a Support Platoon.

- a Panzer Platoon equipped with Panzer III or Panzer IV,
- a Panzergrenadier Platoon
- an Anti-tank Gun Platoon, or
- an Artillery Battery.

You may have up to **two** Support Platoons attached to your company for each Combat or Weapons Platoon you field.

Motivation and Skill

The bersaglieri are Italy's elite infantry. They train hard and fight hard, and have been doing so for more than two years. The platoons of a Compagnia Bersaglieri are rated as **Elite**.

HEADQUARTERS

1 Company HQ

Headquarters

Company HQ	35 points

Options

- Arm any or all Rifle teams with Passaglia bombs for +5 points per team.
- Add Solothurn anti-tank rifles for +20 points per team.
- Add Transport Section for +5 points per vehicle.

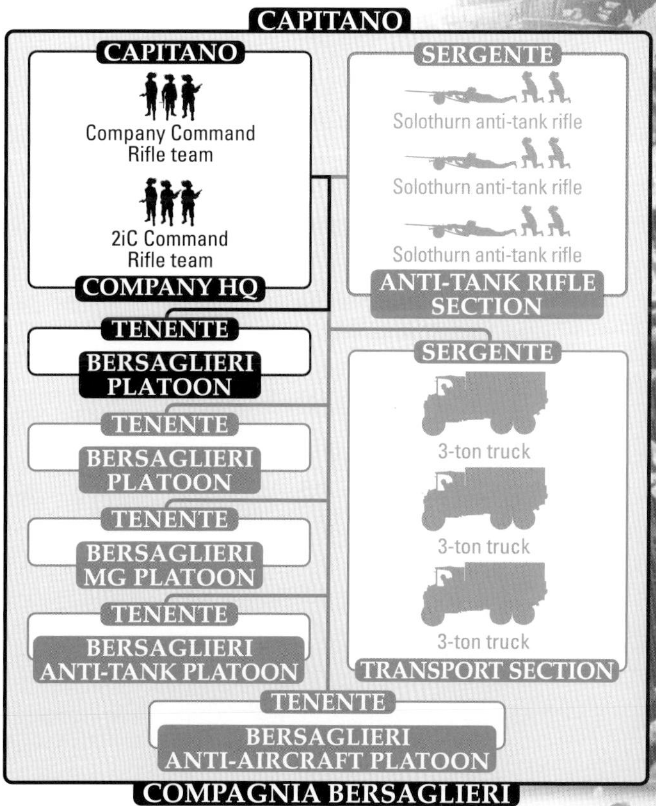

The philosophy of 'few men, many weapons' is the heart of the AS42 organisation. Each company has plenty of weapons with just enough soldiers to man and defend them. In the desert, attacks are made by tanks, not infantry.

101^ Divisione Motorizzata Trieste

The *Trieste* motorised infantry division was the best infantry division in North Africa. Not only was it fully motorised, but it had a regiment of *bersaglieri* as well. Even the *fucilieri*, the infantry, of the division were noted for their excellent performance and used the *bersaglieri* organisation.

COMBAT PLATOONS

1 or 2 Bersaglieri Platoons

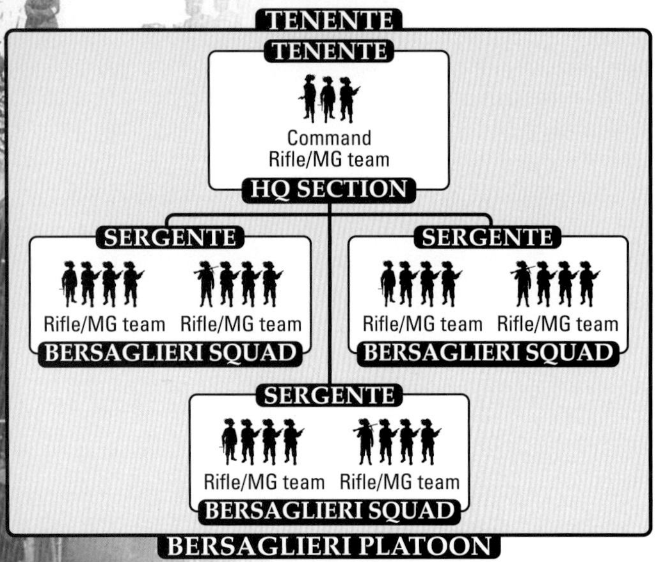

Platoon

HQ Section with:

3 Bersaglieri Squads	150 points
2 Bersaglieri Squads	105 points

Options

- Arm all Rifle/MG teams with Passaglia bombs for +5 points per team.

General Rommel said 'The German soldier impressed the world, the Italian bersaglieri impressed the German soldier!'

The platoon is armed with Breda machine-guns, *bombe Passaglia*, and *bottiglia incendiaria*, Molotov Cocktails, but the absolute dedication of his men is a greater asset to the *tenente*.

0 to 1 Bersaglieri Machine-gun Platoon

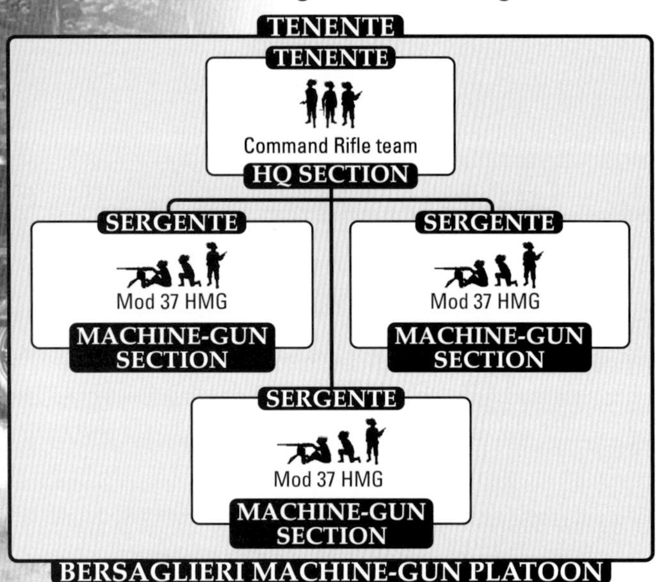

Platoon

HQ Section with:

3 Machine-gun Sections	105 points
2 Machine-gun Sections	75 points

The machine-gun crews gathered around their Breda *modello 37* heavy machine-guns form strongpoints in the Italian battle line. From there they support the *bersaglieri* in their typical flank attacks and break up enemy counter-attacks.

The Breda uses an unusual feed mechanism of twenty-round strips rather than a continuous belt, but a good crew can keep up a good rate of sustained fire.

0 to 1 Bersaglieri Anti-tank Platoon

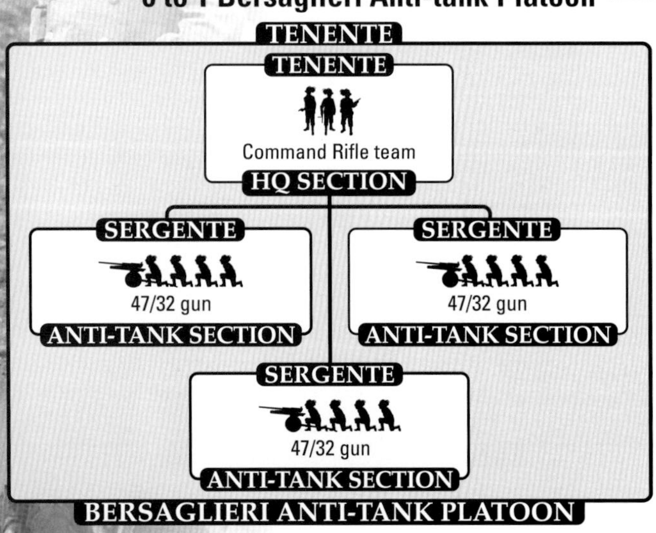

Platoon

HQ Section with:

3 Anti-tank Sections	125 points
2 Anti-tank Sections	90 points

The *Cannone da 47/32 modello 35* gun is known as the *Elefantino*, or little elephant. With the wheels removed, it is only 20"/50cm tall enabling it to take cover in any terrain.

To overcome its limited penetration when shooting at tanks, crews tend to hold their fire until extremely short range where they can hit the flanks, belly, or tracks of enemy tanks.

WEAPONS PLATOONS

0 to 1 Bersaglieri Anti-aircraft Platoon

Platoon
HQ Section with:

3 Anti-aircraft Sections	**100 points**
2 Anti-aircraft Sections	**75 points**

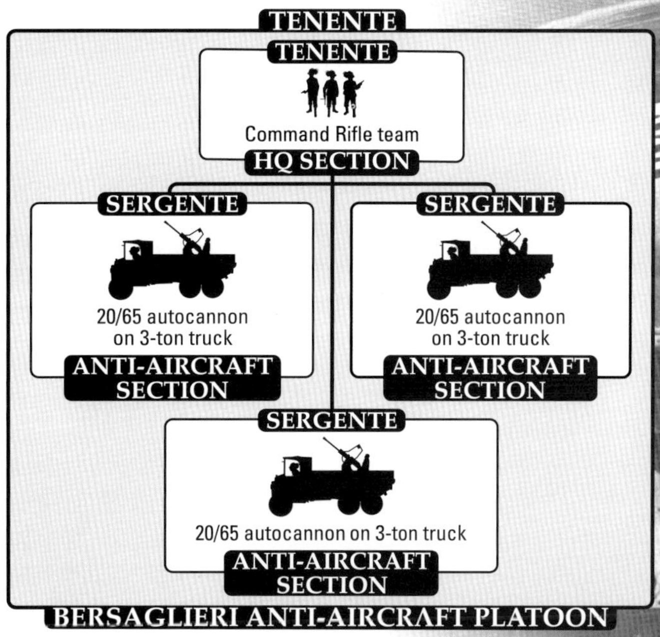

The *cannone-mitragliera Breda da 20/65 modello 35* is the most common anti-aircraft gun in the *Regio Esercito*, the Royal Army. It is a dual-purpose weapon for use against ground and air targets.

It was normally mounted on a truck, but was light enough to be broken down into four pack loads for man or mule carriage. In action the gun required a three-man crew.

As is common in many Italian units, the command team ride in one of the trucks with the guns rather than having their own transport.

SUPPORT PLATOONS

0 to 1 Bersaglieri Mortar Platoon

Platoon
HQ Section with:

3 Mortar Sections	**120 points**
2 Mortar Sections	**95 points**

Options
- Add 3-ton trucks to the platoon at no cost.

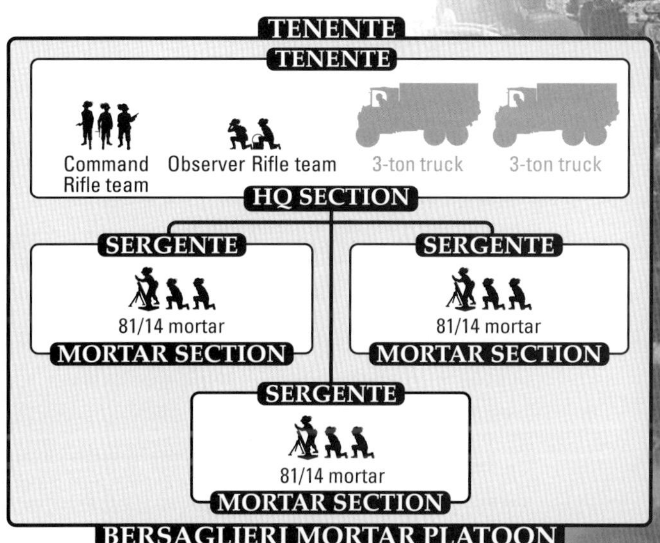

Like the rest of the *Regio Esercito*, the bersaglieri use the 81/14 mortar. Although similar to most other mortars of its size, Italian technology gave it a greater range making it the envy of its foes.

The *bersaglieri* use their Mortar Platoons to pin down distant targets as they manoeuvre to assault them.

0 to 2 Motorised Anti-tank Platoons

Platoon
HQ Section with:

2 Anti-tank Sections	**100 points**

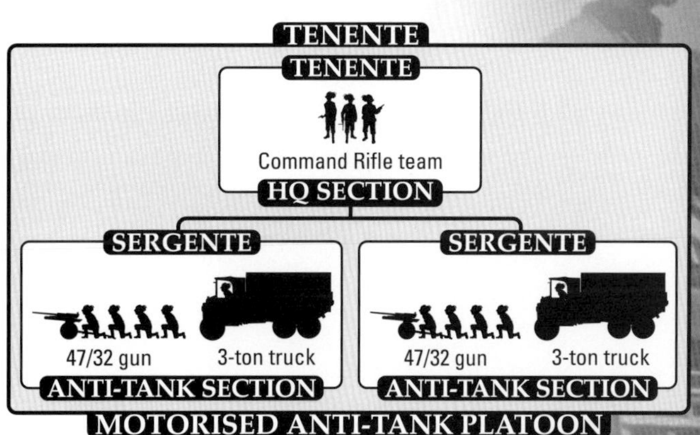

A *plotone anticarro motorizzato*, or motorised anti-tank platoon, is always ready to quickly redeploy to cover dangerous gaps opening in the line. Preventing enemy tanks from breaking through is critical to allow the counterattacks for which the *bersaglieri* have won renown.

COMPAGNIA MOTOCICLISTI

(MECHANISED COMPANY)

At the start of 1942, each bersaglieri regiment and reconnaissance battalion had a Compagnia Motociclisti (pronounced kom-pah-nee-ah moh-toh-cheek-lee-stee, meaning motorcyclist company). These were organised much like the motorised bersaglieri, but with everything in fours rather than threes.

A force based around a Compagnia Motociclisti must contain:

- a Company HQ,
- one Motociclisti Platoon, and
- one to three Motociclisti, Motociclisti Machine-gun, or Motociclisti Anti-tank platoons.

Weapons Platoons available to a Compagnia Motociclisti are:

- a Motociclisti Anti-aircraft Platoon,
- Armoured Car Platoons, and
- Light Tank Platoons.

Support Platoons for a Compagnia Motociclisti can be:

- Carri Platoons,
- a Self-propelled 75/18 Platoon,
- Bersaglieri Platoons,
- a Bersaglieri Mortar Platoon,
- Motorised Anti-tank Platoons, and
- Divisional Support Platoons.

You may also field any of the following platoons from the German section as a Support Platoon.

- a Panzer Platoon equipped with Panzer III or Panzer IV,
- a Panzergrenadier Platoon
- an Anti-tank Gun Platoon, or
- an Artillery Battery.

You may have up to **two** Support Platoons attached to your company for each Combat Platoon you field.

Motivation and Skill

The Motociclisti are exceptionally well trained in every aspect of motorcycling. Their combat performance is equally noteworthy. The platoons of a Compagnia

HEADQUARTERS

1 Company HQ

The Company HQ is organised like that of the Compagnia Bersaglieri on page 75, but with the addition of an optional fourth Solothurn anti-tank rifle for +20 points.

You must equip each Rifle team with Motorcycles for + 5 points and each Solothurn anti-tank rifle with a TL37 truck for +5 points per weapon.

COMBAT PLATOONS

1 or 2 Motociclisti Platoons

A *Plotone Motociclisti* (motorcyclist platoon) is organised as a Bersaglieri Platoon on page 76 with an optional fourth Bersaglieri Squad for +40 points.

You must equip each Rifle/MG team with Motorcycles for +5 points per team.

0 to 1 Motociclisti Machine-gun Platoon

The machine-gun platoon is organised as a Bersaglieri Machine-gun Platoon on page 76 with an optional fourth Machine-gun Section for +30 points.

You must equip each Mod 37 HMG team with Motorcycles for +5 points for the HQ Section and +5 points per Machine-gun Section.

0 to 1 Motociclisti Anti-tank Platoon

The anti-tank platoon is organised as a Bersaglieri Anti-tank Platoon on page 76 with an optional fourth Anti-tank Section for +45 points.

You must equip the HQ and each Anti-tank Section with a TL37 truck for +5 points per section

WEAPONS PLATOONS

0 to 1 Motociclisti Anti-aircraft Platoon

A Compagnia Motociclisti may have an anti-aircraft platoon organised like the Bersaglieri Anti-aircraft Platoon on page 77 as a Weapons Platoon.

0 to 4 Armoured Car Platoons

Platoon	
4 AB41	145 points
3 AB41	110 points
2 AB41	75 points

The *Autoblindo AB41* armoured cars cover the advance, locate the enemy, and work around their flanks to keep the advance moving.

Armoured Car Platoons are Reconnaissance Platoons.

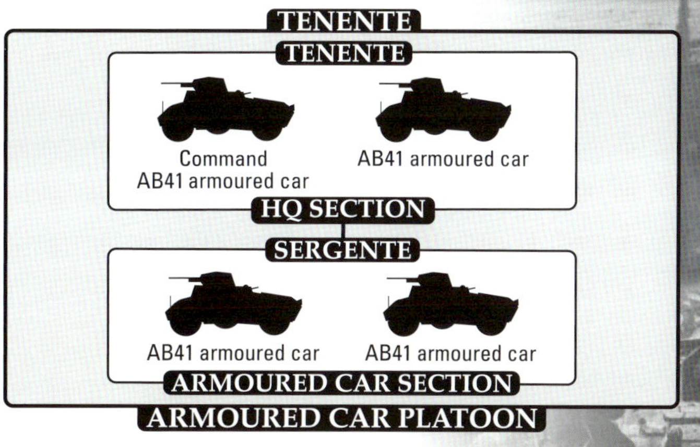

0 to 3 Light Tank Platoons

Platoon	
6 L6/40	200 points
5 L6/40	165 points
4 L6/40	130 points
3 L6/40	95 points

The 6-ton L6/40 light tank was produced in 1940 as the successor to the old L3/35 tankette. The small L6/40 was armed with a 20mm gun with a coaxial 8mm gun making it ideal for cavalry regiments and *bersaglieri* reconnaissance groups where mobility matters more than firepower.

Light Tank Platoons are not Reconnaissance Platoons.

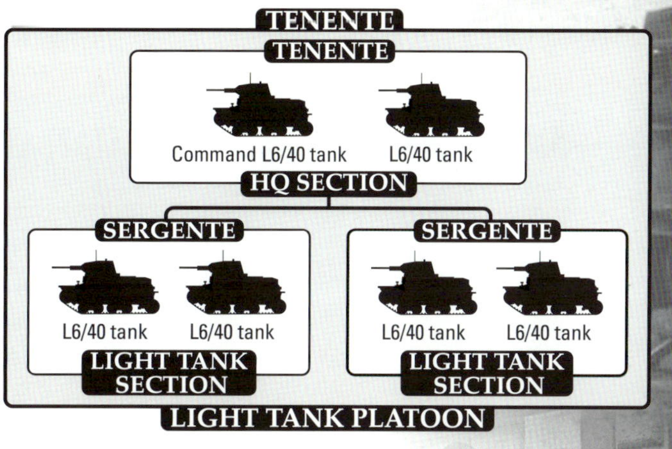

MOTORCYCLES

The *bersaglieri motociclisti* rode the legendary Moto Guzzi *Alce* (pronounced al-cheh), or Elk, introduced in 1938 for military use in reconnaissance and convoy escort. It featured a handlebar-mounting for the squad's Breda 30 light machine-gun. Obviously this machine -gun could only be operated when the motorcycle was stationary!

Equipping a Motociclisti with motorcycles turns them into Cavalry teams except that Motociclisti mounted on motorcycles cannot Launch an Assault, and they move as a Jeep team rather than a Cavalry team.

THE ITALIAN ARMY IN SICILY, 1943

6ª Armata (6th Army)	
Unit	**Battalions and Regiments**
131º Reggimento Corazzata	CI, CII
10º Reggimento Bersaglieri	XXXV, LXXIII
177º Reggimento Bersaglieri Territoriale	DXXV, DXXVI
185º Reggimento Paracadutisti 'Nembo'	III, VIII, XI1
10º Raggruppamento Semovente da 90/53	CLXI, CLXII, CLXIIII
XII Corpo d'Armata	
26ª Divisione da Montagna 'Assietta'	29, 30, XVII CCNN, 25 Artillery
28ª Divisione Fanteria 'Aosta'	5, 6, CLXXI CCNN, 22 'Vespri' Artillery
XVI Corpo d'Armata	
4ª Divisione d'Assalto 'Livorno'	33, 34, 28 'Monvisio' Artillery
54ª Divisione Fanteria 'Napoli'	75, 76, CLXXIII CCNN, 54 Artillery
XIV Panzerkorps (German)	
15. & 29.[1] Panzergrenadierdivision (German)	
Hermann Goring Panzergrenadierdivision (German)	
1. Fallschirmjagerdivision[1] (German)	

[1] Arrived during the campaign as reinforcements.

Regiments are shown in Arabic numerals (1, 2, 3, etc). Battalions are shown in Roman numerals (I, II, III, etc). Unless noted a regiment bears the same name as its parent division. Most infantry regiments have two battalions (I and II) and a weapons battalion (III) unless otherwise noted.

raggruppamento = regiment, *reggimento* = regiment, *divisione* = division, *bersaglieri* = light infantry, *corazzata* = armoured, *d'assalto* = assault, *fanteria* = infantry, *montagna* = mountain, *paracadutisti* = parachute, *territoriale* = territorial militia

FIELDING THE ITALIAN ARMY IN SICILY

The forces defending Sicily were varied, representing almost every type of regiment in the Royal Army and were equipped with some unique equipment. If you want to capture the flavour of this unique campaign, you will find the following guidelines helpful.

The campaign in Sicily was characterised by the scarcity of equipment available to the defenders and the measures taken to remedy this. The most obvious scarcity is modern tanks. Every available Italian tank was being used to form new armoured divisions, so the defenders of Sicily had to make do with old French Renault R.35 tanks as their only tank support.

Recognising this deficiency, *Comando Supremo* had, however, sent the most powerful anti-tank force in its arsenal to compensate. Every single Semovente 90/53 self-propelled anti-tank gun in service fought in the three battalions of *10º Raggruppamento Semovente* supporting the infantry right from the start of the battle. These were backed up by the light Semovente 47/32 in considerable numbers as well.

Aside from this limited, although extremely potent, armoured support, the infantry were pretty much reliant on their own equipment. Artillery was in short supply and ammunition even scarcer, and transport of any sort almost non-existent. There were no trained Guastatori demolisher assault engineers or Lancia da 90/53 *autocannoni* available at all.

What was available in reasonable quantities was riflemen, and these should make up the core of any force. Enough 47/32 and 65/17 guns were available for essential tasks, but few anti-tank rifles were available.

Defeating lavishly-equipped Allied forces with this bare-bones assortment certainly presents challenges. However, well handled, with perhaps a few judicious attachments from the German forces, the defenders of Sicily will definitely win battles against any Allied force.

ROMAN NUMERALS

The Italians commonly used Roman numerals to designate their units, particularly battalions. Although they look unintelligible at first glance, Roman numerals are fairly simple to decipher. There are seven commonly used elements each corresponding to a particular value, I = 1, V = 5, X = 10, L = 50, C = 100, D = 500, and M = 1000. These are combined as needed to produce the required value, so I = 1, II = 2, and III= 3. The tricky bit comes next. Rather than using IIII, four is represented by IV, one less than five. Nine (IX) and ninety (XC) are similar. So continuing our count, IV = 4, V= 5, VI = 6, VII= 7, VIII = 8, IX = 9, X = 10 and XI = 11. For a complex example, DXLIV = 544 (D = 500, XL = 10 before 50 or 40, and IV = 1 before 5 or 4, the total is 544!)

COMPAGNIA FUCILIERI

(INFANTRY COMPANY)

Mussolini has called for 8 Million Bayonets and my countrymen you have answered. The strength and traditions of the fucilieri run in your veins as well as the admiration of your country. The eyes of the world are upon you. Sons of Italy make us proud!
—Colonello Carlo Stormo

A force based around a Compagnia Fucilieri must contain:

- a Company HQ, and
- one to three Fucilieri Platoons.

Weapons Platoons available to a Compagnia Fucilieri are:

- a Machine-gun Platoon, and
- a Light Mortar Platoon.

Support Platoons for a Compagnia Fucilieri can be:

- Mortar Platoons,
- a Regimental Gun Platoon,
- an Anti-tank Platoon,
- a Self-propelled 90/53 Platoon,
- Renault Tank Platoons,
- Bersaglieri Platoons,
- Motociclisti Platoons,
- a Light Tank Platoon,
- Paracadutisti Platoons, and
- Divisional Support Platoons.

You may also field any of the following platoons from the German section as a Support Platoon.

- a Panzergrenadier Platoon,
- a Grenadier Platoon,
- a Fallschirmjäger Platoon,
- an Anti-tank Gun Platoon, or
- an Artillery Battery.

You may have up to **two** Support Platoons attached to your company for each Fucilieri Platoon you field.

Motivation and Skill

The *fucilieri*, the riflemen, are the backbone of the Royal Army. They are not volunteers. They don't want to be heroes. They just want to win this war and return to their farms and villages. The platoons of a Compagnia Fucilieri are rated as **Regular**.

ITALIAN

HEADQUARTERS

1 Company HQ

Headquarters

Company HQ	25 points

Option

- Add Solothurn anti-tank rifles for +15 points per team.

A *capitano dei fucilieri* has a strong role to play in commanding his company-sized portion of the '8 million bayonets' demanded by Mussolini.

As the leader of your company it is up to you to show your men the way. To lead them into danger and out the other side to victory. Your courage and leadership at the critical point on the battlefield makes the difference between glorious victory and ignoble defeat.

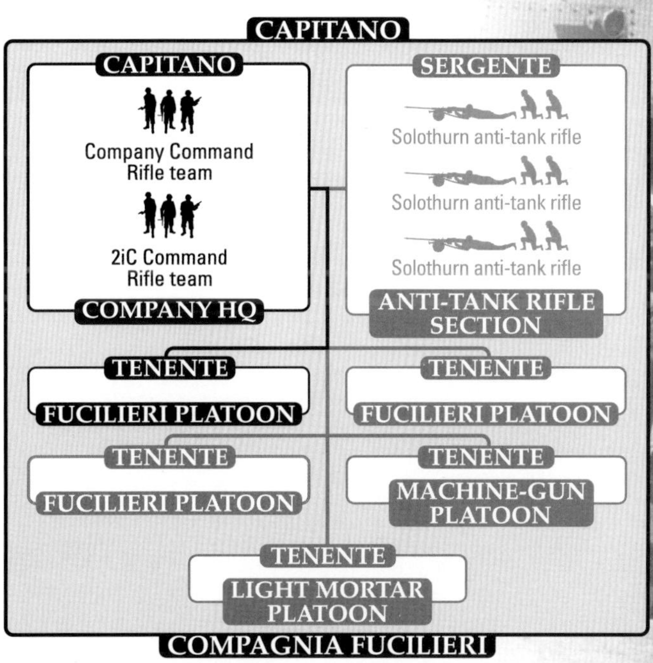

COMBAT PLATOONS

1 to 3 Fucilieri Platoons

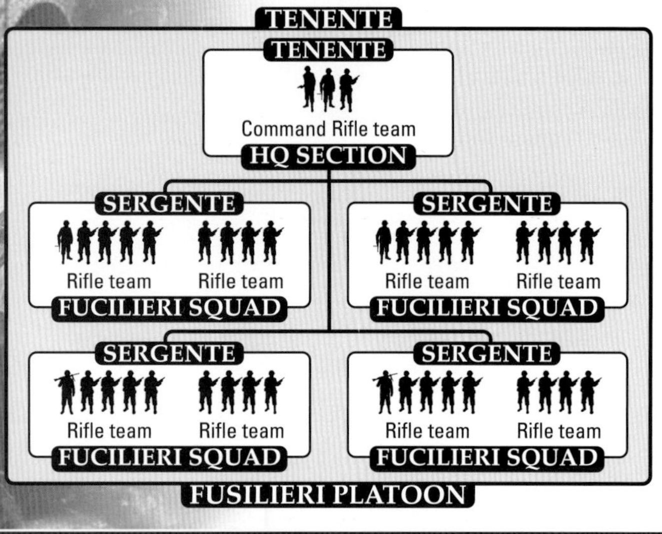

Platoon

HQ Section with:

4 Fucilieri Squads	**95 points**
3 Fucilieri Squads	**75 points**
2 Fucilieri Squads	**55 points**

Options

- Arm all Rifle teams with Passaglia bombs for +5 points per team.
- Upgrade all Rifle teams to Rifle/MG teams for +5 points per Fucilieri Squad.

Armed with the old Carcano 91 rifle and a few new Breda 30 machine-guns, the *fucilieri* must rely on their courage more than on technology.

WEAPONS PLATOONS

0 to 1 Machine-gun Platoon

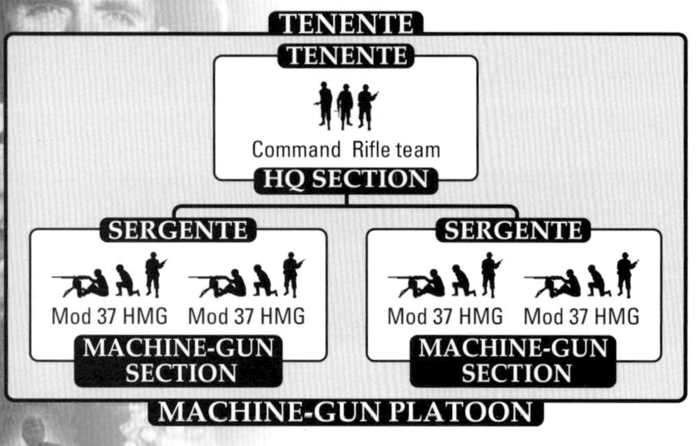

Platoon

HQ Section with:

2 Machine-gun Sections	**95 points**
1 Machine-gun Section	**55 points**

The *8mm Breda modello 37* machine gun laid down an impressive 450 rounds a minute, a big improvement over the old unreliable FIAT-Revelli *modello 35* (nicknamed the 'knuckle-buster' for its exposed recoil mechanism!)

In the hands of an adept gunner, a withering hail of fire could be maintained to support the advancing *fucilieri*.

0 to 1 Light Mortar Platoon

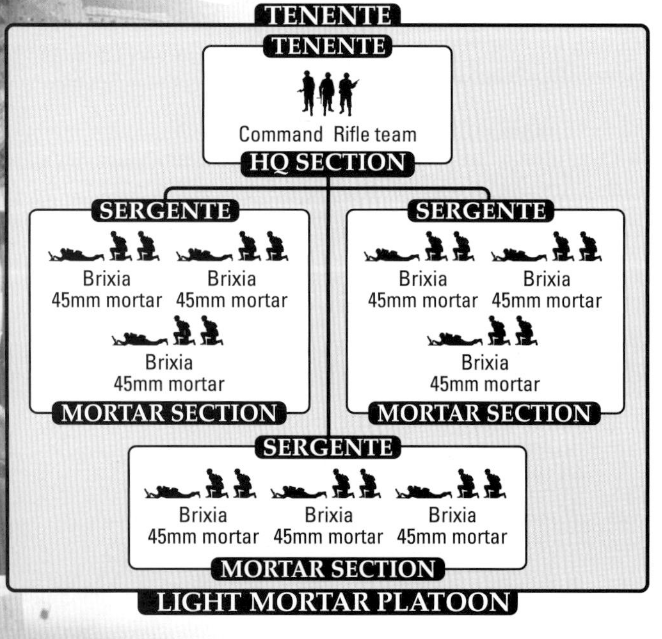

Platoon

HQ Section with:

3 Mortar Sections	**175 points**
2 Mortar Sections	**120 points**
1 Mortar Section	**65 points**

The *45mm Brixia modello 35* light mortar is designed to provide covering fire for the *fucilieri* right up to the point of assault. Unlike machine-guns and medium mortars that have to cease firing early to avoid hitting their own troops, the Brixia fires its small grenades over the attacking infantry allowing it to keep firing until the last few seconds before the assault. This makes the Brixia perfect for supporting infantry assaults.

SUPPORT PLATOONS

0 to 2 Mortar Platoons

Platoon
HQ Section with:

3 Mortar Sections	**80 points**
2 Mortar Sections	**60 points**

The long-ranged *mortaio da 81/14 modello 35* is available in sufficient numbers to give the fucilieri excellent close artillery support. This mortar is great at breaking up attacks and pinning down enemy defenders making them welcomed by all *fucilieri* company commanders.

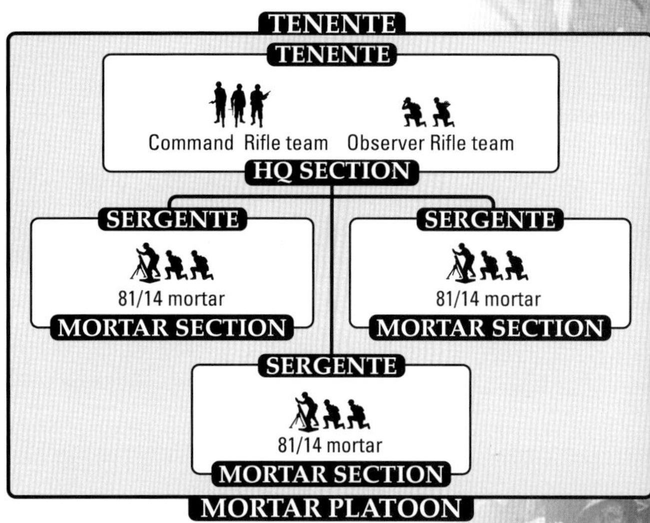

0 to 1 Regimental Gun Platoon

Platoon
HQ Section with:

2 Gun Sections	**85 points**
1 Gun Section	**50 points**

Options
- Add Gun shields to all 65/17 guns for +5 points. 65/17 guns with Gun shields are Heavy guns rather than Light guns.
- Add 3-ton trucks to the platoon at no cost.

The *cannone da 65/17 modello 13* was originally a mountain gun, able to be broken into small loads for transport. Now it is issued as an infantry gun to give the *fucilieri* close-up fire support.

It is a small gun, but with its *effetto pronto* anti-tank round, it is still a threat to enemy tanks.

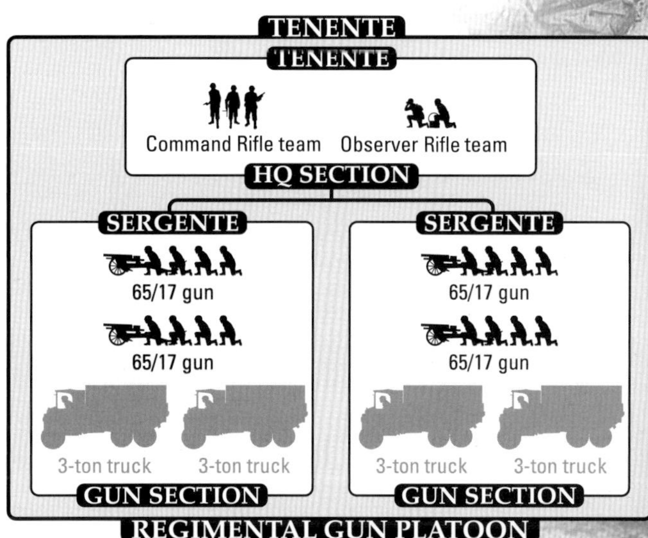

0 to 1 Anti-tank Platoon

Platoon
HQ Section with:

2 Anti-tank Sections	**110 points**
1 Anti-tank Section	**60 points**

Options
- Replace all 47/32 guns with 37/45 (German 3.7cm PaK36) guns for -15 points per Gun Section.
- Add 3-ton trucks to the platoon at no cost.

While most units had the Italian 47/32 gun, less fortunate ones made do with the German 37/45 guns. While far better than nothing, both lacked punch against heavier tanks.

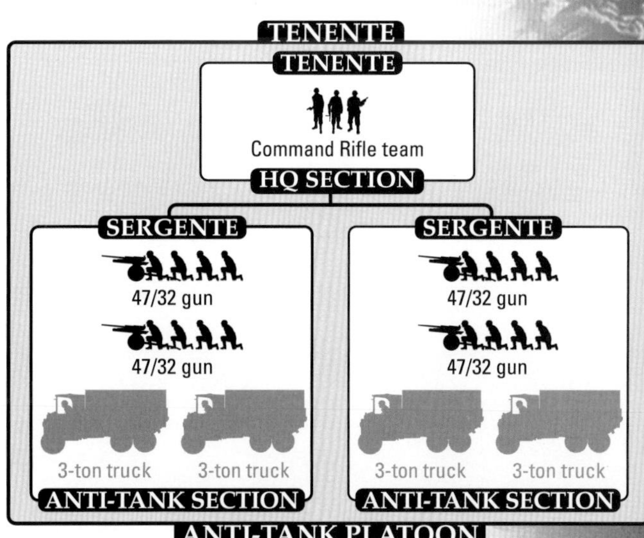

0 to 1 Self-propelled 90/53 Platoon

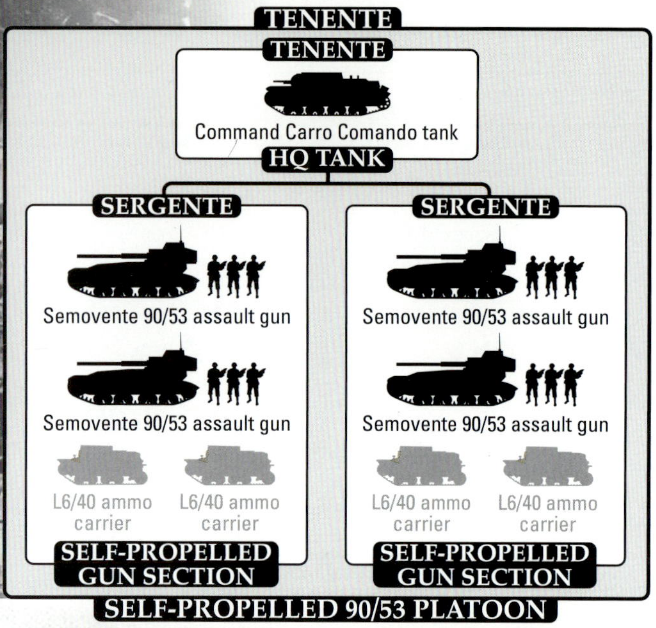

Platoon

1 Carro Comando with:

4 Semovente 90/53	**385 points**
3 Semovente 90/53	**295 points**
2 Semovente 90/53	**205 points**

Options

- Add L6/40 ammo carriers for +15 points per vehicle.
- Arm any or all Carro Comando tanks and L6/40 ammo carriers with an AA MG for +5 points per vehicle.

In 1942, the Italian generals realised that they would need a heavy self-propelled gun to deal with the Soviet T-34 tanks. The result was the *Semovente da 90/53 M41* mounting a 90/53 anti-aircraft gun on a lengthened M14/41tank chassis. With this armament, few enemy tanks can stand in its way. The only drawback is that a mere 6 rounds could be carried, so the *L6/40 trasporto munizioni* ammo carriers provide the main ammunition supply.

Few of these powerful weapons were produced, and when the Italian Army in Russia collapsed before they were ready, all were used to defend Sicily and Italy.

0 to 2 Renault Tank Platoons

Platoon

5 R.35	**125 points**
4 R.35	**100 points**
3 R.35	**75 points**

You may not field both Light Tank Platoons and Renault Tank Platoons.

Italy received over a hundred Renault R.35 light tanks when France surrendered in 1940. They briefly considered sending them to fight in the desert, but sensibly decided to issue them to CI (101st) and CII (102nd) tank battalions garrisoning Sicily instead.

Unfortunately, when the Allies invaded Sicily, these were the only Italian tanks on the island, so they had to fight on, despite their obvious obsolescence.

Sporting a 37mm gun and a co-axial 7.5mm machine-gun, and with a front armour of 45mm, the Renault R.35 was well armed and protected when built, but ridiculously under-gunned compared to the Allied tanks it had to fight.

COMPAGNIA PARACADUTISTI

(INFANTRY COMPANY)

Italy pioneered military parachuting when it resupplied divisions by air way back in 1918. The Regio Esercito, the Royal Army, was amongst the first to create a parachute force. Now these veteran parachutists have created two parachute divisions Folgore and Nembo. Only the best of the best survive the hard training and the three combat-ready practice jumps needed to become a paracadutista, a paratrooper. These few men become a perfect combat team, ready to win victory in many battles.

—Sergente Maggiore Nicolò Da Lio

A force based around a Compagnia Paracadutisti must contain:

- a Company HQ, and
- two or three Paracadutisti Platoons.

Weapons Platoons available to a Compagnia Paracadutisti are:

- a Paracadutisti Machine-gun Platoon, and
- two Paracadutisti Mortar Platoons.

Support Platoons for a Compagnia Paracadutisti can be:

- Paracadutisti Anti-tank Platoons,
- a Paracadutisti Demolisher Platoon,
- Bersaglieri Platoons,
- Fucilieri Platoons, and
- Divisional Support Platoons.

You may also field any of the following platoons from the German section as a Support Platoon.

- a Panzergrenadier Platoon,
- a Grenadier Platoon,
- a Fallschirmjäger Platoon,
- an Anti-tank Gun Platoon, or
- an Artillery Battery.

You may have up to **two** Support Platoons attached to your company for each Paracadutisti Platoon you field.

Motivation and Skill

The parachutists of the Folgore Division are all volunteers. Every one of them has jumped out of a plane from heights as low as 100m. They trained hard and now they fight hard. In such a unit there is no room for cowardice or failure. A Compagnia Paracadutisti does not need to roll on the 8 Million Bayonets table as every platoon in a Compagnia Paracadutisti is rated as **Fearless Veteran**.

HEADQUARTERS

1 Company HQ

Headquarters

Company HQ	45 points

Option

- Arm any or all SMG teams with Passaglia bombs for +5 points per team.

There is no room for bad officers in the *paracadutisti*. Every officer has passed jump training, just like their men. Officers are respected by their soldiers because unlike many, they stick by their men, never abandoning them, no matter how bad the situation.

It is an unwritten rule among paratroopers that the officers always lead attacks from the front. That is where you should be in battle, leading the assault.

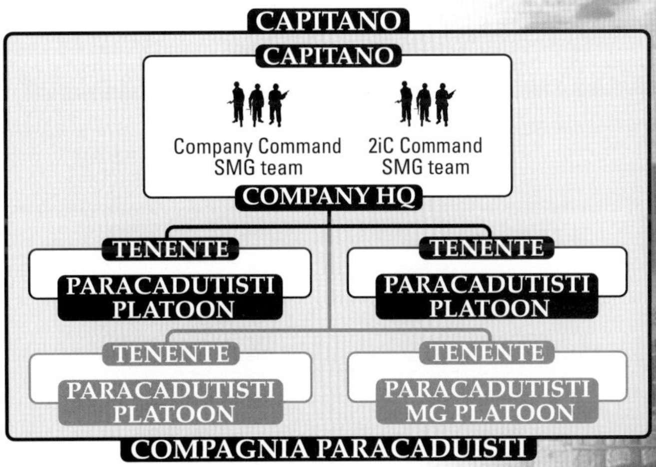

COMBAT PLATOONS

2 to 3 Paracadutisti Platoons

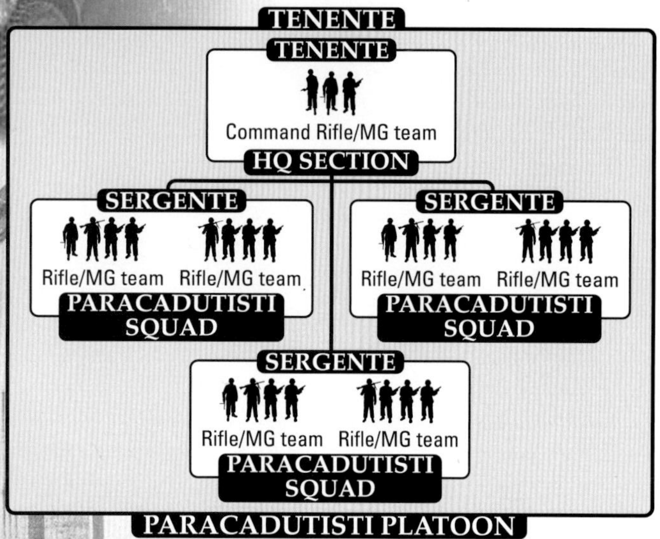

Platoon

HQ Section with:

3 Paracadutisti Squads	185 points
2 Paracadutisti Squads	135 points

Options

- Upgrade Command Rifle/MG team to a Command SMG team at no cost.
- Arm all Rifle/MG and SMG teams with Passaglia bombs for +5 points per team.

The *paracadutisti* were supposed to be armed with Beretta *modello 38* submachine-guns, but there aren't enough so only sergeants and officers have them. Even so, the British shudder when they hear the battle cry '*Folgore!*'.

WEAPONS PLATOONS

0 to 1 Paracadutisti Machine-gun Platoon

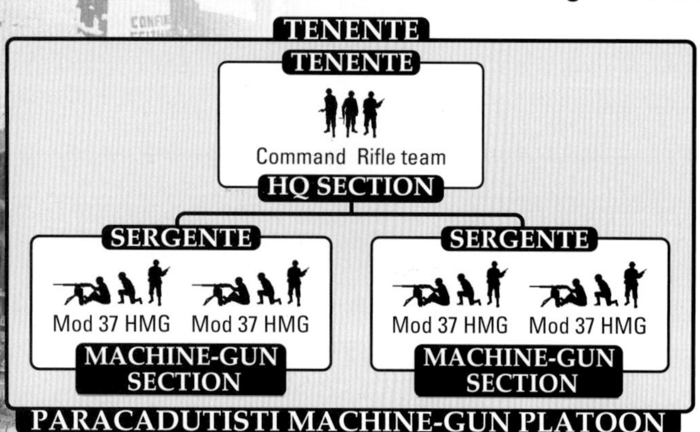

Platoon

HQ Section with:

2 Machine-gun Sections	165 points
1 Machine-gun Sections	95 points

The machine-guns wait until short range to open fire, keeping hidden until then as the *paracadutisti* sneak around the flanks to counterattack.

This technique is very effective and allows the *paracadutisti* to beat many times their numbers. This 'Folgore tactic' has helped create the myth that the Folgore Division will never be overrun.

0 to 2 Paracadutisti Mortar Platoons

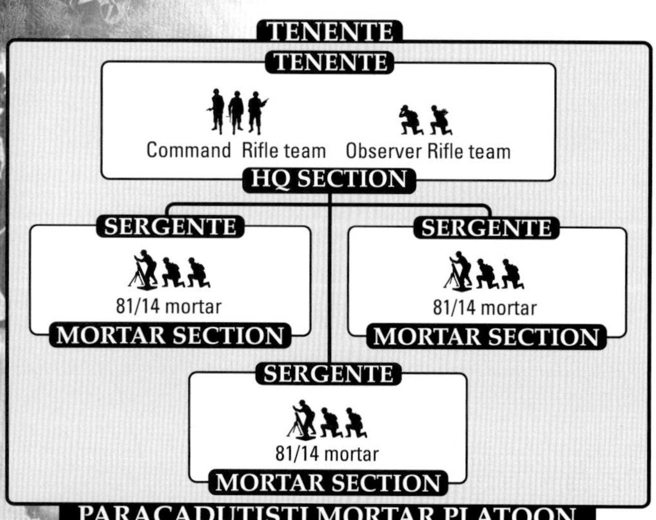

Platoon

HQ Section with:

3 Mortar Sections	130 points
2 Mortar Sections	100 points

Mortars are the perfect weapon for parachutists. They are light enough to parachute into battle, but still deliver a heavy punch at long range.

Every battalion has its own mortar platoon, reinforced by the divisional mortar company as needed. These operate well forward to give the *paracadutisti* the ability to break up enemy attacks and destroy enemy guns.

SUPPORT PLATOONS

Paracadutisti Anti-tank Platoons

Platoon

HQ Section with:

2 Anti-tank Sections	**220 points**
1 Anti-tank Section	**120 points**

The only artillery available to the paratroopers was the little 47/32 '*Elefantino*', not very powerful, but dangerous if used well. The *paracadutisti* 'acquired' extra guns from nearby formations to form their 7th '*Fantasma*' or 'Ghost' battery.

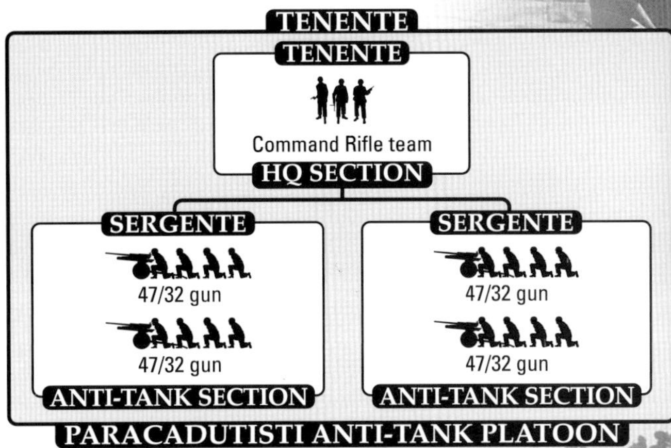

0 to 1 Paracadutisti Demolisher Platoon

Platoon

HQ Section with:

3 Demolisher Squads	**240 points**
2 Demolisher Squads	**170 points**
1 Demolisher Squad	**100 points**

Options

- Upgrade Command Rifle/MG team to Command SMG team at no cost.

Folgore's VIII Battalion was its *guastatori*, its demolition engineers. With satchel charges and flamethrowers they were especially dangerous to marauding Allied tanks.

Replace up to one Pioneer Rifle/MG team per Demolisher Squad with a Flame-thrower team at the start of the game before deployment.

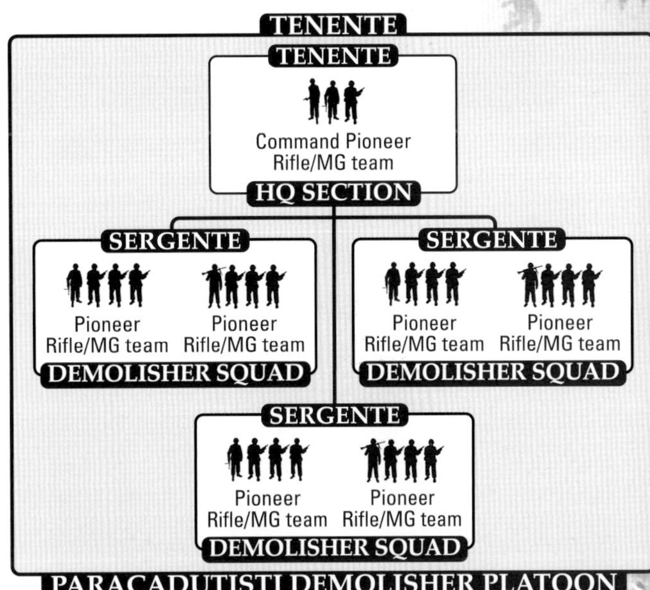

... Haret El Himeimat, 1942...

Soft African sand seeped like water into his uniform. It was everywhere and seemed to have been there forever, like the explosions of British shells all around. Paolo Bettin, caporale, VII battaglione guastatori paracadutisti, pressed his helmet tighter on his head, clenched his teeth and huddled deeper in his buca, his fox-hole. The earth shook so violently his heart missed a beat.

He jumped as a hand touched his right shoulder. Paolo looked up to see capitano Lorenzi in the darkness looking down from the edge of his buca, a sad smile on his face. Paolo couldn't believe it! The young captain was walking around in the maelstrom checking his soldiers and reassuring them with his presence. Lorenzi squeezed his shoulder, winked and dashed on towards the next hole.

Suddenly, like death came silence. The shelling had stopped and the night swallowed all sound. Paolo raised his head to see paratroopers, like ghosts in the darkness, pop up from their buce, fewer than ever. Like his brothers in arms, he checked his trusty 'ninety-one' rifle and arranged the few grenades left to him before daring one last look at the stars overhead. Days ago a mortar round had silenced their last elefantino gun. Grenades and bullets were all that were left, they would have to suffice.

Out in the darkness ahead the creak of tank tracks and the rumble of engines grew nearer. 'FOLGORE!' shouted a nameless voice beside him. Despite the odds, Paolo knew the British would not pass. Should he die, his brothers would fight on to the last.

DIVISIONAL SUPPORT PLATOONS

Any Carri, Bersaglieri, Motociclisti, Fucilieri or Paracadutisti Companies may have the following support platoons:

- a Self-propelled 47/32 Platoon,
- a Light Anti-aircraft Platoon,
- a Heavy Anti-aircraft Platoon,
- a Heavy Anti-tank Platoon,
- Transport Sections,
- Artillery Batteries, and
- Demolisher Platoons.

Motivation and Skill

Divisional support platoons are rated as **Regular**, **Elite** or **Artillery** as indicated in the entry.

Air Support

Aircraft	Limited Air Support	Sporadic Air support
FIAT CR.42 Falco	125 points	90 points
Macchi C.200 Saetta	125 points	90 points
Ju.87 Picchiatello	135 points	100 points

0 to 1 Self-propelled 47/32 Platoon

Platoon

4 Semovente 47/32	195 points
3 Semovente 47/32	145 points
2 Semovente 47/32	95 points

Option

- Arm any or all Semovente 47/32 assault guns with an AA MG for +5 points per assault gun.

Rated as Elite

The *Semovente da 47/32* is a mobile infantry support weapon, perfect for knocking out machine-gun nests holding up the infantry advance. The *semovente* is also useful as an anti-tank weapon against light tanks, although this isn't recommended because of its light armour.

0 to 1 Light Anti-aircraft Platoon

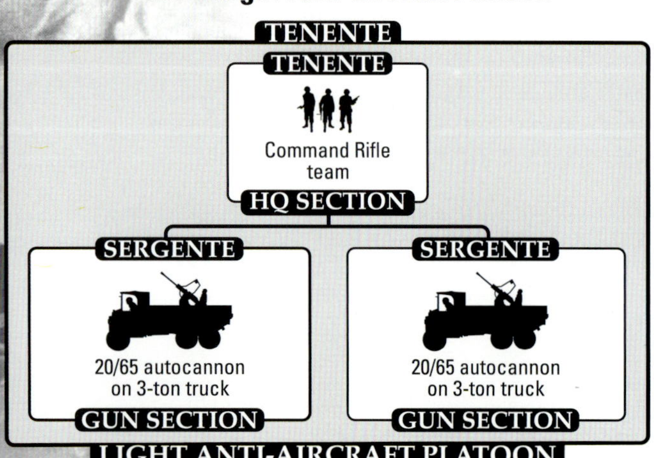

Platoon

HQ Section with:

2 Gun Sections	75 points

Rated as Artillery

The anti-aircraft company keeps enemy aircraft at bay, protecting the vulnerable artillery and tanks, allowing them to destroy the enemy undisturbed.

In mobile operations the guns fire from the back of their trucks, but dismount in static battles.

0 to 1 Heavy Anti-aircraft Platoon

Platoon

HQ Section with:

2 Gun Sections	**280 points**
1 Gun Section	**150 points**

Options

- Replace each Lancia da 90/53 with a towed 90/53 gun and 6-ton truck for -25 points per gun.
- Model towed 90/53 guns with eight or more crew and increase their ROF to 3 for +10 points per gun.

Rated As Artillery

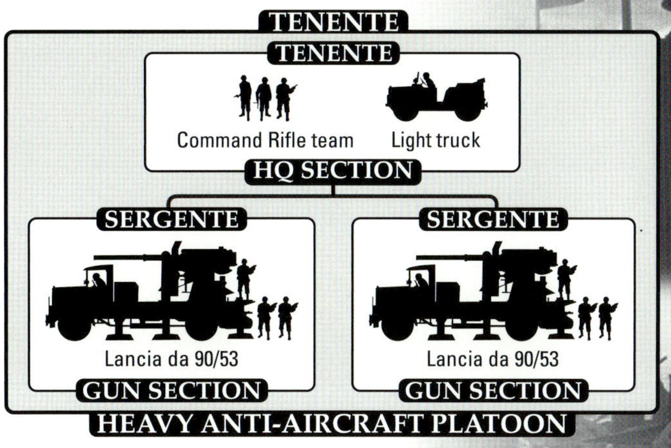

The *autocannone Lancia 3 RO da 90/53* combines mobility with the hitting power of a 90mm anti-aircraft gun.

0 to 1 Heavy Anti-tank Platoon

Platoon

HQ Section with:

2 Gun Sections	**225 points**
1 Gun Section	**125 points**

Options

- Equip 88/56 (German 8.8cm FlaK36) guns with gun shields for +25 points per gun.
- Model 88/56 (German 8.8cm FlaK36) guns with eight or more crew and increase their ROF to 3 for +10 points per gun.

Rated As Artillery

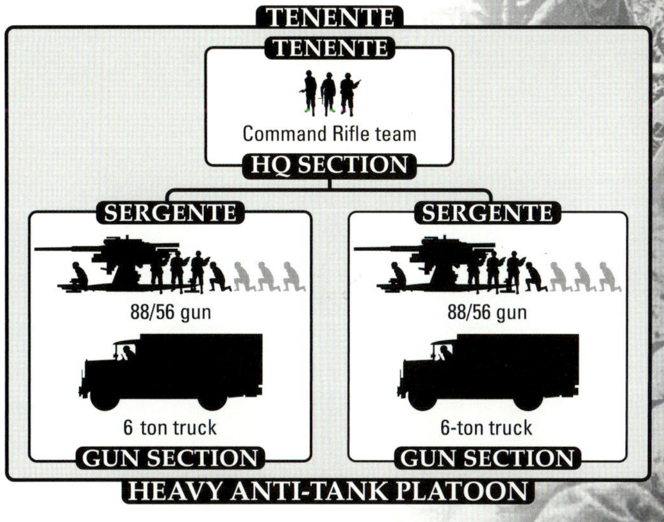

Italy used the excellent German 88/56 anti-aircraft gun as a stopgap anti-tank/anti-aircraft gun until their own 90/53 entered service.

Transport Section

Platoon

HQ Squad with:

1 Transport Squad	**25 points**
No Transport Squads	**15 points**

Rated As Regular

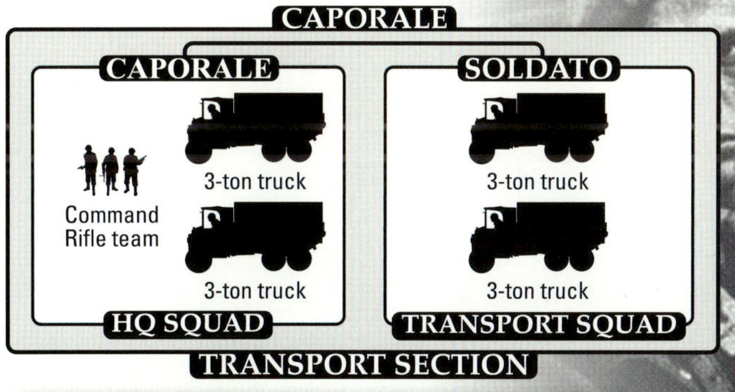

The *Regio Esercito*, the Royal Army, was always short of trucks. The few available were pooled to bring ammunition, food and water to the front. Occasionally they were also allocated to move troops on long marches.

A Transport Section is a Truck Platoon

Artillery Battery

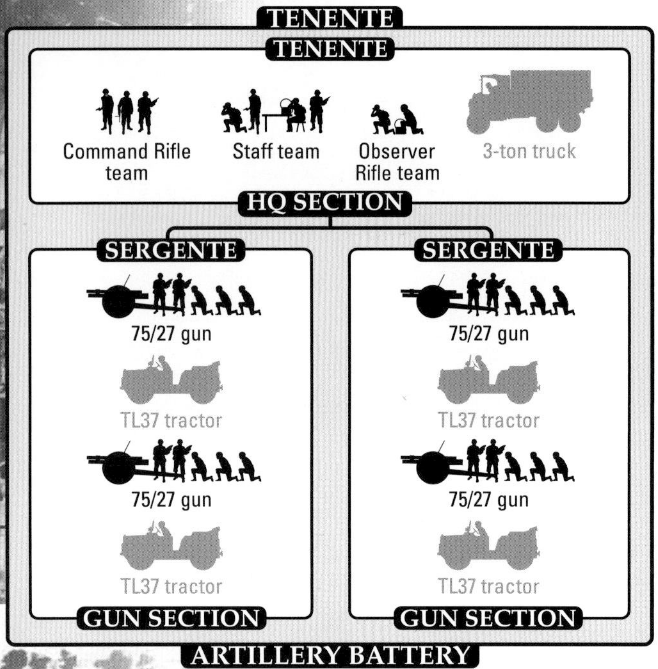

Platoon

HQ Section with:

2 Gun Sections	**190 points**
1 Gun Section	**110 points**

Options

- Replace all 75/27 guns with 100/17 howitzers for +20 points per Gun Section or with captured 25 pdr guns for +20 points per Gun Section.
- Add 3-ton truck and TL37 tractors to the platoon at no cost.

Rated As Artillery

The *artiglieria*, artillery, of the Second World War used the guns that their fathers fired in the First World War. These guns are still the equal of any artillery in the world. The Italian *artigliere* tenaciously fights to the last to preserve the good name of Italy.

Demolisher Platoon

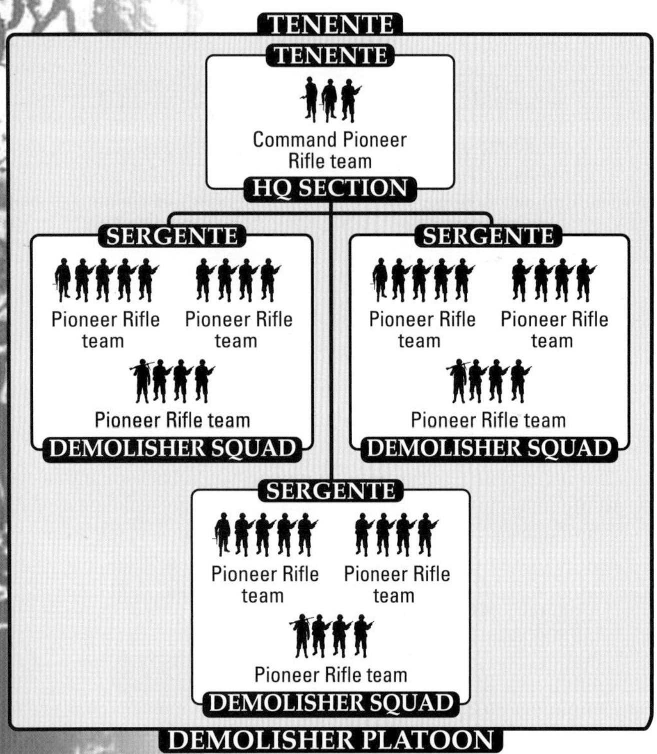

Replace up to one Pioneer Rifle team per Demolisher Squad with a Flame-thrower team at the start of the game before deployment.

Platoon

HQ Section with:

3 Demolisher Squads	**250 points**
2 Demolisher Squads	**175 points**
1 Demolisher Squad	**100 points**

Options

- Upgrade all Rifle teams to Rifle/MG teams for +5 points for the HQ Section and +10 points per Demolisher Squad.

Rated As Elite

The traditions of the *Arditi del Genio*, the assault engineers of the First World War, were resurrected in the Second World War under the honoured name *Guastatori*, demolishers, used since the time of Napoleon.

Organised into companies with names like *Giaguaro* (jee-ahg-wah-roh, Jaguar), *Tigre* (tee-greh, Tiger), *Leone* (leh-oh-neh, Lion), *Folgore* (fohl-gorr-eh, Thunderbolt), *Uragano* (oo-rah-gah-noh, Hurricane), *Tormenta* (torr-mehn-tah, Tormentor), and *Valanga* (vah-lahn-gah, Avalanche), the *Guastatori* led assaults against fortified positions in every theatre. Their battle cry was '*Varco!*', 'Passage!'.

For King & Country

BRITISH FORCES IN THE MEDITERRANEAN

"Before Alamein we never had a victory. After Alamein we never had a defeat."
—Winston Churchill, British Prime Minister.

"I want to impose on everyone that the bad times are over, they are finished! Our mandate from the Prime Minister is to destroy the Axis forces in North Africa...It can be done, and it will be done!."
—General Bernard Law Montgomery.

The 50th (Northumbrian) Infantry Division was a Territorial Division from the north of England, mostly coalminers and workers from the foundries and mills of Durham and Yorkshire. The Division's symbol was two 'T's, one crossing the other, for the Tyne and Tees rivers flowing through the recruiting area.

France

In 1940, after completing its training and filling out its ranks, the Division was sent to join the British Expeditionary Force (BEF) fighting alongside the French. There it was to play a crucial role in facing the German onslaught. After retreating for nearly a week, two battalions of Durham Light Infantry and two battalions of Matilda tanks counterattacked the German 7th Panzer Division under General Rommel at Arras. Although ultimately unsuccessful, the attack bought time for the Division to be evacuated from Dunkirk with the rest of the BEF in June 1940.

Back in England, the 50th Division was rebuilt. Then in 1941 they were sent out to the Middle East to garrison first Cyprus and then Iraq and train for the coming battles.

Brigade Boxes

In 1942 the North Countrymen headed for Libya, where General Rommel had driven the Eighth Army back to Gazala. The 50th Division was deployed in three fortified 'Brigade Boxes' between the South Africans to the north and the Free French and

Indians to the south. Brigade boxes were a uniquely British idea. In theory these islands of infantry scattered in a loose line across the desert would restrict the enemy's movements and provide safe harbours so that the British armour could sally forth and destroy the enemy in a decisive battle.

Gazala

At the end of May 1942, Rommel's *Afrikakorps* drove south through the desert around the Gazala line smashing much of the British armoured strength in the process, but then found itself trapped in the 'Cauldron' with no supply route. It appeared that the British plan was working. 150 Infantry Brigade, supported by the Valentines of 44 RTR, was astride the vital Trigh Capuzzo—the main supply line through to the encircled *Afrikakorps*.

Then, with everything set, the Eighth Army's commanders bickered and dithered. Rommel struck back with everything he had, desperately trying to break back through 150 Brigade and open his supply line. For two days the outnumbered North Countrymen doggedly repelled every attack. On the third day, 1 June, Rommel overran the brigade while Eighth Army looked on.

The defeat of the British armoured divisions and a gallant, but unsupported attack by 5th Indian Division over the next few days left the rest of the Gazala line cut off. The South Africans on the coast managed to slip past Rommel at the last moment, but 50th Division was surrounded. With the *Afrikakorps* lying to the east, a conventional withdrawal was impossible. Instead, 50th Division broke out through the startled Italian infantry to the west. Once clear of the Italian frontline, the Division headed south into the desert. After a retreat of 300 miles, they made it back to friendly lines.

Mersa Matruh

In the meantime, the fortress of Tobruk fell to the German Blitzkrieg, a terrible blow for the British Empire. 50th Division conducted the rearguard of the Eighth Army back to Mersa Matruh in Egypt, the new defensive line. Once more, the North Countrymen were let down by Eighth Army's inept high command. Along with the New Zealand Division and the remnants of 10th Indian Division, the North Countrymen found themselves cut off again. In a confused attack, most of the Division managed to escape and make their way back to the final defence line at Alamein.

First Battle Of Alamein

By the start of July Rommel's *Afrikakorps* was exhausted, but with Alexandria just 60 miles away and the Eighth Army equally tired, they pushed on. Over the next three weeks, South Africans, Australians, New Zealanders, Indians, and the men from Northumbria fought a series of desperate battles that finally stopped Rommel's advance, though at a terrible cost.

Rommel made one more attempt to reach the Suez Canal and the oilfields beyond at the end of August, but this time General Montgomery ('Monty' to his men) was in charge of the Eighth Army. All talk of retreat was banned, a good plan stuck to, and Rommel's attack was defeated.

The 50th Division had meanwhile been withdrawn and reinforced. Monty initially planned on disbanding the Division as since May it had lost an entire brigade, and its two other brigades were under-strength and exhausted. Fortune smiled however, as a new draft of Northumbrian reinforcements arrived just in time to save the Division from its fate.

Second Battle Of Alamein

After nine months of disasters and retreats, the Eighth Army's new general launched its own offensive, Operation Lightfoot, on 23 October, 1942. In the northern sector, the 9th Australian, 51st (Highland), 2nd New Zealand, and 1st South African Divisions attacked the German and Italian lines preceded by a massive artillery barrage. In the south, 44th and 50th Divisions made diversionary attacks, with 50th Division's 69 Infantry Brigade attacking positions held by the elite Italian *Folgore* Division at Munassib Depression. The initial attacks bit deep into the enemy defences, but did not break through. For the next week, much of the fighting was undertaken by the 9th Australian Division on the north coast, drawing the enemy away from the centre where the breakthrough would come.

By 2nd November, Rommel's army was near breaking. Monty launched Operation Supercharge. For this the Northumbrian 151 Infantry Brigade and the Highland 152 Infantry Brigade joined the New Zealand Division for the attack. Following a creeping barrage, the North Countrymen seized their objectives, and opened the way for the following British armour to move through and engage *Afrikakorps* in a tank battle at Tel El Aqqaqir. A few days later, the defeated German and Italian forces began their retreat.

Over the next three months the Eighth Army regained everything they had lost, and they pushed Rommel eastwards all the way out of Libya and into Tunisia. The Eighth Army were helped in this by a new arrival. The First Army, a combined British, French and US force, had landed west of Tunisia in Operation Torch and was closing in on Rommel from the west.

Tunisia

In March 1943, rested and refreshed, 50th Division was summoned back to the front. Rommel had launched an offensive against Eighth Army at Medenine, which had been repelled. Now it was the turn of Eighth Army to resume the offensive with Operation Pugilist. The Axis positions were exceptionally strong, being based around the heavily-fortified Mareth Line. Montgomery selected the 50th Division to make a frontal attack on the line, while the New Zealand Division made a wide outflanking move. The German defences proved too strong for the North Countrymen to overcome, but their fierce attack enabled the New Zealanders to force open the Tebaga Gap with Operation Supercharge II. The 1st Armoured Division dashed through, with Rommel's *Afrikakorps* narrowly escaping the trap.

Advancing on the next Axis position at Wadi Akarit, Montgomery again launched a combined frontal attack and outflanking manoeuvre—Operation Scipio, this time with 69 Brigade and 51st Highland Division attacking, while 4th Indian Division made a brilliant night attack through mountains to outflank the position.

The Axis forces were running out of space to retreat. The First and Eighth Army had linked up. At the start of May, the combined British force smashed through the Axis line at Medjez El Bab in Operation Strike. Tunis fell a few days later, ending the North African campaign.

Sicily

As the North African campaign closed down, 50th Division prepared for the next campaign—Operation Husky, the invasion of Sicily. With Sicily taken, Allied high command hoped that it could force Italy out of the war and secure control of the Mediterranean.

50th Division landed on the south-eastern beaches of Sicily on 10 July, 1943. The North Countrymen were soon pushing northwards towards the main objective of the campaign, Messina, meeting only sporadic resistance from Italian rearguards. Further inland, the 51st (Highland) and 1st Canadian Divisions moved north across rugged terrain, driving back German and Italian forces.

The Division's rapid advance came to a halt when 151 Brigade ran into stiff resistance from elite German paratroops around Primasole Bridge. A bitter battle raged until 17 July before the Division gained control of the strategically vital bridge.

Montgomery continued with attacks further inland to try and turn the German defences around Catania and the southern slopes of Mt Etna, but skilful rearguards and demolitions allowed the German defenders each time to pull back to another position. Eventually, 50th Division reached its final objective of Messina—only to find the last of the Germans had been evacuated and the Americans already there.

It had been more than a year of hard fighting for the men from the Tyne and Tees. While they had not attracted the publicity of other divisions, they had through dogged determination earned a reputation as tough fighters. Monty had been assigned command of the D-Day landings in France, and for that he needed his veteran desert divisions. So in October 1943, 50th (Northumbrian) Division returned to England.

Italy

In the meantime, the other divisions of the Eighth Army continued the war in the Mediterranean, landing in Italy on 3 September, 1943 in Operations Baytown (Calabria) and Slapstick (Taranto). Progress northwards up the Italian peninsula for these troops was slow, hampered by determined German rearguards and demolitions. Operation Avalanche, the landing of a combined US and British Fifth Army at Salerno almost came to disaster when the Germans rapidly counter-attacked, but by the end of 1943 the Allies had closed up to the Gustav Line anchored on Monte Cassino. Deteriorating winter weather and excellent defensive terrain would allow the Germans to hold this line for six months until the middle of 1944.

Normandy

On 6 June, 1944, 50th (Northumbrian) Division returned to battle, landing on Gold Beach in Normandy. For the next six weeks the North Countrymen hammered at the German defences. The Division suffered 4500 casualties, but German strength was ground down. In August German resistance collapsed, and 50th Division advanced across France into Belgium. In September 1944, the line stabilised again, and after a period of static warfare, the Division was withdrawn to England to act as a training formation for fresh troops being sent to the front. For the 50th (Northumbrian) Division the war was over.

The British Empire

Britain has a long and proud history. Her Empire extends around the globe colouring a quarter of the map red. It is true that the sun never sets on the British Empire. Now, once again the German blight is spreading across Europe. Hitler and his Nazi thugs have brought the world to war. Britain will not, can not stand by and watch this happen. Britons Shall never be slaves.

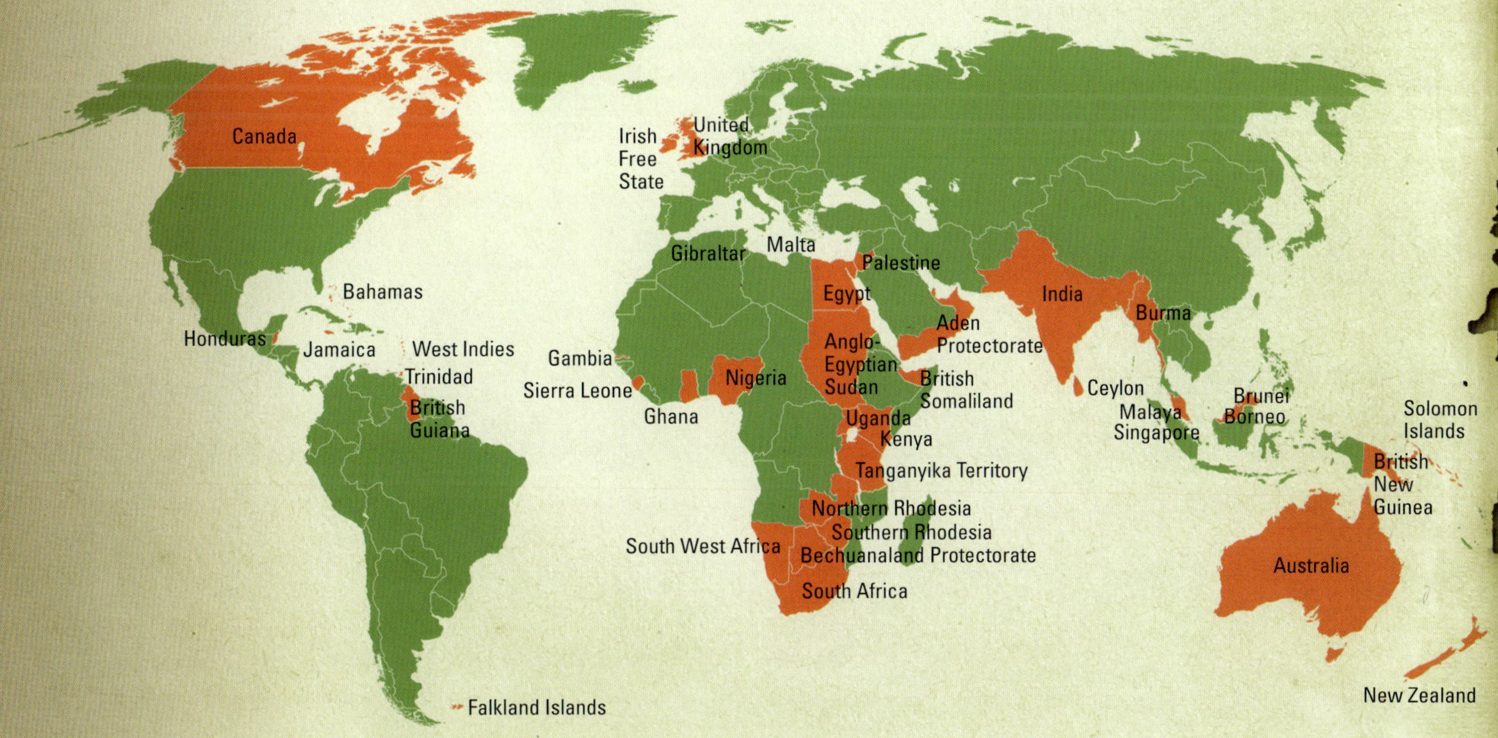

El Alamein

Australian and New Zealand infantry charge under cover of a mammoth artillery bombardment.

A dug-in German '88' halts the British armour, so the Australians take the lead once more.

25 pdr guns turn from the barrage to stop a German counterattack in its tracks.

Oct 23 – Nov 04 1942

Charles Upham leads from the front winning his second VC.

The Maori break through the minefields under the withering fire of the German defenders.

Their speed and tenacity forces the bewildered defenders to retreat.

The artillery screen the Northumbrian Division's attack with a smoke screen.

'Gott in Himmel, die Englanders are so many!'

The North Countrymen fall upon the German defences.

German armoured cars attempt to delay the British advance.

Even the arrival of German Panzers cannot stop the advance.

REGIMENTS OF THE BRITISH ARMY

The British Army is steeped in history and tradition. Many regiments can trace their history back to the Seventeenth Century in the days of Pike and Shot, and most fought in the Napoleonic Wars at the turn of the Nineteenth Century and have battle honours too numerous to list. This long history has produced a number of oddities in the way the army is organised.

In the past, a regiment was the personal property of its Colonel, although sworn to the King's Service. To keep the regiments in being and share the burden of active service, each regiment usually sent one battalion to war, keeping another at home to raise and train replacements.

These battalions are grouped into brigades of three or four battalions as required, with no regard for the regiment of origin (although considerable regard for seniority). Brigades can operate independently or two or three brigades can be grouped into a division, once again as required.

The regiment is the heart and soul of the British Army. A soldier's first loyalty is to his regiment. Battalions are known by the title of their parent regiment, so when you see a reference to The Buffs (Royal East Kent Regiment), it is actually just a single battalion of that regiment. It's worth noting that only certain regiments have been granted the title 'Royal' as a reward for service to the Crown. As a result, the Army as a whole is not a 'Royal Army' in the manner of the Royal Navy.

To complicate matters further, some battalions were actually split to provide the cadre for two new battalions. When this was done, the new battalions simply gained a prefix with the 5th Battalion of The Queen's Royal Regiment becoming the $1/5^{th}$ Queens and the $2/5^{th}$ Queens. Just to make things even more interesting, battalions were sometimes joined gaining a combined title like the $5^{th}/7^{th}$ Gordons, an amalgamation of the fifth and seventh battalions!

There is a strict hierarchy of precedence between regiments. The senior regiments come first, with the Cavalry and Royal Horse Artillery ranking before the Royal Tanks, all before the Royal Artillery, followed by the Foot Guards, the Regiments of the Line, the Yeomanry, and the Territorial Army. The regiments below are given in order precedence.

Foot Guards	
Grenadier Guards (The First or Grenadier Regiment of Foot Guards) 'Bill Browns'	Gren Gds
Coldstream Guards (The Coldstream Regiment of Foot Guards) 'Coldstream', 'Colleys', or 'Lillywhites', never 'Coldstreams'	Coldm Gds
Scots Guards (The Scots Regiment of Foot Guards) 'Jocks', 'Pontius Pilates Bodyguard', 'Kiddies'	SG
Irish Guards (The Irish Regiment of Foot Guards) 'Bob's Own', 'Micks'	IG
Welsh Guards (The Welsh Regiment of Foot Guards)	WG
Regiments of the Line	
The Queen's Royal Regiment (West Surrey) 'Tangerines', 'Mutton Lancers'	Queens
The Buffs (Royal East Kent Regiment) 'Old Buffs', or 'Nutcrackers'	Buffs
The King's Own Royal Regiment (Lancaster)	King's Own
The Royal Northumberland Fusiliers 'Old and Bold', 'Shiners', 'Fighting Fifth'	NF
The Royal Fusiliers (City of London Regiment)	RF
The Lincolnshire Regiment' 'Lincoln Poachers'	Lincoln
The Devonshire Regiment 'Bloody Eleventh'	Devons
The West Yorkshire Regiment (The Prince Of Wales's Own)	W Yorks
The East Yorkshire Regiment (The Duke of York's Own) 'Snappers'	E Yorks
The Bedfordshire and Hertfordshire Regiment	Bedfs Herts
The Leicestershire Regiment 'Bengal Tigers'	Leicesters
The Green Howards (Alexandra, Princess of Wale's Own Yorkshire Regiment)	Green Howards
The Lancashire Fusiliers	LF
The Royal Scots Fusiliers	RSF
The Cheshire Regiment	Cheshire
The South Wales Borderers	SWB
The Cameronians (Scottish Rifles)	Cameronians
The Royal Iniskilling Fusiliers	Innisks
The Worchestershire Regiment 'Eversworded 29th'	Worc R
The East Surrey Regiment	Surreys
The Duke of Cornwall's Light Infantry	DCLI
The Duke of Wellington's Regiment (West Riding)	DWR
The Royal Sussex Regiment 'Belfast Regt', 'Orange Lillies'	R Sussex
The Hampshire Regiment 'Tigers'	Hamps
The Dorsetshire Regiment 'Green Linnets'	Dorset
The Black Watch (Royal Highland Regiment) 'Forty Twa'	Black Watch
The Oxfordshire and Buckinghamshire Light Infantry	Oxf Bucks
The Essex Regiment 'Fighting Fours', 'Pompadours'	Essex
The Sherwood Forresters (Nottinghamshire & Derbyshire Regiment) 'Old Stubborns'	Forresters
The Loyal Regiment (North Lancashire) 'Wolfe's Own'	Loyals
The Northamptonshire Regiment	Northamptons
The Royal Berkshire Regiment (Princess Charlotte of Wales's) 'Biscuit Boys'	R Berks
The Queen's Own Royal West Kent Regiment 'Blind Half-hundred', 'Dirty Half-hundred'	RWK
The King's Own Yorkshire Light Infantry 'Koylis'	KOYLI
The King's Shropshire Light Infantry 'Brickdusts', 'Five and Threepennies'	KSLI
The Middlesex Regiment (Duke of Cambridge's Own) 'Diehards'	Mx
Princess Louise's Kensington Regiment	Kens
The Wiltshire Regiment (Duke of Edinburgh's) 'Springers', 'Moonrakers'	Wilts
The North Staffordshire Regiment (The Prince of Wales's)	N Staffs
The York and Lancaster Regiment 'Cat and Cabbage'	Y&L
The Durham Light Infantry	DLI
The Highland Light Infantry (City of Glasgow Regiment) 'Pig and Whistle Light Infantry'	HLI
The Seaforth Highlanders (Ross-shire Buffs, the Duke of Albany's)	Seaforth
The London Scottish	L Scots
The Gordon Highlanders 'Gay Gordons'	Gordons
The Queen's Own Cameron Highlanders	Camerons
The London Irish	L Irish
The Royal Irish Fusiliers (Princess Victoria's) 'Bird Catchers', 'Old Fogs'	R Ir F
The Argyll and Sutherland Highlanders (Princes Louise's) 'Thin Red Line'	A&SH
Militia Regiments	
North Irish Horse	NIH
Territorial Regiments	
The Royal Tank Regiment*	RTR
The Royal Armoured Corps	RAC
The Recce Corps	Recce

*The regular battalions (1 RTR to 12 RTR) all rank above the infantry, while the territorial battalions rank beneath them.

British Infantry Battalions in the Mediterranean

1st Infantry Division — Tunisia, Italy

2 Infantry Brigade	3 Infantry Brigade	24 Guards Brigade	
1 Loyals	1 DWR	5 Gren Gds	
2 N Staffs	2 Forresters	1 SG	1 Recce
6 Gordons	1 KSLI	1IG	

4th Infantry Division — Tunisia

10 Infantry Brigade	12 Infantry Brigade	21 Tank Brigade[14]	
1 Bedfs Herts	2 RF	12 RTR	
1/6 Surreys	6 Black Watch	48 RTR	4 Recce
2 DCLI	1 RWK	145 RAC	

5th Infantry Division — Sicily, Italy

13 Infantry Brigade	15 Infantry Brigade	17 Infantry Brigade	
2 Cameronians	1 Green Howards	2 RSF	
2 Innisks	1 KOYLI	2 Northamptons	7 Cheshire (MG)
2 Wilts	1 Y&L	6 Seaforth	5 Recce

44th (Home Counties) Division[1] — Alam Halfa, Second Alamein

131 Queens Brigade[2]	132 Infantry Brigade[1]	133 Infantry Brigade[3]	
1/5 Queens	2 Buffs	2 R Sussex	
1/6 Queens	4 RWK	4 R Sussex	6 Cheshire (MG)
1/7 Queens	5 RWK	5 R Sussex	

46th Infantry Division — Tunisia, Salerno, Italy

128 Infantry Brigade	138 Infantry Brigade	139 Infantry Brigade	
2 Hamps[4]	6 Lincolns	2/5 Leicesters	
1/4 Hamps	2/4 KOYLI	2/5 Forresters	2 NF (MG)
2/4 Hamps[5]	6 Y&L	16 DLI	46 Recce
5 Hamps			

50th (Northumbrian) Division — Gazala, First Alamein, Second Alamein, Tunisia, Sicily

69 Infantry Brigade	150 Infantry Brigade[6]	151 Infantry Brigade	
5 E Yorks	4 E Yorks	6 DLI	
6 Green Howards	4 Green Howards	8 DLI	2 Cheshire (MG)
7 Green Howards	5 Green Howards	9 DLI	

51st (Highland) Division 'Highway Decorators' — Second Alamein, Tunisia, Sicily

152 Infantry Brigade	153 Infantry Brigade	154 Infantry Brigade	
2 Seaforth	5 Black Watch	1 Black Watch	1/7 Mx (MG)
3 Seaforth	1 Gordons	7 Black Watch	
5 Camerons	5/7 Gordons	7 A & SH	

56th Infantry Division 'Black Cat Division' — Tunisia, Salerno, Italy

167 London Brigade	168 London Brigade[7]	169 London Brigade	201 Guards Brigade[8]	
8 RF	10 R Berks	2/5 Queens	6 Gren Gds	
9 RF	1 L Scots	2/6 Queens	3 Coldm Gds	6 Cheshire (MG)
7 Oxf Bucks	1 L Irish	2/7 Queens		44 Recce

78th Infantry Division 'Battleaxe Division', 'Churchill's Choppers' — Torch, Tunisia, Sicily, Italy

1 Guards Brigade[9]	11 Infantry Brigade	36 Infantry Brigade	38 Irish Brigade[11]	
3 Gren Gds	2 LF	5 Buffs	6 Innisks	
2 Coldm Gds	1 Surreys	6 RWK	2 L Irish	1 Kens (MG)
3 WG	5 Northamptons	8 A&SH[10]	1 R Ir F	56 Recce

Army Troops

231 Infantry Brigade	1 Army Tank[6,12]	23 Armoured Brigade[13]	25 Army Tank Brigade[14]	32 Army Tank Brigade[6,15]
(Sicily)	(Gazala)	(Desert, Tunisia)	(Tunisia)	(Gazala)
2 Devon	8 RTR[16]	40 RTR	NIH	1 RTR
1 Hamps	42 RTR	46 RTR	51 RTR	4 RTR
1 Dorset	44 RTR	50 RTR	142 RAC	7 RTR

[1] Disbanded after Second Alamein
[2] 7th Armd Div from Second Alamein
[3] 10th Armd Div at Second Alamein
[4] In Italy
[5] In Tunisia
[6] Lost at Gazala
[7] With 50th Div in Sicily
[8] In Salerno
[9] Not in Sicily
[10] With 1 Gds Bde Dec 1942 to Jan 194315
[11] In Sicily, previously 6th Armd Div
[12] Equipped with Valentine II tanks
[13] Equipped with Valentine tanks
[14] Equipped with Churchill tanks
[15] Equipped with Matilda tanks
[16] Switched to 23AB for Alemein Battle

Armoured Divisions In The Mediterranean

There were four armoured divisions fighting in North Africa, Sicily, and Italy in the mid-war period. Each of them had one or two Armoured Brigades, and either a Motor Brigade or a Lorried Infantry Brigade.

The 1st and 7th Armoured Divisions fought at Gazala in May and June 1942, being joined by the 10th Armoured Division for the Alamein battles in October and November. Both 1st and 7th Armoured Divisions then went on to Tripoli and the battles in Tunisia in March to May 1943, leaving the 10th Armoured Division in Egypt.

Meanwhile, the 6th Armoured Division landed in Tunisia in November 1942 as part of the Anglo-American Operation Torch. The Division fought with under-gunned Valentine and Crusader tanks until after the Kasserine Pass battles of February 1943 before being re-equipped with Sherman tanks for the rest of the Tunisian Campaign.

Once Africa was secure, the 7th Armoured Division was rebuilt before fighting in Italy in October to December 1943 where it took part in the capture of Naples.

1st Armoured Division
2 Armoured Brigade
22 Armoured Brigade (Gazala)
201 Guards Motor Brigade (Gazala)
7 Motor Brigade (Alamein)
12th Royal Lancers

6th Armoured Division
26 Armoured Brigade
38 (Irish) Infantry Brigade
1st The Derbyshire Yeomanry

7th Armoured Division
4 Armoured Brigade (until Alamein)
22 Armoured Brigade (Alamein)
7 Motor Brigade (Gazala)
131 Lorried Infantry Brigade (Alamein)
11th Hussars

10th Armoured Division
8 Armoured Brigade
24 Armoured Brigade
133 Lorried Infantry Brigade
1st Household Cavalry Regiment

Armoured Regiments In The Mediterranean

Regiment (by seniority)	Abbrev.	Formation
The Queen's Bays (2nd Dragoon Guards) 'The Bays'	Bays	2 Armd Bde
The Royal Scots Greys (2nd Dragoons) 'The Greys'	Greys	4 Armd Bde
3rd King's Own Hussars 'The Moodkee Wallahs'	3 H	9 Armd Bde
4th Queen's Own Hussars (Amalgamated with 8th Hussars to form 4th/8th Hussars after Gazala)	4 H	4 Armd Bde
8th King's Royal Irish Hussars (Amalgamated with 4th Hussars to form 4th/8th Hussars after Gazala)	8 H	4 Armd Bde
9th Queen's Royal Lancers 'The Delhi Spearmen' or 'The Magpies'	9 L	2 Armd Bde
10th Royal Hussars (Prince of Wales's Own) 'The Shiny Tenth' 'The Brummagem Uhlans'	10 H	2 Armd Bde
17th/21st Lancers 'The Death or Glory Boys', sometimes shortened to 'The Deaths'	17/21 L	26 Armd Bde
1st Royal Tank Regiment	1 RTR	4 Armd Bde 22 Armd Bde[1]
3rd Royal Tank Regiment	3 RTR	4 Armd Bde 8 Armd Bde[1]
5th Royal Tank Regiment	5 RTR	4 Armd Bde 22 Armd Bde[1]
6th Royal Tank Regiment	6 RTR	4 Armd Bde 2 Armd Bde[1]
41st Royal Tank Regiment	41 RTR	24 Armd Bde
45th Royal Tank Regiment	45 RTR	24 Armd Bde
47th Royal Tank Regiment	47 RTR	24 Armd Bde
The Royal Wiltshire Yeomanry (Prince Of Wales's Own)	R Wilts Y	9 Armd Bde
The Warwickshire Yeomanry	Warw Y	9 Armd Bde
The Nottinghamshire Yeomanry (Sherwood Rangers)	SRY	8 Armd Bde
The Staffordshire Yeomanry (Queen's Own Royal Regt)	Staffs Y	8 Armd Bde
2nd Royal Gloucestershire Hussars	2 RGH	22 Armd Bde
2nd Lothians and Border Horse Yeomanry	2 LBH	26 Armd Bde
3rd County of London Yeomanry (Sharpshooters)	3 CLY	22 Armd Bde 4 Armd Bde[2]
4th County of London Yeomanry (Sharpshooters)	4 CLY	22 Armd Bde

[1]After the Gazala battles (July 1942 onwards).

[2]From Sicily (June 1943) onwards.

MOTOR BATTALIONS IN THE MEDITERRANEAN

Regiment (by seniority)	Abbrev.	Formation
3rd Bn, Coldstream Guards (The Coldstream Regt Of Foot Guards) 'The Coldstream', 'The Colleys', or 'The Lillywhites', never 'The Coldstreams'	3 Coldm Gds	201 Gds Bde
2nd Bn, Scots Guards (The Scots Regt Of Foot Guards) 'The Old Buffs' or 'The Nutcrackers'	1 Buffs	8 Armd Bde
14th Bn, The Sherwood Foresters (Nottinghamshire and Derbyshire Regt) 'The Old Stubborns'	14 Foresters	9 Armd Bde
9th Bn, The King's Own Yorkshire Light Infantry Previously the Yorkshire Dragoons	9 KOYLI	2 Armd Bde[2]
1st Bn, The King's Royal Rifle Corps 'The 60th', or less complimentary, 'King's Rich Rude Club'	1 KRRC	4 Armd Bde 7 Mot Bde[3]
2nd Bn, The King's Royal Rifle Corps	2 KRRC	7 Mot Bde 4 Armd Bde[3]
9th Bn, The King's Royal Rifle Corps (The Rangers)	1 Rangers	7 Mot Bde
1st Bn, The Rifle Brigade (Prince Consort's Own) 'The Green Jackets', 'The Sweeps', or less complimentary, 'The Black Mafia'	1 RB	2 Armd Bde[1] 22 Armd Bde[2]
2nd Bn, The Rifle Brigade (Prince Consort's Own)	2 RB	7 Mot Bde
7th (London) Bn, The Rifle Brigade	7 RB	7 Mot Bde
9th Bn, The Rifle Brigade (Tower Hamlets Rifles)	9 RB	201 Gds Bde
10th Bn, The Rifle Brigade (Tower Hamlets Rifles)	10 RB	26 Armd Bde

[1] During the Gazala battles (May and June 1942).
[2] From El Alamein (October 1942) onwards.
[3] From Tunisia (January 1943) onwards.

DESERT RATS TERMINOLOGY

The Desert Rats speak a lingo which the white-kneed chaps from Blighty may have difficulty understanding.

Ack-Ack: Anti-aircraft.

ANZAC: Australian and New Zealand Army Corps, a First World War formation that became a universal name for Australians and New Zealanders.

Batman: Officer's manservant.

Blighty: England.

Box: An all-round defensive position.

Brew-Up: Boil water and make a pot of tea or alternatively destroy a tank with anti-tank fire.

Brigadier: Brigadier General (never addressed as 'General').

Cauldron, The: Area where the Gazala battles were fought.

Chinese Attack: Feint attack made with lots of fireworks.

Churchill: Infantry tank named after the Prime Minister, Winston Churchill.

cwt (hundredweight): A unit of weight equal to a twentieth of a ton (about 50 kg). Measures a truck's load capacity.

Delta, The: The Nile Delta of Cairo, Alexandria, and the Suez Canal. The heart of the British Middle East.

Desert Rat: Jerboa. The symbol of the 7th Armoured Division, which trained and formed in the Egyptian desert, and by extension the Eighth Army.

Digger: Australian or New Zealander.

Djebel: Arabic for a hill, usually steep and rocky.

Eighth Army: The British Army in the Desert, southern Tunisia, Sicily, and Italy.

Eighty-eight ('88'): German 8.8cm FlaK18 anti-aircraft gun. This gun was so feared that any heavy anti-tank gun became an '88' regardless of its actual calibre.

First Army: The British Army in western Tunisia.

Flap: Crisis or panic.

FOO: Pronounced "Foo". Forward Observation Officer - British artillery observer officer.

Full Monty, The: The real thing, the works, everything.

Gazala Gallop: The hurried retreat from Gazala in 1942.

Highway Decorators: The Highland Division. So called for their habit of painting their divisional symbol everywhere.

Jerboa: Small jumping rodent living in the Egyptian desert.

Jock: A Scotsman.

Kiwi: A New Zealander.

Lieutenant: Pronounced 'Lef-tenant' in the British Army.

Lorry: A heavy cargo-carrying truck.

Matilda: Infantry tank named for the early version's similarity to a cartoon duck named Matilda.

Matruh Stakes: A horse-racing reference to the retreat to Mersa Matruh.

Mick: An Irishman.

Monty: General (later Field Marshal) Bernard Law Montgomery. The capable, determined, and victorious commander of the Eighth Army at Alamein and after.

Monty Battle: A well-planned battle that is likely to succeed.

Murder: A quick, intense artillery bombardment relying on the fast calculations of the artillery staff, the accuracy of the gunners, and enough shells swamping the area to hit the target before it can take cover or move away.

Petrol: Called Gasoline by Americans.

pdr (pounder, never 'lbr'): Calibre of a gun measured by the weight of its solid shot. 2 pdr = 40mm. 6 pdr = 57mm. 17 pdr = 76mm. 25 pdr = 88mm.

Quad: 4x4 artillery tractor. From 'quadruped'.

Regiment: A battalion of tanks or armoured cars, or the parent formation of an infantry battalion.

Show: 'A good show'. An attack or battle.

SMLE, Short Magazine Lee Enfield: Standard British rifle.

Springbok: A South African.

Squadron: A company of tanks or armoured cars.

Stonk: An artillery barrage delivered to a set pattern allowing an immediate response to requests for fire.

Subaltern: Lieutenant, particularly a Second Lieutenant.

Tommygun: A Thompson submachine-gun.

Troop: A platoon of tanks.

U/S, Unserviceable: Out of commission.

Up the Blue: In the desert, far from the comforts of the Delta.

VC, Victoria Cross: The highest award for gallantry in the British Empire.

Valentine: Infantry tank made by Vickers. Design was presented to the War Office on Valentines Day.

Wadi: Steep gully.

Wallah: Person responsible for something.

Winkle Out: Clear opposition by a slow careful process.

Wireless: Radio.

Major General GPB 'Pip' Roberts

Major-General George Philip (Pip) Bradley Roberts, MC, DSO and Bar, CB, was the British Army's youngest Major-General at 37, and perhaps their best armoured commander.

Roberts joined 3 Royal Tanks as a subaltern at the age of 19, spending 13 years in Egypt apart from a stint instructing at the Tank Driving and Maintenance School. When the war broke out in 1939, he was promoted to Deputy Assistant Quartermaster General (DAQG) to the Desert Rats. As DAQG he was responsible for ensuring that they had enough supplies to fight.

By late 1940, Roberts was the Brigade Major of 4th Armoured Brigade winning the Military Cross against the Italians in Operation Compass. A year later he was Assistant Quartermaster General to XXX Corps for Operation Crusader against Rommel. He then asked his Corps commander for a regiment, and to his delight was given his old regiment, 3 Royal Tanks.

His first task was to develop tactics for the new Grant tanks. Roberts' contacts at HQ meant that he got his new tanks delivered immediately! Roberts won the DSO commanding 3 Royal Tanks at Gazala where he was unhorsed when his tank 'brewed up'.

After recovering from wounds, Roberts was promoted to Brigadier commanding 22nd Armoured Brigade. His brigade was responsible for stopping Rommel at Alam Halfa and then took part in the pursuit after El Alamein winning a bar to his DSO.

Robert's next appointment was CO of 26th Armoured Brigade in Tunisia. He led the Brigade at Fondouk where the Shermans of the 'Death or Glory Boys' made their famous charge.

His crowning achievement was leading the 11th Armoured Division to victory in Europe.

Characteristics

Pip Roberts is a Warrior and a Higher Command team. He is rated as **Confident Trained**.

Pip Roberts can join any Armoured Squadron for 120 points. This includes the cost of a Grant tank as his mount.

You may replace the Grant tank with a Sherman II or Sherman III tank for +20 points.

Special Rules

Professional: Pip Roberts understands combined arms and moves in the right circles to get the support his troops need. An Armoured Squadron commanded by Pip Roberts may have two Support Choices for each Armoured Platoon, rather than the usual one.

Well In Hand: Pip Roberts has the battle well in hand. Even when things seem to be falling apart, he retains control. Pip Roberts may re-roll failed Company Motivation Checks.

Captain Charles Upham

Captain Charles Hazlitt Upham, Charlie to those who knew him, is unique in the annals of the British Empire. He is the only combat soldier to ever win two Victoria Crosses, the highest award for gallantry in the British Army. A sheep musterer in the high country of New Zealand's Southern Alps before the war, Charlie was a man of contrasts. He had his rough edges, swearing with the best, but also a Diploma in Farm Management and was a qualified Valuer.

When war came, he was one of the first to enlist, determined to halt the Nazi menace as quickly as possible so that he could return and settle on his own farm. By the time the New Zealand Division went into battle, he'd been promoted to Second Lieutenant, despite frequent clashes with the instructors over tactics. On his way back from the course, he picked up his batman, 'Leggy' Le Gros an expert on the mysteries of horse racing and shady deals, but loyal and as rough and ready as his master.

Upham won his first VC on Crete in May 1941. There over a period of a week, despite sickness and wounds, he led his men again and again into the attack. He was always at the front, leading the way, tackling machine-gun nests single-handedly or with his Sergeant, Kirk, armed with as many hand grenades as he could find, looking out for his men and shepherding them to safety.

Charles Upham hated being in the limelight. He had to be ordered to wear the ribbon of his VC on his uniform and hated people bringing attention to it. He was very worried that he might be sent back to New Zealand for a publicity tour and fought as hard to stay with his men as he had against the Germans.

Upham won his second VC twice over as a Captain commanding C Company, 20th Battalion. At Minqar Qaim outside Mersa Matruh he was in the forefront of the midnight charge that saved the New Zealand Division, and then again at Ruweisat Ridge in the Alamein line he led his company into the teeth of the German defences, fighting on with a shattered elbow until he and his men were finally surrounded and captured, Upham unable to walk from a leg wound.

Upham's capture wasn't the end though. He was a bold and persistent escaper and eventually ended up in Colditz, the camp reserved for the most difficult prisoners. Even when liberated, he still wanted to fight, joining an American unit for a few days until ordered back to England.

Characteristics

Captain Upham is an Infantry team, a Warrior and a Company Command team rated as **Fearless Veteran**.

Upham is armed with an Enfield No. 2 revolver and No. 36M 'Mills Bomb' hand grenades. He has Range 4"/10cm, ROF 2 whether he moves or not, Anti-tank 2, and Firepower 4+.

He may join any Rifle Company for +50 points. He becomes the Company Command team replacing the existing Company Command team. Upham may have a Ford V8 car for +5 points.

Special Rules

C'mon, into 'em: Upham is a truly inspirational soldier. He and any platoon he is currently leading always pass Motivation Tests on a roll of 2+.

I'll Get The Bugger: Upham always advanced ahead of his men wiping out machine-gun nests and clearing the way.

Upham may launch a charge from 6"/15cm away from the enemy and moves 6"/15cm when Charging into Contact or Counterattacking. The rest of his platoon still move 4"/10cm, often meaning that they don't get into the fight until the platoon counterattacks.

Keep Your Bloody Head Down: Although Upham took many risks himself, he hated putting his men at risk.

Each turn one Infantry team within 6"/15cm of Upham may roll a die if Destroyed. On a roll of 5+, Upham alerts them to the danger and they duck out of the way and survive unharmed.

Brigadier Peter Young

In 1939 Peter Young was commissioned into the Bedfordshire and Hertfordshire Regiment, with which he went to France in 1940. He joined No. 3 Commando when it was founded and soon became a Captain. His troops took part in raids on the Channel Island of Guernsey, and Lofoten and Vaagso in Norway during 1941. It was during the later raid that he won his first Military Cross (MC). After a period on the staff at Combined Operations HQ, he became second-in-command of No. 3 Commando under Colonel John Dunford-Slater.

In the Dieppe raid of August 19, 1942, Major Young now carrying a US Garand rifle, found himself ashore with only 18 commandos. Despite this, he managed to take his force up the cliffs on a network of barbed wire which, as he put it, 'an over-conscientious German officer had inadvertently provided for them to walk on'. Young was the only Commando officer to reach his objective and bring back all his men. At one point, when they were approaching enemy machine-guns through a cornfield, he encouraged his soldiers by telling them not to worry about bullets as standing corn made effective protection! He was awarded a Distinguished Service Order (DSO) for his part in this raid.

No. 3 Commando's next major battle was Operation Husky, the assault on Sicily. There, due to an inexperienced flotilla commander, his force was landed on the wrong beach behind the infantry it was supposed to lead ashore! Dunford-Slater offered the frustrated Major Young a new challenge to get his teeth into, a fierce action against a fortified farm near Cassibile, taken at the cost of one casualty.

Young's next battle was a raid to secure the Ponte dei Malati bridge ahead of 50th (Northumbrian) Division's advance. This time the landing went according to plan, and the commandos seized the bridge. However, when dawn arrived without any sign of the infantry and increasing pressure from German mobile reserves, the lightly-equipped commandos removed the bridge demolitions and withdrew. Major Young went back to rescue a number of wounded commandos for which he received a Bar to his MC.

On August 1, 1943, Young was promoted to Lieutenant Colonel and given command of No. 3 Commando. He led it through raids in Italy, receiving a second Bar to his MC in the process. He missed the opening of the battle of Termoli (No. 3 Commandos biggest battle to date) being sick at the time, but arrived before the end of the battle.

He led No. 3 Commando in the D-Day landings in Normandy, before taking over a brigade in Burma for the rest of the war.

After the war Brigadier Young was a leading figure in British wargaming, writing *Charge! Or How To Play Wargames*, one of the first books on wargaming.

Characteristics

Peter Young is an Infantry team, a Warrior and a Higher Command team rated as **Fearless Veteran**.

Young is armed with an M1 Garand rifle. He has a Range of 16"/40cm, ROF 1 with no penalty for moving, an Anti-tank rating of 2, and a Firepower rating of 6.

He can join any Commando Troop for +50 points.

Special Rules

MC and Double Bar: No one wins three Military Crosses without being calm in the heat of battle.

Young and any platoon he is currently leading pass all Motivation Tests on a roll of 2+ instead of their normal roll.

Contrary: When faced with the 'impassable' cliff at Dieppe, Young privately agreed that it was, but with a surly growl he tackled it anyway, making it up to his and everyone else's surprise.

Young and any platoon he is currently leading may re-roll any failed Skill Test to cross Impassable Terrain using the Mind and Heart rule.

Cornfields Stop Bullets: To inspire his men's confidence under fire, Young told them that 15 feet of standing corn would stop a bullet. He may well have been right as none were hit. Either way, his men learned to make excellent use of any cover they could find.

Young and any platoon he joins can be Gone to Ground when shooting, as long as they are Concealed and did not move.

Unharmed: Brigadier Young survived five years of war without taking a serious wound.

If Young is Destroyed by enemy fire or in an assault, roll a die. On a roll of 5+ his luck holds and the shot missed. He carries on unharmed. On any other roll, he is hit and counts as Destroyed.

ARMOURED SQUADRON

(TANK COMPANY)

The Royal Tank Regiment dates back to the invention of the tank back in the First World War. We took 'Through Mud and Blood to the Green Fields Beyond' as our creed back then. The tanks have changed a lot since and the Desert's not quite the fields of France, but we never forget 'My Boy Willie' our first tank, still worn proudly on our cap badge.
—Lieutenant Robert Love-Pinecoffin

A force based around an Armoured Squadron must contain:

- a Company HQ, and
- two to four Armoured Platoons.

Weapons Platoons available to an Armoured Squadron can be:

- up to two further Armoured Platoons.

Support Platoons for an Armoured Squadron can be:

- Motor Platoons,
- Scout Patrols,
- Armoured Car Platoons, and
- Divisional Support Platoons.

You may have up to **one** Support Platoon attached to your company for each Light or Heavy Armoured Platoon that you are fielding.

Motivation and Skill

The British armoured regiments have been given a rough handling by Rommel's lot, but they've stuck to their guns, learned their lessons, and are ready to return the favour. An Armoured Squadron is **Confident Trained**.

4TH COUNTY OF LONDON YEOMANRY

The County of London Yeomanry (CLY) were a volunteer cavalry regiment formed in 1901 from veterans of the Boer War. When the Second World War broke out in 1939, the 4th County of London Yeomanry commanded by Lieutenant Colonel Arkwright was formed from part of the old 3rd County of London Yeomanry 'The Sharpshooters'. Both regiments joined the 22nd Armoured Brigade equipped with the new Crusader tanks and went out to join the Eighth Army in the desert.

Their first action was against the Italian *Ariete* armoured division took place at the start of Operation Crusader in November 1941 at El Gubi. One story has it that the regiment's officers went into battle waving riding crops and crying "Tally Ho!" as they charged the Italian guns. Such valour led to very heavy losses putting the brigade out of the battle for several days. The CLY rejoined the battle against the *Afrikakorps* near Sidi Rezegh, displaying considerable gallantry despite continued heavy losses. In May and June 1942 at Gazala, the regiment, now equipped with a mixture of Grants and Crusaders, fought the *Afrikakorps* once more. Again their methods resembled nothing so much as an old-fashioned cavalry charge—brave, but lacking in subtlety and the finer points of armoured tactics.

The regiment, now under Lieutenant Colonel Scott, gained a measure of revenge for its previous defeats when it played a central role in stopping Rommel's attack at Alam Halfa in August. This time their cavalry instincts were kept under a tight rein. They fought from concealed positions using the guns of the Grant tanks to destroy the Germans at long range.

The Yeomanry had a relatively quiet role in the Second Battle of Alamein in October, but as the Axis defences crumbled, the regiment took part in the destruction of *Ariete*—revenge for the rough handling that they received at their hands a year earlier. The regiment then pursued the *Afrikakorps* to Tunisia, where they won a hard-fought battle for Wadi Akarit in April 1943.

The regiment re-equipped with Sherman III tanks and under the command of Lieutenant Colonel, the Viscount Lord Cranley, served briefly in Italy in 1943 before returning to England. It went ashore in Normandy soon after the D-Day landings of June 6, 1944. There it fought a disastrous battle against Tiger tanks at Villers-Bocage. After a month of heavy fighting, the survivors were amalgamated with its equally battered sister regiment, the 3rd County of London Yeomanry to form 3rd/4th CLY.

Heavy Armoured Squadron

HEADQUARTERS

1 Company HQ

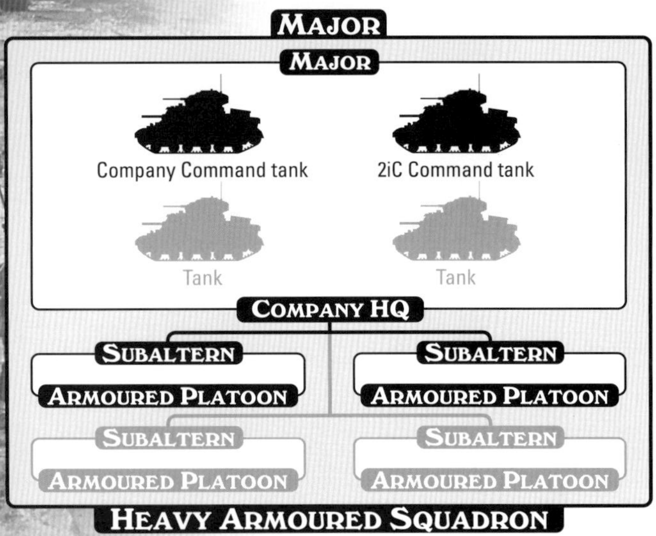

Headquarters
Company HQ with:

2 Grant tanks	**190 points**

Options

- Add up to two Grant tanks for +95 points per tank.
- Fit any or all Grant tanks with Lee turrets with a cupola MG for +5 points per tank.
- Upgrade any Grant tanks to Sherman II or III tanks for +20 points per tank.
- Arm any or all Sherman tanks with a 0.5" AA MG for +5 points per tank.

Note: The Company Command tank must be the first tank upgraded to a Sherman tank.

The Heavy Armoured Squadrons are the backbone of any armoured regiment. Their big 75mm guns finally give the British Army an answer to the Jerry Panzers and their wicked long-range 88's.

COMBAT PLATOONS

2 to 4 Heavy Armoured Platoons

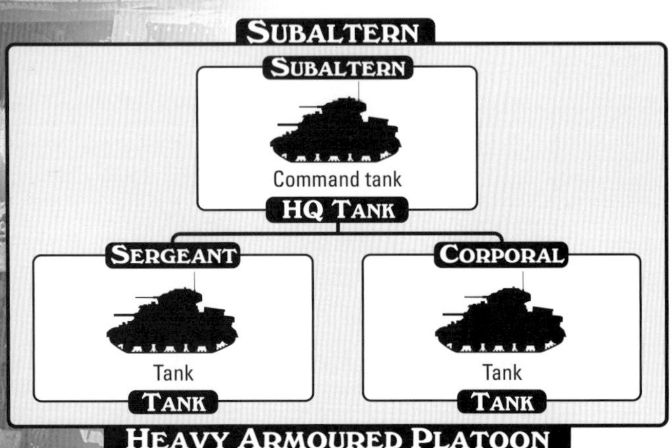

Platoon

3 Grant	**285 points**

Options

- Fit any or all Grant tanks with Lee turrets with a cupola MG for +5 points per tank.
- Upgrade any Grant tanks to Sherman II or III tanks for +20 points per tank.
- Arm any or all Sherman tanks with a 0.5" AA MG for +5 points per tank.

Note: The Command tank must be the first to be upgraded to a Sherman tank.

Remember that your Grant tanks can fire both their 75mm main gun and their 37mm turret gun at the same time using the Multiple Guns rule in the Flames Of War rulebook.

Grant tanks may be modelled as either the British-style Grant or the US-style M3 Lee with a machine-gun cupola on the top of the turret. Both were used interchangeably and referred to as Grants without distinction.

WEAPONS PLATOONS

0 to 2 Light Armoured Platoons

A Heavy Armoured Squadron may include up to two Light Armoured Platoons as an advance guard or for flank protection.

LIGHT ARMOURED SQUADRON

HEADQUARTERS

1 Company HQ

Headquarters
Company HQ with:

2 'Honey' Stuart I or III	**100 points**

- Add up to two 'Honey' Stuart tanks for +50 points per tank.
- Arm any or all 'Honey' Stuart tanks with an AA MG for +5 points per tank.

2 Crusader II	**105 points**

- Add up to two Crusader II tanks for +50 points per tank
- Upgrade any or all Crusader II tanks to Crusader II CS tanks at no cost, or Crusader III tanks for +5 points per tank.

Note: The Company Command and 2iC Command tanks may not be Crusader III tanks.

A Light Armoured Squadron may not have both 'Honey' Stuart and Crusader tanks.

The squadrons equipped with the light 'Honey' Stuart tanks use their high speed to move from position to position firing from brief halts. They protect the flanks of the heavies allowing them to get on with the destruction of the enemy.

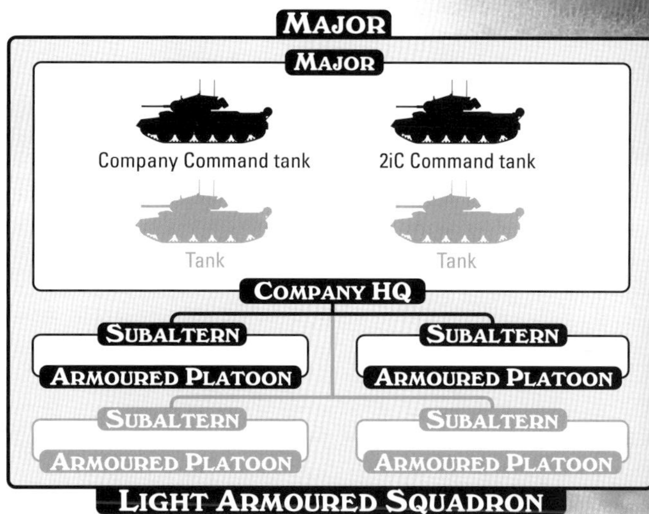

Light armoured squadrons are the regiment's fast, mobile troops. Their speed enables them to get amongst the enemy where they can really make themselves felt. Light squadrons won't win in a gun duel, but using hit-and-run tactics they are deadly.

Crusader squadrons tend to be more aggressive. Their cruiser tanks are ideally designed for swirling, close-quarters tank battles. Although they are outgunned, the Crusaders give a good account of themselves once they get amongst enemy tanks.

BRITISH

COMBAT PLATOONS

2 to 4 Light Armoured Platoons

Platoon

3 'Honey' Stuart I or III	**150 points**

- Arm any or all 'Honey' Stuart tanks with an AA MG for +5 points per tank.

3 Crusader II	**155 points**

- Replace the command tank with a Crusader II CS tank at no cost.
- Upgrade any or all Crusader II tanks to Crusader III tanks for +5 points per tank.

Note: The Command tank must be the last tank upgraded to a Crusader III.

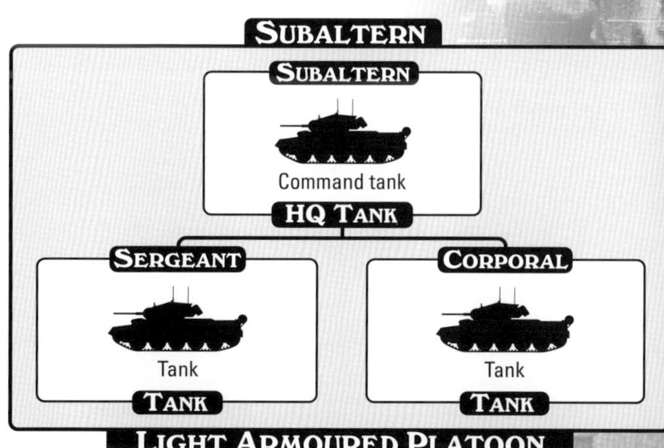

WEAPONS PLATOONS

0 to 2 Heavy Armoured Platoons

Light Armoured Squadrons were sometimes backed up by their heavier cousins. They may include up to two Heavy Armoured Platoons for anti-tank support.

Motor Company

(INFANTRY COMPANY)

Along with the Royal Horse Artillery, the Rifle Brigade plays a vital role in modern mobile warfare. We provide the foundation on which the tanks manoeuvre. We occupy key positions well forward on the battlefield where the gunners can really get stuck into Jerry. Together we give the tanks a clear run at the Hun.

—Captain Sebastian Playfair

A force based around a Motor Company must contain:

- a Company HQ, and
- two or three Motor Platoons.

Weapons Platoons available to a Motor Company are:

- three Scout Patrols,
- a Motor Machine-gun Platoon, and
- two Anti-tank Platoons.

Support Platoons for a Motor Company can be:

- Armoured Platoons,
- Armoured Car Platoons, and
- Divisional Support Platoons.

You may have up to **two** Support Platoons attached to your company for each Motor Platoon that you are fielding.

Motivation and Skill

The rifle regiments have been cracking around the desert 'up the blue' for most of the war. They are confident of their ability to handle the enemy and ready to prove it. A Motor Company is **Confident Veteran**.

HEADQUARTERS

1 Company HQ

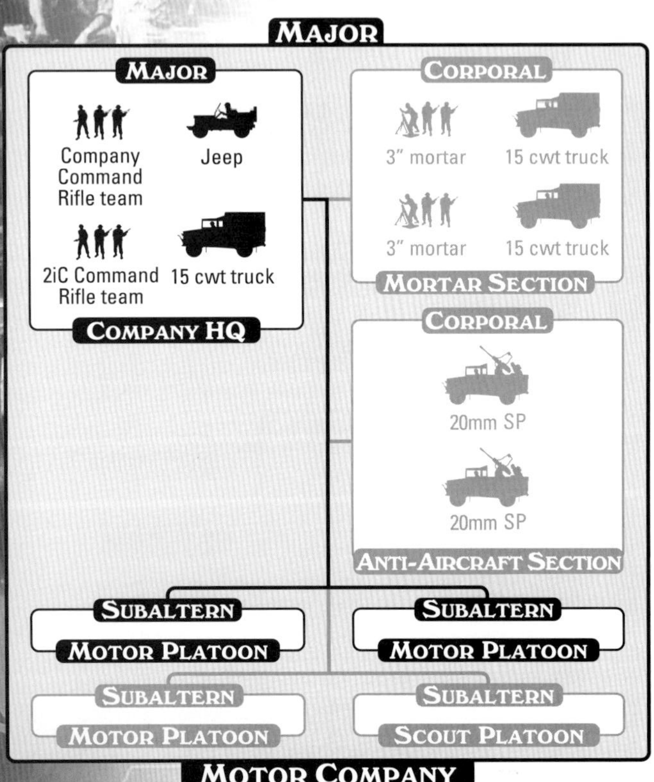

Headquarters

Company HQ	40 points

Options

- Equip all Rifle teams with Sticky Bombs for +5 points per team.
- Replace either or both the Jeep and 15 cwt truck in the HQ Section with White scout cars for +5 points for the platoon.
- Add a Mortar Section for +60 points.
- Replace both 15 cwt trucks in the Mortar Section with Mortar Carriers for +5 points.
- Add an Anti-aircraft Section for +55 points.

For such a small unit, a motor company commander has a large amount of firepower at his disposal. Their machine-guns, anti-tank guns and plentiful artillery support allow them to beat almost any opposition.

Use this firepower wisely, inflicting maximum damage on the enemy while conserving your own strength. Your platoons are small and you cannot afford to take heavy casualties.

COMBAT PLATOONS

A Motor Company must have two or three Combat Platoons. There are two styles of Motor Platoon, trucked and lorried. All of your Motor Platoons must be of the same style.

Trucked Motor Platoons

Platoon

HQ Section with:

3 Motor Squads	**125 points**
2 Motor Squads	**95 points**

Options

- Equip all MG teams with Sticky Bombs for +5 points per team.
- Add a Light Mortar team for +10 points.
- Add Anti-tank Rifle teams for +20 points per team.
- Upgrade up to one Anti-tank Rifle team to a PIAT team for +10 points.

You may not field more than one PIAT team in your company.

The riflemen of the motor platoons use their mobility to take their objective before digging in with their supporting anti-tank guns to hold it against all-comers.

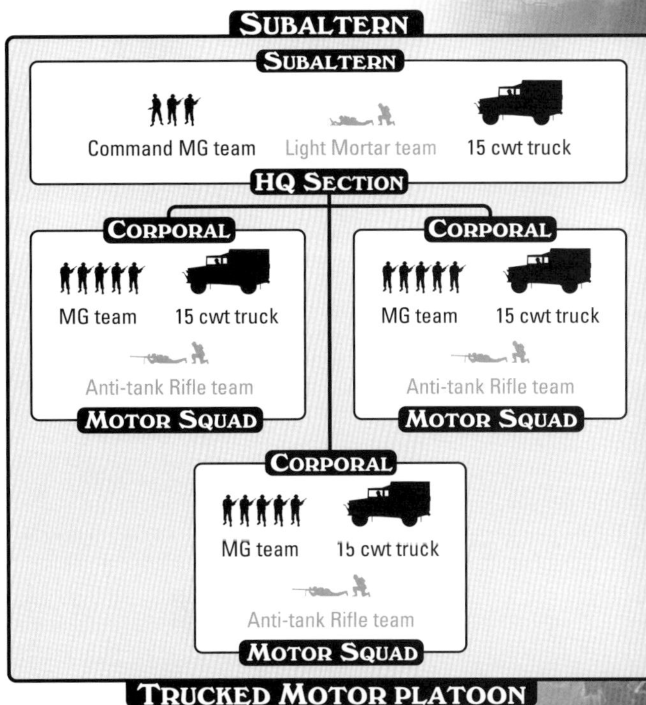

Lorried Motor Platoons

Platoon

HQ Section with:

2 Motor Squads	**150 points**
1 Motor Squad	**95 points**

Options

- Equip all MG teams with Sticky Bombs for +5 points per team.
- Add a Light Mortar team for +10 points.
- Add an Anti-tank Rifle team for +20 points or a PIAT team for +30 points.

Light Mortar, Anti-tank Rifle and PIAT teams ride in the Motor Squads' trucks.

You may not field more than one PIAT team in your company.

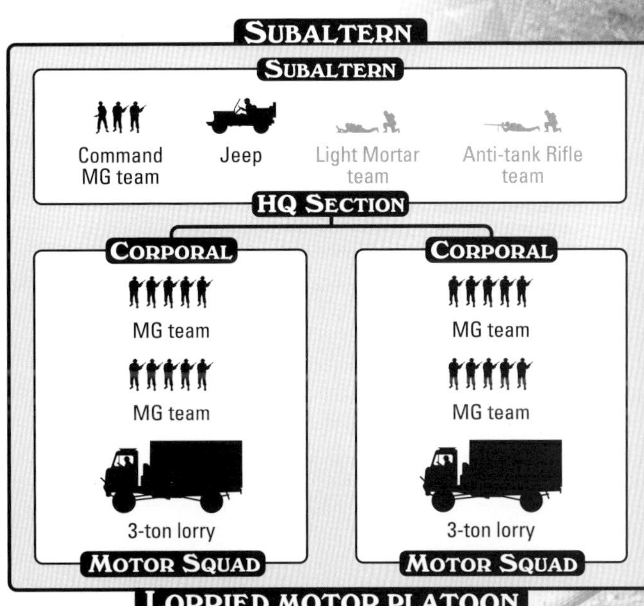

After the defeat at Gazala some Motor Battalions were reorganised to use two 3-ton lorries rather than four small 15 cwt trucks. This reduced the amount of petrol and other supplies (not to mention drivers and mechanics) needed to keep the battalion in battle.

PIAT—Projector Infantry Anti-tank

The PIAT is the British equivalent of the Bazooka. Whereas the Bazooka is a rocket launcher, the PIAT is an ingenious shoulder-fired, inside-out, flat-trajectory mortar. With the PIAT, a tube on the back of the bomb acts as the barrel. A large spring flings a rod or spigot up the tube detonating the charge, launching the bomb at the enemy tank and re-cocking the spring (not to mention bruising the operator's shoulder!)

The PIAT came into service with the First Army late in the Tunisian campaign and was widely used in Sicily and Italy. By this time the Boys anti-tank rifle had long been discarded as a useless encumbrance and the No. 74 Sticky Bomb abandoned as being too dangerous. A company with PIAT teams may not have Anti-tank Rifle teams or Sticky Bombs.

WEAPONS PLATOONS

0 to 3 Scout Patrols

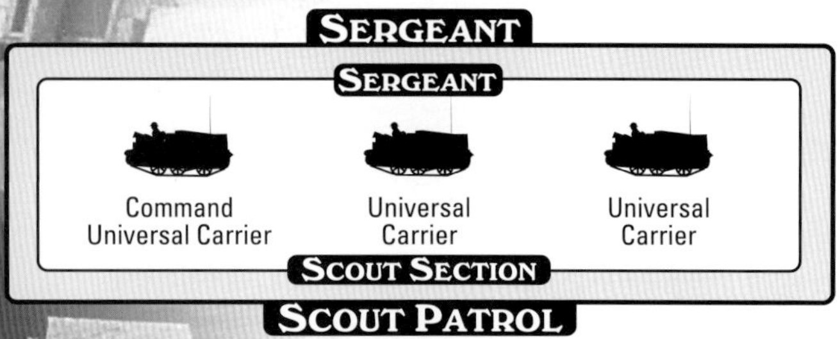

Although purchased as separate platoons, all of your Scout Patrols deploy as a single platoon at the same time. Treat the Scout Patrols as a single platoon when calculating the number of platoons held in Ambushes or Reserve.

Platoon

3 Universal Carrier	90 points

Options

- Arm any or all Universal Carriers with an extra hull-mounted MG for +5 points per carrier or 0.5" MG for +10 points per carrier.
- Replace up to one extra hull-mounted MG with a Boys anti-tank rifle at no cost.

The motor company's scout platoon scouts ahead of the company in advances and covers the flanks in battle. In defence they form the mobile reserve.

Scout Patrols are Reconnaissance Platoons.

0 to 1 Motor Machine-gun Platoon

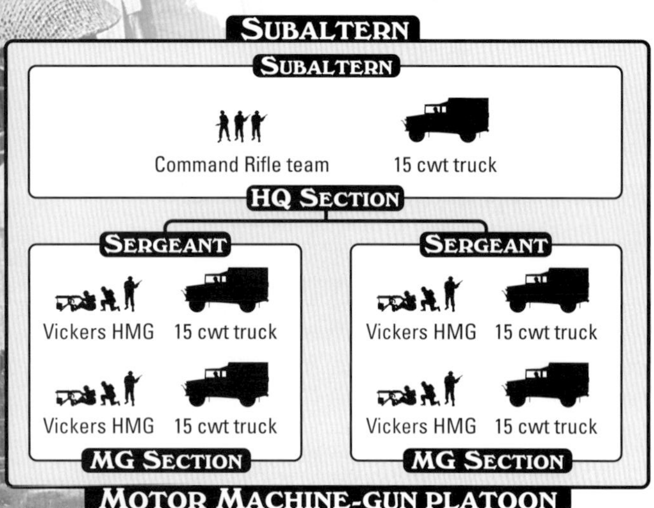

Platoon

HQ Section with:

2 Machine-gun Sections	150 points
1 Machine-gun Section	80 points

Options

- Replace the HQ Section 15 cwt truck with a Troop Carrier for +5 points and all other 15 cwt trucks with MMG Carriers for +5 points per MG Section.
- Equip all Rifle and Vickers HMG teams with Sticky Bombs for +5 points per team.

Vickers HMG teams from Motor Companies are not trained in indirect fire techniques, so they cannot fire Artillery Bombardments.

The Vickers medium machine-guns of the machine-gun platoon pin the enemy down while the motor platoons manoeuvre to deliver the knock-out blow. On the defensive, no enemy infantry can approach the Vickers without first weathering a storm of lead.

0 to 2 Anti-tank Platoons

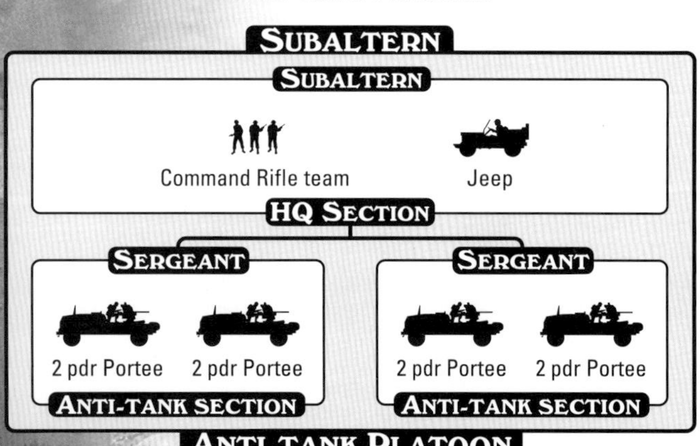

It is impossible for infantry to survive in the desert without anti-tank support. The guns in the motor battalion's anti-tank platoons are handy enough to be brought right up into the front line, keeping enemy armour at a distance.

Platoon

HQ Section with:

2 Anti-tank Sections	135 points
1 Anti-tank Section	75 points

Options

- Upgrade any or all 2 pdr portees to 6 pdr portees for +15 points per gun.
- Replace all 2 pdr portees with 6 pdr guns towed by Jeeps for +30 points per section.
- Equip all Rifle teams, Gun teams and Portees with Sticky Bombs for +5 points per team.

Portee guns are issued Sticky Bombs for use when they dismount. They are of no use while the guns remain mounted.

ARMOURED CAR SQUADRON

(RECONNAISSANCE MECHANISED COMPANY)

Armoured car squadrons replace the light cavalry of the past. Ranging far across the desert, they keep a watch on Rommel making sure he doesn't get up to any tricks. The squadrons are almost entirely equipped with armoured cars making them mobile and hard-hitting if they have to fight.

A force from an Armoured Car Squadron must contain:

- a Company HQ, and
- two to five Armoured Car Platoons.

Weapons platoons available to an Armoured Car Squadron are:

- an Assault Platoon, and
- a 75mm Gun Platoon.

Support platoons available to an Armoured Car Squadron are:

- Armoured Platoons
- Motor Platoons, and
- Divisional Support Troops

You may only have **one** Support Platoon attached to your company for each Armoured Car Platoon in your force.

Motivation and Skill

Only soldiers of the highest calibre are chosen for the difficult and dangerous job of intelligence gathering. An Armoured Car Squadron is rated as **Confident Veteran**.

HEADQUARTERS

1 Company HQ

Headquarters

Company HQ with:

2 Marmon Herrington III	**60 points**

- Add up to two Marmon Herrington III armoured cars for +30 points per armoured car.
- Arm any or all Marmon Herrington armoured cars with an AA MG for +5 points per armoured car.

2 Humber II or III	**70 points**

- Add up to two Humber II or III armoured cars for +35 points per armoured car.

2 Daimler I	**90 points**

- Add up to two Daimler I armoured cars for +45 points per armoured car or Daimler Dingo scout cars for +30 points per scout car.
- Replace AA MG on any Daimler Dingo scout cars with 0.5" AA MG for +5 points.

2 AEC I	**120 points**

- Add up to two AEC I armoured cars for +55 points per armoured car.

Option

- Add an Anti-aircraft Section for +80 points.

British armoured cars are heavily armed enabling them to keep their German and Italian counterparts at a respectful distance. The lack of infantry in the squadron can however make things tricky in dense terrain.

The Company HQ Platoon is a Reconnaissance Platoon.

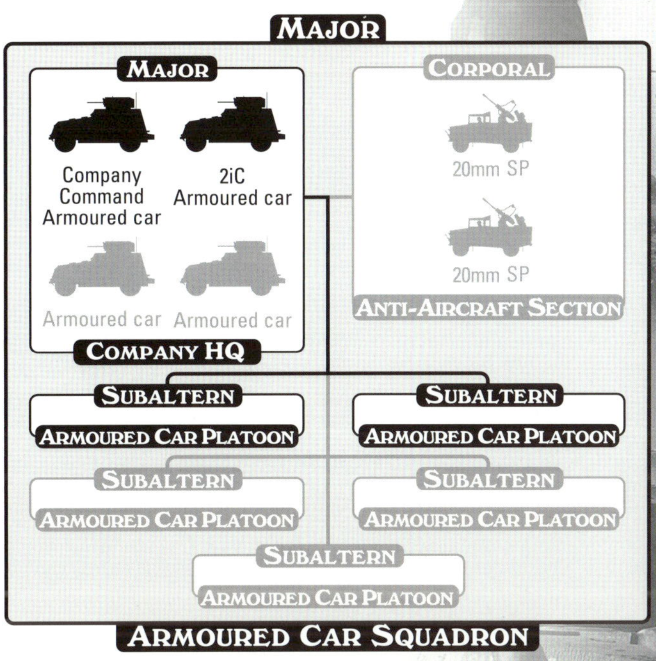

COMBAT PLATOONS

2 to 5 Armoured Car Platoons

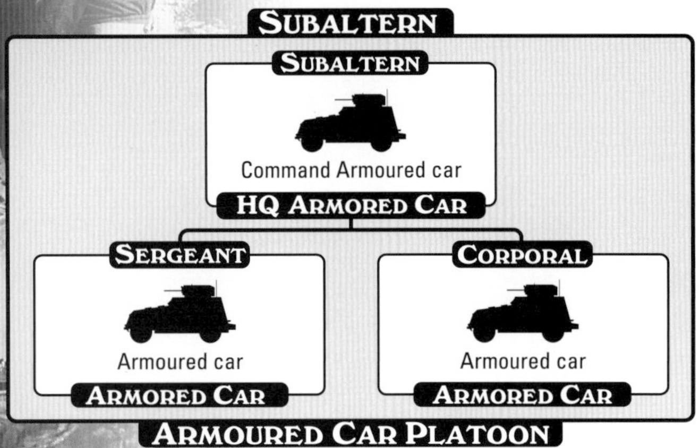

Armoured car platoons roam far ahead of the tanks observing enemy dispositions and reporting their movements.

In pursuits they lead the chase, harassing the enemy, ambushing convoys and generally creating havoc with the retreating enemy.

In retreats they are the rearguard, delaying the enemy advance and covering the withdrawal of the fighting forces.

Captured Guns

The armoured car regiments equipped with the Marmon Herrington found themselves out-gunned by their German opposition. Their solution used typical Desert Rats ingenuity. They took the turrets off their cars and mounted guns they'd captured in their place. They used a wide variety of weapons including 20mm Solothurn and 2.8cm sPzB41 anti-tank rifles, and 3.7cm PaK36 anti-tank guns.

Platoon

3 Marmon Herrington III	**90 points**

- Upgrade any or all Marmon Herrington armoured cars by replacing the Boys anti-tank rifle and turret MG with a hull-mounted captured anti-tank gun for +10 points per armoured car.
- Arm any or all Marmon Herrington armoured cars with an AA MG for +5 points per armoured car.
- Replace one Marmon Herrington armoured car with a Daimler I armoured car for +15 points, or an AEC I for +30 points.

3 Humber II or III	**105 points**

- Replace one Humber armoured car with an AEC I armoured car for +20 points.

3 Daimler I	**135 points**

- Replace one Daimler armoured car with a Daimler Dingo scout car for -15 points.
- Replace AA MG on the Daimler Dingo scout car with 0.5" AA MG for +5 points.

3 AEC I	**170 points**

Armoured Car Platoons are Reconnaissance Platoons.

WEAPONS PLATOONS

0 to 1 75mm Gun Platoon

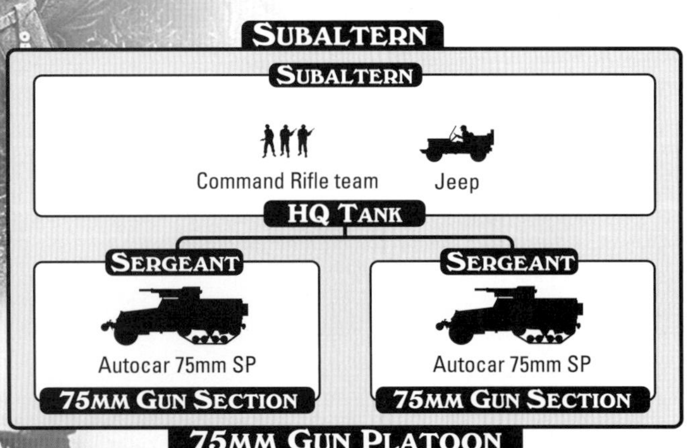

Platoon

HQ Section with:

2 Autocar 75mm SP	**150 points**

When the armoured car squadrons arrived in Tunisia, they found themselves coming face-to-face with the enemy far more often than they had in the desert.

Ex-American M3 75mm GMC half-tracks, known as Autocar 75mm SP in British service, gave them their own artillery to pin the enemy down while the armoured cars withdrew.

0 to 1 Assault Platoon

Platoon

HQ Section with:

3 Assault Sections	**155 points**
2 Assault Sections	**115 points**

Option

- Replace all Jeeps with White scout cars for +5 points for the platoon.

The close and difficult terrain of Tunisia and Italy made it necessary to reconnoitre on foot on many occasions, so most squadrons formed an assault platoon. Despite their aggressive name, the assault platoon's main role was dismounted reconnaissance. They used Jeeps or White scout cars to get as close as they safely could before dismounting.

Assault Platoons are Reconnaissance Platoons.

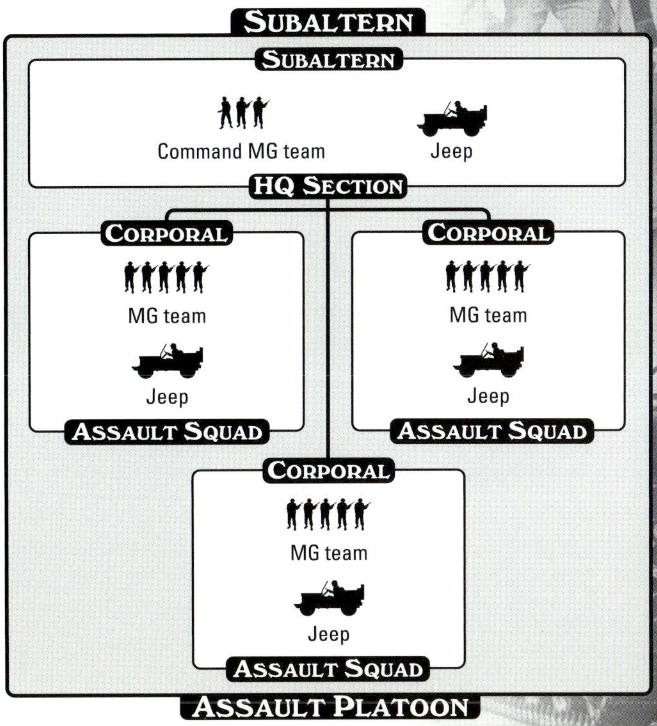

Royal Wiltshire Yeomanry

This regiment began the war as a horsed Yeomanry regiment, and was sent to Palestine where it was thought that cavalry might still be useful in modern war. By 1941 it was obvious that the days of horsed cavalry were over, and the regiment became a motorised regiment in trucks. It saw service in Iraq and then against the Vichy French in Syria. In 1942 the Wilts Yeomanry, under Lieutenant Colonel Sykes, was urgently sent to Egypt. It received Honey tanks to train with, but it only received its full complement of fifty Sherman, Grant and Crusader tanks a few days before it was sent into action at Alamein on the night of 23 October. The regiment had a bad start, with mines taking a heavy toll. But despite the losses, the Wilts Yeomanry pressed forward, overrunning German anti-tank guns, and the next day engaging in a ferocious tank duel with the tanks of the *Afrikakorps*. However, by mid-day of the 24th the regiment had lost its colonel and was down to one Sherman and two Grant tanks. That afternoon the survivors were withdrawn. The following week the regiment regrouped, got fresh replacements, and new tanks. On the night of 2 November, now under Lieutenant Colonel Gibb, it was sent into action again. The charge of the regiment at Tel El Aqqaqir ridge overran the enemy gunline, but in a fierce melee with German '88s' most of the tanks were destroyed. The four battered tanks which survived the battle were withdrawn. The regiment spent the next year rebuilding before it was sent to Italy, where it fought from mid-1944.

BRITISH

107th (South Nottinghamshire Hussars) Royal Horse Artillery

The South Notts Hussars were originally a part-time volunteer Yeomanry cavalry regiment, but in the 1920's it was converted into an artillery regiment. It was raised from men from Nottinghamshire, and commanded by Lieutenant Colonel Bill Seely who, like many other armoured or RHA commanders, was Master of Hounds for the local fox hunt, a prestigious position in the local aristocracy.

The South Notts' stand at Gazala was to be a tragically common experience for British artillery in 1942-1943. The battle of Gazala began badly for the South Notts Hussars. In the *Afrikakorps'* first attack, a battery found itself isolated and was overrun after a fierce fight with the German tanks. The regiment fought on, however. The remaining two batteries supported a major attack on the *Afrikakorps*, trapped in the Cauldron. As the day wore on, though, a steady stream of wounded and weary men made their way back through the regiment's positions, a sure sign the battle was not going well. That evening the General drove up and announced that he was now withdrawing, but the regiment should 'stand and fight to the last man and the last round.'

The next morning the *Afrikakorps* began a ferocious bombardment of the regiment's position with tanks, artillery and Stuka dive bombers. Having learnt from previous experience the cost of attacking British field artillery, they were cautious about charging the South Notts Hussars without weakening them first. After a stiff fight in which the gunners knocked out ten German tanks, E Troop was overrun. By midday the position was a shambles of burning vehicles, ammunition boxes, and dead and wounded men, but the guns continued to fire. Repeated flank attacks by tanks and infantry were beaten off as the gunners swung their guns around on their platforms. By the afternoon German tanks were able to close in using the smoke and wreckage of the regiment's blazing transport as cover. Colonel Seely was killed while conducting the defence from his 'Honey' Stuart tank. After the command posts were overrun, the guns fought individually until their crews were machine-gunned or the guns crushed under the tracks of the marauding tanks.

When the regiment returned to the Cauldron after the battle, every gun of the 107th RHA was still in position, surrounded by burnt out vehicles and tanks. The gunners lay where they had fallen, the layers still crouched over their sights.

... Pip Roberts, Gazala 1942 ...

'Large numbers of tanks to our front,' reports the Honey Squadron commander, '100 tanks, 3000 yards away, moving north west' he continued.

'A whole ruddy Panzer Division is quite obviously in front of us', mused Pip Roberts, switching to intercom. 'Peter,' addressing the adjutant in the tank below, 'report to Brigade, about 100 enemy tanks moving north west, and then get ready to load the 75. Operator, pass up my tin hat and stow my beret in an un-oily spot.'

Switching to the regimental net, he orders, 'Hullo, regimental orders. B and C Squadrons take up battle line with your Grants on the small ridge 300 yards to our front. A Squadron pull back and try to get in on the enemy's left flank.'

Leaning out the hatch to the left, Pip yells down to the officer standing in the turretless Marmon Harrington pulling up alongside, 'Charles, would appreciate a little artillery support.'

'No problem, sir,' the artillery officer replies. 'Two minutes. Keep your head down.'

Back to the intercom, 'Driver, advance slightly with the other tanks. 75 gunner, enemy tank straight ahead receiving no attention—engage. First shot just over, come down half a tank height Still over—come down a whole tank's height. Good shot—continue firing.'

Slam! The Grant rocks back on its suspension. Pip's head swings left, just the job for the 37.

'37 gunner traverse left, traverse left, on. Enemy tank broadside on 500—fire! 37 gunner—good —a couple more shots and then the co-ax.'

Back to the regimental net. 'Hullo C Squadron—what's the matter—you're going the wrong way.' Several tanks, including the CO's are pulling out of line.

'Sorry,' replies C Squadron's CO, 'but I can't see a damned thing with blood in my eyes and all of my periscopes are smashed. I think the same thing has happened to my other tanks, the two I have left. Also, I have no more ammunition.'

'OK, well done—carry on.'

It's going to be tricky, B Squadron's Grants, what's left of them, will be getting short of ammunition.

'Peter, tell Brigade that if we are achieving a great deal by staying here, I think we can, but it may be expensive.'

The reply is quick. 'Pip, Brigade says to join them,' Peter's voice is distorted by the intercom.

'Regimental orders, B and C Squadrons rally on the high ground to the north east. A Squadron hold up the enemy tanks while we get clear. Peter, see if you can get the ammunition lorries to meet us.'

'Driver, reverse very slowly. 75 and 37 gunners continue firing at suitable targets.'

' Only two rounds left for the 75,' the 75 gunner replies. The 37 gunner adds 'Down to five here.'

Rifle Company

(INFANTRY COMPANY)

The 'Poor Bloody Infantry' always cop it in the neck. The General says take so and so, an' the squaddies pick up their rifles and walk through hell to take it, nothing but a tin hat to protect them. Just another day in the army. Still got to shave in the morning, still get bully and biscuits for dinner.
—Private Tom 'Lefty' Wright

A force based around a Rifle Company must contain:

- a Company HQ, and
- two or three Rifle Platoons.

Weapons Platoons available to a Rifle Company are:

- four Carrier Patrols,
- a Mortar Platoon,
- an Anti-tank Platoon,
- an Anti-aircraft Platoon,
- a Pioneer Platoon, and
- an additional Rifle Platoon.

Support Platoons for a Rifle Company can be:

- Machine-gun Platoons,
- a Heavy Mortar Platoon,
- Tank Platoons,
- Transport Platoons,
- Recce Platoons,
- Commando Platoons, and
- Divisional Support Platoons.

You may have up to **two** Support Platoons attached to your company for each Rifle Platoon you field.

Motivation and Skill

The British Army has been fighting for three years now. Early mistakes have been corrected and new tactics introduced. A Rifle Company is rated as **Confident Veteran**.

HEADQUARTERS

1 Company HQ

Headquarters	
Company HQ	30 points
Option	
• Add Jeep or Troop Carrier for +5 points.	

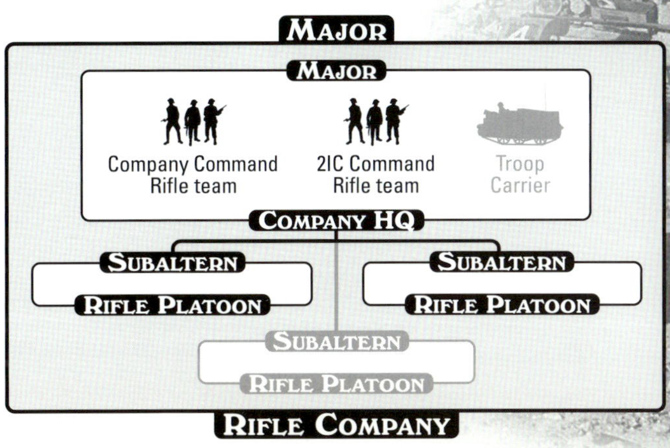

As the company commander, the Major represents your influence on the battle more than any other. The Major's presence at the critical point in battle is essential. There he can lead by example and inspire his men to greater efforts.

Troop Carrier

The British Army developed a wide range of light tracked carriers. The most common was the Universal Carrier, so called because it replaced the earlier Scout and Bren Carriers and added a whole slew of new roles as well.

The basic Universal Carrier is modified for different roles. As the troop carrier it lacks armament as its role of commander's runabout makes weapons unnecessary. As the mortar carrier, it has fittings for stowing the mortar on the rear and ammunition inside. As the MMG carrier it has fittings for the Vickers MMG on the engine deck. As the OP carrier it has reels for cable and a ladder. In the basic scouting role it carries a Bren light machine-gun and in many cases a Boys anti-tank rifle as well.

COMBAT PLATOONS

2 or 3 Rifle Platoons

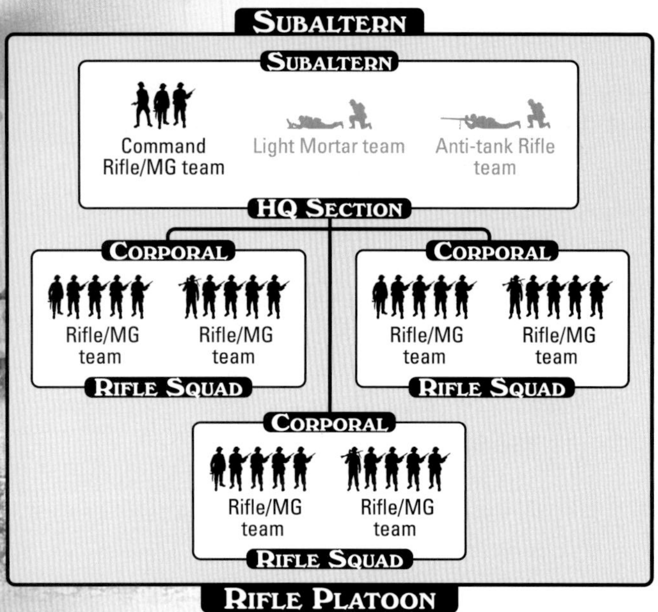

Platoon

HQ Section with:

3 Rifle Squads	150 points
2 Rifle Squads	105 points

Options

- Equip all Rifle/MG teams with Sticky Bombs for +5 points per team.
- Add Light Mortar team for +10 points.
- Add Anti-tank Rifle team for +20 points or PIAT team for +30 points.

The infantry have been the backbone of the British Army since its inception three hundred years ago. These days the 'Thin Red Line' wears khaki, and Lee-Enfield rifles and Bren light machine-guns have replaced the old Brown Bess musket, but their reputation for tenacity remains.

With a 2" mortar to knock out machine-gun pits, and a Boys anti-tank rifle or one of the new PIAT anti-tank launchers for taking out tanks, the lads in a Rifle Platoon can take anything Jerry throws at them.

WEAPONS PLATOONS

0 to 4 Carrier Patrols

A Rifle Company's Carrier Patrols are organised like the Scout Patrols of a Motor Company, see page 110.

0 to 1 Mortar Platoons

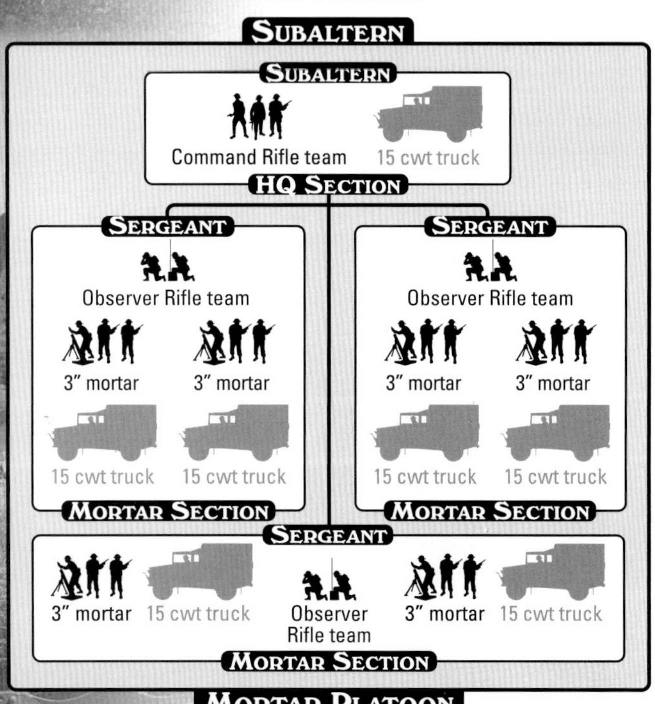

Platoon

HQ Section with:

3 Mortar Sections	195 points
2 Mortar Sections	135 points
1 Mortar Section	75 points

Options

- Add 15 cwt trucks to the platoon at no cost.
- Replace the HQ Section 15 cwt truck with a Troop Carrier for +5 points and all other 15 cwt trucks with Mortar Carriers for +5 points per Mortar Section.
- Equip all Rifle and Mortar teams with Sticky Bombs for +5 points per team.

While not as deadly as its big-barrelled counterparts in the artillery, the mortar platoon is a highly mobile and effective alternative. A rifle platoon with an observer attached can be assured of quick, reliable and accurate support.

0 to 1 Anti-tank Platoon

A Rifle Company's Anti-tank Platoon is organised like those of a Motor Company, see page 110.

0 to 1 Anti-aircraft Platoon

Platoon

2 Anti-aircraft Sections	110 points
1 Anti-aircraft Section	55 points

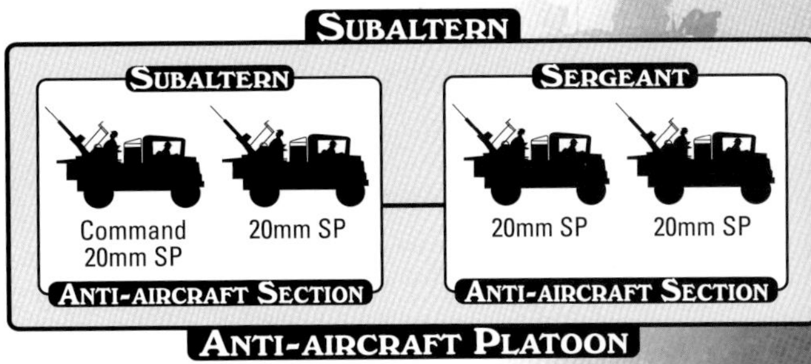

The battalion anti-aircraft platoon initially had four twin-mounted Bren guns. Many battalions disbanded the platoon when its machine-guns proved ineffective in stopping German air attacks, but others replaced them with captured Italian Breda 20mm anti-aircraft guns.

Meanwhile, the official solution, the Oerlikon 20mm portee, was under development and arrived in time for Sicily and Italy.

0 to 1 Pioneer Platoon

Platoon

Pioneer Section with:

2 Assault Squads	100 points
1 Assault Squad	75 points

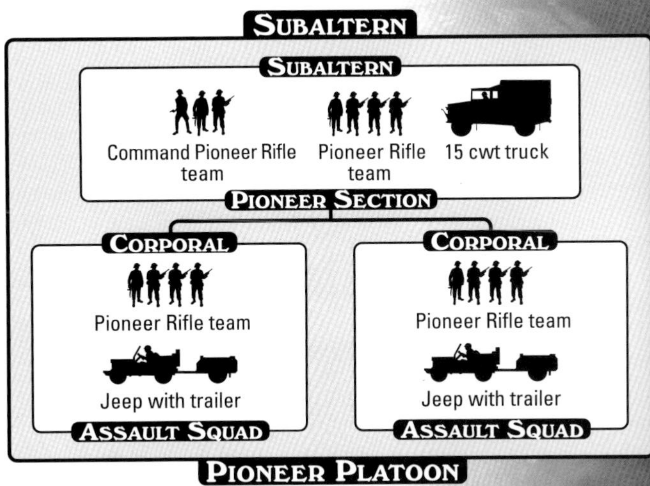

Pioneers were initially the battalion's labourers and many platoons were disbanded to reinforce the rifle platoons. By 1943 minefields and fortifications were much more common and pioneer platoons resurfaced in the role of mine-clearing in assaults and similar work.

SUPPORT PLATOONS

0 to 3 Machine-gun Platoons

Platoon

HQ Section with:

2 Machine-gun Sections	155 points
1 Machine-gun Section	85 points

Options

- Replace HQ Section 15 cwt truck with a Troop Carrier for +5 points and all other 15 cwt trucks with MMG Carriers for +5 points per MG Section.
- Equip all Rifle and HMG teams with Sticky Bombs for +5 points per team.

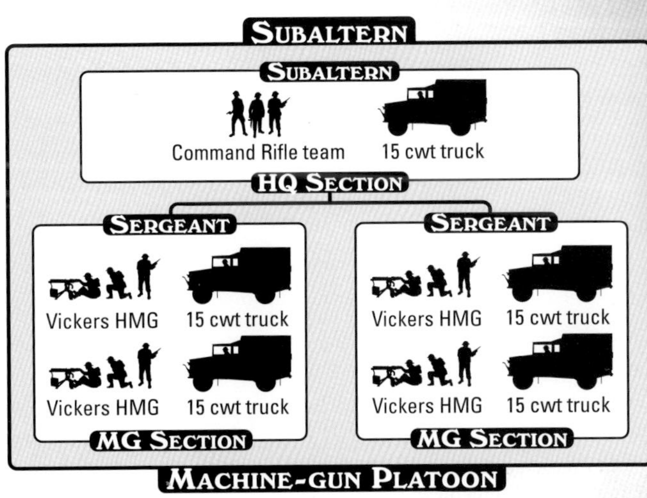

The British Army is unusual in retaining large numbers of specialist machine-gun battalions, one for each infantry division. In part this is due to the sophistication of the machine-gun tactics developed in the First World War and continued in the current one.

Machine-gun platoons don't just support the infantry with direct fire. They also fire overhead barrages using artillery methods when needed.

BRITISH

0 to 1 Heavy Mortar Platoon

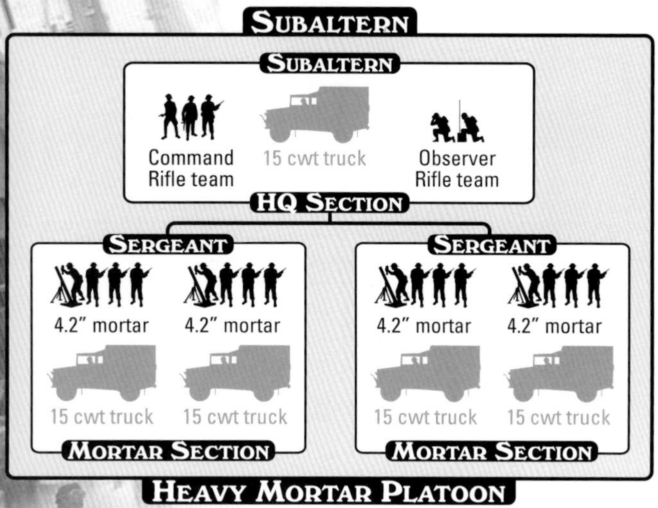

Platoon

HQ Section with:

2 Mortar Sections	**175 points**
1 Mortar Section	**100 points**

Options

- Add 15 cwt trucks to the platoon at no cost.
- Replace all 15 cwt trucks with Troop Carriers for +5 points for the HQ Section and +5 points for each Mortar Section.
- Equip all Rifle and Mortar teams with Sticky Bombs for +5 points per team.

The 4.2" heavy mortar first appeared in the Battle of El Alamein and is starting to replace the heavy machine-guns of one company. It is an excellent infantry support weapon firing a heavy shell over a useful distance.

0 to 2 Tank Platoons

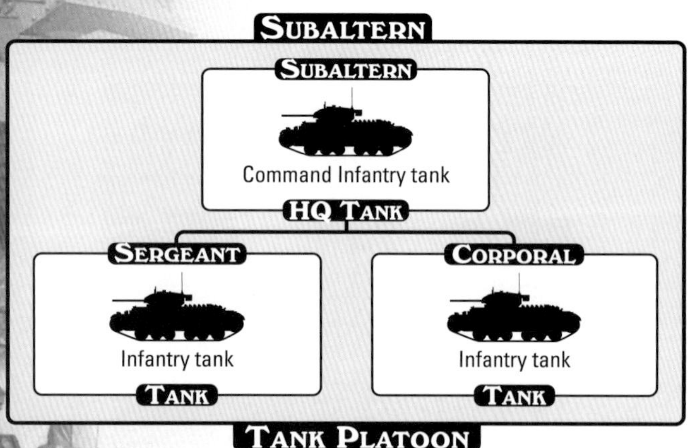

The Army Tank Brigades were very successful in their role of infantry support. They assisted the infantry in most battles in North Africa.

The Eighth Army started 1942 with plenty of Valentine II tanks and a few old worn-out Matilda tanks and retained its Valentines (with a few upgunned ones arriving after El Alamein) until the end of the campaign in Tunisia.

The First Army was supported by the massively armoured Churchill infantry tank.

The Valentine was outdated and Montgomery preferred the versatile Sherman to the lumbering Churchill, so all infantry support in Sicily and Italy during 1943 was provided by diesel-engined Sherman III tanks.

Platoon

3 Matilda II	**200 points**

- Replace up to two tanks with Matilda II CS tanks for +20 points per tank.

3 Valentine II	**150 points**

- Either: upgrade one Valentine II tank to a Valentine VIII tank for +20 points, or replace up to two tanks with Matilda II CS tanks for +40 points per tank.

3 Churchill III	**370 points**

- Replace up to two tanks with Churchill I tanks for -20 points per tank.

3 Sherman III	**345 points**

- Arm any or all Sherman tanks with a 0.5" AA MG for +5 points per tank.

A force may combine Matilda and Valentine tanks, but otherwise must have only one type of tank.

No more than one Tank Platoon in your force may be equipped with Matilda II CS or Churchill I tanks.

Confident Trained Armour

British tank battalions suffered numerous defeats at the hands of Rommel and are still rebuilding their pool of experienced crews and capable commanders. Tank Platoons are rated as **Confident Trained**.

Transport Section

Platoon	
HQ Squad with:	
1 Transport Squad	25 points
No Transport Squad	15 points

The transport companies of the RASC (Royal Army Service Corps) bring food and petrol up to the front lines. They also carry the infantry on long marches, in which case a transport company is assigned to each brigade. Individual Transport Sections are detailed to each company to carry its platoons.

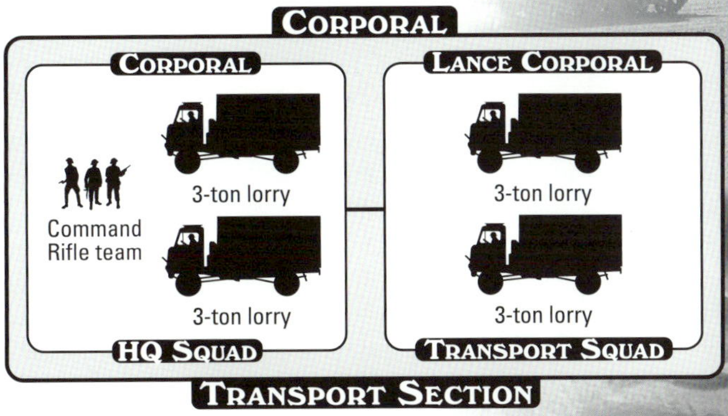

A Transport Section is a Transport Platoon.

...Charlie Upham, Egypt 1942...

'Now the bullets were really flying!' Leggy continued, dramatic hand gestures accompanying his tale to two young Privates. 'Charlie and me, we were pinned down see, couldn't move left, couldn't move right, stuck fast. Now these bastards are becoming a right pain in the starting handle if you catch my drift.'

'But Charlie's boys are in trouble and those machine-guns have to go. An' if any Jerry heroes decide to get in his way, that's their business!'

He paused to check on the steaming billy. 'Almost done, can't wait for a good cuppa.'

'So, bullets are whizzing past me an' the boss', he returned to his tale, 'The rock we're hunkered behind is taking a right royal bloody hammering, there's noise, there's shouting, there's smoke! By Crikey, it was hot. Now Charlie has been around a long time, and knows those buggers have to reload sometime—you can't keep those dogs barking all day! When they stopped, we moved!'

'I give 'em the bad news with the trusty old Enfield. Charlie is off like the proverbial off a bloody shovel! Even with a busted shoulder that fella moves faster'n I can. And there he was you see, shoulder smashed by a Jerry bullet, wouldn't go see the doctor, no, not Upham, he's still bloody chasing Jerries! So now I'm up and running then boom! I don't know what his grenade hit but it was bloody loud I can tell you! When my head finally decides it isn't last week anymore, I see Charlie getting to his feet, uniform smoking with a bloody great grin on his face. So now I'm thinking, Christ, if we hadn't pissed 'em off before then we certainly have now!'

'So there we are, in the middle of a nice Jerry get together, most bloody scary! Charlie's just tossed a grenade into another truck and boom that goes up too! Everything seems to be going up, trucks, barrels, ammo, the whole bloody lot. I came far too close for my liking to having my noggin taken off by a chunk of metal and suddenly I'm thinking this is getting a bit too hairy! Jerry must have thought the whole bloody army was after 'im, the rate Charlie was going at it! Then a bloody great tank rolls up out of the dark! Well that was it for me; I thought we were goners for sure!'

'We were down behind one of the trucks when Charlie yells out 'Keep your bloody head down' and the next thing I know he's off towards the tank.'

Leggy poured himself a cup of the strong sweet brew that passed for tea and rocked back on his heels. 'Anyway, as ...'

'You're boring these poor sods Leggy,' interrupted Captain Upham walking up. 'Lay off the bullshit, it wasn't that big a deal. Now, what's a bloke got to do 'round here to get a bloody cuppa?'

RECCE SQUADRON

(RECONNAISSANCE MECHANISED COMPANY)

With the armoured cars of the cavalry needed for the armoured divisions, the infantry formed its own recce regiments. Most divisions have one and their role is well summed up by their motto 'Only the enemy in front (every other beggar behind)'. The recce regiment is always first in advances and last in retreats. Stealthy work is their speciality, but if need be, they'll fight to achieve their objectives yelling their battle cry 'Bash on Recce'!

A force based around a Recce Squadron must contain:

- a Company HQ, and
- two or three Recce Platoons.

Weapons Platoons available to a Recce Squadron are:

- an Assault Platoon,
- a Mortar Platoon,
- an Anti-tank Platoon,
- an Anti-aircraft Platoon.

Support Platoons for a Recce Squadron can be:

- Rifle Platoons,
- Machine-gun Platoons,
- Heavy Mortar Platoons,
- Commando Platoons, and
- Divisional Support Platoons.

You may have up to **one** Support Platoon attached to your company for each Recce Platoon that you field.

Motivation and Skill

The Reconnaissance Corps prides itself in its skill and esprit de corps. Its troopers are well-trained and know their job like the back of their hands. A Recce Squadron is rated as **Confident Veteran**.

HEADQUARTERS

1 Company HQ

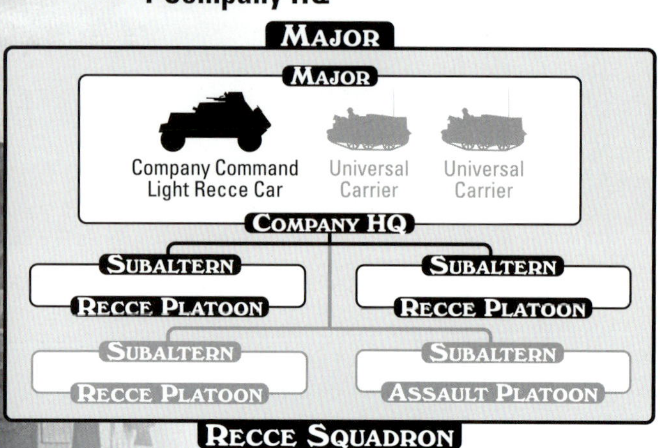

The Company HQ of a Reconnaissance Squadron is a Reconnaissance Platoon.

Headquarters

Company HQ	30 points

Option

- Add Universal Carriers for +30 points per carrier.
- Arm any or all Universal Carriers with an extra hull-mounted MG for +5 points per carrier or 0.5" MG for +10 points per carrier.

The Major must use all his skill and experience to coordinate the actions of his troops, many small platoons often scattered far and wide over the battlefield, as they seek out the enemy. He must judge when they should fight and when it is more sensible to simply observe and leave the fighting to the rest of the Division.

COMBAT PLATOONS

2 or 3 Recce Platoons

Platoon
LRC Patrol with:

5 Humber LRC III	150 points
4 Humber LRC III	120 points
3 Humber LRC III	90 points

Options

- Replace up to three Humber LRC with Humber II or III armoured cars at no cost.
- Add Scout Patrols for +90 points per patrol.
- Arm any or all Universal Carriers with an extra hull-mounted MG for +5 points per carrier or 0.5" MG for +10 points per carrier.
- Replace up to one extra hull-mounted MG per Scout Patrol with a Boys Anti-tank Rifle at no cost.

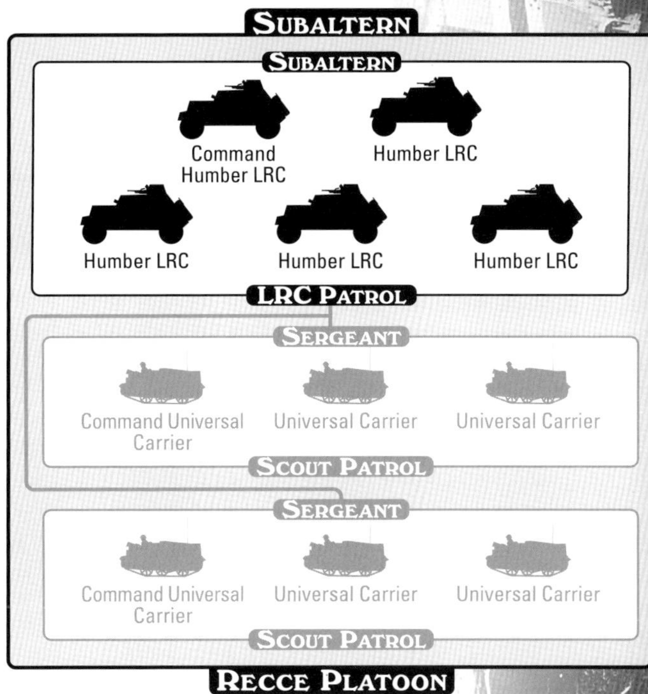

The LRC Patrol and Scout Patrols operate as separate platoons, each with their own Command team. Although its sections count as separate platoons for all other purposes, a Recce Platoon deploys all at the same time as a single platoon. Treat the entire Recce Platoon as a single platoon when calculating the number of platoons held in Ambush or Reserve.

The Recce Platoons are light, fast and mobile, and armed with many machine-guns and anti-tank rifles.

LRC and Scout Patrols are Reconnaissance Platoons.

WEAPONS PLATOONS

0 to 1 Assault Platoon

Platoon
HQ Section with:

4 Assault Squads	155 points
3Assault Squads	125 points
2 Assault Squads	95 points

Option

- Equip all MG teams with Sticky Bombs for +5 points per team.
- Add Anti-tank Rifle team for +20 points or PIAT team for +30 points.

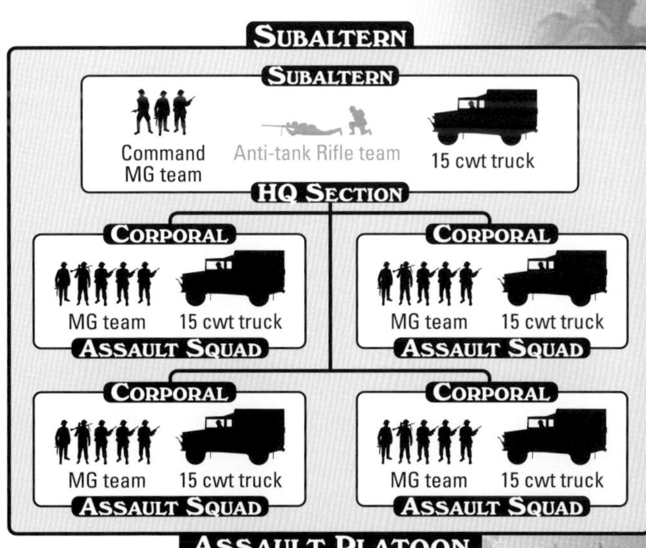

When enemy positions cannot be bypassed, the Assault Platoon can be called upon to clear them out, allowing the squadron to keep rolling forwards rather than waiting for the Rifle battalions to catch up and do the job.

0 to 1 Mortar Platoon

The Mortar Platoon is shown on page 116.

0 to 1 Anti-tank Platoon

The Anti-tank Platoon is shown on page 110.

0 to 1 Anti-aircraft Platoon

The Anti-aircraft Platoon is shown on page 117.

COMMANDOS

After the withdrawal of all British units from mainland Europe after Dunkirk, Prime Minister Winston Churchill ordered the formation of irregular raiding units or Commandos to take the fight back to the German enemy in occupied Europe with 'butcher and bolt' raids.

The Commandos conducted many small raids against the French and Norwegian coasts, but their most successful action was Operation Chariot by No.2 Commando, which wrecked the dry dock at St Nazaire, forcing the giant battleship Tirpitz to return to Germany for repairs.

The Commandos further distinguished themselves at Dieppe in August 1942, where No. 3 and No. 4 Commandos were the only units to successfully complete their assignments, despite initial setbacks.

Later than year, No. 1 and No. 6 Commandos were in the vanguard of the Operation Torch landings in French North Africa on 8 November, 1942. The Commandos fought their way to within miles of Tunis before being turned back by the newly arrived 10th Panzer Division.

The next big action by the Commandos in the Mediterranean was Operation Husky, the liberation of Sicily on July 10, 1943. There No. 3 Commando, and No. 40 ('forty') and No. 41 ('four-one' not 'forty one'!) Royal Marine Commandos led the Canadian and British invasion force ashore. No. 3 Commando was then assigned to take the Ponte dei Malati bridge ahead of 50th (Northumbrian) Division who would then go on to relieve the 1st Parachute Brigade dropping on Primasole bridge, key to the advance to Catania. The Commandos succeeded, but German counterattacks forced them off the bridge before the delayed 50th Division arrived.

No. 3 and No. 40 (RM) Commandos then took part in Operation Baytown, the Eighth Army's landings on the toe of Italy early in September, 1943. Later, on 9 September, No. 2 and No. 41 (RM) Commandos covered the left flank of the Salerno landings near Naples in Italy. At the start of October No. 3 Commando was into action again, landing to seize the town of Termoli on the Adriatic coast ahead of 78th Infantry Division.

The Commandos continued raiding and made numerous landings in the Mediterranean throughout 1944 and 1945, contributing greatly to the Allied victory.

COMMANDO SPECIAL RULES

Know The Plan

Commandos are expected to be independent-minded (if not downright unconventional) sorts and every man is drilled in the plan before an attack. That way if the officers are killed, an NCO, or even a private can take over as needed.

Commando Platoons use the German Mission tactics special rule.

Fairbairn-Sykes

Under Captains W E Fairbairn and A E Sykes, a pair of tough Shanghai policemen, Commandos were trained in every imaginable method of killing and avoiding being killed in close combat. The Fairbairn-Sykes dagger they designed for the Commandos is still in use today.

Commando Infantry teams hit on a roll of 2+ in assault combat.

Mind And Heart

The men trained at the Commando Basic Training Centre at Achnacarry, Scotland never forgot their instructors' chant of 'It's all in the mind and the heart' as they scaled impossible cliffs and swam rivers in full kit.

All Commando Infantry and Man-packed Gun teams are Mountaineers.

No British Bulldog

Commandos are fearless, but they are also raiders. Their job is to get in, strike hard, and get out. Prolonged combats simply delay their mission, so the British Bulldog rule does not apply to Commando platoons.

You Are Not Alone

Commandos are small, hard-hitting strike forces. As each commando troop has only two small platoons, they must operate together to win. Every commando knows that no matter what happens, they are not alone. Even if their troop runs into insurmountable trouble, another troop will be there to help them out or take over their part in the operation.

A Commando Troop never has to take a Company Morale Check for being below half strength. They still take Platoon Morale Checks as normal though.

However, if the total number of destroyed Commando Platoons from all troops exceeds the number still on the table, the Commando player must roll a die at the start of each turn. On a roll of 3+ the force fights on, heedless of its losses. On any other roll the remaining commandos withdraw to conserve their remaining strength and the game ends. If there are no remaining Commando Company Command teams then this roll is automatically failed.

COMMANDO TROOP

(INFANTRY COMPANY)

We are the men who bring the war home to Germans all over fallen Europe. We 'butcher' and when necessary we 'bolt' as Mr. Churchill has told us to. They're so scared of us they daren't even take us alive! So be it. Let them tremble, as they should, at the name Commando!
—Sergeant Richard 'Chalkie' White

A force based around a Commando Troop must contain:

- a Company HQ and
- one or two Commando Platoons.

Weapons Platoons available to a Commando Troop are:

- a Commando Mortar Platoon, and
- a Commando Machine-gun Platoon.

Support Platoons for a Commando Troop can be:

- Rifle Platoons,
- Machine-gun Platoons,
- a Heavy Mortar Platoon,
- Tank Platoons,
- Recce Platoons, and
- any Divisional Support Platoons.

You may attach up to **one** Support Platoon to your Commando Troop for each Commando Platoon you field.

Motivation and Skill

Commandos are highly trained, experienced and motivated volunteers who know that Hitler has ordered them executed if captured alive. A Commando Troop is rated as **Fearless Veteran**.

HEADQUARTERS

1 Company HQ

Headquarters

Company HQ	25 points

Option

- Add PIAT team for +35 points.

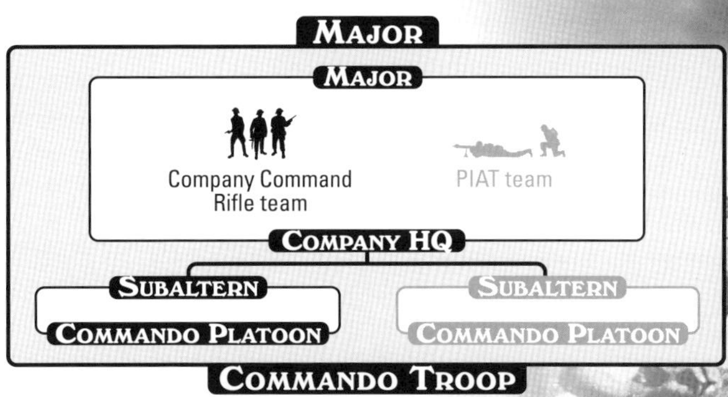

Only one of your Commando Troops may have a single Commando Platoon. All others must have two Commando Platoons.

The men of the Army and Royal Marine Commandos are all highly trained volunteers with experience from successful raids in occupied Europe under their belts. They are the most devastating assault force on the face of the planet and excel in their chosen area of expertise. They are light raiders however and require support from regular army units if they are to hold against enemy forces in a defensive posture for long.

In *Flames Of War* you can field multiple companies in the same force. This is particularly useful with the commandos as a Commando troop is quite small and they usually operate in groups of up to a full five-troop Commando. Two or three Commando troops of two Commando Platoons each with a little divisional support make for a very tough force.

Commandos in the Mediterranean

Commando	Battle Honours
1 Commando	Pointe de Saire 1941, Le Touquet 1942, Torch 1942, Sedjenane 1942, Burma 1944, Kangaw 1945.
2 Commando	Vaagso 1941, St Nazaire 1942, Sicily 1943, Vis 1944, Solta 1944, Spilje 1944, Lake Comacchio 1945, Argenta 1945.
3 Commando	Guernsey 1940, Lofoten Islands 1941, Vaagso 1941, Dieppe 1942, Husky 1943, San Venere 1943, Termoli 1943, Normandy 1944, Linne 1945, Rhine 1945, Leese 1945, Aller 1945, Lauenburg 1945.
6 Commando	River Ardour 1942, Torch 1942, Normandy 1944, Maasbracht 1945, Wesel 1945, Leese 1945, Lauenburg 1945.
40 (RM) Commando	Dieppe 1942, Sicily 1943, Italy 1943, Adriatic 1943 – 1944, Corfu 1944.
41 (RM) Commando	Sicily 1943, Salerno 1943, Normandy 1944, Walcheren 1944.

COMBAT PLATOONS

1 or 2 Commando Platoons

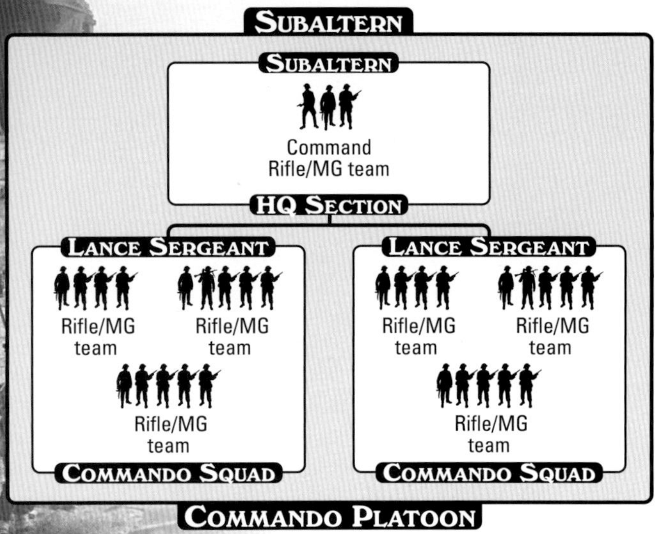

Platoon

HQ Section with:

2 Commando Squads	**230 points**

Options

- Replace one Rifle/MG team with a Light Mortar team at no cost.
- Replace one Rifle/MG team with an Anti-tank Rifle team or PIAT team at no cost.
- Upgrade up to two Rifle/MG teams to SMG teams at no cost.

Each Commando troop is made up of two Commando 'sections' or platoons. Commando Sections are well armed, however it is their daggers and silent-killing techniques which make them such a terrifying force in close assaults.

WEAPONS PLATOONS

0 to 1 Commando Machine-gun Platoon

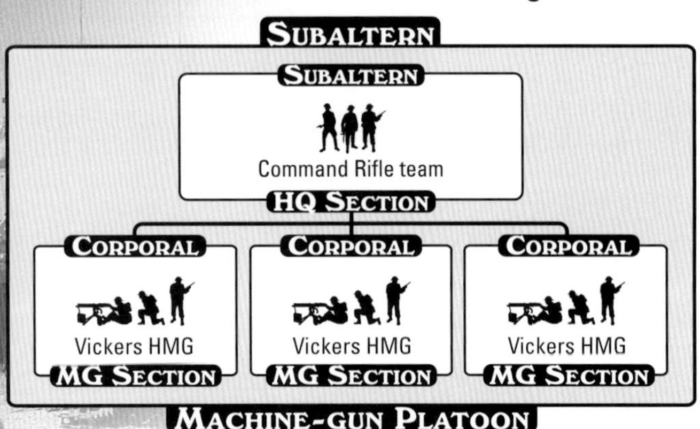

Platoon

HQ Section with:

3 Machine-gun Sections	**155 points**
2 Machine-gun Sections	**110 points**

A force may not have more than one Commando Machine-gun Platoon.

Each Commando troop has one machine-gun platoon that gives their mates heavy fire support to cover them in the last phase of assaults. They also break up enemy counter-attacks with their sustained fire.

Commandos were specialists in quick attacks. They neither had the ammunition nor the time for prolonged machine-gun bombardments.

The Vickers HMG teams of a Commando Machine-gun Platoon may not fire Artillery Bombardments.

0 to 1 Commando Mortar Platoon

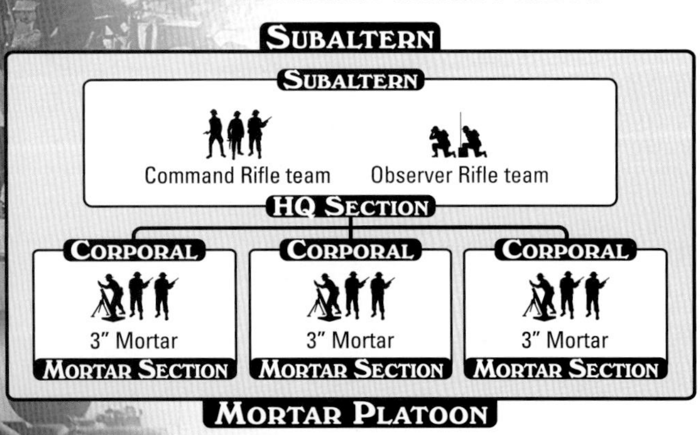

Platoon

HQ Section with:

3 Mortar Sections	**125 points**
2 Mortar Sections	**90 points**

A force may not have more than one Commando Mortar Platoon.

The Commando's heavy troop has a mortar platoon to go with its machine-gun platoon. The mortar platoon gives the Commando light artillery support of its own.

Divisional Support

Your force may have the following support platoons:

- Field Platoons, Royal Engineers,
- Mine Flail Platoons,
- Artillery Batteries,
- Anti-tank Platoons, Royal Artillery,
- Light Anti-aircraft Platoons,

Motivation and Skill

The divisional troops supporting the tanks and riflemen are all old hands who long ago 'got their knees brown' from the harsh desert sun. All Divisional Support Platoons are rated as **Confident Veteran** unless otherwise noted.

Air Support

Aircraft	Limited Air Support	Sporadic Air support
Hurricane IIC	140 points	105 points
Hurricane IID	135 points	100 points
Kittyhawk	130 points	95 points

0 to 1 Field Platoon, Royal Engineers

Platoon

HQ Section with:

4 Field Squads	150 points
3 Field Squads	120 points
2 Field Squads	95 points

Options

- Add Pioneer Supply 3-ton truck for +25 points.

When you deploy your force at the start of a game you may elect to replace a Field Platoon, Royal Engineers with a Rifle Platoon of the same or lower points value.

The Field Platoons of the Royal Engineers are highly trained experts and far too valuable to waste as infantry. Their main roles are mine laying and clearing, along with construction work. If they find themselves under assault they will withdraw to allow the infantry to clear the position and then continue their work.

Field Platoons, Royal Engineers may not launch assaults, nor may they Counterattack if assaulted. Field Platoons, Royal Engineers will always attempt to Break Off at the earliest opportunity.

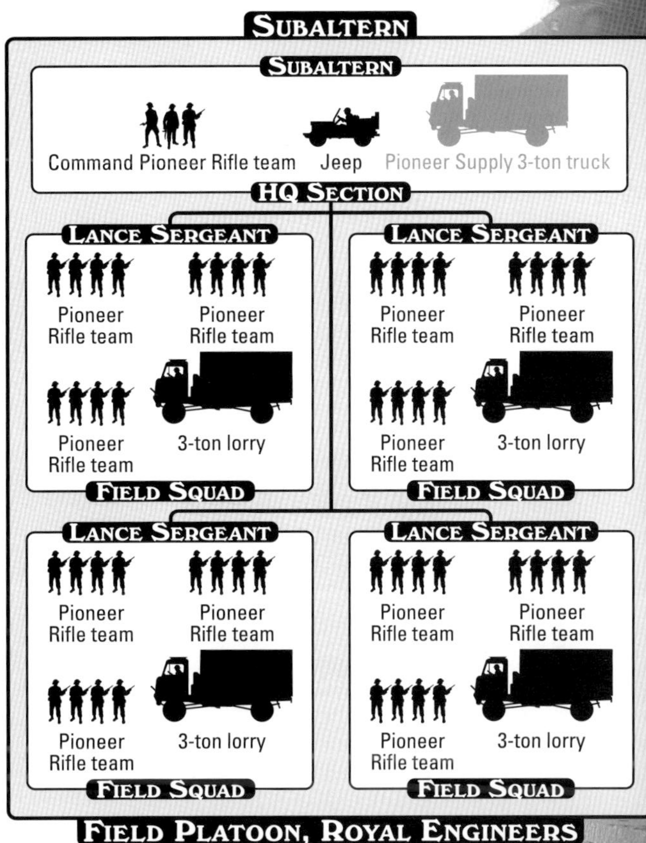

0 to 1 Mine Flail Platoon

Platoon

3 Matilda Scorpion	205 points
2 Matilda Scorpion	135 points
1 Matilda Scorpion	70 points

Option

- Remove the 2 pdr gun from all Matilda Scorpion mine flail tanks making room for the flail's engine controls and operator inside the tank instead of in the sponson for -35 points per tank.

Trained Tank Crews

The top secret flail tanks have just finished testing and are rated **Confident Trained**.

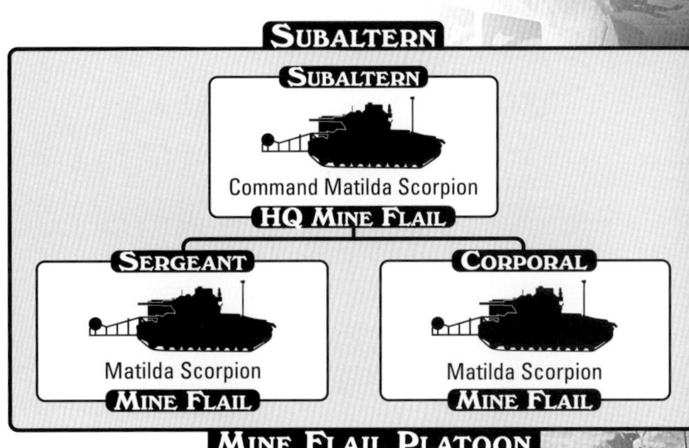

BRITISH

Royal Artillery

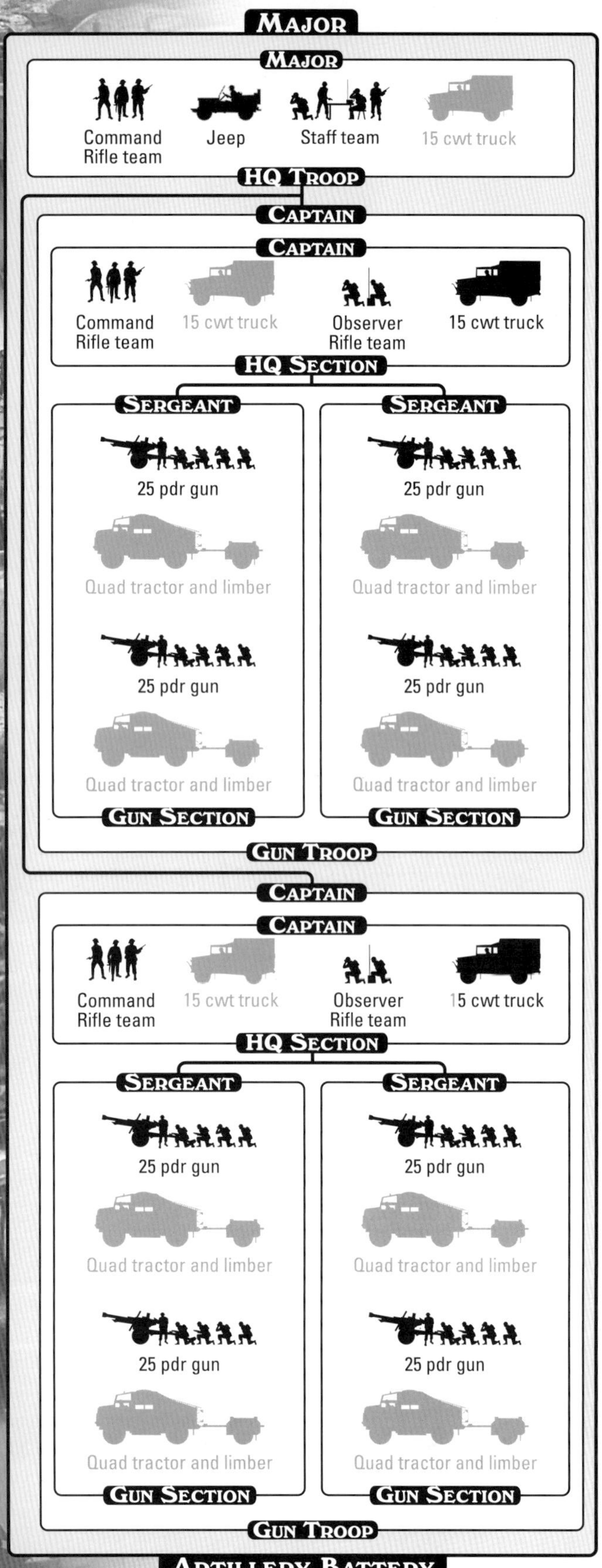

... The Cauldron, 1942 ...

The 25 pounder gun barks and rocks back, sending another shell towards its target somewhere in the distance. The horizon is a vision of hell—the desert littered with burning vehicles. Columns of thick black smoke cast bizarre shadows across the yellow sand. Overhead Stuka dive-bombers wheel like carrion birds. About a hundred yards behind the gun, several Quad tractors burn.

Lieutenant Smith runs over yelling something inaudible in the din of battle, pointing behind him at several tanks nosing their way through the blazing transport, turrets swiveling as if sniffing for prey. The sweating gunners, stripped to the waist, need no orders.

'Two Six Heave!' yell the gunners as they heft the trail of the 25 pounder, dragging the gun about on its turntable to face the sudden threat from the rear. Jones, the number two, rams sinister black shot into the still-smoking breech, followed by a brass case. The breech slams shut as Richards, the number three, his face pressed against the gunsight, frantically traverses onto the target. The gun barks, jerking back once more. The German tank slews about and stops.

B Troop's other three guns fire in rapid succession and another tank erupts in flames. The rest continue to advance, machine-guns chattering, bullets zipping about the gun, pinging off the shield. Gunners carrying cartridges to the guns fall, but still the guns fire as if the crews are parts of an automatic machine. The tanks still come on, turrets turning, guns blazing.

'There's no more AP!' yells a gunner bringing up a box of ammunition. 'Then we fire HE!' Smith yells back. The 25 pounder barks again. The shell strikes the front of a tank's turret with a deafening bang. The tank stops, hatches open and the crew bails out. The other tanks stop and begin to reverse.

Each Gun Troop operates as a separate platoon with its own Command team. The HQ Troop Command team and Staff team are Independent teams. If the HQ Troop Command team joins a Gun troop, it becomes the Platoon Command Team

Although they count as separate platoons for all other purposes, an Artillery Battery deploys as a single platoon, all at the same time. Treat both Gun Troops as a single platoon when calculating the number of platoons held in Ambush or Reserve.

There are two styles of Artillery Batteries, the Royal Horse Artillery Battery and the Field Battery, Royal Artillery. Both are organised identically as shown opposite, but operate differently as shown below.

Royal Horse Artillery Battery

The Royal Horse Artillery, or RHA, has a long and illustrious history. The gunners are superbly trained and will fight to the last in defence of their guns.

Their fast and accurate bombardments have crushed many German counterattacks saving their accompanying Motor Companies from being overrun.

Platoon

HQ Troop with:

Two Gun Troops with a total of:

4 Gun Sections	**465 points**

One Gun Troop with:

2 Gun Sections	**270 points**
1 Gun Section	**165 points**

Options

- Add 15 cwt trucks and Quad tractors at no cost.
- Replace the HQ Troop jeep with a White scout car for +5 points.
- Replace the HQ Troop jeep with a Command Marmon Herrington armoured car for +25 points, or a Command 'Honey' Stuart I or III tank for +75 points.
- Replace any or all Observer team's 15 cwt trucks with OP Carriers or White scout cars for +5 points for the battery.
- Replace any or all Observer Rifle teams and their 15 cwt trucks with Observer Marmon Herrington armoured cars for +25 points per armoured car, or Observer 'Honey' Stuart tanks for +75 points per tank.
- Equip all Rifle and Gun teams with Sticky Bombs for +5 points per team.
- Replace all 25 pdr guns and their Quad tractors with Priest self-propelled guns for +35 points per section.

A Royal Horse Artillery Battery can only be taken as a support choice for an Armoured Squadron, a Death or Glory Squadron, a Motor Company, or an Armoured Car Squadron

Royal Horse Artillery Batteries are rated as **Fearless Veteran** *and are Horse Artillery Platoons. They may not use the Mike Target special rule.*

Field Battery, Royal Artillery

The Royal Artillery are experts at providing quick fire support to the infantry. With the entire division's artillery on call, they rely on volume more than pin-point accuracy or heavy shells.

The results are devastating for the enemy. Attacks are destroyed before they reach the infantry's positions and defences shattered ahead of the infantry's attacks.

Platoon

HQ Troop with:

Two Gun Troops with a total of:

4 Gun Sections	**415 points**

One Gun Troop with:

2 Gun Sections	**240 points**
1 Gun Section	**145 points**

Options

- Add 15 cwt trucks and Quad tractors at no cost.
- Replace the HQ Troop jeep with a White scout car for +5 points.
- Replace the Command Rifle team and its jeep with a Command Marmon Herrington armoured car for +20 points.
- Replace any or all Observer team's 15 cwt trucks with OP Carriers or White scout cars for +5 points for the battery.
- Replace any or all Observer Rifle teams and their 15 cwt trucks with Observer Marmon Herrington armoured cars for +20 points per armoured car.
- Equip all Rifle and Gun teams with Sticky Bombs for +5 points per team.
- Replace all 25 pdr guns and their Quad tractors with Bishop self-propelled guns for +5 points per section, or with Priest self-propelled guns for +35 points per section.

A Field Battery, Royal Artillery can only be taken as a support choice for a Rifle Company, a Recce Squadron, a Commando Troop, or a Divisional Cavalry Squadron.

The Royal Artillery is not so flash as the RHA, their speciality is massed fires, not showy manoeuvres. They remain Confident Veteran but can use the Mike Target special rule.

Anti-tank Platoon, Royal Artillery

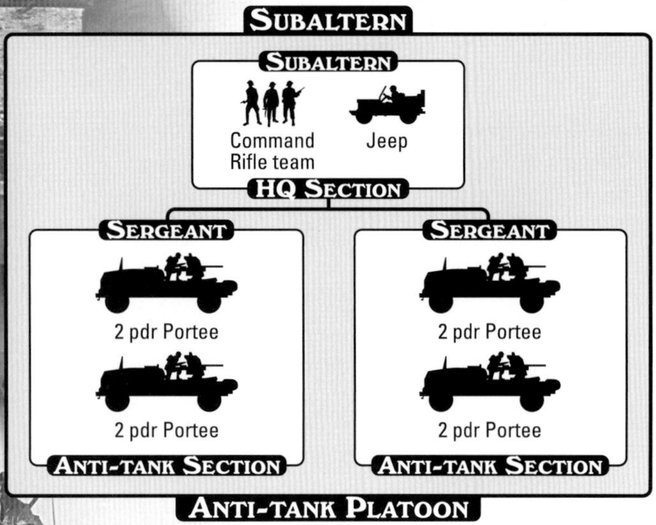

The Royal Artillery's anti-tank platoons are the first to get new weapons. They started receiving 6 pdr anti-tank guns during the Gazala battles of June 1942. By the time of the Mareth Line battles in March 1943, a few batteries of 17/25 pdr guns were on hand as well.

Platoon

HQ Section with:

2 Anti-tank Sections	135 points
1 Anti-tank Section	75 points

Options

- Replace all 2 pdr portees with 6 pdr portees for +30 points per section.
- Replace all 2 pdr portees with 6 pdr guns towed by Jeeps for +30 points per section.
- Replace all 2 pdr portees with Deacon self-propelled guns for +65 points per section.
- Replace all 2 pdr portees with 17/25 pdr guns towed by Quad tractors for +95 points per section.
- Equip all Rifle and Gun teams with Sticky Bombs for +5 points per team.

Deacon self-propelled guns may only support an Armoured Squadron, a Motor Company, or an Armoured Car Squadron.

You may not field more than one Anti-tank Platoon armed with 17/25 pdr guns.

0 to 1 Light Anti-aircraft Platoon

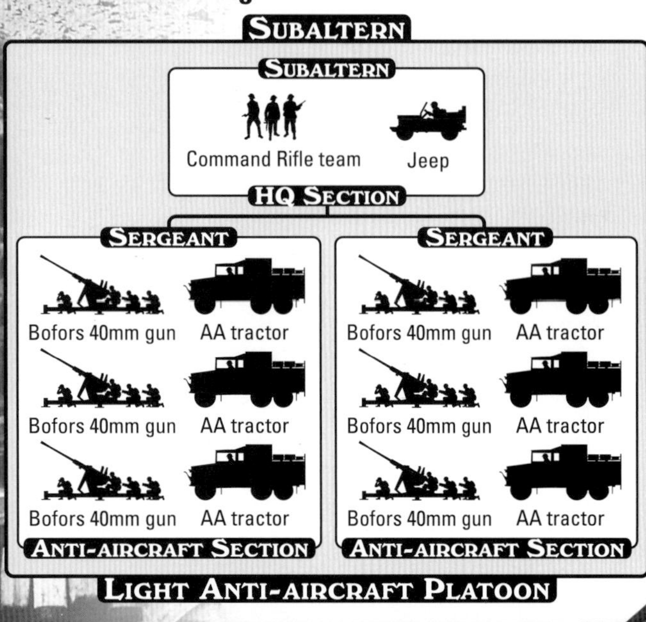

Platoon

HQ Section with:

2 Gun Sections	195 points
1 Gun Section	110 points

The divisional light anti-aircraft regiment protects the infantry against the German Air Force's incessant Stuka attacks. It performs a vital role in keeping the artillery firing as well as protecting the front-line troops.

THE BRITISH EMPIRE

The British Empire is the largest the world has ever seen. It occupies a quarter of all the lands of the Earth and includes a quarter of the planet's population. The sun never sets on the British Empire.

When war broke out volunteers from throughout the Empire flocked to the flag ready to fight. Australians, Burmese, Canadians, Englishmen, Indians, Irishmen, New Foundlanders, New Zealanders, Nigerians, Rhodesians, Scotsmen, South Africans, Ugandans, and Welshmen fought side by side against Hitler's unfounded aggression.

Although all once British colonies, the various countries making up the Empire have very different characters. All of the armies in the Empire were organised the same way and all had the same basic training and equipment, yet the circumstances of their employment, their fortunes in battle, and perhaps most importantly the backgrounds of their soldiers gave them all a distinct identity and character.

This section attempts to reflect some of this character on the battlefields of *Flames Of War* by providing various rules for you to customise your force as some of the various armies making up the Empire's armed forces.

Of course, you don't have to use these variations if you don't want to. Your Australians, Indians, or South Africans can use the normal rules for British troops instead.

BRITISH

No. 1 Company, 3rd Battalion, Welsh Guards

Raised in 1941, No.1 Company of the 3rd Welsh Guards (the Welsh Guards numbered their companies rather than use letters) landed in North Africa in 1943 as part of the British First Army. It went into its first battle on 8 April 1943 at Fondouk, in Tunisia, a strategically important pass. Dominating the road through the pass was a steep rocky hill, Djebel ain el Rhorab, the high point being called 'the Razor-back'. The Welsh Guards were ordered to take and hold the Razor-back which was defended by the German *27. Marsch Battalion*.

Just after dawn No.1 Company formed into open order and started off. The Company crossed Wadi Rhouil without loss, but as it began climbing towards its objective came under rifle fire from a village on the right flank and machine-gun fire from the hill itself. The Carrier platoon under Captain McVittie moved through the infantry to provide covering fire, but No.1 Company was pinned down 600 yards short of the hill. The attack seemed to have bogged down.

Then two troops of Sherman tanks from the Lothians and Border Horse moved up going around the hill on the left flank to rake German positions on the reverse slopes of the Razor-Back. Lance-Sergeant K G Summers set up his section of 3" mortars, and began bombing the German machine-guns. Artillery from 152nd Field Regiment quickly joined in. The 21-year-old Battalion Adjutant, Captain G.D. Rhys-Williams went forward in his Carrier to get No.1 Company attacking again. Ignoring enemy fire, Rhys-Williams moved along the front line, regrouping the platoons, encouraging the men, and giving orders. Picking up a rifle, Rhys-Williams urged the Company into the assault again. Shouting to the men 'Keep your distances' and 'Come on boys—we can do it', Rhys-Williams led No.1 Company into the German positions and stormed Razor-back ridge. More than a hundred Germans were taken prisoner. However, the gallant Rhys-Williams was killed at the moment of victory.

SCOTS REGIMENTS

Scots regiments no-longer wear their kilts on active service, however they still have their bagpipes. Although the use of bagpipes on the field of battle was banned between the wars, numerous pipers ignored orders and piped the attack home often wearing their kilt.

You may field a Scots Rifle Company. If you do, add a bagpiper to the company's 2iC Command team for +10 points.

Bagpipes

If the 2iC Command team is Destroyed by enemy shooting, roll a die. On a roll of 4+, the piper's music inspires the surviving team members to keep going and the team is returned to play immediately. On any other roll, the piper and his officer meet a heroic end.

Any hits on the 2iC Command team do not count towards Pinning Down the platoon.

THE EIGHTH ARMY IN THE DESERT AND ITALY

When the Second World War began, Egypt seemed an unlikely battlefield, that was until Mussolini's ambition led to the ill-fated Italian invasion. The Western Desert Force that defeated him grew into the Eighth Army as it faced the German Afrikakorps under General Rommel.

The Eighth Army always had a high proportion of colonial divisions, most with considerable battle experience by 1942. By contrast its British Divisions were rather less experienced.

At Gazala in June 1942 the Eighth Army was mishandled by its own generals and roughly treated by Rommel. All of the divisions that got away from that battle had lost a brigade in battle except the 1st South African Division which made a daring escape in the north. The retreat to the Alamein line cost the army the 2nd South African Division and the 10th Indian Division, and very nearly the 2nd New Zealand Division as well.

The Alamein battles of the second half of 1942 showed the mettle of the colonial troops and the new British divisions quickly learned to handle themselves in battle under the careful eye of their new commander, General Montgomery.

By the time the Eighth Army reached the Tunisian border in February 1943, it was a veteran fighting machine that beat the best the Germans and Italians could field in every battle it undertook. Fighting alongside the First Army they pushed the Germans and Italians back. Within three months a quarter of a million Axis troops surrendered and the fighting in Tunisia was over.

July 1943 saw the Eighth Army invading Sicily alongside General Patton's Seventh Army. After a victorious campaign, the Eighth Army invaded Italy, fighting their way up from the toe to join General Clark's Fifth Army in the liberation of Italy.

The main part of this section represents the veteran Eighth Army at its peak.

FIELDING A FRESHLY ARRIVED EIGHTH ARMY FORCE

You may field your force as one of the newer divisions in the Eight Army who have yet to 'get their knees brown' by making the Skill rating of the entire company and its supporting troops Trained rather than Veteran.

If you do this, the number of points available to spend on a Freshly Arrived Rifle Company increases as follows:

Normal Force	Freshly Arrived Force
1000 points	1300 points
1500 points	1950 points
2000 points	2600 points

In addition:

- You may not take Recce or Commando Platoons.
- Platoons may not have PIAT teams.
- Anti-tank Platoons may not be equipped with 17/25 pdr guns.
- Tank Platoons must be equipped with Matilda or Valentine tanks. Those equipped with Matilda tanks cost an extra +60 points per platoon, while those equipped with Valentine tanks cost an extra +45 points per platoon.
- Mine Flail Platoons cost an extra +20 points per mine flail tank.

Freshly Arrived Rifle Companies may also be Scots Rifle Companies.

THE FIRST ARMY IN TUNISIA

The First Army under General Anderson was formed in December 1942 from Eastern Task force set up for the Operation Torch landings to liberate Algeria and Tunisia.

It was the first army to combine British, American, and French troops under one commander. Unfortunately, none of its divisions or senior officers had any experience in the current war. Worse still, they faced some of Germany's best, and initially suffered accordingly.

Despite this, they learned quickly and by April 1943 had defeated two major German counterattacks and were ready for the final advance on Tunis.

One of the oddities of war was that the First Army, having sailed directly from Britain, was actually better equipped than the Eighth Army and tended to field newer equipment sooner. They had the heavy Churchill tank in place of the lighter Valentine, and received the PIAT anti-tank launcher and 17/25 pdr heavy anti-tank gun sooner.

FIELDING A FIRST ARMY FORCE

You may field your force as one of the inexperienced regiments that made up the First Army by making the Skill rating of the entire company and its supporting troops Trained rather than Veteran.

If you do this, the number of points available to spend on a First Army Rifle Company or Recce Squadron increases as follows:

Normal Force	First Army Force
1000 points	1300 points
1500 points	1950 points
2000 points	2600 points

In addition:

- Platoons may not be equipped with Sticky Bombs.
- Commando Platoons cost 300 points per platoon, but remain Veteran.
- Tank Platoons must be equipped with Churchill or Sherman tanks. Those equipped with Churchill tanks cost an extra +110 points per platoon, while those equipped with Sherman III tanks cost an extra +105 points per platoon
- Mine Flail Platoons cost an extra +20 points per mine flail tank.

First Army Rifle Companies may also be Scots or Irish Rifle Companies.

BRITISH

IRISH REGIMENTS

Conscription was never introduced into Northern Ireland and Britain couldn't conscript Irishmen from the Irish Free State (Eire)—so the Irish regiments were largely volunteers from all over Ireland.

As well as having the strong esprit de corps typical of volunteer units, the 'Fighting Irish' loved a good brawl. This fighting spirit quickly gained them a reputation as close-in fighters.

You may field an Irish Rifle Company. If you do, your Company HQ and all of your Combat and Weapons Platoons are Irish Platoons.

Fighting Irish

The Irish love a good fight and don't take the enemy's attempts to hold them at bay well. No matter how heavy the fire, the Irish will follow their motto '*Faugh a Ballagh*' (Clear the Way) and find a way to get into the fight.

Irish Platoons do not use the British bulldog special rule. Instead, any Irish Platoon that is Pinned Down may re-roll failed Motivation tests to rally from being Pinned Down.

GUARDS REGIMENTS

The five Regiments of Foot Guards are the most prestigious infantry units in the British Army. Their standards are very high in all respects. Their most outstanding quality on the field of battle is their steadiness.

You may field a Guards Rifle Company. If you do, your Company HQ and all of your Combat and Weapons Platoons are Guards Platoons at an additional cost of +25 points per platoon.

Unflappable

When all around them are in a 'flap', the Guards will still be following orders immaculately.

Guards Platoons fight to the last and may re-roll any failed Platoon Morale Checks. If you are fielding a Guards Rifle Company, your Company Command team may re-roll Company Morale Checks.

THE DEATH OR GLORY BOYS

26TH ARMOURED BRIGADE

Britain also sent an armoured division to fight in Tunisia under the British First Army. This was the 6th Armoured Division equipped with a unique mixture of Valentine and Crusader tanks. Its three armoured regiments were the 16th/5th Lancers, the 17th/21st Lancers, and the 2nd Lothian and Border Horse. The lancers were both old regiments with illustrious histories. The 16th/5th were an amalgamation of the old 16th Lancers and the newer (and therefore less senior and listed second) 5th Lancers. Likewise, the 17th/21st Lancers were an amalgamation of the old 17th and 21st Lancers. The Lothian and Border Horse, on the other hand, were a yeomanry regiment that only dated back to just before the turn of the century.

The cap badge of the 17th/21st Lancers embodies the cavalry spirit of these regiments. It shows a skull and cross bones with the motto 'Or Glory' underneath. They have earned their nickname 'The Death or Glory Boys' many times over. Perhaps their most famous exploit was to lead the Charge of the Light Brigade at Balaklava during the Crimean War.

The 6th Armoured Division began landing in North Africa in November 1942. Blade Force, based around 17th/21st Lancers, raced ahead to seize Tunis. They came close to taking their goal, but were forced back by strong German counterattacks. In February 1943, the 6th Armoured Division rushed south to stop the German breakthrough at Kasserine Pass. Here they gallantly pitted their Valentines and Crusaders against more powerful German Panzer IV and Tiger tanks.

In March 1943, the armoured regiments re-equipped with Sherman III tanks. Then they joined the armoured divisions of the Eighth Army for the final drive on Tunis.

FIELDING A DEATH OR GLORY FORCE

When the 6th Armoured Division first arrived in Tunisia, it had spent years in training, but had no actual combat experience. To reflect this, all platoons (including infantry, guns and armoured cars) in a force containing Armoured Platoons from a Death or Glory Squadron are rated as **Trained**, regardless of the ratings given elsewhere in the book.

In compensation, when forming a Death or Glory force the number of points available to a Death or Glory Squadron increases as follows

Normal Force	Death or Glory Squadron
1000 points	1300 points
1500 points	1950 points
2000 points	2600 points

You also have the following restrictions:

- No Light or Heavy Armoured Platoons.
- No Lorried Motor Platoons.
- Only Daimler I armoured cars and Daimler scout cars.
- No Assault Platoons.
- No 75mm Gun Platoons.
- No Deacons, no 17/25 pdr guns.
- No Mine Flail Platoons.
- No Priest Self-propelled guns.

17TH/21ST LANCERS

A regiment renowned for having taken part in the Charge of the Light Brigade and at Omdurman, the 17th/21st Lancers lived up to their reputation for cavalry élan in Tunisia. It was one of the first armoured units ashore in Operation Torch in 1942. Inexperienced, its obsolete Valentines and Crusaders nevertheless performed well against the panzers in the early fighting in Tunisia. With 26th Armoured Brigade, it fought with great determination at Thala, pitching their now 'tragically useless' Crusaders and Valentines against German Panzer IV Specials, being reduced down to twelve tanks. The regiment, re-equipped with Sherman III's, attacked the Fondouk gap in April 1943, living up their nickname of 'the Death or Glory Boys'. The regiment lost two squadrons to mines and anti-tank fire within an hour of fighting, but with help from the 16th/5th Lancers and the 10th (London) Rifle Brigade, managed to overcome the opposition and clear the way for the advance. At Djebel Kournine the regiment, working closely with 12th (Honourable Artillery Company) Royal Horse Artillery, destroyed a panzer unit with little loss, and the regiment led the way in the final advance on Tunis. The regiment then fought in Italy, garnering further laurels to its already glorious reputation.

DEATH OR GLORY SQUADRON

(TANK COMPANY)

A force based around a Death or Glory Squadron must contain:

- a Company HQ,
- one to three Valentine Armoured Platoons, and
- up to two Crusader Armoured Platoons.

Support Platoons for a Death or Glory Squadron can be:

- Motor Platoons,
- Scout Patrols,
- Armoured Car Platoons, and
- Divisional Support Platoons,

You may have up to **one** Support Platoon attached to your company for each Armoured Platoon that you are fielding.

Motivation and Skill

The men of the 26th Armoured Brigade have spent years training for battle, but still lack practical experience. Death or Glory Squadrons are rated as **Confident Trained**.

HEADQUARTERS

1 Company HQ

Headquarters	
Company HQ with:	
2 Valentine III	**155 points**
• Add up to two Crusader II CS tanks for +70 points per tank.	
3 Grant (Lee turret)	**360 points**

There are no Valentine CS tanks, so your Company HQ uses Crusader CS tanks instead.

The Company HQ and Armoured Platoons of a Death or Glory Boys Squadron are organised like those of a normal Light Armoured Squadron (see pages 97).

In early 1943 26th Armoured Brigade acquired a small number of M3 Lee tanks from the US 1st Armoured Division (Old Ironsides).

COMBAT PLATOONS

1 to 3 Valentine Armoured Platoons

Platoon	
3 Valentine III	**225 points**
You must have at least as many Valentine platoons as Crusader platoons in your force.	

Although the Valentine was originally designed as an infantry support tank, the lack of other tanks has put it in the cruiser tank role. Here its thick armour compensates for its lack of speed.

You may not have a total of more than four Valentine and Crusader Armoured Platoons in a squadron.

1 to 2 Crusader Armoured Platoons

Platoon	
3 Crusader III	**205 points**

The 6 pdr-armed Crusader tanks give the Death or Glory Boys a decent punch against enemy tanks. Their big weakness is their light armour, so use cover and speed to protect them.

MIXED SQUADRON ORGANISATION

The 6th Armoured Division arrived in Tunisia with mixed squadrons of Valentine and Crusader tanks. This unusual arrangement came about when the Valentine-equipped regiments were offered the new Crusader III tanks armed with 6 pdr guns. The regiments preferred the Valentines because of their thicker armour, so rather than totally re-equipping with the light Crusaders, they used the Crusader tanks as heavy gun tanks making up one or two platoons in each squadron.

After fighting at Kasserine Pass the regiments re-equipped with new American Sherman III tanks, much to the disgust of American tankers still using the older M3 Lee. Once re-equipped the 6th Armoured Division used the normal Heavy Armoured Squadron organisation shown on page 96.

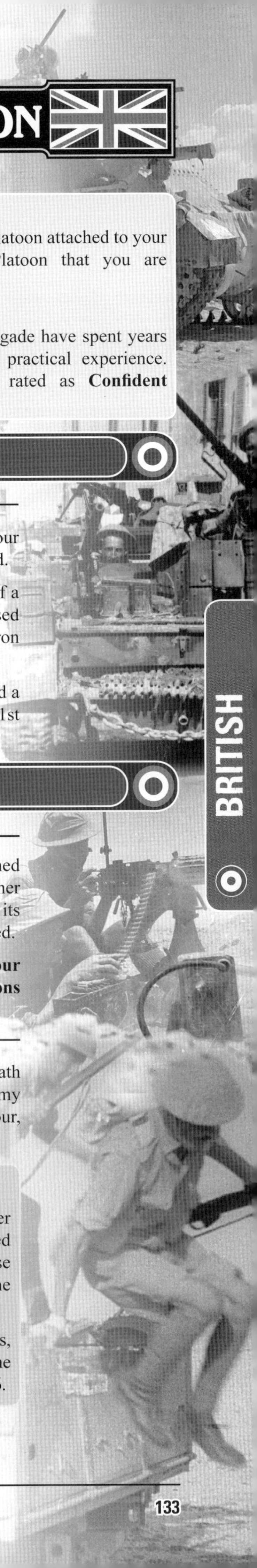

AUSTRALIAN ARMY

Australia responded to Britain's declaration of war on Germany by promising five new divisions for Imperial service. As the first Australian Imperial Force also had five divisions, the five new divisions in the second AIF were numbered 6th to 9th and 1st Armoured.

The first into battle was the 6th Australian Division, who destroyed the Italian Army in Libya in 1940, then fought in Greece. The 7th Australian Division then fought briefly against the French in Syria, before both divisions were recalled to defend Australia from the Japanese.

It was the 9th Australian Division that would earn everlasting fame. Not only halting Rommel's first offensive in 1941 and holding Tobruk for six months against the Afrikakorps, but then halting his second major offensive and saving the day at El Alamein in 1942.

9TH AUSTRALIAN DIVISION IN THE DESERT

9th Australian Division — **First and Second Alamein**

20 Infantry Brigade	24 Infantry Brigade	26 Infantry Brigade	
2/13th Battalion	2/28th Battalion	2/23rd Battalion	2/2nd (MG) Battalion
2/15th Battalion	2/32nd Battalion	2/24th Battalion	2/3rd Pioneer Battalion
2/17th Battalion	2/43rd Battalion	2/48th Battalion	9th Divisional Cavalry

The '2/' in front of each battalion's number indicates that these are the second incarnation of these battalions, the originals having served with the AIF in the First World War.

AUSTRALIAN BATTALIONS

By the start of 1942, the Australians had established an enviable record in the Western Desert, so when they were called to the front to stop the German *Afrikakorps* at El Alamein, they were very confident of their ability to do so. Their victories there did nothing but increase their morale even further.

As the only complete experienced division in the field, and with plenty of replacements waiting in the Nile Delta, the Australian General, 'Ming the Merciless' Morshead, was as willing as his men to fight hard and keep fighting until they won, regardless of cost.

You may field an Australian Rifle Company or Divisional Cavalry Squadron. If you do, all of your platoons (including supporting platoons) become Australian Platoons and their Motivation rating changes to **Fearless** rather than Confident. However, to reflect this, the number of points available to spend on your force decreases as follows:

Normal Force	Australian Force
1000 points	835 points
1500 points	1250 points
2000 points	1670 points

In addition:

- You may not equip any platoons with PIAT anti-tank launchers.
- You may not take Commando, or Recce Platoons as part of your force.
- You may take one Machine-gun Platoon as a Weapons Platoon choice as well as those taken as Support choices.
- Heavy Mortar Platoons are not Australian Platoons and remain Confident, but decrease in cost by -20 points per Mortar Section.
- Anti-tank Platoons may not be equipped with 17/25 pdr guns.
- Tank Platoons are not Australian Platoons and remain Confident. They must be equipped entirely with Valentine II tanks, but decrease in cost to 125 points per platoon.
- Mine Flail Platoons are not Australian Platoons and remain Confident, but decrease in cost by -10 points per mine flail tank.
- Field Artillery Batteries may not be equipped with Bishop or Priest self-propelled guns.
- You may take Light Tank and Carrier Platoons from a Divisional Cavalry Squadron as support choices for an Australian Rifle Company.
- You may not have more than one Light Tank Platoon equipped with Stuart tanks.

Disorderly Conduct

Australian soldiers have a strong disrespect for authority. They'll do what they are told if it makes sense to them, but if not, they'll do their own thing instead. In one famous incident a Private greeted a Colonel with "How's it going Bill?" much to the surprise of British officers present. It turned out that the Private had been the Colonel's boss before the war!

One benefit of this was that when officers became casualties, there was usually someone able to take over the leadership.

Australian Platoons do not use the British Bulldog special rule. Instead, they use the German Mission Tactics special rule.

DIVISIONAL CAVALRY SQUADRON

(TANK COMPANY)

Unlike the British divisions which had a recce regiment, the Australian and New Zealand divisions had a divisional cavalry regiment as their reconnaissance force. The 'Div Cav' operated a mixture of light tanks and reconnaissance carriers in the desert. They were lightly equipped, so they avoided combat where they could, gathering information by stealth and guile rather than force.

A force based around a Divisional Cavalry Squadron must contain:

- a Company HQ,
- one or two Light Tank Platoons, and
- two to four Carrier Platoons.

Support Platoons for a Divisional Cavalry Squadron can be:

- Rifle Platoons, and
- Divisional Support Platoons.

You may have up to **two** Support Platoons attached to your company for each Light Tank Platoon that you field.

Motivation and Skill—Australian

An Australian Divisional Cavalry Squadron is rated as **Fearless Veteran**, but has the benefits and restrictions on Australian Battalions from the previous page, including reduced points available.

Motivation and Skill—New Zealand

A New Zealand Divisional Cavalry Squadron is rated as **Confident Veteran**, but costs an additional +20 points per platoon and has all of the benefits and restrictions on New Zealand Battalions shown on page 136.

HEADQUARTERS

1 Company HQ

Headquarters	
2 'Honey' Stuart	125 points
2 Crusader II	135 points

Options

- Arm any or all 'Honey' Stuarts with an AA MG for +5 points per tank.
- Add Universal Carriers for +30 points per carrier.
- Arm any or all Universal Carriers with an extra hull-mounted MG for +5 points per carrier or 0.5" MG for +10 points per carrier.

The Divisional Cavalry spearhead assaults and lead pursuits against the defeated enemy. In static battles, they guard the division's HQ.

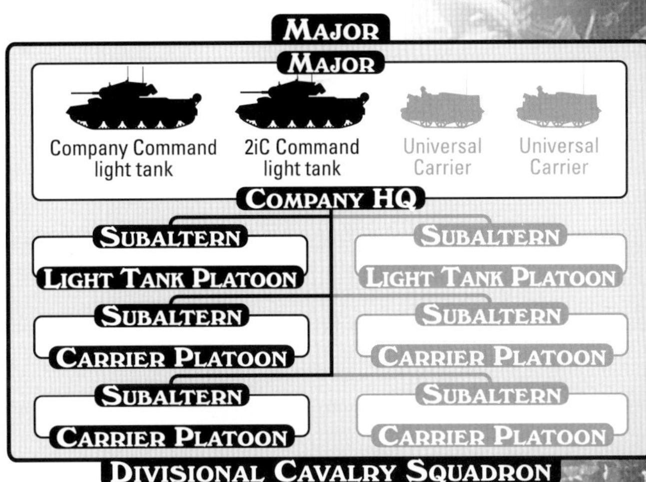

BRITISH

COMBAT PLATOONS

1 or 2 Light Tank Platoons

Platoon	
3 'Honey' Stuart	190 points
3 Crusader II	200 points

Option

- Arm any or all 'Honey' Stuarts with an AA MG for +5 points per tank.

Every Div Cav Squadron was allocated two platoons of light tanks organised like the Light Armoured Platoon on page 107.

They provide heavier firepower to back up the carriers. The New Zealanders fielded the small and fast Stuart, while the Australians preferred the larger British-built Crusader II, but had a few Stuarts as well.

1 to 4 Carrier Platoons

The Carrier Platoons of the Divisional Cavalry are organised like the Scout Patrols on page 110.

Carrier Platoons are Reconnaissance Platoons.
You must field at least one Carrier Platoon for every Light tank Platoon that you field.

New Zealand Army

When New Zealand went to war alongside Britain, it raised its Second New Zealand Expeditionary Force (2 NZEF). The first NZEF had served with distinction in Gallipoli and with the ANZAC Corps in France in the First World War. The new division became the 2nd New Zealand Division and the battalions were numbered 18 to 28 following on from those of the territorial divisions defending New Zealand.

The New Zealand Division's first taste of battle was in Greece in April 1941 where they took part in the evacuation of the country after the ill-fated British intervention. The evacuation left the majority of the Division on the island of Crete. There, short of weapons, communications, and even shovels, they faced the German airborne invasion. Despite some hard fought battles, early mistakes doomed the defence and once more the New Zealand Division fled by sea, this time to Egypt.

After rebuilding, the New Zealand Division went into battle once more. In the disorganised chaos of Operation Crusader in December 1941, the British relief of Tobruk, the New Zealand Division occupied the vital Sidi Rezegh airfield. Then cut off and surrounded, they broke through to the Tobruk garrison. The cost was enormous, but Rommel was forced to retreat for the first time.

When Rommel struck again at Gazala, the New Zealand Division was still rebuilding in Syria. It raced forward to Mersa Matruh, taking up positions at Minqar Qaim on the southern flank on 24 June, 1942. When Rommel attacked, chaos ruled once more with conflicting orders from the British Generals and lack of support from the armour. The three divisions holding the position were surrounded and lost heavily as they broke out to the Alamein position a hundred miles to the rear.

In the confused fighting of the First Battle of El Alamein, the New Zealand Division destroyed much of the Italian *Ariete* Division's artillery in one attack, but lost a brigade to the German *Afrikakorps* when British armour failed to support their attack on Ruweisat Ridge on 15 July. Their distrust of British armour grew to outright disgust when the same thing happened at El Mreir barely a week later.

Fortunately for the division, now down to one brigade, the battle petered out as both sides were exhausted. By the time Rommel attacked again at Alam Halfa at the end of August, the Division was back up to two brigades. When Rommel retreated, the New Zealand Division attacked to cut him off, but lacked the strength to halt two full armoured corps on its own.

From then on, under the new British commander, General Montgomery, the fortunes of the New Zealand Division looked up. The Division received its own armoured brigade, and made the breakout in the Second Battle of Alamein. It pursued Rommel the breadth of Libya in a series of battles, then outflanked his main defensive line at Mareth, before closing in for the kill in Tunisia. The Division went on to Italy at the end of 1943, and fought there until it was victorious.

2nd New Zealand Division in the Desert, Tunisia, and Italy

2nd New Zealand Division — **Alamein, Alam Halfa, Tunisia, and Italy**

4 Infantry Brigade[1]	5 Infantry Brigade	6 Infantry Brigade	
18th Battalion	21st Battalion	24th Battalion	27th (MG) Battalion
19th Battalion	22nd Battalion	25th Battalion	28th (Maori) Battalion
20th Battalion	23rd Battalion	26th Battalion	Divisional Cavalry Regiment[2]

4 Light Armoured Brigade[3]	8 Armoured Brigade[4]	9 Armoured Brigade[5]
The Royal Scots Greys	3rd Royal Tank Regiment	3rd King's Own Hussars
1st The King's Dragoon Guards*	The Nottinghamshire Yeomanry	The Royal Wiltshire Yeomanry
11th Hussars (Prince Albert's Own)*	The Staffordshire Yeomanry	The Warwickshire Yeomanry
2nd Bn, KRRC**		14th Bn, The Sherwood Foresters**

* Armoured Car Regiment.

** Motor Battalion.

1 Destroyed at Ruweisat Ridge and rebuilt as an Armoured Brigade for the Italian campaign.

2 Not present in Italy until the very end of 1943 as re-equipping with Staghound armoured cars.

3 Attached during advance into Tunisia.

4 Attached for Tunisian battles.

5 Attached for the Battle of Alamein.

NEW ZEALAND BATTALIONS

By 1942, the New Zealand Division lacked the dash of their Australian counterparts. It had lost most of a brigade at Crete and another at Sidi Rezegh in 1941, and was to lose the best parts of two more at Ruweisat Ridge and El Mreir in 1942. Bearing in mind that the division only ever had three brigades, their battle experience was hard-won and their enthusiasm slightly dampened. However, despite the setbacks, the division remained one of the most experienced and effective divisions in the Eighth Army.

You may field a New Zealand Rifle Company or Divisional Cavalry Squadron. If you do, all of its platoons (including supporting platoons) become New Zealand Platoons at an additional cost of +20 points per platoon or Carrier Patrol.

In addition:

- You may not take Commando or Recce Platoons as part of your force.
- Heavy Mortar and Mine Flail Platoons are not New Zealand Platoons.
- Field Artillery Batteries may not be equipped with Bishop or Priest self-propelled guns.
- You may take Light Tank and Carrier Platoons from a Divisional Cavalry Squadron as support choices.
- You may take Light or Heavy Armoured Platoons. They may not be equipped with 'Honey' Stuart tanks and are British Platoons, or instead you may take Tank Platoons equipped with Sherman III tanks as New Zealand Platoons. You may not take any other Tank Platoons.

4 by 2 and No. 8 Wire

New Zealand is a small remote country and its soldiers had to learn to make do or do without while they were growing up. As they say in New Zealand, they could make anything with a bit of 4 by 2 timber and some No. 8 fencing wire! This independence carried over to their military operations. Everyone was told the plan before each attack, and if an officer was killed, there'd always be someone to work out what to do now.

New Zealand Platoons use the German Mission Tactics special rule

28TH MAORI BATTALION

When the war began the Maori (indigenous population) of New Zealand asked to be allowed to form their own battalion. This was formed with regional companies. A Company was from the Far North and gained the nickname Nga Kiri Kapia (nah kee-rree kah-pee-ah), 'the Gumdiggers'. B Company came from the central North Island (famous for the Rotorua Lakes, a tourist destination) and was known as Nga Rukukapa (nah rruh-kuh-kah-pah), 'the Penny Divers'. C Company from the East Coast became Nga Kaupoi (nah kow-poy), 'the Cowboys'. D Company came from a mixture of South Island tribes and was called 'Ngati Walkabout'.

The Maori Battalion was an extra battalion in the New Zealand Division, not part of any brigade, and tended to be assigned where it was most needed. The Battalion is most famous for its many daring assaults and its rather casual attitude to weapons and equipment acquired from the enemy. At one point members of the Maori Battalion were seen racing around the rear areas with a German staff car and an '88' and its tractor!

You may field a Maori Rifle Platoon as the additional Rifle Platoon in a New Zealand Rifle Company, or a full Maori Rifle Company.

If you field a full Maori Rifle Company, your Company HQ and all of your Combat Platoons are Maori Platoons.

Maori Platoons are New Zealand Platoons with all of the special rules applying to New Zealand Platoons above plus the following special rules for the same cost of +20 points per platoon or Carrier Patrol.

The Maori were brave and daring soldiers, however their eagerness for battle often overtook the caution of their training. Maori Platoons are rated as **Fearless Trained** instead of the usual Confident Veteran, and must make a Breakthrough Assault if they are able to.

Haka

The Maori often performed a haka or war dance within earshot of the enemy before launching an attack. This, combined with their fearsome reputation, would have their foes quaking in their boots. Maori soldiers frequently swapped their issue rifles for German submachine-guns and any other automatic they could find. To their way of thinking the old bolt-action Lee Enfield didn't make enough noise, and the more noise the better when launching a charge!

Any platoon that is attempting to fire Defensive Fire against a Maori Platoon must take a Motivation test before doing so.

- If they pass the Motivation Test, they conduct Defensive Fire as normal.
- If they fail, the soldiers quail in fear and must re-roll all successful rolls to hit from the Defensive Fire assigned to Infantry teams.

Canadian Army

Canadian soldiers established an outstanding record in the First World War where the Canadian Corps was used as an elite assault unit. When the Second World War began, thousands volunteered for a new Canadian Corps.

By the middle of 1942, three Canadian Infantry Divisions, a Canadian Armoured Division, and a Canadian Army Tank Brigade were all training in Britain. The 2nd Canadian Infantry Division conducted the one-day raid on the port of Dieppe in August 1942, suffering heavy losses before returning to training.

It wasn't until July 1943 in the Sicily landings that the Canadians finally reached the main battlefields. 1st Canadian Infantry Division landed in the first wave and went on to fight throughout the rest of the campaign with the support of the Sherman tanks of the 1st Canadian Armoured Brigade. The Canadians then transferred to the eastern coast of Italy where they fought a bloody Christmas battle at Ortona.

The Canadians fought on throughout 1944 and 1945. Their contribution to Allied victory in Europe enhanced the reputation of the Canadian soldier even further.

1st Canadian Infantry Division in Sicily and Italy

1st Canadian Infantry Division — **Sicily and Italy**

1 Infantry Brigade	2 Infantry Brigade	3 Infantry Brigade	1 Armoured Brigade	
The Royal Canadian Regiment	Princess Patricia's Canadian Light Infantry	Le Royal 22e Regiment	11th Canadian Armd Regt (The Ontario Regiment)	Saskatoon Light Infantry (MG)
The Hastings and Prince Edward Regiment	The Seaforth Highlanders of Canada	The Carleton and York Regiment	12th Canadian Armd Regt (The Three Rivers Regiment)	4th Canadian Recce Regt
The 48th Highlanders of Canada	The Loyal Edmonton Regiment	The West Nova Scotia Regiment	14th Canadian Armd Regt (The Calgary Regiment)	(4th Princess Louise Dragoon Guards)

Canadian Battalions

The Canadians were well-trained, but lacking in experience when they landed in Sicily. To reflect this the Skill rating of Canadian Rifle Companies and Recce Squadrons and their supporting troops is **Trained** rather than Veteran. The number of points available to spend on a Canadian force increases as follows:

Normal Force	Canadian Force
1000 points	1175 points
1500 points	1760 points
2000 points	2350 points

In addition:

- You may not use Anti-tank Rifle teams or Sticky Bombs.
- Commando Platoons cost 300 points per platoon, but remain Veteran.
- Tank Platoons must be equipped entirely with Churchill or Sherman tanks. Those equipped with Churchill tanks cost an extra +65 points per platoon. Those equipped with Sherman tanks must replace their Sherman III tanks with Sherman V tanks at a cost of an extra +60 points per platoon.
- Mine Flail Platoons cost an extra +20 points per mine flail tank.

Assault Troops

The Canadians have maintained their enviable reputation as aggressive assault troops.

Canadian Platoons do not use the British Bulldog special rule. Instead any Canadian Platoon that is Pinned Down may re-roll failed Motivation tests to rally from being Pinned Down.

Woodsmen

Although Canada has been settled for centuries, it was not until the Nineteenth Century that its population underwent significant growth and it remains a largely rural country.

Canadian Platoons use the German Mission Tactics special rule.

Canadian Army Equipment

Otter I Light Recce Cars

One of the light armoured vehicles produced for the Canadian army was the Otter I LRC. The Otter was Canada's answer to the Humber III LRC. Of a similar design, it was based on a Ford 15 cwt truck chassis rather than a Humber Snipe car.

A Canadian Recce Squadron replaces all Humber III LRC recce cars with Otter I LRC recce cars at no cost.

Indian Army

The Indian Army is a separate entity from the British Army. It has its own officers, ranks, and traditions dating back to the days of 'John Company', the Honourable East India Company, a British company that grew to dominate the Indian subcontinent. Within one hundred years of its creation in the early 1600's, the John Company already had its own army and in the 1740's fought several wars with French troops.

By 1857, the John Company controlled much of India, either directly or through puppet rulers. However, in this year dissatisfaction with British rule boiled over into open war with the Indian Mutiny. In the wake of the Mutiny, Queen Victoria dissolved the Honourable East India Company and assumed direct rule over India. The Company's armed forces became the Indian Army. Although prior to the Mutiny recruiting had been widespread across India's many cultural, religious and ethnic population, the new Indian Army restricted recruiting to groups seen as 'martial races' (and more importantly reliably loyal to the Crown).

The Indian Army provided troops for many of the Empire's colonial wars, acquitting itself well in the process. The best graduates from the Royal Military Academy at Sandhurst vied for positions in the Indian Army where pay was higher and battle more likely.

The Indian Army made a massive contribution in the First World War with over a million men in arms and 115 battalions serving overseas, fighting in every theatre of that war from France to Gallipoli, Palestine, and Persia.

In the Second World War, the Indian contribution was even greater with nearly two million soldiers in arms. 4th and 5th Indian Divisions defeated the Italians in the Western Desert and Somalia in 1940, then fought in Syria, Iran, and Iraq. They returned to the desert in 1942, joining 10th Indian Division as Rommel launched his attack on the Gazala Line. There, abysmal British generalship saw brigade after brigade overrun as they faced Rommel's entire *Afrikakorps* one at a time.

Under General Montgomery, 4th Indian Division went on to win acclaim at Alamein and in the Tunisian Campaign before handing the torch to 8th Indian Division for the battles in Italy.

BRITISH

Indian Regiments

A *jawan*, or soldier, is recruited from the so-called 'martial races', chosen because of their loyalty and military qualities. Soldiering is an honourable profession in India and there is never any shortage of volunteers. Most are recruited from the Punjab and noted for their personal honour and strong faith.

Indian Army soldiers have no particular hatred of their enemies, and they aren't fighting for democracy or any other ideology. What motivates them is pride in their regiment, their sense of honour as professional soldiers, a *jawan* who abandons his post or his weapon or turns his back on the enemy is shunned for life as a *bhagoda* or coward, and the unquestioning trust between the men and their officers.

When added to the extensive training of Indian soldiers (they had to learn many new things to fight in a foreign war against modern technology, but this also meant more practical training too) and considerable combat experience on the North-west Frontier between the wars, Indian soldiers have earned a reputation for being tough, reliable soldiers in campaigns in North Africa, Syria and Eritrea.

You may field an Indian Rifle Platoon as the additional Rifle Platoon in a standard British Rifle Company, or you may field a full Indian Rifle Company or Recce Squadron.

If you field a full Indian company, your Company HQ and all of your Combat and Weapons Platoons are Indian Platoons. Your Machine-gun Platoons may also be Indian Platoons if you wish.

Although Indian soldiers are brave and well trained. Indian Platoons are rated as **Fearless Trained** instead of the usual Confident Veteran.

If you field an Indian company, there are several other restrictions.

- Instead of additional Indian Rifle Platoons, you may field additional British Rifle Platoons.
- If you are fielding an Indian Recce Squadron, you may not have an Assault Platoon.
- You may not field Commando Platoons.

GURKHA REGIMENTS

The Gurkhas of Nepal have a superb reputation as first-class fighting men. They are recruited from hardy hill tribes in the Himalayan mountains. Their ferociousness using their heavy-bladed *khukuri* knives in close combat is legendary. So to is their determination not to abandon their weapon while still alive.

You may field a Gurkha Rifle Platoon as the additional Rifle Platoon in a standard British or Indian Rifle Company, or you may field a full Gurkha Rifle Company.

If you field a full Gurkha Rifle Company, your Company HQ and all of your Combat and Weapons Platoons are Gurkha Platoons. Your Machine-gun Platoons may be either British or Indian Platoons.

Gurkha Platoons are Indian Platoons with addition of the Khukuri special rule for +20 points per platoon or Carrier Patrol.

Khukuri

Every Gurkha carries a heavy-bladed recurved knife called a *khukuri*. They use this for everything from cutting food and wood to chopping off the heads of their foes.

> Gurkha Platoons re-roll failed To Hit rolls in assault combat against Infantry, Gun, or Transport teams.

INDIAN ARMY SPECIAL RULES

Indian Platoons do not use the British Bulldog special rule Instead they have two special rules of their own.

War Cry

Indian soldiers always charge shouting war cries to gain the blessings of the gods and intimidate their enemies. Weak-hearted foes hearing this fearsome cry will flee before a shot is fired.

> Any platoon that is attempting to fire Defensive Fire against an Indian Platoon must take a Motivation Test before doing so.
>
> - If they pass the Motivation test, they conduct Defensive Fire as normal.
> - If they fail, the soldiers quail in fear and must re-roll all successful rolls to hit from the Defensive Fire assigned to Infantry teams.

North-west Frontier

The Indian Army fought continuous wars against rebellious Pathan tribes on the famous (and mountainous) North-west Frontier. At the same time they fought the Naga tribes of the equally mountainous (but less well-known) North-east Frontier. As a result they were specialists at mountain warfare.

> All Indian Infantry and Man-packed Gun teams are Mountaineers.

INDIAN ARMY EQUIPMENT

Indian Pattern Carriers

India lacked a heavy vehicle industry, so when called upon to provide carriers for their infantry, they adopted a wheeled version known appropriately enough as the Indian Pattern Carrier.

> An Indian Rifle Company or Recce Squadron replaces all Universal Carriers with Indian Pattern Carriers, and all Troop, MMG, and OP Carriers with Indian Pattern Troop Carriers at no cost.
>
> Indian Recce Platoons also replace their Humber III LRC recce cars with Indian Pattern Carriers at no cost.

Blacker Bombards

The Indian Army was always short of equipment, especially anti-tank weapons. When a shipment of Blacker Bombards (a spigot mortar like a huge PIAT) turned up at Cairo, they were happy to grab them. Despite their cumbersome nature, the Indians were very impressed with their destructive capability and longed for a chance to try them out against German Panzers.

> An Indian Rifle Company may add up to two Blacker Bombards to the Company HQ for +25 points each.

INDIAN DIVISIONS IN THE MEDITERRANEAN

4th Indian Division 'Red Eagles' — Benghazi, Second Alamein, Tunisia

5 Indian Brigade[1]	**7 Indian Brigade**	**161 Indian Brigade**[1, 2]	
1/4 Essex 4th (Outram's) Bn, 6th Rajputana Rifles 3rd Bn, 10th Baluch[3] 1st Bn, 9th Gurkha Rifles[4]	*1 R Sussex* 4th Bn, 16th Punjab* 1st Bn, 2nd King Edward VII's Own Goorkha Rifles (Simoor Rifles)	*1 A & SH*[3] 1st Bn, 1st Punjab 1st Bn, 2nd Punjab[4] 3rd (DCO) Bn, 7th Rajput[4] 4th Bn, 7th Rajput[3]	5th (Napier's) Bn, 6th Rajputana Rifles (MG) The Central India Horse (21st King George V's Own Horse)[2]

5th Indian Division 'Ball of Fire' — Gazala, First Alamein

9 Indian Brigade	**10 Indian Brigade**[5]	**11 Indian Brigade**[7]	**29 Indian Brigade**
2 W Yorks 3rd Bn, 9th Jats[5] 3rd Royal Bn, 12th Frontier Force*[5] 3rd Bn, 14th Punjab*[6]	*1 DCLI*[5] *2 HLI* 4th (DCO) Bn, 10th Baluch[5] 2nd Bn, 4th Prince of Wales's Own Gurkha Rifles[5]	*2 Camerons* 2nd , 5th Mahratta Light Infantry 2nd Bn, 7th Gurkha	*1 Worc R*[5] *2 HLI*[6] 3rd Bn, 2nd Punjab* 1st Bn, 5th Mahratta Light Infantry

8th Indian Division — Italy

17 Indian Brigade	**19 Indian Brigade**	**21 Indian Brigade**	
1 RF 1st (Prince Of Wales's Own) Bn, 12th Frontier Force* 1st Bn, 5th Royal Gurkha Rifles (Frontier Force)	*1/5 Essex* 3rd Bn, 8th Punjab 6th Royal (Scinde) Bn, 13th Frontier Force Rifles*	*5 RWK* 1st Bn, 5th Mahratta Light Infantry 3rd Bn, 15th Punjab*	5 Royal/5th Mahratta Light Infantry (MG) 6th Duke Of Connaught's Own Lancers (Watson's Horse)**

10th Indian Division[7] — Tobruk

20 Indian Brigade	**21 Indian Brigade**	**25 Indian Brigade**	
1 SWB 1st (Wellesley's) Bn, 6th Rajputana Rifles 3rd B n, 18th Royal Garhwal Rifles	*1 DCLI* 4th (Wilde's) Bn, 13th Frontier Force Rifles* 2nd Bn, 4th Prince of Wales's Own Gurkha Rifles	*1 King's Own* 2nd Bn, 5th Mahratta Light Infantry 2nd (Ludhiana) Bn, 11th Sikh*	*1 NF (MG)* The Guides Cavalry (10th Queen Victoria's Own Frontier Force)

3 Indian Motor Brigade[5]	**18 Indian Brigade**[8]
2nd Royal Lancers (Gardner's Horse)** Prince Albert Victor's Own Cavalry (11th Frontier Force)** 18th King Edward VII's Own Cavalry**	*2/5 Essex* 2nd Bn, 3rd Queen Alexandra's Own Gurkha Rifles 4th Bn, 11th Sikh*

* Sikh or partly Sikh regiments.
** Recce Regiment
[1] Loaned to 4th Indian Division for First Alamein and Alam Halfa.
[2] Withdrawn after El Alamein.
[3] Added after Alam Halfa.
[4] Removed after Alam Halfa.
[5] Lost at Gazala.
[6] Added after Gazala.
[7] Lost at Tobruk and Mersa Matruh.
[8] Lost at First Alamein.
Italics indicate British Army regiments

BRITISH

INDIAN ARMY TERMINOLOGY

Allah Ho Akbar (ahl-lah ho ak-bar): God is great. Punjabi war cry.
Ayo Gurkhali (ai-oh goor-kha-lee): The Gurkhas are here. Gurkha war cry.
Badri Vishal Lal Ki Jai (bah-drree vish-ahl lahl kee jay): Victory to the great Lord Badri Nath (avatar of Vishnu, god of protection and balance). Garhwali war cry.
Bhagoda (bah-go-da): Coward. One who abandons their post.
Bol Bajrang Bali Ki Jai (bohl bahj-rrang bah-lee kee jay): Cry victory to Lord Hanuman (monkey god, warrior and helper of Rama). Rajput war cry.
Bol Shri Chakrapati Shivaji Maharaj Ki Jai (bohl shree chak-rrah-pah-tee shee-vah-jee mah-hat-raj kee jay): Cry victory to Emperor Shivaji (ancient hero). Mahratti war cry.
Bole So Nihal Sat Siri Akal (bol-ey so nee-hal saht see-ree ahk-ahl): He who cries God is truth, is ever happy. Sikh war cry.
Daffidar (dah-fah-dhar): Indian cavalry sergeant.
Dushmen (dhush-mahn): Enemy.
Ghari (garr-ih): Truck or other vehicle.
Gurkha (goor-kha): Nepalese soldier. Modern spelling Gorkha.
Havildar (hav-ahl-dhar): Indian sergeant.
Hindi (hin-dee): National language of India.
Hindu (hin-doo): India's main religion.
Jai Ma Kali (jay mah kah-li): Hail mother Kali (goddess of strength and courage against evil). Gurkha battle prayer.
Jat (jat): Punjabi who is not a sardarji.
Jat Balwan, Jai Bhagwan (jat bahl-van jay bhag-van): Brave Jat, victory to God. Jat war cry.
Jawan (ja-van): Soldier.
Jemadar (jah-mah-dhar): VCO officer.
Johnny Gurkha: British nickname for Gurkha soldiers.
KCO: King's Commissioned Officer. 'British' officer (whether British or Indian).
Khukuri (khook-ur-ee): Broad-bladed Gurkha knife.
Naik (nai-ak): Indian corporal.
Opley (orp-lay): Cowpat: Brigade box.
Pugree (pah-grrih): Indian turban.
Rajput (rrej-put): Hindu sect renown as brave and honourable warriors from Rajastan.
Raja Ram Chandra Ki Jai (rraj-ah rram chand-rrah kee jay): Victory to king Ram Chandra (avatar of Vishnu). Rajput war cry.
Sahib (sah-hihb): Sir.
Sardarji (Sur-dar-jee): Respectful Indian name for a Sikh.
Sepoy (se-pah-hi): Indian soldier.
Shahbash (sheh-bahsh): Good work.
Sikh (seek): Turban-wearing Indian warrior sect.
Subedar (sue-beh-dhar): VCO junior officer.
Tikh hai (tee-kay): OK.
Urdu (urr-doo): Common language of the Indian Army. A version of Hindi from the Pakistan region with many Persian words.
VCO: Viceroy's Commissioned Officer. Indian officer.
Vijay Ya Virgati (vee-jay yah vir-gah-tee): Victory or death. Creed of Rajput.

SOUTH AFRICAN ARMY

South Africa found itself in a difficult position at the start of the war. The Union of South Africa was founded after the end of the Boer War (1899 to 1902). The new country combined the British Cape colonies with the recently conquered Boer (Afrikaans) Transvaal and Orange Free State. Since Germany had helped the Boers against the British, many Afrikaans felt more loyalty to them than Britain. As a result, South Africa fielded a relatively small volunteer army in the Second World War, keeping the dissenting soldiers in South Africa for home defence.

After a successful campaign against the Italians in East Africa in 1940 and 1941, the South African divisions were sent to Libya to face Rommel. Here they met with disaster after disaster.

Most of the problem can be blamed on poor British generalship. In November 1941, the 1st South African Division fought in Operation Crusader. The British plan had brigades being scattered all over the desert and a South African Brigade was overrun by the German 15th Panzer Division and the Italian *Ariete* Division.

In the next major battle at Gazala, the 1st South African Division held the line closest to the coast. There, after launching diversionary attacks against the Italians, they were virtually abandoned by the British and barely escaped being cut off and surrounded. The 2nd South African Division which had been training in Tobruk suddenly found itself surrounded and ordered to hold the port at all costs. Its position was untenable and within days, the whole division was captured. By this time the South Africans were understandably concerned about the possibility of losing their entire army!

When Rommel reached El Alamein, the 1st South African Division was the only battleworthy formation still facing him. The division was once more entrenched in a 'box' on the coast. Rommel attempted to outflank the box and continue the advance as he had earlier at Mersa Matruh. This time however, the massed South African artillery stopped his elite 90th Light Africa Division dead, buying time for the Australian, Indian, New Zealand, and Northumbrian Divisions to extend the line southwards, halting Rommel for good.

The 1st South African Division had one more part to play before returning to South Africa to rebuild as an armoured division. In the Second Battle of Alamein, it formed the southern wing of the main attack on the German/Italian lines, helping to win this historic victory.

SOUTH AFRICAN BATTALIONS

The South Africans had plenty of experience, but little confidence in the British generals. This combined with the need to be cautious if the remains of their army weren't to be squandered resulted in them being reluctant to take unnecessary risks.

To reflect this the Motivation rating of South African Rifle Companies and their supporting troops is **Reluctant** rather than Confident. However, the number of points available to spend on a South African force increases as follows:

Normal Force	South African Force
1000 points	1200 points
1500 points	1800 points
2000 points	2400 points

In addition:

- Platoons may not have PIAT teams.
- Your force may not include Recce, or Commando Platoons.
- Anti-tank Platoons may not have 17/25 pdr guns.
- Tank Platoons must be equipped with Matilda or Valentine II tanks. Those equipped with Matilda tanks cost an extra +40 points, while those equipped with Valentine tanks cost an extra +30 points per platoon. They remain Confident Trained.
- Field Artillery Batteries may not be equipped with Priest self-propelled guns.
- Mine Flail Platoons cost an extra +15 points per mine flail tank.
- Your force may include Armoured Car Platoons equipped with Marmon Herrington armoured cars from an Armoured Car Squadron as Support choices.

SOUTH AFRICAN DIVISIONS IN THE DESERT

1st South African Division — **Gazala, First and Second Alamein**

1 Infantry Brigade	2 Infantry Brigade	3 Infantry Brigade	
1st Duke of Edinburgh's Own Regiment	1st Cape Town Highlanders	1st Imperial Light Horse	Regiment President Steyn (MG)
1st Royal Natal Carabiniers	1st Natal Mounted Rifles	1st Rand Light Infantry	2nd Regiment Botha
1st Transvaal Scottish	1st/2nd Field Force Battalion	1st Royal Durban Light Infantry	3rd South African Armoured Car Regiment[1]

2nd South African Division[2] — **Tobruk**

4th Infantry Brigade	6th Infantry Brigade	
2nd Royal Durbin Light Infantry	1st South African Police	De Middlandse Regiment (MG)
The Kaffrarian Rifles	2nd South African Police	7th South African Recce Regiment
The Umvoti Mounted Rifles	2nd Transvaal Scottish	

[1]Detached to Eighth Army.

[2]Destroyed in Tobruk

STARS&STRIPES

AMERICAN FORCES IN THE MEDITERRANEAN

"For you at home who think the African campaign was small stuff, let me tell you this one thing—the First Division did more fighting then than it did through all of World War I."
—War Correspondent Ernie Pyle.

The badge of the 1st Infantry Division was a large red '1' on a green background, giving the Division its nickname—'Big Red One'. The Division consisted of three infantry regiments, the 16th, 18th and 26th. The 16th and 18th Infantry Regiments had a long history having fought in the American Civil War, the Spanish American War, and the First World War. The history of the 26th Infantry Regiment was nearly as illustrious. It was formed in 1901 and had fought in the Philippines and in the First World War, where these regiments first came together as a permanent division.

When Germany invaded Poland in 1939 and sparked the Second World War, the 1st Infantry Division was undermanned and scattered across a variety of barracks. It was hurriedly brought up to strength along with the three other divisions then in existence (Germany had over a hundred divisions ready for battle!) The National Guard was called up for Federal service and new divisions were authorised as fast as troops could be trained to man them.

In 1942 the Division was sent to England, where it trained for the invasion of Europe. However, in November 1942, Big Red One was sent to North Africa instead.

OPERATION TORCH

Big Red One's first battle was an amphibious assault on Oran in Vichy French (pro-German) Algeria. The landing on 8 November 1942 making it the first US division to see combat in the European Theatre, living up to its reputation of 'the First was first'. Many French soldiers welcomed the US troops as liberators, while others fought back hard, especially at the town of St Cloud. The divisional commander, Major General 'Terrible' Terry de la Mesa Allen, a tough, aggressive soldier, ordered that 'Nothing in Hell must delay or stop 1st Division'. By 10 November Oran had fallen to Big Red One.

Fresh from their victory over the French, Big Red One moved east into Tunisia. There the division fought across the whole front with 18th Infantry Regiment clashing with the German 10th Panzer Division at Longstop Hill in the north over Christmas, the 16th and part of the 26th Infantry Regiment supporting the pro-Allied French in the Ousseltia Valley in the centre, and part of the 26th Infantry Regiment taking Gafsa in the south. Over the following five months, difficult terrain and skirmishes with veteran German troops taught Big Red One many lessons.

KASSERINE PASS

On Valentine's Day 1943 the German Field Marshall Rommel launched an attack against US forces at Kasserine Pass, throwing back the 1st 'Old Ironsides' Armored Division. Big Red One held the line with the survivors of Old Ironsides and a small British force, stopping the German offensive.

EL GUETTAR

In March 1943 Big Red One took the offensive, advancing through mountainous hills around El Guettar. Their old foes, the 10th Panzer Division, counterattacked, overrunning some artillery. The battle raged on the dusty El Guettar plain as the 18th Infantry Regiment and 601st Tank Destroyer Battalion eventually drove back the German attack. It was the first clear American victory in the campaign. The US Commander in the field, Major General George S. Patton Jr., wrote 'This has been a great day for the American Army. The 1st Div stopped the famous 10th Panzer cold in two attacks.'

BIZERTE

Big Red One launched another offensive in northern Tunisia in late April, using a deadly combination of devastating artillery barrages and sudden attacks to drive the enemy from fortified hill positions. It was tough fighting, but 1st Infantry Division proved itself again in the capture of the city of Bizerte. All Axis forces in North Africa surrendered days later. Big Red One had learned its lessons well.

OPERATION HUSKY

With North Africa free of Axis troops, the Allied governments decided that the next step would be to invade Sicily, the island off the toe of Italy, in Operation Husky. The invasion began in the early hours of 10 July 1943. Preceded by an airdrop of 82nd Airborne Division and a landing by Darby's Rangers, Big Red One hit the beach at Gela, at 0245 hours. Outnumbered and outgunned, the Italian troops manning the coastal defences quickly surrendered. Late in the morning the Italian *Livorno* Division attempted to drive the Americans back into the sea. The infantry's bazookas and fire from the supporting warships held off the attacks, securing the beachhead.

THE BATTLE FOR GELA

The next day *Livorno* attacked again, this time with more than sixty tanks of the *Hermann Göring* Panzer Division, including several massive Tiger heavy tanks. Big Red One was still landing their supporting tanks and artillery, and by mid-morning German tanks had overrun many of the forward companies getting within several hundred yards of the beach. Field guns were rushed ashore to fire at close range at the advancing panzers, while Sherman tanks went straight into combat as they landed. Offshore the cruisers USS Boise and USS Savannah opened fire. As darkness descended, the attacks petered out. The bridgehead still held.

LIBERATION OF PALERMO

Over the next few days the Allies went on the offensive. On 13 July, Big Red One began its advance across Sicily. Gibilscemi, Niscemi, and Barrafranca were taken after heavy fighting. Supported by the speedy M5 Stuart light tanks of the 70th Light Tank Battalion, they forged ahead. Whereever enemy resistance was hardest, the crushing power of Big Red One's artillery, followed by determined infantry assaults drove the enemy back. By 17 July the Division was in Enna, the vital road junction in the centre of Sicily.

From there resistance stiffened. It wasn't until 22 July that 45th 'Thunderbird' Infantry Division reached the northern shores of Sicily, cutting the island in half, and the main city of Sicily, Palermo, fell to 2nd 'Hell On Wheels' Armored Division and General Truscott's 3rd 'Marne' Infantry Division. It took nearly another week for Big Red One to take its next town with the Italian *Aosta* and *Assietta* Divisions refusing to give up Nicosia until 28 July.

THE BATTLE FOR TROINA

While the US Army struggled forward, the Germans and Italians were preparing a well-fortified defence line—the Etna Line—across the island's north-eastern corner from San Fratello on the north coast, through the town of Troina, past Mount Etna, and to Catania on the east coast. Troina, a hill town, was the central pillar of the Etna Line and its capture fell to Big Red One and the Marne Division. For seven days, the Americans launched attacks and fended off counterattacks from the German 15th *Panzergrenadier* Division and the Italian *Aosta* Division. Finally, on 6 August they entered Troina. The Etna line had been cracked.

VICTORY

The US commander, General George S. Patton was obsessed with the idea of reaching Messina before the British General Montgomery. 'This is a horse

race in which the prestige of the US Army is at stake,' Patton wrote. 'We must take Messina before the British.' Big Red One was exhausted after 28 days of continuous fighting, so the Marne and Thunderbird Divisions took the lead. On the morning of 17 August 1943, the 3rd Infantry Division entered Messina.

Less than a month later on 9 September 1943, the Italians surrendered and the US and British Armies landed at Salerno on the mainland of Italy in Operation Avalanche. Less than a month later, despite ferocious German resistance, Naples fell to the Allies on 1 October. Then, halfway to Rome, the advance stalled at Monte Cassino. Even Operation Shingle, an outflanking landing at Anzio in January 1944, failed to break the line. Rome would hold out until 5 June 1944.

BLOODY OMAHA

Meanwhile, Big Red One, the most battle-hardened division in the US Army was needed for the invasion of France and in November 1943 it returned to England with a new commander, Major General Clarence Huebner. After six-months hard training, yet again 'the First was first', landing at Omaha beach—where the German defences were strongest—on D-Day, 6 June 1944. The first assault waves were massacred before they could get off the beach. By sheer guts, the survivors assaulted the German defences and that evening, Big Red One had carved out a shallow bridgehead.

Big Red One led all the way to Germany fighting in the hedgerows of Normandy, the city streets of Aachen, and in the hellish battle in Hurtgen Forest. There was no rest for the Big Red One. When Hitler launched an offensive through the Ardennes forest, Big Red One rushed south to plug the gap. In January 1945 Big Red One resumed the offensive, crossing the Rhine at Remagen on 25 March marching deep into Germany before the final surrender.

WHY WE FIGHT

"Men, this stuff that some sources sling around about America wanting out of this war, not wanting to fight, is a crock of bullshit. Americans love to fight, traditionally. All real Americans love the sting and clash of battle. You are here today for three reasons. First, because you are here to defend your homes and your loved ones. Second, you are here for your own self respect, because you would not want to be anywhere else. Third, you are here because you are real men and all real men like to fight. When you, here, every one of you, were kids, you all admired the champion marble player, the fastest runner, the toughest boxer, the big league ball players, and the All-American football players. Americans love a winner. Americans will not tolerate a loser. Americans despise cowards. Americans play to win all of the time. I wouldn't give a hoot in hell for a man who lost and laughed. That's why Americans have never lost nor will ever lose a war; for the very idea of losing is hateful to an American.

An Army is a team. It lives, sleeps, eats, and fights as a team. This individual heroic stuff is pure horseshit. The bilious bastards who write that kind of stuff for the Saturday Evening Post don't know any more about real fighting under fire than they know about fornication!

We have the finest food, the finest equipment, the best spirit, and the best men in the world. Why, by God, I actually pity those poor sons-of-bitches we're going up against. By God, I do. ... All of the real heroes are not storybook combat fighters, either. ... One of the bravest men that I ever saw was a fellow on top of a telegraph pole in the midst of a furious fire fight in Tunisia. I stopped and asked what the hell he was doing up there at a time like that. He answered, "Fixing the wire, Sir." I asked, "Isn't that a little unhealthy right about now?" He answered, "Yes Sir, but the Goddamned wire has to be fixed". I asked, "Don't those planes strafing the road bother you?" And he answered, "No, Sir, but you sure as hell do!" Now, there was a real man. A real soldier.

I don't want to get any messages saying, "I am holding my position." We are not holding a Goddamned thing. Let the Germans do that. We are advancing constantly and we are not interested in holding onto anything, except the enemy's balls. We are going to twist his balls and kick the living shit out of him all of the time. Our basic plan of operation is to advance and to keep on advancing regardless of whether we have to go over, under, or through the enemy. We are going to go through him like crap through a goose; like shit through a tin horn!

There is one great thing that you men will all be able to say after this war is over and you are home once again. You may be thankful that twenty years from now when you are sitting by the fireplace with your grandson on your knee and he asks you what you did in the great World War II, you won't have to cough, shift him to the other knee and say, "Well, your Granddaddy shovelled shit in Louisiana." No, Sir, you can look him straight in the eye and say, "Son, your Granddaddy rode with ... a son-of-a-goddamned-bitch named Georgie Patton!"

General George S. Patton

The M4 Sherman is more than a match for any Axis tank in the desert.

An armored LMG squad halts an enemy attack.

M10 3" GMC tank-destroyers ambush a Panzer III.

KASSERINE

In ten days of gruelling battle, US forces halted and turned back the last major German offensive in North Africa and won their first clear victory in the Tunisian desert
—Tunisia, 14 February, 1943.

Mortars smoke the enemy out from their fortifications.

Water-cooled machine-guns can keep up a high rate of fire to keep the enemy at bay

M3 Stuart light tanks clear the flanks

Half-tracks get soldiers to the battle quickly

Firing on the move, US infantry keep the Germans' heads down as they assault the enemy position.

Anti-tank guns engage approaching enemy armor.

Ambushed! The enemy tanks's fate is sealed

TROINA

Troina was the pivot of the Etna line. When it fell, victory in Sicily was certain with the capture of Messina almost assured.
—Sicily, 31 July, 1943.

Working closely with the infantry as a combined arms force, tanks can easily overwhelm enemy positions.

M5 Stuart light tanks move through a wood to support an infantry attack

A machine-gun platoon faces a German attack.

Rifle platoons clear enemy from the town.

Ranger light infantry move quickly through a vineyard as they close with the enemy

'El Darbo' leads his Rangers from the front

T19 105mm half-tracks fire in support.

Armored cavalry in M3A1 armored cars and jeeps scout ahead of the advance.

Infantry cautiously scout the way for an M10 3" GMC tank-destroyer.

US INFANTRY DIVISIONS

IN THE MEDITERRANEAN

OPERATION TORCH AND TUNISIA

Division	Nicknames & Mottos	Battles
1st Infantry Division	Big Red One, Fighting First *No Mission Too Difficult, No Sacrifice Too Great, Duty First*	Operation Torch, Tunisia, Sicily, Normandy, Bulge, Germany.
16th Infantry Regiment	*Semper Paratus (Always Prepared)*	
18th Infantry Regiment	*In Omnia Paratus (In All Things Prepared)*	
26th Infantry Regiment	*Palmam Qui Meruit Ferat (The Palm Of Victory To He Who Earned It)*	
9th Infantry Division	The Varsity, The Old Reliables	Operation Torch, Tunisia, Sicily, Cotentin Peninsular, Germany.
39th Infantry Regiment	*D'une Vaillance Admirable (Of Admirable Valour)*	
47th Infantry Regiment	*Ex Virtute Honos (From Virtue, Honour)*	
60th Infantry Regiment	*To The Utmost Extent Of Our Power*	
34th Infantry Division	Red Bull *Attack! Attack! Attack!*	Tunisia, Cassino, Gothic Line.
133rd Infantry Regiment	*Avauncez (Advance)*	
135th Infantry Regiment	*To The Last Man*	
138th Infantry Regiment	*St Louis' Own*	
1st Ranger Bn	Darby's Rangers	Operation Torch, Tunisia, Sicily, Salerno, Anzio.
509th Parachute Infantry Bn *All The Way, and Here I Am - Here I Stay*	The Geronimos	Operation Torch, Tunisia, Salerno, Anzio, Southern France, Rhineland, Ardennes.

OPERATION HUSKY AND SICILY

Division	Nicknames & Mottos	Battles
1st Infantry Division	(see above)	
3rd Infantry Division	Rock of the Marne *Nous Resterons La (We Will Stay There)*	Sicily, Cassino, Anzio, Colmar Pocket, Munich.
7th Infantry Regiment	*Volens Et Potens (Willing and Able)*	
15th Infantry Regiment	*Can Do*	
30th Infantry Regiment	*Our Country, Not Ourselves*	
9th Infantry Division	(see above)	
45th Infantry Division	Thunderbird *Semper Anticus (Always Forward)*	Sicily, Salerno, Cassino, Belfort Gap.
157th Infantry Regiment	*Eager For Duty*	
179th Infantry Regiment	*In Omnia Paratus (In All Things Prepared)*	
180th Infantry Regiment	*Tanap Nanaiyakia Altaiyaha (Ready in Peace or War)*	
82nd Airborne Division	All American *In Air, On Land*	Sicily, Salerno, Normandy, Nijmagen, Ardennes.
504th Parachute Infantry Regiment	*Strike Hold*	
505th Parachute Infantry Regiment (Panthers)	*Ready*	
Ranger Force	Darby's Rangers	Sicily, Salerno, Anzio

OPPERATIONS AVALANCHE AND SHINGLE, SALERNO, CASSINO AND ANZIO

Division	Nicknames & Mottos	Battles
3rd Infantry Division	(see above)	
34th Infantry Division	(see above)	
36th Infantry Division	Texas, Lone Star, T-Patchers	Salerno, Cassino, Anzio, Southern France, Vosges, Germany.
141st Infantry Regiment	*(First Texas) Remember The Alamo*	
142nd Infantry Regiment	*I'll Face You*	
143rd Infantry Regiment	*Arms Secure Peace*	
45th Infantry Division		(see above)
82nd Airborne Division		(see above)
6615th (Provisional) Ranger Force		(see above)
509th Parachute Infantry Battalion		(see above)

UNITED STATES

US ARMORED DIVISIONS

IN THE MEDITERRANEAN

1ST ARMOURED DIVISION 'OLD IRONSIDES'

Unit	Tanks	Battles
1st Armored Regiment (formerly 1st Cavalry, Mechanized)		
1st Battalion (Light)	M3 Stuart	Operation Torch, Tunisia, Anzio, Rome
2nd Battalion (Medium)	M4 Sherman	Tunisia, Anzio, Rome
3rd Battalion (Medium)	M4 Sherman	Tunisia, Anzio, Rome, Gothic line
13th Armored Regiment (formerly 13th Cavalry, Mechanized)		
1st Battalion (Light)	M3 Stuart	Operation Torch, Tunisia, Anzio, Rome
2nd Battalion (Medium)	M3 Lee	Operation Torch, Tunisia, Anzio, Rome, Gothic line
3rd Battalion (Medium)	M3 Lee	Tunisia, Anzio, Rome
6th Armored Infantry Regiment		Operation Torch, Tunisia, Monte Cassino, Anzio, Rome, Po Valley

Light tank battalions replaced their M3 and M3A1 Stuart tanks with M5A1 Stuart tanks and medium tank battalions replaced their M3 Lee tanks with M4 Sherman tanks when the campaign in Tunisia ended.

2ND ARMOURED DIVISION 'HELL ON WHEELS'

Unit	Battles
66th Armored Regiment (formerly 66th Infantry, Light Tanks)	Sicily, Normandy, Siegfried Line, Ardennes, Ruhr, Elbe
67th Armored Regiment (formerly 67th Infantry, Medium Tanks)	Operation Torch, Sicily, Normandy, Siegfried Line,
41st Armored Infantry Regiment	Sicily, Normandy, Siegfried Line, Ardennes, Ruhr, Elbe

US ARMY TERMINOLOGY

AAA: Anti-aircraft Artillery. Pronounced 'Triple A'.

AAA (AW): AAA equipped with Automatic Weapons (.50 cal AA MG's and 37mm or 40mm cannon).

AAA (AW) (SP): AAA (AW) with Self-propelled mounts.

A&P: Ammunition and Pioneer.

Avalanche: Codename for the invasion of Italy at Salerno.

BAR: Browning Automatic Rifle, said be-ay-ar.

Bazooka: Anti-tank rocket launcher named after comedian Bob Burns' home-made trombone-kazoo.

Beep: Big jeep, the 3/4-ton truck.

Blitz Buggy: Jeep.

Blitzdough: A term used by the American press for armored infantry, from Blitzkrieg and Doughboy.

Blitzkrieg: German for 'Lightning War'.

C Rations: Pre-packaged light-weight field rations.

Cal, Calibre: The diameter in inches of the round fired by a gun, e.g. .50 cal = half inch or 12.7mm.

Carbine: A short rifle firing a .30 cal pistol round issued as a replacement for pistols.

CCA: Combat Command A.

CCB: Combat Command B.

CCR: Combat Command Reserve.

Chow: Food.

CGMC, Combination Gun, Motor Carriage: A self-propelled anti-aircraft gun.

CO: Commanding Officer.

Coastal Artillery (AA) Battalion: Anti-aircraft Battalion. At the start of the war anti-aircraft artillery was the responsibility of the coast defence branch of the artillery.

Combat Command: A brigade-level command which is assigned battalions from regiments as required for its mission. US armored divisions had two main combat commands (CCA & CCB).

Dogface: Infantryman.

Dope: Information, military intelligence.

Doughboy: Traditional US Army nickname for infantry.

Dozer: Bulldozer.

FUBAR: Fouled Up Beyond All Recognition.

Garand: M1 Garand semi-automatic rifle.

GI: US soldier, from 'GI' (Government Issue) stamped on their uniforms.

GMC, Gun, Motor Carriage: A self-propelled gun.

GMC: General Motors Corporation.

Grant: British codename for M3 Medium Tank.

Gyrostabilizer: a device using gyroscopes to keep the gun level allowing shooting on the move.

HMC, Howitzer, Motor Carriage: A self-propelled howitzer.

Husky: Codename for the invasion of Sicily.

I&R: Intelligence and Reconnaissance.

K Rations: Front-line canned rations.

Lee: British codename for M3 Medium Tank.

Lieutenant: Pronounced loo-tenant in the US Army.

MGMC, Machine-gun, Motor Carriage: A self-propelled anti-aircraft gun.

MMC, Mortar, Motor Carriage: A self-propelled mortar.

Peep: Reconnaissance Jeep.

Purple Heart: US wound badge.

Purple Heart Box: M3 half-track, reference to cramped inside and light armor.

Ranger: US Army commando.

Red Leg: Artilleryman, from red stripe on dress trousers.

RCT: Regimental Combat Team.

Recon: Short for reconnaissance.

Regiment: Command consisting of three battalions.

Ronson: Nickname for the M4 Sherman referring to the slogan of Ronson cigarette lighters "Lights First Time".

Scott: British codename for M8 75mm HMC.

Sherman: British codename for M4 Medium Tank.

Shingle: Codename for the landings at Anzio.

SNAFU: Situation Normal, All Fouled Up.

Squadron: US term for a cavalry battalion.

Stabilizer: see Gyrostabilizer.

Stars & Stripes: The US Army newspaper.

Stuart: British codename for M3 or M5 Light Tank.

Tank destroyer: Self-propelled anti-tank gun.

Torch: Codename for the invasion of North Africa.

TO&E: Table of Organisation and Equipment.

TOT, Time On Target: Artillery bombardment in which the first round fired from each gun is timed to impact on the target simultaneously.

Troop: US cavalry company.

TRV: Tank Recovery Vehicle.

TECHNICAL SERGEANT
CHARLES 'COMMANDO' KELLY

Chuck Kelly was the third of nine brothers growing up in the rough north-side Irish tenements of Pittsburgh to enlist in the Army. After training he was assigned to L Company, 143rd Infantry Regiment, in the 'T-Patchers', the Texan 36th Infantry Division. After guard duty in Algiers, the T-Patchers led the way ashore on 9 September 1943 at Salerno on the Italian mainland. Four days later, PFC Kelly went out on a reconnaissance of Hill 315 with three other soldiers, only to be surrounded and cut off.

'I brought my BAR up and pulled the switch. There were three men working the Jerry machine-gun, and as my bullets socked into them they hit the ground twitching. I had fired only 10 rounds. The 60 or 70 other Germans coming over the knoll were only 50 feet away. I wasn't cool, calm and collected then. I pointed my BAR at them as if it were an extension of my arm, and bullets jetted out of it. I wasn't even conscious of aiming, but it didn't seem I could miss.'

By the time the Germans retreated, Kelly had accounted for 40 of them.

The next day Kelly virtually single-handedly defended the Mayor's house in nearby Altavilla. In doing so he 'fired every weapon the infantry uses. You don't have to know anything about them. Just keep on pushing them and they'll shoot.' His feat earned him the nickname Commando Kelly from the army newspaper, Stars & Stripes.

Over the next six months he was promoted to Technical Sergeant earning his country's highest award, the Congressional Medal of Honor, and nine other medals to become his country's most decorated soldier before returning to the United States as a hero.

CHARACTERISTICS

Kelly is an Infantry team and a Warrior. He can replace a Rifle or Rifle/MG team in any Rifle, Ranger, or Parachute Rifle Platoon for +25 points.

SPECIAL RULES

One Man Army: Kelly uses his BAR and every other weapon that comes to hand, from rifles to bazookas and even 37mm guns. His characteristics are: Range 16"/40cm, ROF 3, Anti-tank 2, and Firepower 5+.

When shooting at armoured vehicles, if Kelly scores more than one hit he may discard a hit to increase the Anti-tank rating of another hit to 5, or two hits to increase it to 7.

Every hit caused by Kelly counts as two hits for the purposes of Pinning Down the enemy.

No Braver Man: Kelly ignores all the effects of being Pinned Down. If Kelly's platoon fails a Platoon Morale Check, roll a die. On a roll of 4+, Kelly fights on alone, although the rest of the platoon are Destroyed. With no Command team, Kelly cannot move or counterattack in assaults and will never flee, but he can fight where he stands.

STAFF SERGEANT
COLE 'REB' JACKSON

..Reb Jackson...

Sergeant Cole Jackson Senior fought with Patton's US Tank Corps in the First World War. Inspired by tales of 'The Great Crusade', Cole Jackson Junior joined the army on his eighteenth birthday.

Jackson was a corporal in the tanks when the war began and took part in the Louisiana Manoeuvres of 1940, being promoted to Sergeant when the 1st Armored Division, 'Old Ironsides' was formed. When he learned that he was scheduled to transfer to the newly formed 6th Armored Division while Old Ironsides left for Europe, Jackson went AWOL (absent without leave). On his return, he was busted to Private, but shipped out with Old Ironsides.

Jackson's tank landed in North Africa on the first day of Operation Torch. By Christmas he was a Sergeant again, had three tanks shot out from under him, and been wounded twice. At Kasserine Pass, Jackson made Staff Sergeant after leading his platoon in a counterattack that stopped a German thrust.

Jackson went on to fight in every major action that Old Ironsides fought, surviving the destruction of four more tanks.

CHARACTERISTICS

Jackson is a Warrior. He is always mounted in a tank, but never the platoon commander's tank.

Jackson can be part of any Tank Platoon for +25 points.

SPECIAL RULES

Go Fix It: If the Platoon Command team is Destroyed, treat Jackson as the Platoon Command team.

Like A Rock: If Jackson's tank is required to take a Motivation test and fails, re-roll the test. If Jackson's platoon is required to take a Motivation test and fails, Jackson can re-roll the test for his tank. If the re-roll passes, treat Jackson's tank as passing the test, but the rest of the platoon as failing it. This can lead to Jackson fighting on alone after the rest of the platoon fail a Platoon Morale Check.

MAJOR GENERAL
ERNEST N HARMON

Known by his troops as 'Old Gravel Voice', Major General Ernest N Harmon gained a reputation as a dashing and aggressive leader. Frequently seen leading from the front, Harmon inspired confidence with his presence.

During the First World War he led a cavalry troop in the Meuse-Argonne battles. Between the wars he competed as a pentathlete in the Paris Olympics, before rising to command a light tank battalion as a Lieutenant Colonel.

Given command of 2nd Armored Division in July 1942 as a temporary Major General, Harmon led them during the Operation Torch landings in November. As part of Patton's Western Taskforce he landed near Casablanca, defeating a French column before racing to secure the city.

Ordered to the front by Eisenhower at the height of the Kasserine Pass battle in February 1943, Harmon took command of the battle. Setting off in a jeep, he toured the front visiting key commanders and assessing the situation first hand. Within days he turned the rout into a successful defence.

After the danger had passed, Harmon turned down command of II Corps, instead recommending Patton for that position. Harmon was given command of 1st Armored Division in April 1943, leading them from Tunisia to Italy, taking part in the Salerno and Anzio landings and capturing Rome in June 1944.

With the fall of Rome, Harmon was sent Stateside to become a corps commander, but requested a return to combat in Europe. From September 1944, he led 2nd Armored Division in combat, including the Battle of the Bulge. By the time the war ended, Harmon was commanding XXII Corps.

CHARACTERISTICS

Harmon is a Warrior and a Higher Command team rated as **Fearless Trained**.

Harmon is always mounted in a Jeep. He can join any Tank or Armored Rifle Company for +50 points.

SPECIAL RULES

Old Gravel Voice: At the start of the Shooting step Harmon may attempt to rally one platoon within 6"/15cm.

- If the platoon is Pinned Down, roll a Motivation test. If it is successful, the platoon rallies and is no longer Pinned Down.
- Any Bailed Out vehicles in the platoon take a Motivation test and if successful remount immediately.

Get Moving: Each turn one platoon that is not Pinned Down and is within 6"/15cm of Harmon may attempt to move again at the end of the Movement step after all other movement. Roll a die. On a roll of 4+ the platoon may move a further 4"/10cm. All of the normal rules apply for this movement. The platoon may still shoot and assault after making this extra move.

COLONEL
WILLIAM 'BILL' O DARBY

Captain William Orlando Darby had been an artillery officer for eight years when appointment as aide-de-camp to General Hartle led to promotion to Lieutenant Colonel in charge of forming the first Ranger battalion.

'El Darbo', as he became known, hand picked his officers and men before submitting them to the Commando Depot in Scotland for rigourous training. Soon after, they boarded ship for Oran in Algiers for their first assault landing. This success was followed by more when they moved to southern Tunisia to raid Sened and then take part in the battle of El Guetar.

Their achievements earned the Rangers a position in the first assault wave in Operation Husky. In preparation, Darby's Rangers as they were known were quickly expanded to a three-battalion Ranger Force before landing at Licata and Gela.

Ranger Force then took part in Operation Avalanche where they took the vital Chiunzi Pass and held it against all comers. Once again, Darby's love of being right up front was noted, with one officer recalling approaching a Ranger on the beach and asking 'Do you know where I can find Colonel Darby?' The Ranger grinned and replied, 'You'll never find him this far back.'

Ranger Force continued its tradition of being first ashore in Operation Shingle, the landings at Anzio. However, here they suffered a disaster at Cisterna where the 1st and 3rd Rangers were wiped out.

Ranger Force was disbanded and Darby returned to the United States as a Colonel to train new units. Darby soon wangled a posting back to Italy as deputy commander of the 10th Mountain Division only to be killed days before the end of the war. He was posthumously promoted to Brigadier General.

CHARACTERISTICS

Darby is an Infantry team, a Warrior and a Higher Command team rated as **Fearless Trained**.

He is armed with an M1 Garand rifle rated as follows: Range: 16"/40cm, ROF: 1, Anti-tank: 2, Firepower: 6, with the Automatic Rifle special rule.

Darby can join any Rifle, Ranger or Parachute Rifle Company for +50 points.

SPECIAL RULES

Red Leg: Darby's artillery background showed in the amount of firepower his Rangers amassed.

He does not suffer the usual +1 to hit penalty for being a Command team rather than an Observer team when ranging in artillery. All mortar platoons ranged in by Darby count as Veteran when rolling to hit teams under the template.

Keep Moving: Each turn Darby and one platoon that is not Pinned Down and is within 6"/15cm of Darby may attempt to move again at the end of the Movement step after all other movement. Roll a die. On a roll of 4+ the platoon may move a further 4"/10cm. All of the normal rules apply for this movement. The platoon may still shoot and assault after making this extra move.

TANK COMPANY

Everyone in Old Ironsides wears the armored forces patch, see, 'cos we are an armored division, and that means tanks. Without tanks, this division ain't nothin'. The tanks lead the way. The tanks do the fightin' and if they have to, the tanks do the dyin'. It don't matter none tho', 'cos we always win in the end. We're the First and we're the best—Old Ironsides!
—Lieutenant Dan Thomas, Arkansas

A force based around a Tank Company must contain:
- a Company HQ, and
- two or three Tank Platoons.

Weapons Platoons available to a Tank Company are:
- an Armored Mortar Platoon,
- Recon Platoons, and
- Assault Gun Platoons.

Support Platoons for a Tank Company can be:
- Armored Rifle Platoons,
- Armored Recon Platoons, and
- Divisional Support Platoons.

You may have up to **two** Support Platoons attached to your company for each Tank Platoon that you are fielding.

Motivation and Skill

The US may be new to the war, but the tankers are keen, well-trained, and learning fast. A Tank Company is **Confident Trained**.

HEADQUARTERS

1 Company HQ

Headquarters
Company HQ with

2 M3 or M3A1 Stuart	**105 points**

- Equip all M3A1 Stuart tanks with stabilisers for +10 points for the platoon.

2 M5A1 Stuart	**120 points**
2 M3 Lee	**180 points**

- Fit any or all M3 Lee tanks with long M3 75mm guns in place of short M2 75mm guns for +10 points per tank.

2 M4 or M4A1 Sherman	**230 points**

Option
- Add an M31 TRV recovery vehicle to a Company HQ with M4 or M4A1 Sherman tanks for +10 points.

Your company must include at least one Tank Platoon equipped with the same type of tank as the Company HQ.

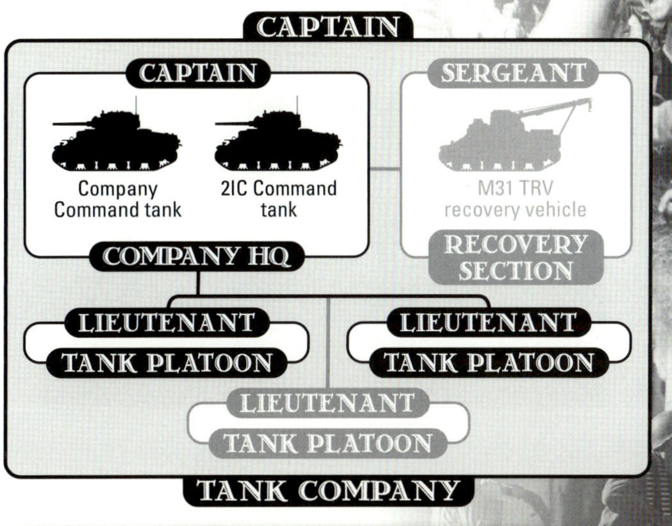

Following your battle plan, the tank platoons outmanoeuvre and outfight the enemy. When the going gets tough, you'll have the Captain leading from the front, keeping the fight going until you are victorious.

The M31 TRV is invaluable for fixing tanks bogged down in rough terrain using the vehicle recovery rules.

COMBAT PLATOONS

2 or 3 Tank Platoons

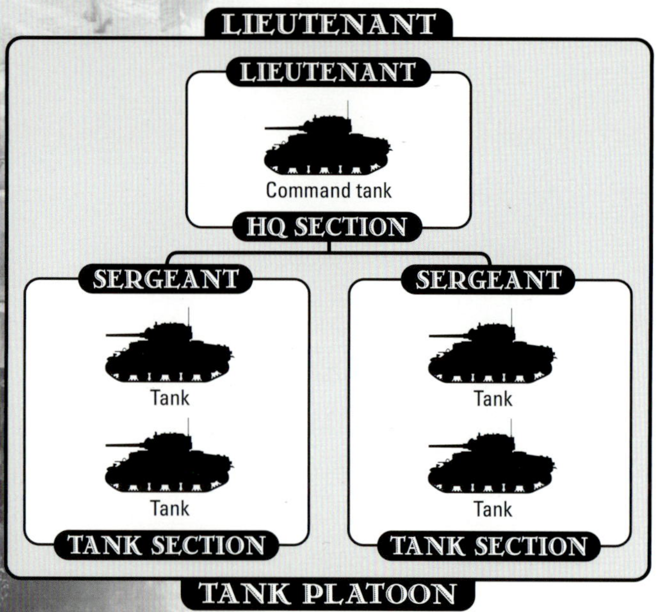

Platoon	
5 M3 or M3A1 Stuart	260 points
4 M3 or M3A1 Stuart	210 points
3 M3 or M3A1 Stuart	160 points
• Equip all M3A1 Stuart tanks with stabilisers for +10 points for the platoon.	
5 M5A1 Stuart	305 points
4 M5A1 Stuart	245 points
3 M5A1 Stuart	185 points
5 M3 Lee	455 points
4 M3 Lee	365 points
3 M3 Lee	275 points
• Fit any or all M3 Lee tanks with long M3 75mm guns in place of short M2 75mm guns for +10 points per tank.	
5 M4 or M4A1 Sherman	575 points
4 M4 or M4A1 Sherman	460 points
3 M4 or M4A1 Sherman	345 points

The USA provides its tankers with some of the best and most reliable tanks in the world. The light tank battalions with their fast M3 Stuart tanks and the medium tank battalions with the powerful M3 Lee and M4 Sherman tanks both outmanoeuvre any enemy that they don't outgun.

Don't forget that your M3 Lee tanks can fire both their 75mm main gun and the 37mm turret gun at the same time using the Multiple Guns rule.

WEAPONS PLATOONS

0 to 1 Armored Mortar Platoon

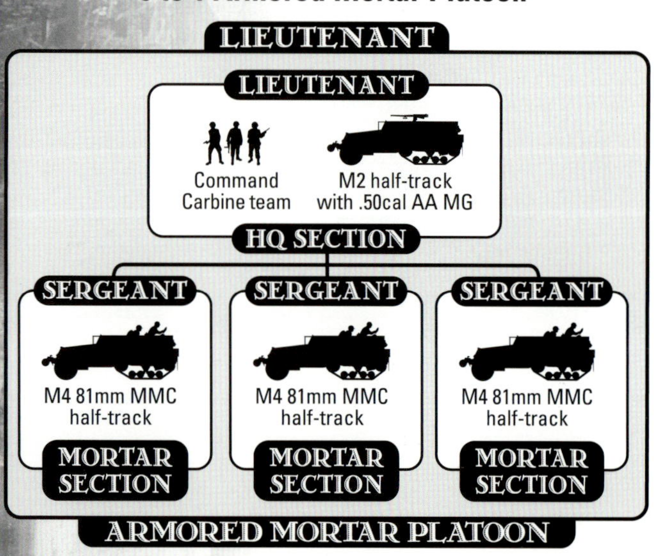

Platoon	
HQ Section with	
3 Mortar Sections	125 points
2 Mortar Sections	90 points
Option	
• Arm any or all M4 81mm MMC half-tracks with a .50 cal AA MG for +5 points per half-track.	

The one thing tanks aren't well equipped to handle are anti-tank guns. They leave them to the battalion mortar platoon. Firing from behind cover, the mortars can bombard and smoke out or destroy anti-tank guns without fear of retribution.

0 to 3 Recon Platoons

Platoon

HQ Section with

2 Recon Squads	**70 points**
1 Recon Squad	**50 points**

Options

- Add a Bazooka team for +15 points.
- Arm any or all Jeep teams with an AA MG for +5 points per Jeep team.

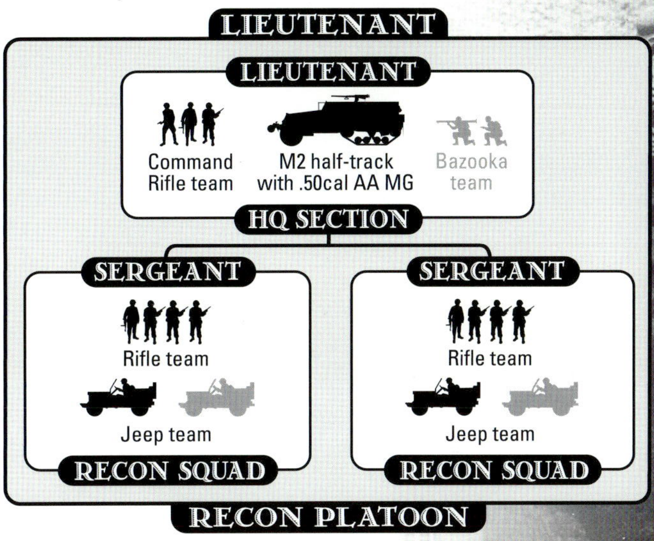

The soldiers of the regimental recon platoons are known as Intelligence Agents. They are equally capable of spying out enemy positions or fighting them. Their task is to locate enemy ambushes and scout suitable routes for tank attacks.

Recon Platoons are Reconnaissance Platoons.

TANK DESIGNATIONS

The US Army used a simple system to designate its equipment. The first type of a piece of equipment (say a medium tank) was designated M1. If a new design replaced the old one, it would be called M2, and a third design M3, and so on. If changes were made to a design, it gained a suffix, so the M4A1 Medium Tank was the first variant of the fourth design.

In the early stages of the war many experimental designs were rushed into battle without being standardised. These used T codes, such as the T19 HMC, and added the suffix E for variants, producing the T28E1 CGMC for instance.

However, despite its apparent simplicity, this system caused considerable confusion in war-time since there was a M3 Light Tank, an M3 Medium Tank, an M3 GMC, and an M3 Submachine-gun. To resolve this, numbers were later skipped to avoid duplication and the British codenames were used unofficially.

Assault Gun Platoon

Platoon

3 T30 75mm HMC	**110 points**
2 T30 75mm HMC	**75 points**

- Arm any or all T30 75mm HMC assault guns with a .50 cal AA MG for +5 points per assault gun.

3 M8 Scott HMC	**155 points**
2 M8 Scott HMC	**105 points**

Assault gun platoons are versatile. They usually operate as artillery firing long-range bombardments. However, when necessary, they close with particularly tough targets and destroy them with point-blank fire.

UNITED STATES

ARMORED RIFLE COMPANY

(MECHANISED COMPANY)

Us armored infantry call ourselves Blitzdoughs, you know, put blitzkrieg and doughboy together, you get Blitzdoughs. Like it says, we're doughboys fighting in the mud, shedding our blood. But once the tanks start moving, it's all on. We mount our half-tracks and move out, leading the blitz all the way to Hitler's bedroom!

—Lieutenant Jebidiah Hope, Kentucky

A force based around an Armored Rifle Company must contain:

- a Company HQ, and
- two or three Armored Rifle Platoons.

Weapons Platoons available to an Armored Rifle Company are:

- an Armored Machine-gun Platoon,
- an Armored Mortar Platoon,
- a Recon Platoon, and
- an Assault Gun Platoon.

Support Platoons for an Armored Rifle Company can be:

- Tank Platoons,
- Armored Recon Platoons, and
- Divisional Support Platoons.

You may have up to **two** Support Platoons attached to your company for each Armored Rifle Platoon that you are fielding.

Motivation and Skill

The Blitzdoughs are ready and eager to prove their training in the heat of battle. An Armored Rifle Company is **Confident Trained**.

HEADQUARTERS

1 Company HQ

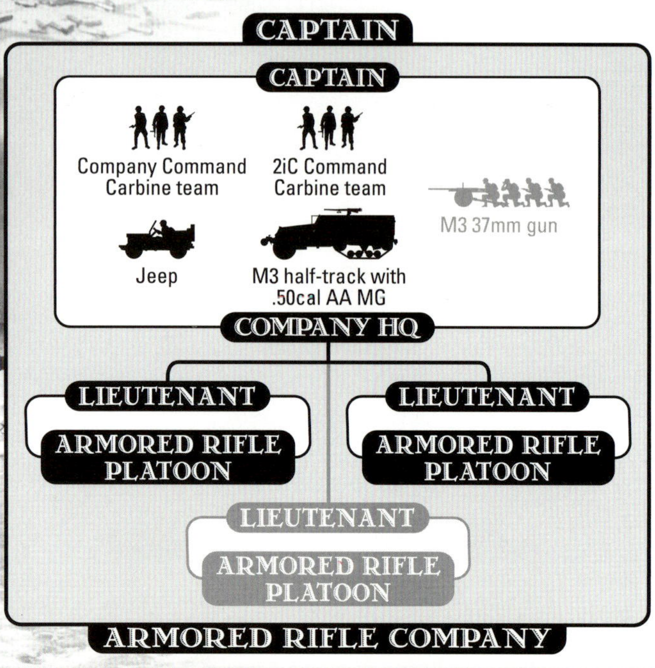

Headquarters	
Company HQ	**45 points**

Options

- Add an M3 37mm gun for +15 points.
- Replace M3 37mm gun with a Bazooka team at no cost.
- Arm the Jeep with an AA MG for +5 points.

Your half-tracks may look like Gypsy caravans, but your men will follow you anywhere. In the heat of battle, the Captain is at the hottest point, directing the battle and urging the men on.

COMBAT PLATOONS

2 or 3 Armored Rifle Platoons

Platoon

HQ Section with
Light Machine-gun Squad,
60mm Mortar Squad, and

2 Rifle Squads	**195 points**
1 Rifle Squad	**155 points**

Options

- Replace M3 37mm gun with a Bazooka team at no cost.
- Add Bazooka teams for +15 points per team.

Armored rifle platoons have more weaponry than any other infantry platoon in the world. As well as two .50 cal heavy machine-guns and five .30 cal machine-guns, they have a 37mm anti-tank gun, a 60mm mortar and four bazookas! That doesn't count the fifty semi-automatic rifles, carbines and submachine-guns carried as personal weapons.

With this much firepower and mobility, the platoon is ideal for both offensive and defensive operations. In the attack the riflemen assault under cover of the machine-guns of the half-tracks and the mortar, while on the defence, their light machine-guns and mortar allow them to dominate the terrain around them.

...Kasserine Pass, 1943...

As the rising sun burns away the early dawn mist, Lieutenant Haywood anxiously focuses his field glasses on the pass. 'Mason!' he calls, 'get on the horn to Battalion! We've got company. There's hundreds of them!'

Haywood ducks as explosions shake his half-track. The air is filled with the shriek of shrapnel and the deadly hiss of fragments of stone, as mortar bombs crash into the rocks around them. 'Tell them we need some artillery on the pass, right now!' he yells over the noise.

The rattle of splinters against the half-track's sides count the interminable seconds. Then, with a flash, the sky behind them lights up as the armored division's self-propelled artillery fires as one. As the pass below erupts in flames and smoke, the German mortar fire slackens.

Risking a quick glance, Haywood spots German infantry fanning out across the slopes. 'Johnson!' he yells to his driver, 'Get us moving, they're trying to flank us!'

Johnson hits the starter and the half-track's engine roars into life. Haywood clambers over to the machine-gun mount. 'Get us up that slope to the right,' he shouts, cocking the massive .50 cal. Standing up, he waves 'follow me' to the rest of the platoon.

Johnson whips the half-track around. Lurching and bouncing, it scrambles up the rocky slope, Haywood clinging on for dear life.

They crest the ridge and Johnson hits the brakes. Haywood swings the big machine-gun toward a squad of Germans. His hands grip the trigger and the gun spews tracer fire down the hillside. Mason's Garand blazes away beside him.

The Germans stampede back towards the road, vainly seeking cover as the platoon's light mortar lobs shells amongst them; chasing them back the way they came. Beyond, Haywood sees German armor forming up. 'Let's move out,' he says to Johnson. 'We've won this round, but the main event is just getting started.'

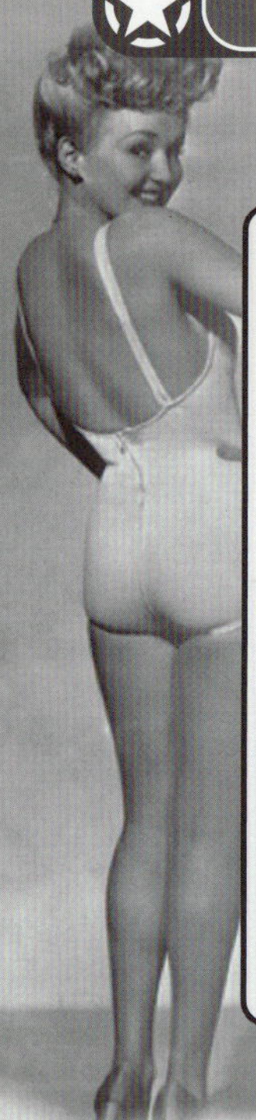

WEAPONS PLATOONS

0 to 1 Armored Machine-gun Platoon

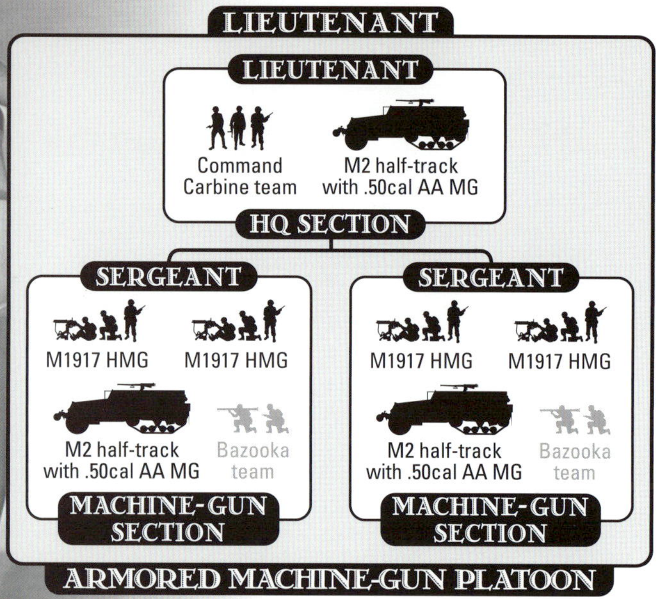

Platoon

HQ Section with

2 Machine-gun Sections	120 points
1 Machine-gun Section	70 points

Option

- Add Bazooka teams for +15 points per team.

The machine-gun platoon forms the bastion of the armored infantry battalion's defence. Its heavy machine-guns have the range and rate of fire to stop infantry attacks in their tracks.

In offensive operations, the machine-gun platoon covers an open flank or provides long-range fire support to dismounted attacks.

Armored Machine-gun Platoons may make Combat Attachments to Combat Platoons.

0 to 1 Armored Mortar Platoon

Each armored infantry battalion also fields an Armored Mortar Platoon identical to that of a tank battalion. The organisation is shown on page 158.

0 to 1 Recon Platoon

Armored infantry Recon Platoons are organised the same as those of the tanks. The organisation is shown on page 159.

0 to 1 Assault Gun Platoon

The Assault Gun Platoons are also the same as those of the tanks. The organisation is shown on page 159.

TRUCK-BORNE COMPANY

McGuinness' 2nd Battalion, 6th Armored Infantry lost most of its half-tracks during the retreat from Teboura in northern Tunisia in early December 1942. McGuinness was quickly sacked and replaced with Lieutenant Colonel Ringsak. With no replacement half-tracks available, the 2nd Battalion was mounted in trucks for the remainder of the campaign.

You can field troops from Ringsak's battalion as a Truck-borne Company. To do this replace all of the M3 half-tracks in Armored Rifle Platoons with three $2^1/_2$-ton trucks for the whole platoon at a cost of -10 points per half-track, and all M2 half-tracks in the Machine-gun Platoon with two $2^1/_2$-ton trucks for the whole platoon at a cost of -10 points per half-track.

The Armored Mortar, Recon and Assault Gun Platoons remain as before.

ARMORED RECON COMPANY

(RECONNAISSANCE MECHANISED COMPANY)

A force from an Armored Recon Company must contain:

- a Company HQ, and
- two or three Armored Recon Platoons.

Weapons Platoons available to an Armored Recon Company are:

- an Assault Gun Platoon, and
- two Light Tank Platoons.

Support Platoons for an Armored Recon Company can be:

- Tank Platoons,
- Armored Rifle Platoons, and
- Divisional Support Troops.

You may only have **one** Support Platoon attached to your company for each Armored Recon Platoon in your force.

Motivation and Skill

The cadre of experienced cavalry troopers around which Armored Recon Companies are formed are well-trained and proud of their history. An Armored Recon Company is rated as **Confident Trained**.

HEADQUARTERS

1 Company HQ

Headquarters

HQ Section with

2 Security Squads	**115 points**
1 Security Squads	**75 points**
No Security Squad	**35 points**

Option

- Arm the M2 half-track with an AA MG for +10 points.

Like the US Cavalry of old, your recon captain has the eyes of a hawk and the cunning of a weasel. Using his wits and fieldcraft, the commander of an armored recon company can defeat larger, more heavily armed forces.

The Company HQ Platoon of an Armored Recon Company is a Reconnaissance Platoon.

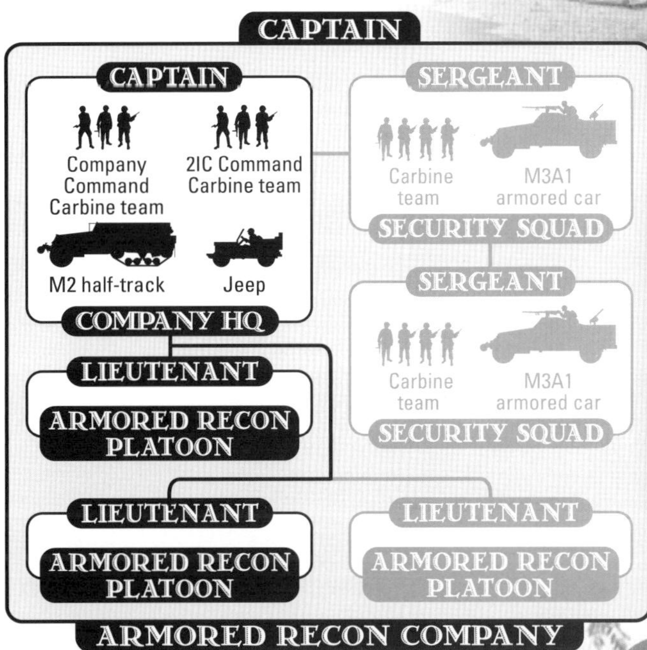

M2 .50cal Heavy Machine-gun (.50 cal MG)

Initially designed as an anti-tank weapon after the First World War, the Browning '.50 cal' found its niche as an anti-aircraft machine-gun in the Second World War, and is still in use today.

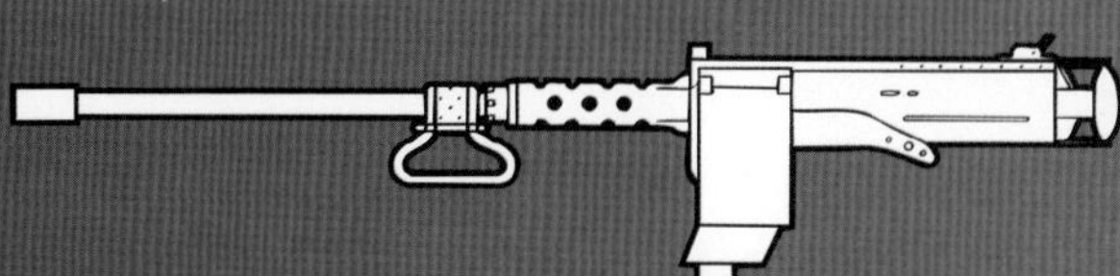

The M2 .50 cal heavy machine-gun is one of the most powerful machine-guns in the world. 5'4" (165cm) long and weighing in at 84lb (38kg) without its 44lb (20kg) tripod, its rounds are nearly 5.5" (14cm) long and weigh over a quarter of a pound (116gm) each! A complete 110 round belt weighs over 28lb (13kg).

M1919A3 .30 cal Machine-gun (LMG or AA MG)

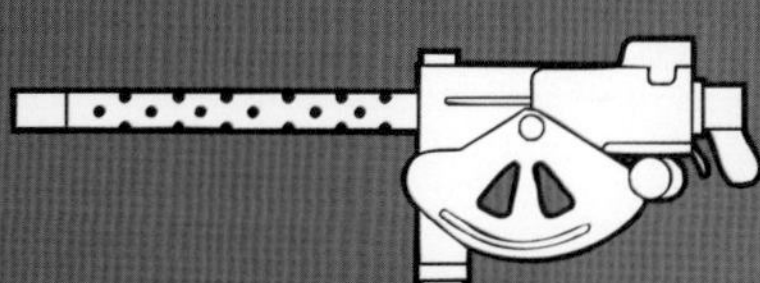

The M1919 .30 cal light machine-gun is a lightened, air-cooled version of the First World War M1917 Browning heavy machine-gun.

The M1919 was much handier than the heavy M2 being only 3'5" (104cm) long and weighing only 41lb (18.5kg) complete with tripod. The rounds are also handier and lighter being only 3.15" (8cm) long. A 250 round belt weighs in at 14lb (6.4kg).

COMBAT PLATOONS

2 to 3 Armored Recon Platoons

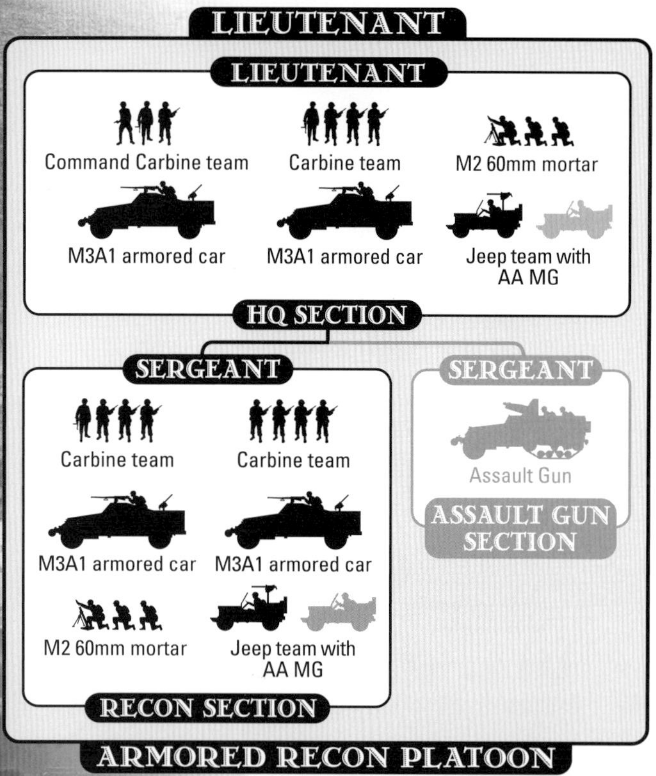

Armored Recon Platoons are Reconnaissance Platoons.

Platoon

HQ Section with

1 Recon Section	**175 points**
No Recon Section	**90 points**

Options

- Replace one Carbine team per section with a Bazooka team at no cost.
- Replace one Bazooka team with an M3 37mm gun at no cost.
- Mount M2 60mm mortars in Jeep teams as Portees at no cost.
- Add a T30 75mm HMC assault gun for +35 points or an M8 Scott HMC assault gun for +45 points.
- Arm the T30 75mm HMC with a .50 cal AA MG for +5 points.

Although each regiment had its own recon company for local reconnaissance, the divisional armored recon battalion probes deep behind enemy lines for essential intelligence.

Armored recon platoons are lightly equipped and stealthy. They can operate mounted from their M3A1 armored cars or on foot, sneaking forward to gather information covered by the platoon's mortar.

Before the game begins, a player fielding an Armored Recon Company may elect to operate the Recon Sections of their Armored Recon Platoons as separate platoons. If they do so, one of the Carbine teams in the Recon Section becomes a command team and the section counts as a separate platoon in every respect except that they deploy together and count as a single platoon when determining the number of platoons held in Ambush and Reserve. The Assault Gun Section, if present, joins the platoon formed from the HQ Section.

WEAPONS PLATOONS

0 to 1 Assault Gun Platoon

The Assault Gun Platoon is organised like the one in the Tank Company on page 159. You may only field an Assault Gun Platoon if none of your Armored Reconnaissance Platoons have Assault Gun Sections.

0 to 2 Light Tank Platoons

All Light Tank Platoons taken as Weapons Platoons options must be equipped with M3, M3A1, or M5A1 Stuart light tanks. The Light Tank Platoons are organised like those of the Tank Company on page 158.

RIFLE COMPANY

(INFANTRY COMPANY)

The GI's slice of battle is the most mixed up, confused and bewildering thing anybody can imagine. One thing he does know. When he sees the enemy he kills him, then snakes forward as far as he can and holds his gain if it's humanly possible. If it's suicide to hold it, he works his way back, to take it some other time.

—Technical Sergeant Charles E Kelly, Pennsylvania

A force based around a Rifle Company must contain:

- a Company HQ, and
- two or three Rifle Platoons.

Weapons Platoons available to a Rifle Company are:

- a Weapons Platoon,
- two Anti-tank Platoons, and
- two Machine-gun Platoons,
- an Ammunition & Pioneer Platoon.
- a Mortar Platoon,

Support Platoons for a Rifle Company can be:

- an Intelligence and Recon Platoon,
- a Cannon Platoon,
- Tank Platoons,
- Armored Recon Platoons,
- Ranger Platoons,
- Parachute Rifle Platoons, and
- Divisional Support Platoons.

You may attach up to **two** Support Platoons to your company for each Rifle Platoon you field.

Motivation and Skill

Although GI's are citizen soldiers new to battle, their training is thorough and they perform well. A Rifle Company is rated as **Confident Trained**.

HEADQUARTERS

1 Company HQ

Headquarters

Company HQ	20 points

Option

- Add Bazooka teams for +15 points per team.

An American CO has many responsibilities to handle, coordinating support platoons as well as directing his own combat platoons. However, good training and even better communications ensure control over his portion of the battlefield at all times.

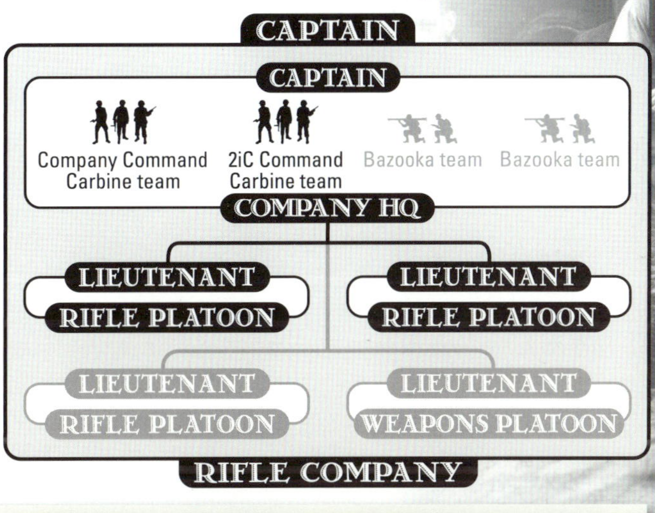

COMBAT PLATOONS

2 or 3 Rifle Platoons

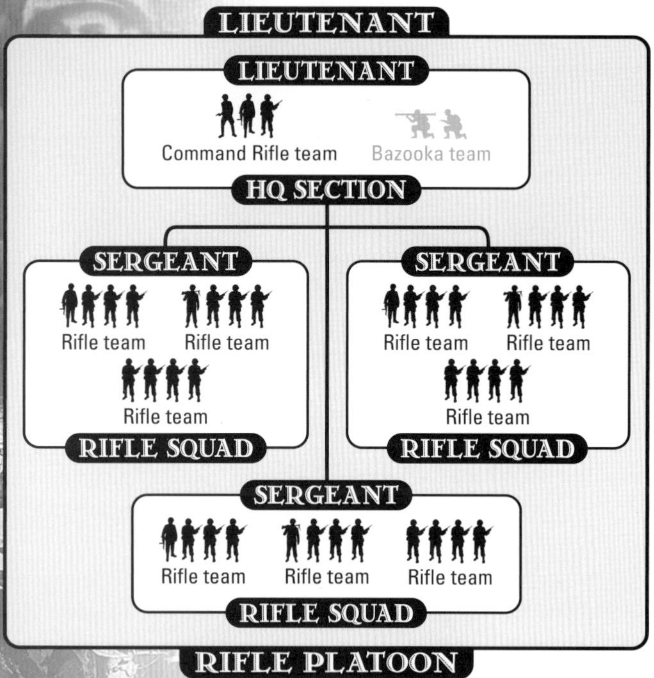

Platoon

HQ Section with:

3 Rifle Squads	**130 points**
2 Rifle Squads	**90 points**

Option

- Add Bazooka team for +15 points.

The M1 Garand semi-automatic rifle and Browning Automatic Rifle (BAR) allow the Doughboys to put out a steady rate of fire, whether standing still or on the move. When well supported, a Rifle Platoon is tough in both defensive and offensive operations.

WEAPONS PLATOONS

0 to 1 Weapons Platoon

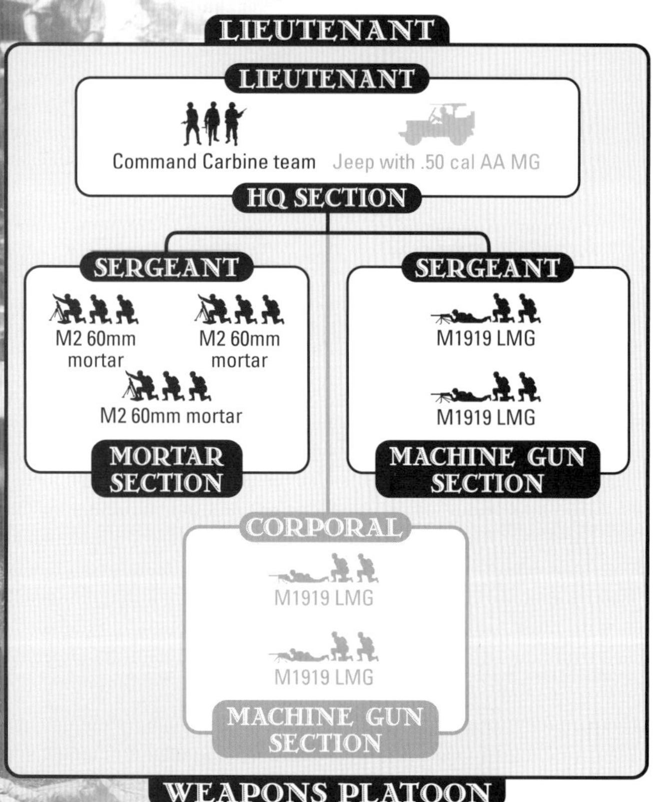

Platoon

HQ Section with Mortar Section and:

2 Machine-gun Sections	**135 points**
1 Machine-gun Section	**100 points**

Option

- Add Jeep with .50cal AA MG for +15 points.

The Weapons Platoon lays down a base of fire, covering the Rifle Platoons as they advance on the enemy. Although the platoon only has two machine-guns officially, it wasn't unusual for quartermasters to issue 'replacements' for 'lost' guns to increase their firepower.

Weapons Platoons may make Combat Attachments to Combat Platoons.

0 to 2 Machine-gun Platoon

Platoon

HQ Section with:

2 Machine-gun Sections	**100 points**
1 Machine-gun Section	**55 points**

Options

- Add Bazooka teams for +15 points per team.
- Add Jeep with .50cal AA MG for +15 points.
- Add Jeeps with trailers at no cost.

Although a battalion only officially had two machine-gun platoons, many collected 'replacement' weapons to double their strength so they could cover the entire front line.

Machine-gun Platoons may make Combat Attachments to Combat Platoons.

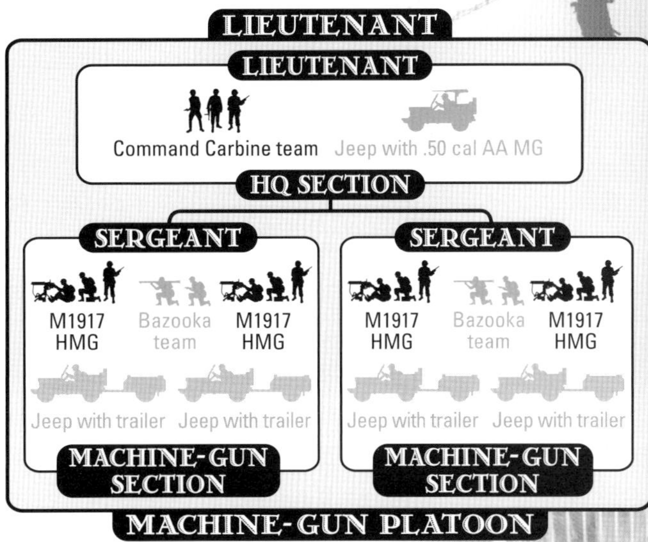

0 to 1 Mortar Platoon

Platoon

HQ Section with

3 Mortar Sections	**135 points**
2 Mortar Sections	**90 points**
1 Mortar Section	**55 points**

Options

- Add Bazooka teams for +15 points per team.
- Add Jeep with .50cal AA MG for +15 points.
- Add Jeeps with trailers at no cost.

Mounted in their jeeps, the mortar platoon will never be too far away from the CO or his radio. Carried on the backs of their crews, the mortars can go places the field artillery's 105's can't. This means they're always there to give the rifle platoons decisive artillery support the instant they need it.

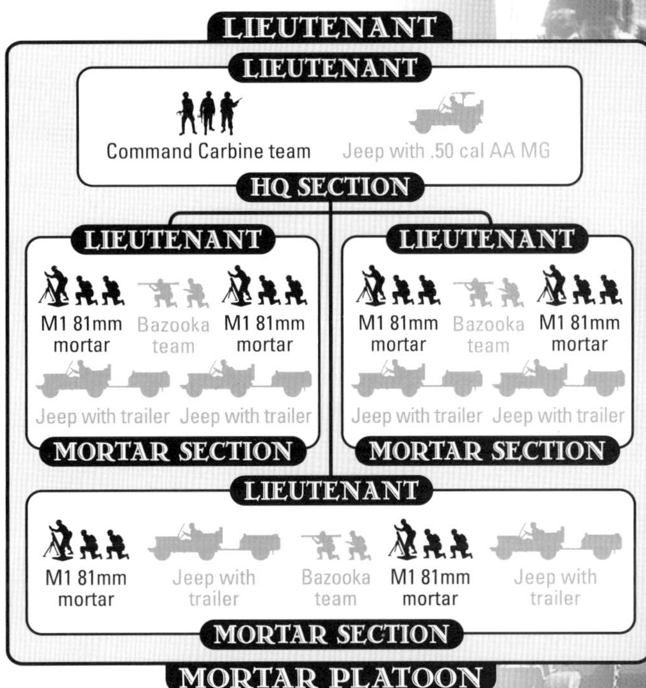

0 to 2 Anti-tank Platoons

Platoon

HQ Section with

4 M3 37mm	**110 points**
3 M3 37mm	**85 points**
2 M3 37mm	**60 points**

Options

- Upgrade any or all M3 37mm guns to M1 57mm guns for +10 points per gun.
- Add up to one Bazooka team per gun for +15 points per team.

You may not field more than one platoon equipped with M1 57mm guns.

The M3 37mm gun was good against light tanks, but the M1 57mm seen in small numbers in Sicily was better against medium tanks.

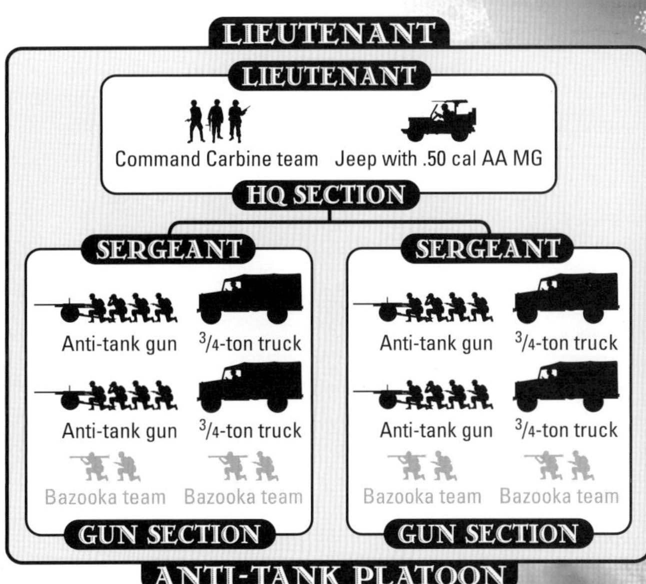

0 to 1 Ammunition & Pioneer Platoon

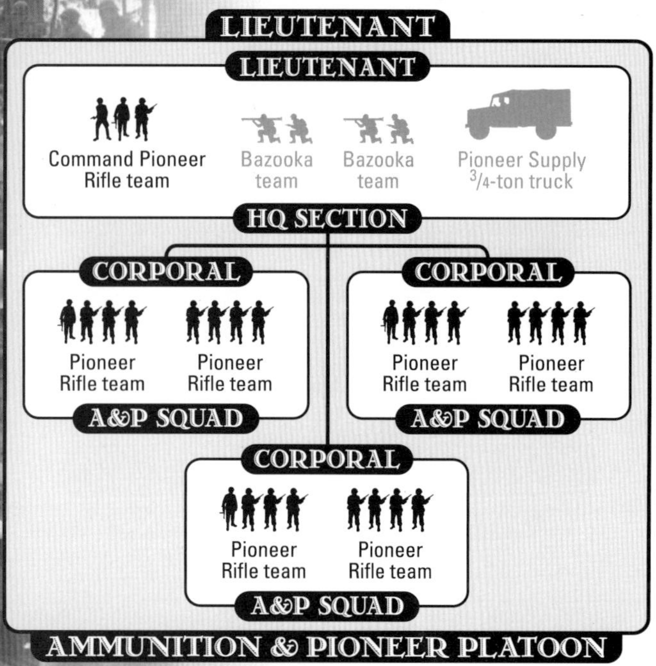

Platoon

HQ Section with

3 A&P Squads	130 points
2 A&P Squads	95 points

Options

- Add Bazooka teams for +15 points per team.
- Add Pioneer Supply truck for +5 points.

Every rifle battalion had an Ammunition and Pioneer (A & P) Platoon whose job was to keep the front line troops supplied with ammunition and help them prepare fortifications when they took up defensive positions.

In attacks they had the unpleasant task of clearing mines and booby traps so that the supporting arms could catch up with the riflemen.

SUPPORT PLATOONS

0 to 1 Intelligence & Recon Platoon

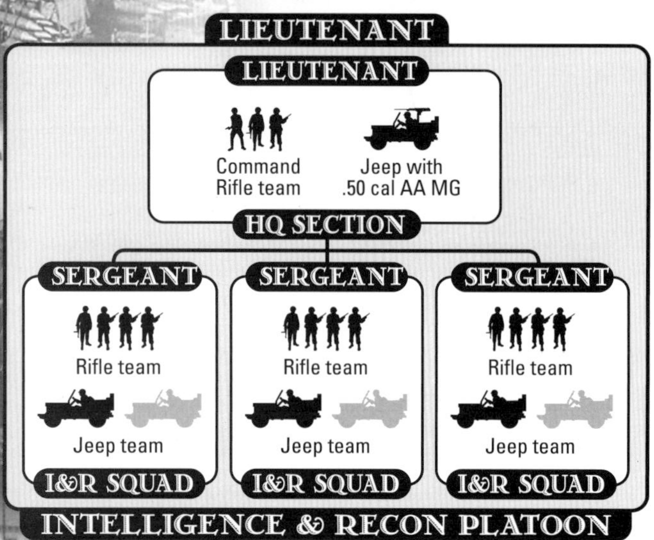

Platoon

HQ Section with

3 I&R Squads	95 points
2 I&R Squads	75 points

Option

- Arm any or all unarmed Jeep teams with an AA MG for +5 points per Jeep team.

The infantry regiment's Intelligence and Recon (I & R) Platoon's task was to find the enemy, take prisoners, and bring them back.

Intelligence and Recon Platoons are Reconnaissance Platoons.

0 to 1 Cannon Platoon

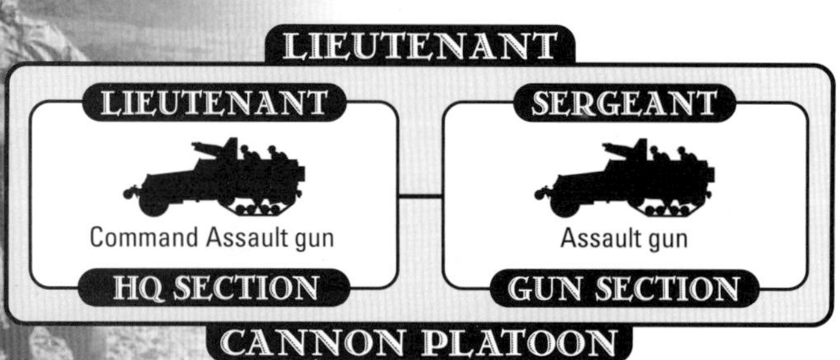

Platoon

2 T30 75mm HMC	75 points
2 T19 105mm HMC	95 points

Option

- Arm any or all T30 75mm HMC or T19 105mm HMC assault guns with a .50 cal AA MG for +5 points per assault gun.

Every infantry regiment had a cannon company on the German model with three cannon platoons with T30 75mm HMC assault guns and one with T19 105mm HMC assault guns.

RANGER COMPANY

(INFANTRY COMPANY)

We are Rangers, specially-trained light infantry raiders. We are America's answer to the famous British Commandos. Us Rangers are a very flexible force. We get the most dangerous missions. High Command sees us as elite infantry, so when there's no raiding to be done, we lead the way for the regular Joes.

—Sergeant Benjamin Walters, Texas

A force based around a Ranger Company must contain:

- a Company HQ, and
- one or two Ranger Platoons.

Weapons Platoons available to a Ranger Company are:

- a Mortar Platoon.

Support Platoons for a Ranger Company can be:

- Tank Platoons,
- Armored Recon Platoons,
- Rifle Platoons,
- Parachute Rifle Platoons, and
- Divisional Support Platoons.

You may attach up to **one** Support Platoon to your company for each Ranger Platoon you field.

Motivation and Skill

Rangers are well motivated, tough volunteers, but heavy casualties, rapid expansion, and the shorter training time of the newer members has diluted the combat experience of the older survivors. A Ranger Company is **Fearless Trained**.

HEADQUARTERS

1 Company HQ

Headquarters	
Company HQ	**10 points**

Option

- Upgrade Command Carbine team to a Command SMG team for +5 points.
- Add Bazooka teams for +20 points per team.

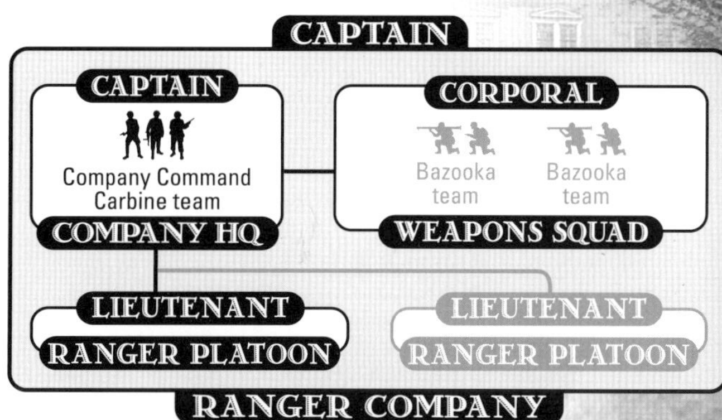

When they need it Rangers have plenty of support. Ranger Force had 83rd Chemical Mortar Battalion, their own Self-propelled Anti-tank Platoon with M3 75mm GMC tank-destroyers, and even a borrowed Armoured Field Artillery Battery under command in Sicily!

Only one of your Ranger Companies may have a single Ranger Platoon. All others must have two Ranger Platoons.

In *Flames Of War* you can field multiple companies in the same force. This is particularly useful with the rangers as a ranger company is quite small and they usually operate in groups of up to five-platoon ranger companies. Two or three Ranger Companies of two Ranger Platoons each with a little divisional support make for a very tough force.

I Shall Never Fail My Comrades

Ranger units are close-knit organisations. In order to fit into landing craft for raiding operations, each company has only two small platoons. These companies are too weak for independent operations, but the rangers' comradeship allows them to work closely together.

A Ranger Company never has to take a Company Morale Check for being below half strength. They still take Platoon Morale Checks as normal though.

However, if the total number of destroyed Ranger Platoons exceeds the number still on the table, the Ranger player must roll a die at the start of each turn. On a roll of 3+ the force fights on, heedless of its losses. On any other roll the remaining rangers withdraw to conserve their remaining strength and the game ends. If there are no remaining Ranger Company Command teams then this roll is automatically failed.

UNITED STATES

COMBAT PLATOONS

1 or 2 Ranger Platoons

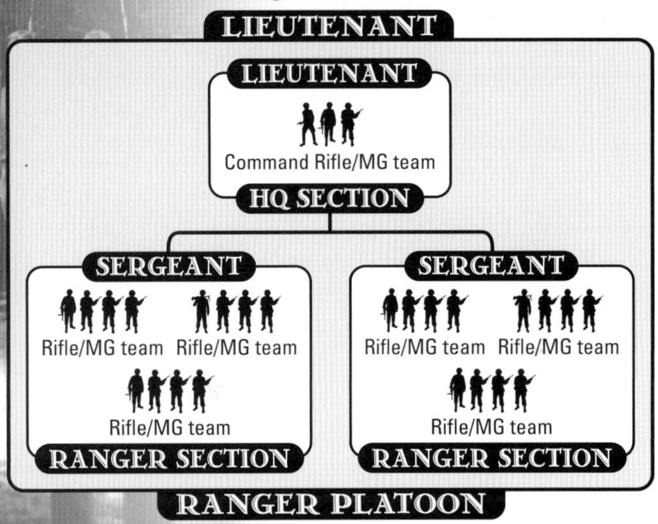

Platoon

HQ Section with:

2 Ranger Sections	135 points

Options

- Upgrade the Command Rifle/MG team to a Command SMG team at no cost.

Darby was an artilleryman and wanted his Rangers to have plenty of firepower, as every squad has its own light machine-gun! This gives them a considerable punch for a light infantry force.

WEAPONS PLATOONS

0 to 1 Ranger Mortar Platoon

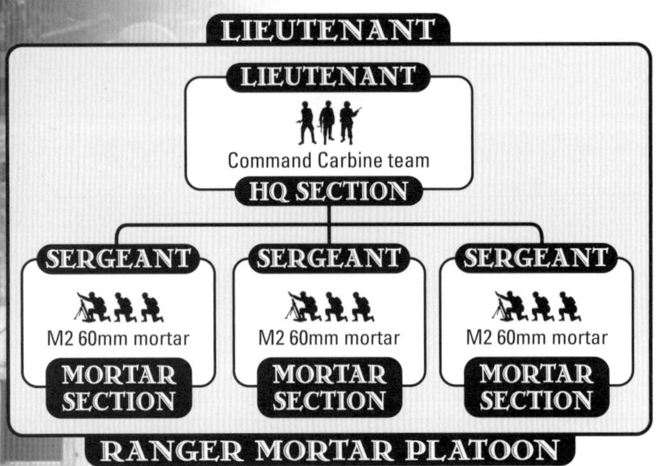

Platoon

HQ Section with:

3 Mortar Sections	80 points
2 Mortar Sections	55 points

Options

- Upgrade Command Carbine team to Command SMG team for +10 points.

Ranger Mortar Platoons used either light or medium mortars depending on the situation.

You may replace all Ranger M2 60mm mortars with M1 81mm mortars at the start of any game before deployment.

RANGER SPECIAL RULES

Rangers Lead The Way

While the infantry practised speed marching, the rangers took it a step further. They speed marched through the toughest terrain they could find!

Ranger Infantry teams may move At the Double (using the Truscott Trot) through Difficult Going.

No Obstacle Too Tough

Rangers are trained in climbing cliffs and other seemingly impassable obstacles allowing them to go anywhere.

All Ranger Infantry and Man-packed Gun teams are Mountaineers.

PARACHUTE RIFLE COMPANY

(INFANTRY COMPANY)

Why sign up to be Airborne? Well son, simply put we are the best! Every one of us is a volunteer—no cowards in our companies, lets face it, when things are really FUBAR, you want the man in the foxhole next to you to be the best. 'Sides which, we're the best-trained, the best-paid, and the best-dressed troopers in the US Army. Now that's how you pull the ladies, son, jump wings and fifty dollars a month in your pocket.

—Lieutenant John T Hancock, South Carolina

A force based around a Parachute Rifle Company must contain:

- a Company HQ, and
- two or three Parachute Rifle Platoons.

Weapons Platoons available to a Parachute Rifle Company are:

- a Parachute Machine-gun Platoon, and
- a Parachute Mortar Platoon.

Support Platoons for a Parachute Rifle Company can be:

- a Parachute Field Artillery Battery,
- a Parachute Engineer Combat Platoon,
- a Parachute Anti-aircraft Artillery Platoon,
- Tank Platoons,
- Armored Recon Platoons,
- Rifle Platoons,
- Ranger Platoons, and
- Divisional Support Platoons.

You may attach up to **one** Support Platoon to your company for each Parachute Rifle Platoon that you field.

Motivation and Skill

Parachute Rifle Companies are simply the best-trained troops in the US Army. Extremely rigorous training has created hardy, independent-thinking soldiers who believe in themselves and the men beside them. A Parachute Rifle Company is **Fearless Veteran**.

HEADQUARTERS

1 Company HQ

Headquarters

Company HQ	30 points

Option

- Add Bazooka teams for +25 points per team.

Parachute Rifle Companies are the bravest of the brave. No one else would leap out of a perfectly good aircraft deep over enemy-held territory. The Company HQ represents you, leading these brave men into battle, pitting these lightly armed, but highly dangerous, soldiers against the foe.

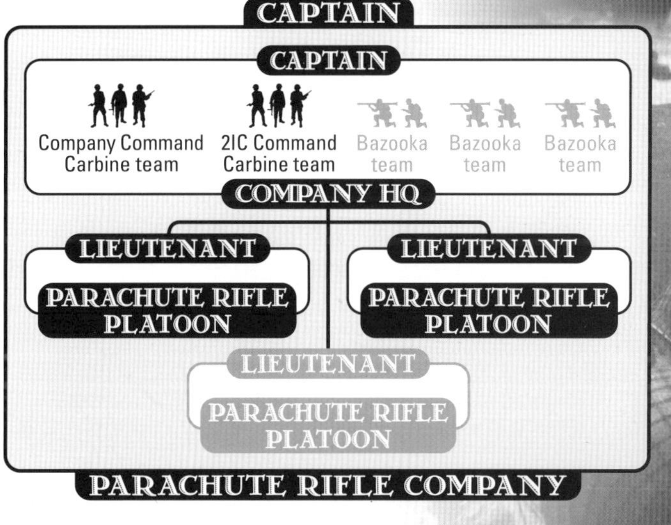

Parachute Operations In Tunisia, Sicily and Italy

The 504th and 505th Parachute Infantry Regiments were part of the 82nd 'All American' Airborne Division, the Army's first airborne division, and the first to be sent overseas. However, the first combat jump was made by the independent 509th Parachute Infantry Battalion in November 1942 as part of Operation Torch. The 509th then dropped on the airfield at Youks les Bains and raided a bridge at El Djem before fighting the rest of the North African campaign as regular infantry.

The first combat drop of the 504th and the 505th was Operation Husky, the invasion of Sicily, in July 1943. Their second combat drop reinforced the Salerno beachhead in mid-September, where they captured Altavilla before liberating Naples on 1 October 1943.

UNITED STATES

COMBAT PLATOONS

2 or 3 Parachute Rifle Platoons

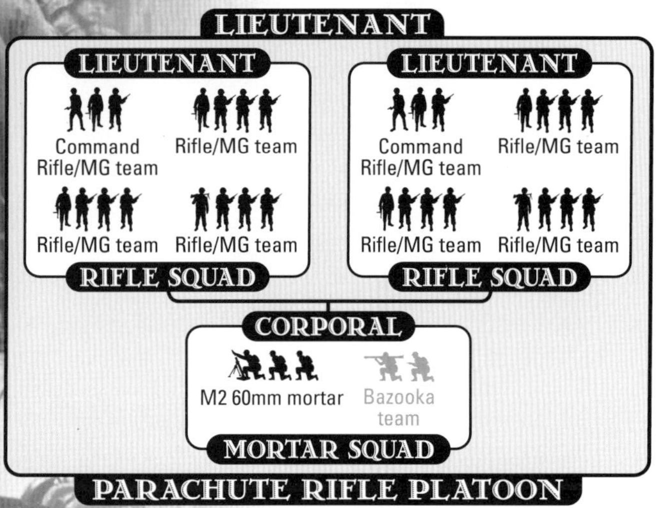

Platoon	
Mortar Squad with:	
2 Rifle Squads	240 points
1 Rifle Squad	140 points

Option

- Add Bazooka team for +25 points.

Armed with M1 Garand rifles and M1919A4 machine-guns parachute rifle platoons contain some of the best-armed squads in any army, capable of laying down an impressive amount of firepower.

Parachute platoons operate with both a first and second lieutenant because they are split across two aircraft when they jump. That way both aircraft have an officer aboard.

To reflect this, parachute platoons have two Command teams. Only the first of these teams acts as the Platoon Command team while it survives. The other counts as a normal rifle team until the first Command team is Destroyed. When the first Command team is Destroyed, the second Command team immediately takes over as the Platoon Command team.

WEAPONS PLATOONS

0 to 1 Parachute Machine-gun Platoon

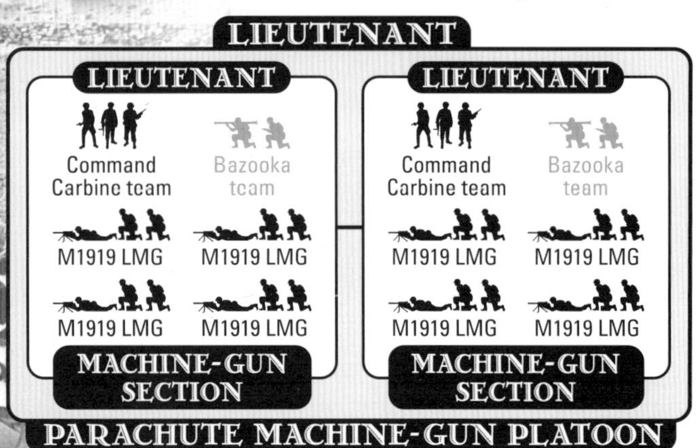

Platoon	
2 Machine-gun Sections	250 points
1 Machine-gun Section	125 points

Option

- Add Bazooka teams for +25 points per team.

Unlike the infantry who have heavy water cooled M1917A1 machine-guns in their battalion machine-gun platoons, the airborne forces use the lighter air-cooled M1919A4 machine-gun.

Parachute Machine-gun Platoons may make Combat Attachments to Combat Platoons.

0 to 1 Parachute Mortar Platoon

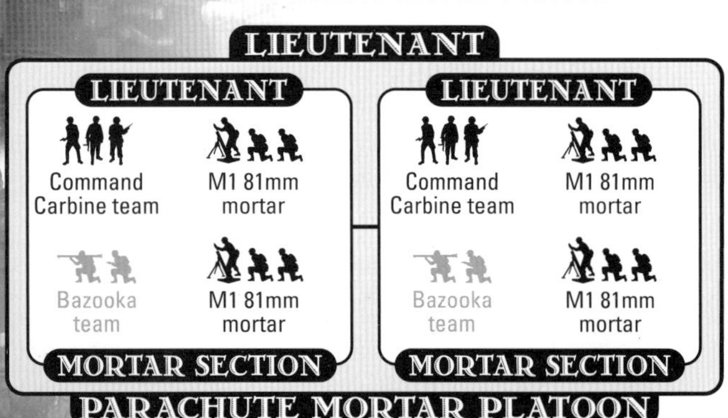

Platoon	
2 Mortar Sections	150 points
1 Mortar Section	75 points

Option

- Add Bazooka teams for +25 points per team.

The main form of artillery support for the airborne forces is the parachute mortar platoon's M1 81mm mortars. They tow their M1 81mm mortars and ammunition in a small handcart to give them greater mobility.

SUPPORT PLATOONS

0 to 1 Parachute Field Artillery Battery

Platoon
HQ Section with:

2 Gun Sections	205 points
1 Gun Section	110 points

Option
- Add $2^1/_2$-ton trucks to the platoon at no cost.

Parachute field artillery batteries use a pack howitzer that can be broken down into six loads for airdrops and then quickly assembled ready for action. When the battery goes into battle on land, they often have trucks attached to carry the pack howitzers (they are too fragile to tow) on long-distance marches.

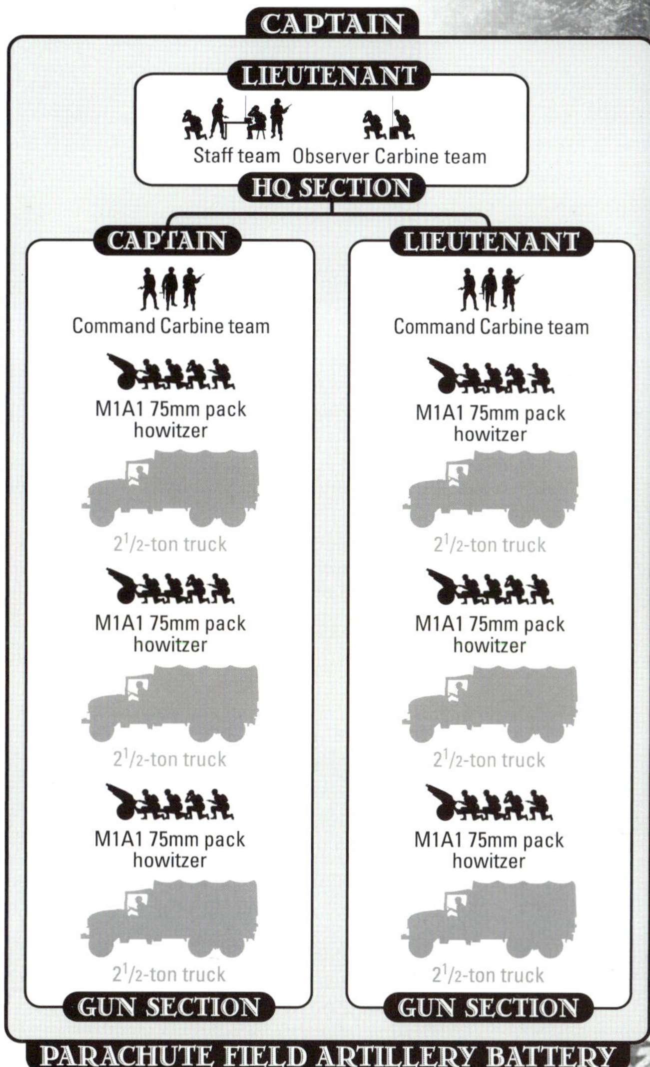

0 to 1 Parachute Engineer Combat Platoons

Platoon

HQ Squad	75 points

Options
- Add Operating Squad for +75 points.
- Add Weapons Squad for +70 points.
- Replace all Pioneer M1919 LMG teams with Pioneer Rifle teams at no cost.
- Add Bazooka teams for +25 points per team.

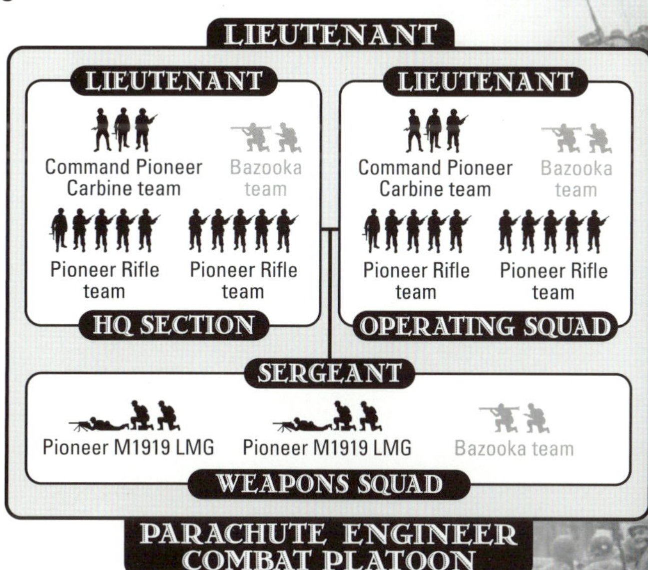

0 to 1 Parachute Anti-aircraft Artillery Platoon

A Parachute Anti-aircraft Artillery Platoon is organised like the Anti-aircraft Artillery Platoon on page 177, except that it has it has no vehicles and must replace all M1 Bofors guns with M2 .50 cal AA guns at no cost. If the platoon has two Automatic Weapons Sections, add a second Command carbine team at no cost.

UNITED STATES

DIVISIONAL SUPPORT PLATOONS

US Companies may have the following support platoons:

- Self-propelled Anti-tank Platoons,
- Field Artillery Batteries,
- Armored Field Artillery Batteries,
- Chemical Mortar Platoons
- Anti-aircraft Artillery (Self propelled) Platoons,
- Truck Sections, and
- Anti-aircraft Artillery Platoons, and
- Engineer Combat Platoons.

Motivation and Skill

The psychological profiling of new recruits makes sure that the specialists are as good as the front-line troops. Divisional Support Platoons are classed as **Confident Trained** unless otherwise noted.

Air Support

Aircraft	Limited Air Support	Sporadic Air support
P38 Lightning	130 points	95 points
P40 Warhawk	130 points	95 points

0 to 1 Self-propelled Anti-tank Platoon

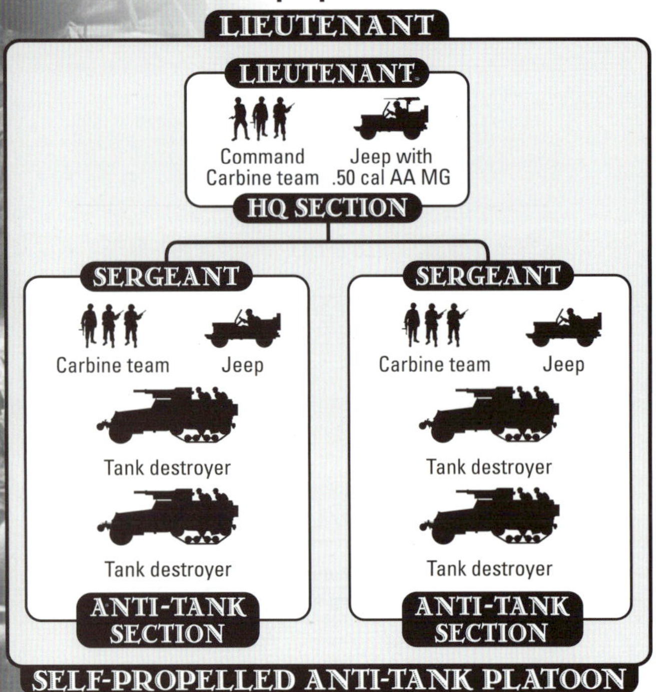

Platoon

With M6 37mm GMC:

2 Anti-tank Sections	**170 points**
1 Anti-tank Section	**95 points**

With M3 75mm GMC:

2 Anti-tank Sections	**300 points**
1 Anti-tank Section	**160 points**

- Arm any or all M3 75mm GMC tank destroyers with a .50 cal AA MG for +5 points per tank destroyer.

With M10 3in GMC:

2 Anti-tank Sections	**450 points**
1 Anti-tank Section	**235 points**

Option

- Arm any or all unarmed Jeeps with an AA MG for +5 points per Jeep.

No more than one platoon in your force may be equipped with M6 37mm GMC tank destroyers.

Like a big game hunter, tank destroyers use their powerful guns to bring down the most dangerous foes, all the while avoiding destruction by remaining hidden until they are ready to deliver the fatal shot.

The jeeps act as trackers, following the target and guiding the tank destroyers into the best hide from which to ambush their prey. Once they have fired, tank destroyers quickly move to another concealed position ready to strike again.

Field Artillery Battery

Platoon

HQ Section with:

2 Gun Sections	**165 points**
1 Gun Section	**95 points**

Option

- Add $^{3}/_{4}$-ton and $2^{1}/_{2}$-ton trucks at no cost.

A Field Artillery Battery may only support a Rifle, Ranger, or Parachute Rifle Company.

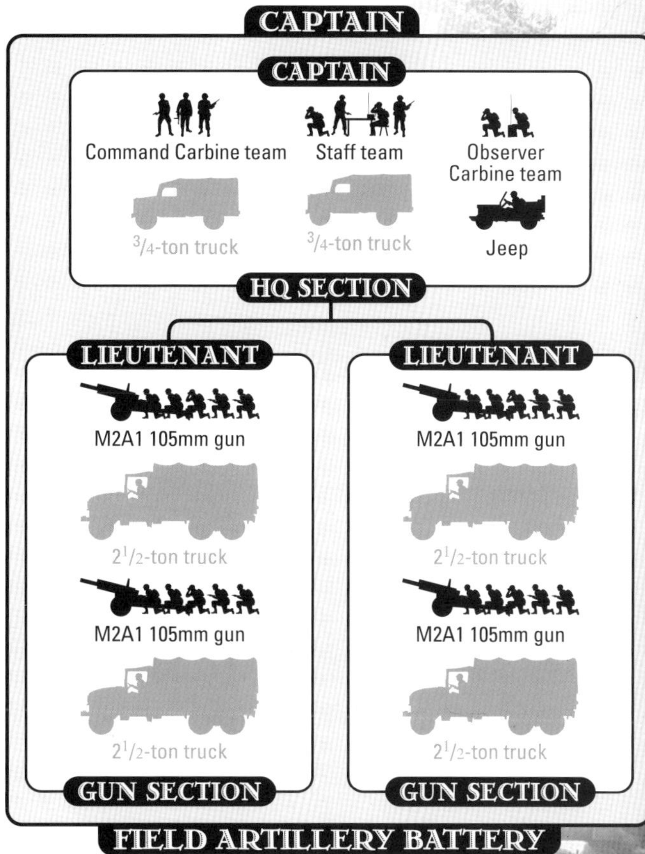

Cheap and plentiful hard-hitting artillery is easily one of the infantry commander's most powerful tools. When defending, massed artillery bombardments smash the enemy attacks, causing casualties and dislocating their plans. It breaks up concentrated attacks allowing them to be dealt with piecemeal.

When attacking artillery is even more valuable. Few enemy soldiers can maintain effective fire with 42 pound (19 kg) shells falling on their positions, and over time their casualties mount up making the infantry's job much easier.

Armored Field Artillery Battery

Platoon

With T19 105mm HMC:

2 Gun Sections	**295 points**
1 Gun Section	**165 points**

- Arm any or all T19 105mm HMC half-tracks with a .50 cal AA MG for +5 points per half-track.

With M7 Priest:

2 Gun Sections	**325 points**
1 Gun Section	**180 points**

Options

- Add Jeep for Command team at no cost.
- Replace any Jeeps with unarmed M2 half-tracks for +5 points per half-track.
- Arm any or all unarmed Jeeps or M2 half-tracks with an AA MG for +10 points per vehicle.

An Armored Field Artillery Battery may only support a Tank, Armored Rifle, Armored Recon, or Ranger Company.

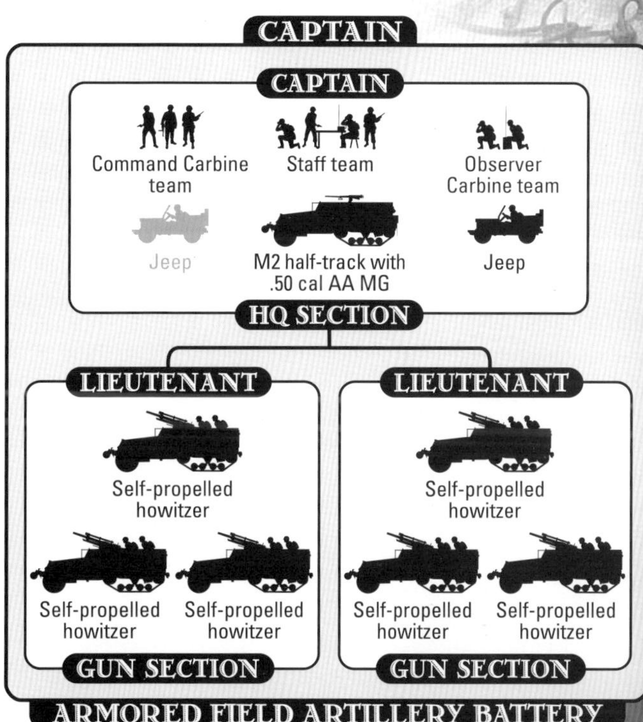

Artillery is an essential part of an armored force. Only artillery has the ability to contribute across the whole battlefield, delivering its firepower against critical targets on call.

The combination of the armored forces' extensive radio network and the excellent fire control system of the US artillery mean a quick response to requests for fire. The artillery bring sudden death to enemy anti-tank guns and infantry caught under their devastating bombardments.

Chemical Mortar Platoon

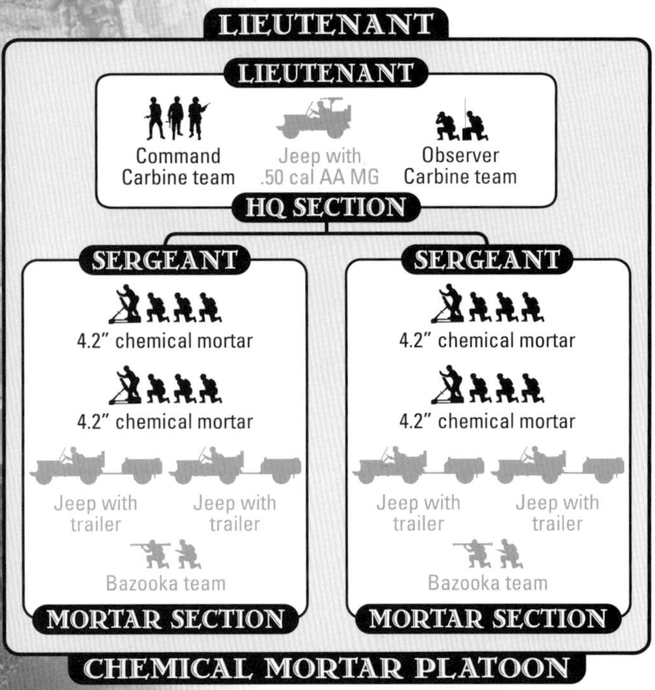

Platoon

HQ Section with:

2 Mortar Sections	125 points
1 Mortar Section	70 points

Option

- Add Bazooka teams for +15 points per team.
- Add Jeep with .50cal AA MG for +15 points.
- Add Jeeps with trailers at no cost.

A Chemical Mortar Platoon may only support a Rifle, Ranger, or Parachute Rifle Company.

With a high rate of fire, long range, and a heavy shell, these weapons provide excellent fire support for the infantry. They can keep up with the infantry in almost any terrain as the crews are well trained in moving their weapons in handcarts when they can't use their jeeps.

Anti-aircraft Artillery (Self-propelled) Platoon

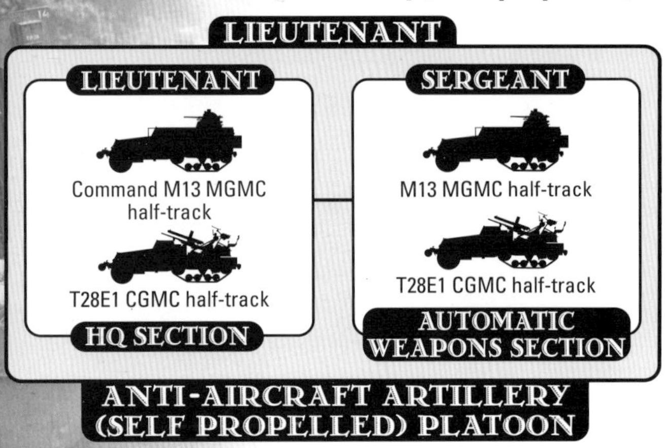

Platoon

2 Auto Weapons Sections	180 points
1 Auto Weapons Section	90 points

Options

- Replace all M13 MGMC with T28E1 CGMC at no cost.
- Replace all T28E1 CGMC with M15 CGMC at no cost.

Anti-aircraft artillery (AAA) is vital to keep the Stuka divebombers of the German Air Force at bay and the new self-propelled mountings are proving their usefulness in mobile battles. The M13 MGMC is particularly versatile, performing equally well against ground and air targets.

Truck Section

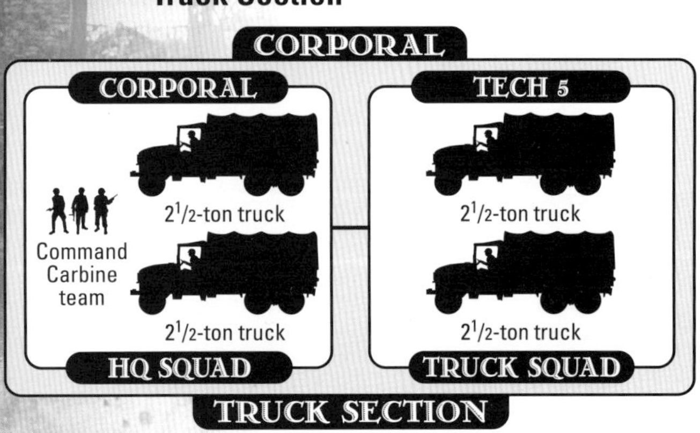

Platoon

HQ Squad with:

1 Truck Squad	25 points
No Truck Squad	15 points

The Quartermasters Company provided trucks to carry the infantry on road marches.

A Truck Section is a Transport Platoon.

Anti-aircraft Artillery Platoon

Platoon

HQ Section with

2 Auto Weapons Sections	**105 points**
1 Auto Weapons Section	**60 points**

Option

- Replace one M1 Bofors gun per section with an M2 .50 cal AA gun for -20 points per section.

M2 .50 cal AA guns are carried Portee on their trucks.

While the self-propelled AAA quickly proved themselves in battle, the majority of AAA cover was provided by towed weapons. Strangely, all anti-aircraft troops were initially part of the Coastal Artillery, but served in the field none the less.

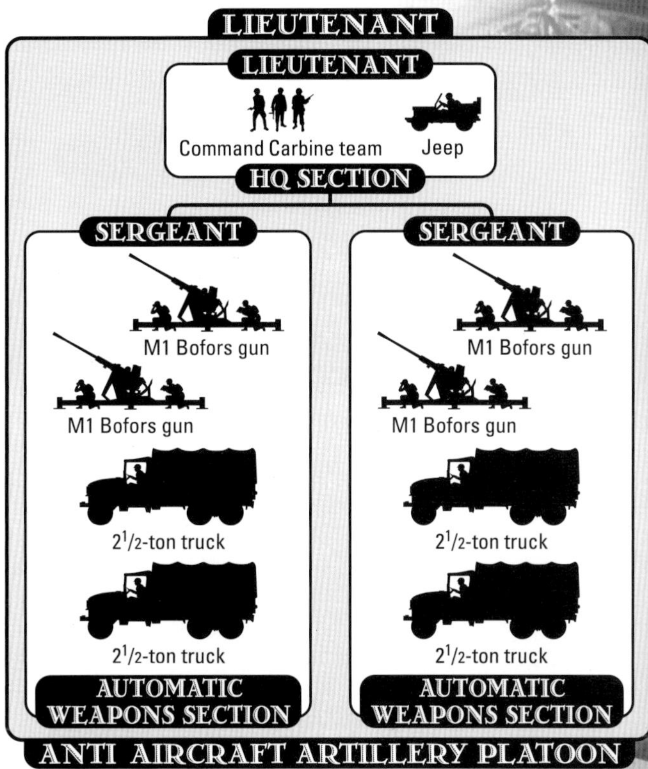

... Bizerte ...

Staff Sergeant Cole 'Reb' Jackson scrambles up on the platoon's number three tank. Briscoe, its commander, looks up out of the turret at him. 'Reb, we gotta call in some artillery,' Briscoe says, his face pale. 'We'll be slaughtered if we go out there again.' Jackson snorts and glances at a column of black smoke rising above the ridge, marking the grave of his tank. 'We just have to duck and weave, boy' he says. 'Pin 'em, flank 'em, punch 'em on the nose.'

He turns as a dusty jeep screeches to a halt. 'What the hell do you sons of bitches think you're doing!' barks the red-faced little man that bounces out of it. Jackson curses silently. General Ernie Harmon, Old Gravel Voice. 'You waiting for those German bastards to die of old age?' Harmon continues, striding across to the M4 Sherman tank and clambering onto it. 'Sergeant, I want this goddamn platoon moving, and I want it moving, now!'

Jackson sketches a salute. 'There's a German gun just over the ridge, General,' he says calmly. 'It just popped our two lead tanks. We're just about to go fix it.'

"Go fix it"?' Harmon snorts. 'Horseshit, it looks more like you're having a goddamn coffee break! I want this godawful platoon on that godforsaken piece of real estate right now! Where the hell's your goddamned officer?'

Jackson cocks a thumb towards the other pillar of smoke. 'Lieutenant's in that one, sir.'

Harmon pauses, and then clears his throat. 'I still want you on that damned road, Sergeant. Now, you form your platoon up and you damn well follow me!' Harmon gestures to his driver who brings the jeep up alongside the Sherman.

'General,' Jackson says. 'You go racin' over the hill in that thing, and you'll get your dang fool head shot off. You leave that gun to me, an' I'll leave the generalling to you, and we'll take your hill. Now get the hell off my tank!'

Harmon stares at him, speechless for a moment. And then he grins. 'You just do it, Sergeant.' He snaps a salute and climbs into his jeep.

As Harmon's jeep races off, Jackson turns, 'Briscoe, out! I need your tank.'

Pressing the mic button, Jackson quickly issues orders. Cautiously, the other two tanks roll towards the ridge, just poking their guns over as they fire on the trees hiding the German gun.

'Left, slow and steady, Joe,' Jackson directs his driver. 'Ain't no use if you drop a track.'

Emerging from a gully, Jackson spots his target. The 75 cracks. An HE round rips the gun apart. 'That's how you do it, boys,' he says. 'Pin 'em, flank 'em, kick 'em in the ass.'

Engineer Combat Platoon

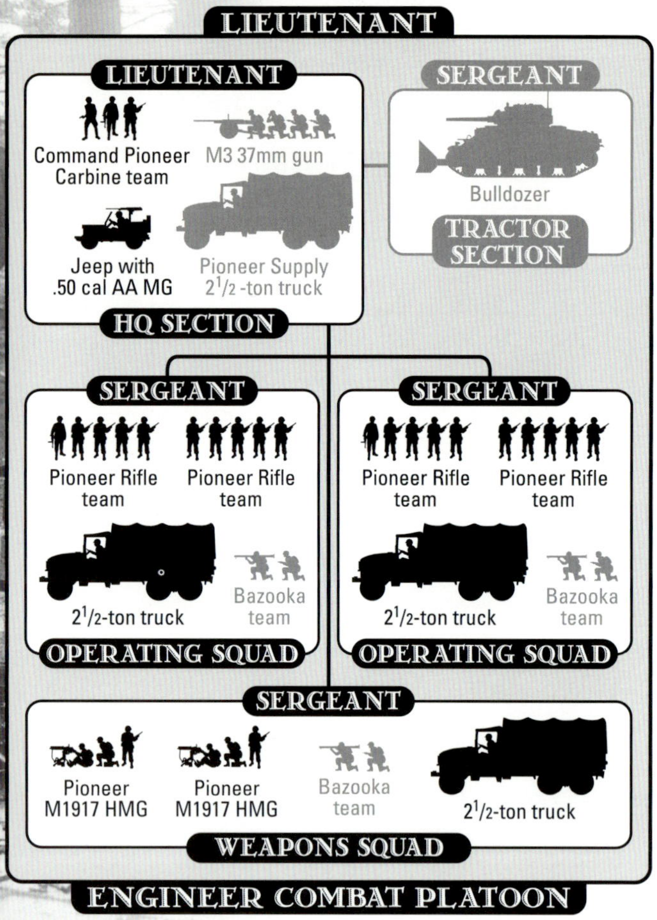

Platoon

HQ Section with Weapons Squad and

2 Operating Squads	**165 points**
1 Operating Squad	**125 points**
No Operating Squads	**85 points**

Options

- Replace all Pioneer M1917 HMG teams with Pioneer Rifle teams at no cost.
- Add M3 37mm gun for +15 points.
- Replace the M3 37mm gun with a Bazooka team at no cost.
- Add Bazooka teams for +15 points per team.
- Add Pioneer Supply $2^{1}/_{2}$-ton truck for +25 points.
- Add a Bulldozer for +10 points, a turretless M4 Sherman dozer for +15 points, or an M4 Sherman tank fitted with a dozer blade for +120 points.

Engineer Combat Platoons clear and lay mines barbed wire and other obstacles. To do this with a minimum of interference, they have machine-guns and anti-tank guns to keep the enemy's heads down.

Although the engineers' trucks looked like normal cargo carriers, they were actually dump trucks fitted with a tipping load bed.

Armored Engineer Combat Platoons

Armored divisions had an Armored Engineer Battalion instead of the infantry's Engineer Combat Battalion. Despite the new name, the only difference was that one platoon in each company was mounted in armoured half-tracks instead of dump trucks.

You may field an Armored Engineer Platoon to support your Tank or Armored Rifle Company by replacing the $2^{1}/_{2}$-ton trucks with M3 half-tracks for +10 points per half-track. All half-tracks have an AA MG.

KASSERINE PASS

FEBRUARY 14, 1943

Dateline: 12 February 1943

From our correspondent, Tom Grossman, somewhere in Tunisia

I moved up to the front yesterday, and have been catching up on all the recent action with the boys from 2nd Battalion, 13th Armored Regiment. Led by Colonel Henry E Gardiner, this unit has been in the thick of the fighting ever since arriving on these African shores.

Captain Mike Bradshaw, of Santa Rosa California, told me of an encounter with the Germans in the Ousseltia Valley late last month. Driving to the rescue of trapped French troops, an American force with Gardiner's battalion at its head not only stopped a major enemy offensive, but then drove the Germans out of the valley. Major General Paul Robinett was awarded the French Croix de Guerre in recognition of the achievements of our troops.

Dateline: 15 February 1943

From our correspondent with 1st Armored Division, Tunisia

Yesterday was St Valentines Day, but love was conspicuous by its absence. The front has come alive again. A new German offensive is sweeping forwards like a wave, breaking over our positions all along this sector of the front. Driving to where the action was hottest, the little-known town of Sidi Bou Zid, I witnessed the bravest act I shall probably ever see.

All that stood between the massed Panzer divisions and victory were the new M4 Sherman tanks of 3rd Battalion, 1st Armored Regiment, commanded by Lt Col Louis Hightower. Heavily outnumbered, beset from all sides yet refusing to surrender, this fine unit fought to the last, buying invaluable time for our defences to be strengthened in preparation for the approaching storm.

This morning our forces struck back. The roar of dozens of armored vehicles could not drown out the stirring call of "The Star Spangled Banner", played as Lt Col James Alger's 2nd Battalion, 1st Armored Regiment lead a taskforce out to do battle with the enemy.

Driving out into the desert in perfect formation, this mighty phalanx has but one goal: evicting the enemy from the real estate they seized the day before.

Early progress has been good. Official reports indicate that Alger has reached the main body of enemy troops. The sound of a fierce battle is reaching me even as I write this. The gunfire proof that our flag is still flying here.

Dateline: 18 February 1943

Tom Grossman, from the battlefields of Tunisia

After the indescribable heroism of the last two days, I have rejoined Lt Col Henry Gardiner's 2nd Battalion, 13th Armored Regiment, a unit which faces a stern test in the days to come.

The Germans are fielding their latest secret weapons. Lt Col James Alger's brave counter-attack ran foul of the enemy's new super-heavy 'Tiger' tanks and 'Screaming Meemee' rockets. The Allied forces are rolling with the punch, and the enemy has been slow to consolidate his gains. His next target is the town of Sbeitla, and there I had the privilege of seeing Gardiner's men in action.

In a masterful defence, Gardiner's M3 Lee tanks held the Panzers at bay, not giving an inch until ordered to do so. There have been many casualties, but the enemy has been forced to pay a far heavier price. Leading from the front as always, Colonel Gardiner's tank was hit, and his fate was unknown for several hours. I am glad to report that he escaped on foot and is back with slightly wounded but still full of fight.

2nd Battalion disengaged once the next line of defence was prepared, falling back through Kasserine Pass. The Germans will sure have a fight on their hands getting through here. Engineers are laying minefields and barbed wire, tank destroyers and artillery are settling into position. Reinforcements are rushing here from all over Tunisia. Gone is the confusion of four days ago. This is a steady, well-planned withdrawal, buying time, waiting for the right moment to strike back. us,

Dateline: 21 February 1943

From our special correspondent, Tom Grossman in Tunisia

The final showdown is approach-ing. After several days of hard fighting, the defenders of Kasserine Pass fell back on Major General Robinett's force defending at Tebessa.

Once again the Germans haven't lived up to their reputation. Their advance has been very hesitant, allowing Colonel Henry Gardiner's 2nd Battalion, 13th Armored Regiment plenty of time to conceal themselves in the Foussana Valley at Tebessa.

When the enemy finally arrived yesterday they were reluctant to attack, sending in their air force first. It did no good. Not 200 yards from me are the wrecks of two Stuka divebombers, still smoking after being brought down by our anti-aircraft fire.

Dawn has brought a new attack, the enemy showing more deter-mination than yesterday. The enemy made steady progress up the valley, but finally the storm of artillery fire was too much for them. This time, however, there was no escape.

When the Germans turned to flee, they ran straight into Gardiner's battalion closing the door. The American tanks poured out their vengeance, repayment for the weeklong retreat, a tribute to the brave men of Sidi Bou Zid.

As I write this, the sound of battle has faded, there is no sign of the enemy except the abandoned tanks, the charred skeletons of burned trucks, and the hundreds of prisoners who have been rounded up. Today was the finest day in the entire Tunisian campaign, a day where Americans took on the very best that Hitler had to offer, held their ground, and gave it right back.

Dateline: 25 February 1943

From Tom Grossman in Tunisia

Yesterday morning, American forces in Tunisia recaptured the strategically important Kasserine Pass.

Lead by men of 1st Armored Division, the counterattack has reclaimed nearly all of the ground lost during last week's battles. With the enemy reeling all along the front, it is only a matter of time before a knock-out blow is delivered, freeing North Africa from beneath the Nazi jackboot at last.

Gallantry Awards

Distinguished Service Cross
Lt Col H Gardiner, Feb 18.
Silver Star
Capt J Meredith, Feb 22.
Bronze Star
Maj D D Unsworth, Feb 20.
Lt J M Brown, Feb 21.

Painting Afrikakorps

Due to the extreme conditions in the desert, the colour of the Afrikakorps uniform varied depending on how long the individual has been in the desert sun. By adding a small amount of white to the uniform colour on your mixing palette you can simulate the sun-bleaching of the uniforms. Add more white for veterans of many battles, but don't add any white at all to represent newly-arrived soldiers who have spent little time under the blazing sun.

	Vallejo Acrylic	Games Workshop
Infantry		
Uniform	Russian Uniform (924)	Camo Green
Helmet and gasmask		
(1941-1942)	Green Brown (879)	Desert Yellow
(1942-1943)	Iraqi Sand (819)	Kommando Khaki
Boots	Beige Brown (875)	Bestial Brown
Boot uppers	German Camo Beige (821)	Kommando Khaki
Webbing	Stone Grey (884)	Rotting Flesh
SMG ammunition pouches and bread bag	German Camo Beige (821)	Kommando Khaki
Waterbottle and entrenching tool	Beige Brown (875)	Bestial Brown
Tanks		
(1941-1942)	Green Brown (879)	Desert Yellow
(1942-1943)	Iraqi Sand (819)	Kommando Khaki
Camouflage		
Panzer Grey	German Grey (995)	Codex Grey
Standard Colours		
Faces and hands	Flat Flesh (955)	Dwarf Flesh
Rifle butt	Beige Brown (875)	Bestial Brown
Machine-guns, rifle barrels, goggles, and tracks	Gunmetal Grey (863)	Boltgun Metal
Tyres	Black (950)	Chaos Black

Painting Afrikakorps Infantry

1

After preparing your figures for painting, undercoat them with a black spray-can primer or thinned primer paint. Paint a base coat of **Russian Uniform (924)** on the uniforms and paint the helmets **Green Brown (879)** (1941-1942) or **Iraqi Sand (819)** (1942-1943).

2

Next highlight the uniforms. Mix a little **White (951)** with the **Russian Uniform (924)** and dry brush this onto the raised parts of the uniform to add depth to the figures. See the *Flames Of War* book or the *Quartermasters Painting Guide* for dry brushing techniques.

3

Finish the figures by painting the details with a 2/0 brush. Paint faces and hands in **Flat Flesh (955)**, rifles and boots in **Beige Brown (875)**, and machine-guns in **Gunmetal Grey (863)**. Now your troops are ready for battle. All you need to do now is to mount them on their bases. See the *Flames Ofwar* book or the *Quartermasters Painting Guide* for basing ideas.

Expert

Once you have painted your army you may want to go back and add more details to your figures. Only do this if you wish to put a lot more time into your painting. You can paint the webbing, water bottle, goggles and webbing, adding highlight for more depth.

Painting Afrikakorps Guns

1

After assembling your guns using the supplied instructions, undercoat them with a black spray-can primer or thinned primer paint. Base coat your guns with **Green Brown (879)** (1941-1942) or **Iraqi Sand (819)** (1942-1943).

2

Mix a little **White (951)** into the **Green Brown (879)** or **Iraqi Sand (819)** and highlight the top surfaces of the gun. Dry brushing is an excellent method for this as it picks out the guns' details and gives the impression of light and shadow.

3

Paint the tyres **Black (950)**. Now paint the crew as described above and you are ready to mount your weapon and its crew to its base. Your gun is now ready for its first battle.

Expert

Adding battlefield wear and tear, mud on the wheels and smoke stains at the end of the barrel all add up to a weapon that will stand out on the battlefield.

Painting Afrikakorps Tanks

1

Assemble your tanks using the diagram in the pack. Undercoat them with a black spray-can primer or thinned primer paint. Base coat your tanks with **Green Brown (879)** (1941-1942) or **Iraqi Sand (819)** (1942-1943).

2

Mix a little **White (951)** into the base colour. Dry brush this on the top surfaces and raised details of the tank to highlight them. Scale miniatures benefit from accentuating detail in this way that would otherwise be lost to the eye.

3

Finish off your tanks by painting your tracks **Gunmetal Grey (863)** and the tyres on the road wheels **Black (950)**. Your tanks are now ready to stalk their prey across the battlefield.

Expert

To take your tank to the expert level, you can paint the tools. Paint the tracks with a rusty brown and highlight with metal. Adding decals for unit numbers, crosses and army symbols gives your tank its final touches.

Recognising Afrikakorps Vehicles

Sd Kfz 254 Saurer

The wheel-cum-track Sd Kfz 254 armoured observation post is a unique vehicle developed by Saurer for the Austrian army. For road movement it lowers its wheels, while its tracks give excellent cross-country mobility.

The frame radio aerial and unusual arrangement of wheels and tracks make it easy to recognise.

Sd Kfz 250/5 'Greif'

Rommel's half-track is a Sd Kfz 250/5 armoured observation post named *Greif* (meaning *Attack* or *Griffin*).

The frame radio aerial and bold lettering of the word *'Greif'* make this half-track very easy to spot.

Panzer III J

The Panzer III J is the most common German tank until the retreat from El Alamein. It has a 5cm (2") gun and 5cm (2") of armour.

It is recognisable by the stowage bin on the back of the turret, no spaced armour on the mantlet (only on the L model), and most importantly, its six road wheels.

Panzer IV F2

The Panzer IV provides the lighter Panzer III tanks with heavy fire support. The long-barrelled Panzer IV F2 and G have anti-tank guns capable of penetrating any tank in existence.

The Panzer IV can be recognised by eight small road wheels and hatches above the driver and radio operator's positions.

Tiger I E (Tunisia)

The super-heavy Tiger I E tank has a massive 8.8cm (3.45") gun and 10cm (4") of armour. It is almost invulnerable to any Allied gun.

It is hard to miss the big square hull with a circular turret, long barrel, and interleaved road wheels of this vehicles.

Diana

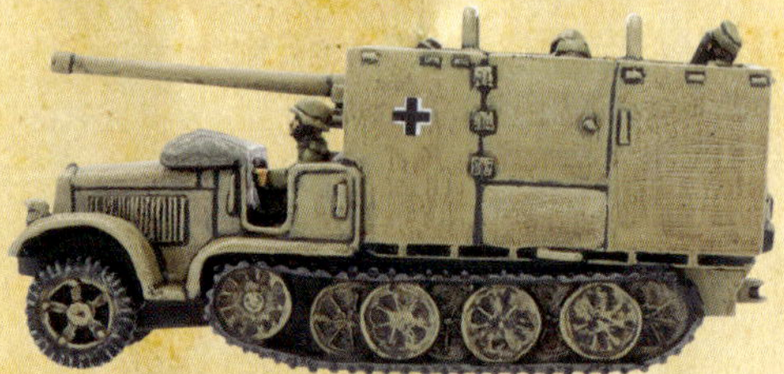

The 7.62cm FK36(r) auf Panzerjäger Sf Zgkw 5t tank hunter is better known by the codename Diana. It is a Soviet 7.62cm (3") field gun mounted on the chassis of a Sd Kfz 6 (5t) half-track.

It is easy to recognise with its high square box superstructure and half-tracked chassis.

15cm (Sf) Lorraine Schlepper

The 15cm (Sf) Lorraine Schlepper is a combination of a captured French infantry carrier and a First World War German 15cm sFH13/1 (L/17) howitzer.

The small Lorraine Schlepper is easy to spot with its fighting compartment set well back on the chassis and the recoil spade suspended from the rear.

Bison (15cm sIG)

The Bison has a 15cm sIG33 (L/12) infantry gun mounted on a highly modified Panzer II chassis. The Panzer II chassis was both widened and lengthened.

The key recognition feature of this vehicle are the long, low chassis with six road wheels.

Afrikakorps Tank Markings

Army Symbols

Every vehicle displayed combinations of the German cross or Balkenkreuz, the Afrikakorps palm (usually displayed on the left front guard or vehicle sides), and divisional symbols. Most vehicles were originally grey, so when they were repainted in desert colours, a contrasting grey patch was sometimes left behind the markings.

When using captured vehicles it is essential to distinguish them in the battlefield, so they usually had oversized crosses painted on the doors and any other flat surface.

Common Tank Numbering System

This diagram shows the numbering system for a complete company of combat vehicles. The first number '2' indicates the 2nd company, the second number is the platoon number and the third number is the tank number in the platoon.

15. Panzerdivision

Wolfsangel

15. Panzerdivision is unusual in only showing a single oversized red digit for the company number, omitting the platoon and tank numbers. The divisional symbol was commonly found on the turret sides and the rear of the turret bin. Tank crews often thought of themselves as the elite regiment of the division and had their own symbol. For *Panzerregiment 8* this was the *Wolfsangel*, usually displayed next to the divisional symbol. The *Afrikakorps* palm was displayed on the front drivers plate and the *Balkenkreuz* on the hull sides.

21. Panzerdivision

21. Panzerdivision used the common 3 digit numbering system as described above. The numbers were normally red with white outlines painted on the turret sides. The divisional symbol was commonly found on the front plate with the *Afrikakorps* palm and this was repeated on the rear plate.

This tank is from 2nd company, 3rd platoon, and is the 3rd tank.

10. Panzerdivision

10. Panzerdivision usually followed the same practice as *15. Panzerdivision* in only painting the company number on the turret side and rear, although some companies later added the platoon and tank numbers in smaller white numerals.

The Bison symbol of *Panzerregiment 7* was usually shown on the turret sides and rear. The divisional symbol was displayed front and rear.

90. leiche Afrikadivision

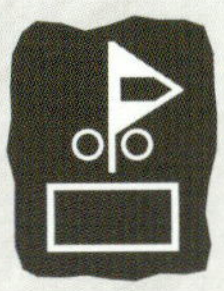

90. leichte Afrikadivision had few armoured vehicles of its own. However its trucks and gun tractors displayed the divisional symbol front and rear.

164. leiche Afrikadivision

164. leichte Afrikadivision had relatively few vehicles of its own as it was newly formed at Alamein. Those it had displayed the divisional symbol front and rear.

PAINTING ITALIANS

	Vallejo Acrylic	Games Workshop
Desert Vehicles		
Yellow Sand	Green Ochre (914)	Desert Yellow
Camouflage		
Grey Green	German Fieldgrey (830)	Catachan Green
Sicily & Italy Vehicles		
Grey Green	German Fieldgrey (830)	Catachan Green
Camouflage		
Yellow Sand	Green Ochre (914)	Desert Yellow
Sicily Semovente 90/53		
Grey Green	German Fieldgrey (830)	Catachan Green
Camouflage		
Red Brown	Beige Brown (875)	Scorched Brown
Dark Green	Olive Grey (888)	Dark Angels Green
Infantry		
Uniform	Desert Yellow (977)	Desert Yellow
Puttees	Olive Grey (888)	Dark Angels Green
Helmets, Artillery	Green Ochre (914)	Desert Yellow
Sicily & Italy Infantry		
Uniform, Puttees	Olive Grey (888)	Dark Angels Green
Helmets, Artillery	German Fieldgrey (830)	Catachan Green
Common		
Webbing	Yellow Green (881)	Desert Yellow
Boots, Rifle butt	Beige Brown (875)	Scorched Brown
Faces and hands	Flat Flesh (955)	Dwarf Flesh
Officers Sahariana jackets	Khaki (988)	Kommando Khaki
Vehicle tracks and gun barrels	Gunmetal Grey (863)	Boltgun Metal

Paint your Italian infantry and vehicles following the guide for Afrikakorps, substituting the colours in the above list.

ITALIANS AT THE FRONT

Italian soldiers that were sent to North Africa and Tunisia were issued with desert uniforms. Use the techniques shown in the Afrikakorps painting guide for your desert infantry.

Italian infantry that served on the battlefields of Sicily and Italy wore the standard green uniform of the Italian Army. Use the Sicily & Italy section of the paint list to paint your force.

Due to a shortage in paint, transport vehicles in Africa were generally left green (German Fieldgrey). Crews often painted patches of Green Ochre for Camouflage.

Various camouflage schemes were applied to Italian tanks during the Sicily campaign. This three-tone Semovente 90/53 uses a German Fieldgrey basecoat with Beige Brown and Green Ochre blotches painted over the top.

RECOGNITION

RECOGNISING ITALIAN ARMOURED VEHICLES

Carro Camando

Visually similar to the Semovente 75 it commands, the distinguishing features of the Carro Cammando is the 13.2mm machine-gun in place of the 75mm gun, and the artillery range-finder in front of the hatch.

L6/40

The L6/40 is smaller than most other Italian vehicles. It has 4 road wheels on canter-levered suspension and is armed with a 20mm main gun and co-ax machine gun. The Semovente 47 is built on the same chassis, with a hull mounted 47mm gun and no turret.

AB41

The Autoblindo is a reconnaissance vehicle that features the same turret as the L6/40 fitted to an armoured car. This armoured car also features an 8mm machine-gun fitted to the rear of the drivers compartment.

M13/40 or M14/41

The M13/40 and M14/41 are virtually indistungishable from each other. The M14/41 features a larger engine and different radiator arangement, but has the same armourment and armour as the M13/40. The M13/40 and M14/41 retained the 4 double-wheeled bogie suspension of its predecessor, the M11/39.

Lancia da 90/53

Mounting the huge 90/53 (90mm) gun on the back of a Lancia 3 RO 6-ton truck makes this beast hard to miss on the battlefield. It is easily distinguished by the 6 massive supporting legs that keep the gun stable during combat.

Semovente 75/18

Using the M14/41 hull to mount a 75mm gun gives the Semovente 75/18 a very low silhouette. It is easily recognised by the lack of turret and flared muzzle break of the 75mm gun.

Semovente 90/53

A lengthened and heavily modified M14/41 hull and the huge 90mm gun makes the Semovente 90/53 an easy vehicle to recognise and fear on the battlefield.

RECOGNISING YOUR BROTHERS IN BATTLE

Fucilieri

The backbone of the Royal Army, the Fucilieri shown wear their desert-coloured uniforms.

Bersaglieri

Italy's elite forces are the Bersaglieri, recognised by the plume of feathers adorning their helmets.

Folgore

The fearless parachutists fight with unequalled tenacity. Their green or camouflaged helmets are easy to spot and feared by Allied forces.

MARKINGS

The Italians used a simple method of coloured rectangles to identify the three different companies of an Armoured Battalion. Red= 1st Company, Sky Blue= 2nd Company, Yellow= 3rd Company.

White vertical bars within the coloured rectangles denotes the platoon number in the company. The Company Command tank would have a solid rectangle, the first platoon would have a single white bar, the second platoon would have two white bars and the third platoon would have three.

Numbers carried above the coloured rectangles distinguish individual tanks within the platoons. The first tank of the platoon would carry a number '1' through to the fifth tank carrying the number '5'.

This marking system was common on Italian armoured vehicles throughout the war and on all fronts and was usually displayed on both sides and the rear of the turret.

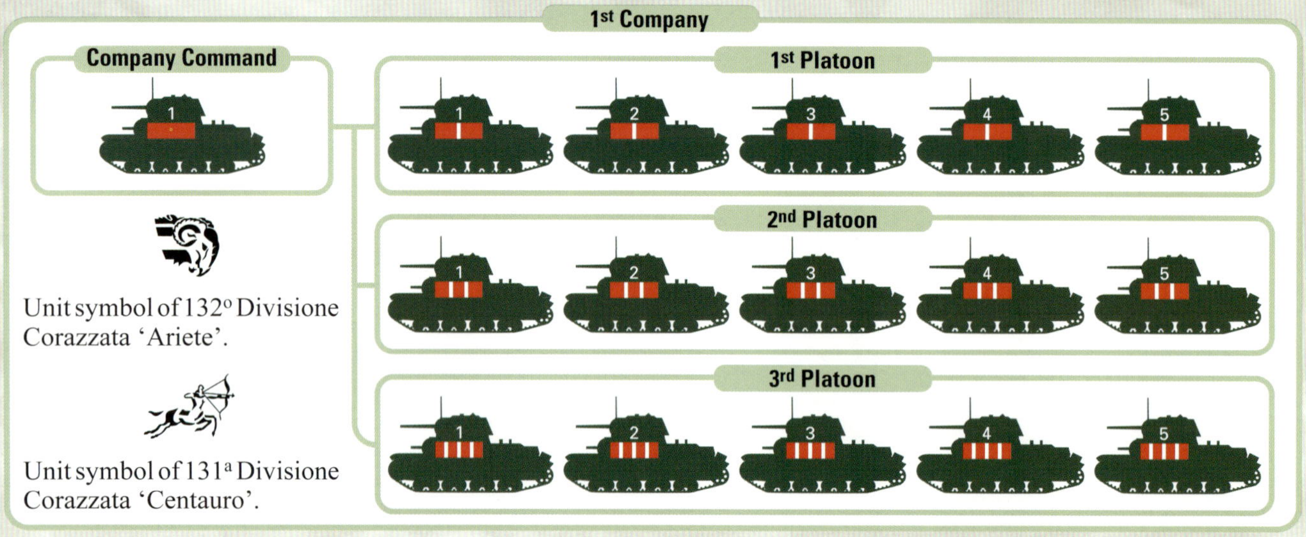

Unit symbol of 132º Divisione Corazzata 'Ariete'.

Unit symbol of 131ª Divisione Corazzata 'Centauro'.

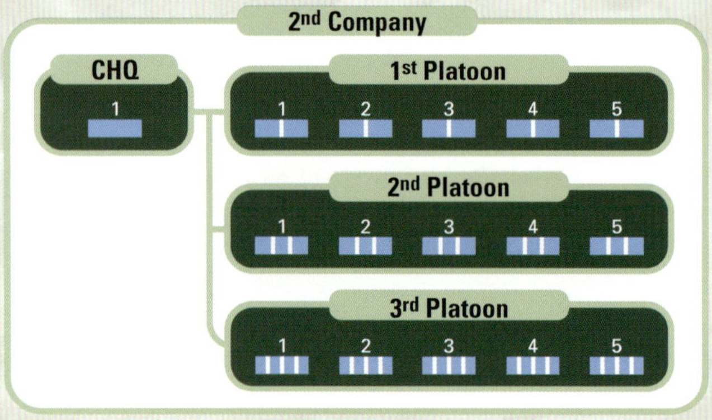

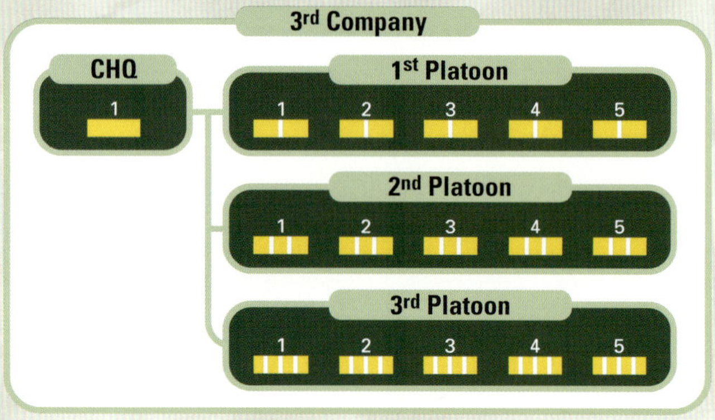

The Semovente 90/53 used a silhouette of itself as a unit symbol. This was usually painted on both sides of the gun shield.

This M14/41 bears the red rectangle of the 1st Company of the Battalion. A single white bar and the number '3' indicates this is the 3rd tank of 1st platoon.

Sometimes unit symbols like Ariete's 'Ram' and Centauro's 'Centaur archer' were painted on the hull sides.

Semovente 47/32 and 75/18 self-propelled guns used a triangle split in half vertically, with either the top half black and the bottom yellow or vice-versa. Different platoons were distinguished by rotating the triangle 180º and/or swapping the yellow and black colours allowing for a variety of combinations.

Painting British Forces

	Vallejo Acrylic	Games Workshop
Desert Vehicles		
Light Stone	Dark Sand (847)	Desert Yellow
Camouflage*		
Dark Green	Bronze Green (897)	Catachan Green
Olive Drab	Brown Violet (887)	Catachan Green
Tunisia Vehicles		
Service Colour	Khaki Grey (880)	Graveyard Earth
Camouflage*		
Very Dark Brown	Germ. Camo Med Brown (826)	Dark Flesh
Sicily & Italy Vehicles		
Light Mud	Khaki (988)	Kommando Khaki
Camouflage*		
Black	Black (950)	Chaos Black
Faded Black	German Grey (995)	Codex Grey
Desert Infantry		
Uniform	Iraqi Sand (916)	Kommando Khaki
Socks	Khaki (988)	Graveyard Earth
Helmets, Vickers MG's, mortars	Dark Sand (847)	Desert Yellow
Tunisia, Sicily, & Italy Infantry		
Trousers	English Uniform (921)	Graveyard Earth
Shirts	Khaki (988)	Kommando Khaki
Helmets, Vickers MG's, mortars	Khaki Grey (880)	Graveyard Earth
or	Khaki (988)	Kommando Khaki
Common		
Webbing	Stone Grey (884)	Rotting Flesh
Boots	Black (950)	Chaos Black
Faces and hands	Flat Flesh (955)	Dwarf Flesh
Rifle butt	Beige Brown (875)	Scorched Brown
Vehicle tracks and gun barrels	Gunmetal Grey (863)	Boltgun Metal

* Any of the camouflage colours given can be used in the desert.

Paint your British infantry and vehicles following the guide for Afrikakorps, substituting the colours in the above lists.

Applying Markings

EXPERT TIP

You may notice that the clear area around the edge of decals is sometimes visible. This is called 'silvering' and occurs because air is trapped under the decal. You can avoid this by painting the area where the decal will sit with gloss varnish or future floor polish and allowing it to dry. Apply the decals using Micro Sol to mould the decal on to the models shape. When the decal is dry, paint with matt varnish to remove the gloss.

Step 1: First cut out the decals you need for your tank. Then put the decal you're planning to add to your tank into warm water. After about 20 seconds the decal will start to slide away from the backing paper.

Step 2: Use your brush to separate the decal from the paper. Then use the brush to pick the decal from the water, make sure the decal is face up on the brush. Sometimes the decal will try and wrap around the brush, it can be flattened by brushing it along a flat surface

Step 3: Use the brush to float the decal onto the tank surface. Once the decal is floating in a small pool of water the brush can be slid out from under it. While the decal is floating use the brush to adjust its position by sliding it around.

Step 4: Once in position, dry the brush on a paper towel or similar, then use it to soak up the excess water on and around the decal. The decal can be flattened out during this process as well. Leave to dry.

INFANTRY DIVISION MARKINGS

British vehicles generally carried few markings. The most obvious of those were the divisional symbol and the battalion code number. These were carried on the front and rear of the vehicle with the battalion code on the driver's side (that's the right-hand side in Britain) and the divisional code on the other side.

Other markings carried would be a registration number carried on the bonnet or door and (less common in the desert) a bridging number giving the weight of the vehicle. Transport vehicles were rarely camouflaged, giving them a spartan appearance.

The truck shown below belongs to the 27th Machine-gun Battalion (51 on red on the driver's side) of the 2nd New Zealand Division (silver fern on a black diamond on the left-hand side).

Battalion marking

Divisional marking

INFANTRY DIVISIONS

Every infantry division had its own symbol painted on its vehicles to identify them. Although some were simply geometric symbols, many had a connection to the origin of the division. Some like the HD of the Highland Division are obvious. Others like Dick Whittington's cat for the London-based 56th Division are less so. One of the oddest is the choice of a platypus for the 9th Australian Division, chosen because the nine-penny stamp showed a platypus!

1st Infantry Division; 4th Infantry Division; 5th Infantry Division

44th Infantry Division; 46th Infantry Division; 50th Infantry Division

51st Infantry Division; 56th Infantry Division; 78th Infantry Division

9th Australian Division; 1st Canadian Division; 4th Indian Division

5th Indian Division; 2nd New Zealand Division; 1st South African Division

BATTALION CODE NUMBERS

The battalion code numbers were used to identify vehicles from each battalion during road marches. To make it easier for traffic controllers, they were painted on the driver's side (right-hand side in Britain) front and rear.

The colour of the background reflected the brigade or arm of service of the unit—red for the senior brigade, green for the second and brown for the junior, red over blue for artillery, green over blue for recce, and blue for the Royal Engineers.

The numbers were randomised to make it more difficult for enemy spies to decipher them and report which units are moving where.

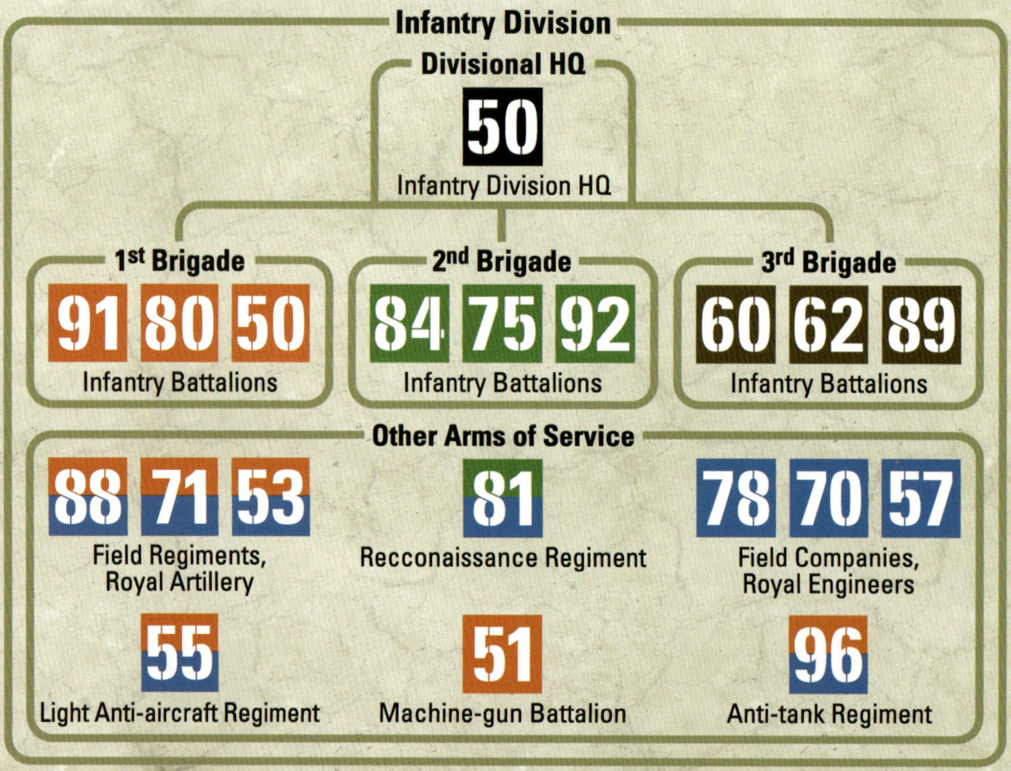

Recognising British Vehicles

Churchill III

Although its design is reminiscent of the First World War, the Infantry Tank Mark IV, the Churchill III, is an outstanding vehicle. Its thick armour protects it from most anti-tank weapons in the heat of battle allowing it to support the infantry at all times.

6pdr Portee

The war in the desert is all about mobility. If anti-tank guns can't keep up with the speed of the battle, they are useless. That is why the 6 pounder anti-tank gun is mounted 'portee-style' on the back of a 3-ton truck enabling it to fight the mobile battle.

Oerlikon 20mm Portee

By mounting the Oerlikon 20mm anti-aircraft gun on a light truck chassis the War Office has finally provided the infantry with much-needed anti-aircraft protection from the marauding German Air Force.

Indian Pattern Carrier

Indian industry is not yet up to the task of providing the expanding Indian Army with tracked carriers. The Indian Pattern Wheeled Carrier replaces the Universal Carrier in their regiments.

Humber LRC III

Based on the Humber Snipe, the LRC gives the infantry an effective scout car at a time when industry is strained producing enough equipment for the armoured divisions.

Humber III

Sufficient Humber armoured cars are now on hand to allow issue to some infantry recce regiments as heavy cars to support the LRC's.

Otter LRC I

The Otter is the Canadian version of the infantry's Light Recce Car (LRC) based on a Ford truck chassis.

Recognising British Carriers

Universal Carrier

The Universal Carrier is the basic version of the carrier family. It is used as a scout carrier and as a troop carrier.

OP Carrier

The OP Carrier is fitted for artillery observation post (OP) work. It is distinguished by a cable reel on the front and a ladder on the side.

Mortar Carrier

The Mortar Carrier holds plenty of ammunition for the 3" mortar, while the mortar itself is strapped on the rear plate.

MMG Carrier

The MMG Carrier gives the Vickers medium machine-gun mobility on the battle-field. The gun sits on the engine cover when moving.

ARMOURED DIVISION MARKINGS

Armoured Division Insignia

1st Armoured | 6th Armoured | 7th Armoured | 10th Armoured

Each division had its own symbol which was painted on every vehicle. In most cases the symbol appeared on the front and rear sand guards on the left-hand side of the vehicle.

7th Armoured Division

99 — Divisional HQ

Armoured Divisions

Senior Brigade

- 71 — Brigade HQ
- 40, 86, 67 — Armoured Regiments
- 60 — Motor Battalion

Junior/Motor Brigade

- 49 — Brigade HQ
- 65, 68, 83 — Armoured Regiments
- 87 — Motor Battalion

Other Arms of Service

- 50 — Anti-tank Regiment, Royal Artillery
- 54 — Light Anti-aircraft Regiment
- 76 — Armoured Car Regiment
- 77, 55, 44 — Royal Horse Artillery Regiments
- 33, 22 — Field Squadrons, Royal Engineers

Each battalion showed a unit sign on its right-hand sand guards. The colour of the sign indicates the type of unit (red for armour, red over blue for artillery etc.) and the white number identifies a particular battalion.

22nd Armoured Brigade - 7th Armoured Division (Desert Rats)

Brigade HQ

71

1RTR - Senior Regiment

40

Regimental HQ (4 tanks)

A Squadron (16 tanks) | B Squadron (16 tanks) | C Squadron (16 tanks)

5RTR - 2nd Regiment

86

Regimental HQ (4 tanks)

A Squadron (16 tanks) | B Squadron (16 tanks) | C Squadron (16 tanks)

4CLY - Junior Regiment

67

Regimental HQ (4 tanks)

A Squadron (16 tanks) | B Squadron (16 tanks) | C Squadron (16 tanks)

1RB - Motor Battalion

60

Tanks used geometric symbols painted on the turret sides to identify their position in the regiment and brigade. The colour of the symbol gave the regiment (senior red, second yellow and junior blue) while the shape gave the squadron. Some units (like the 16th/5th Lancers and 4CLY opposite) painted troop numbers inside the symbol.

TANK CAMOUFLAGE

Many 'Honey' Stuart light tanks were painted all-over Light Stone with no camouflage, like this one of 5RTR.

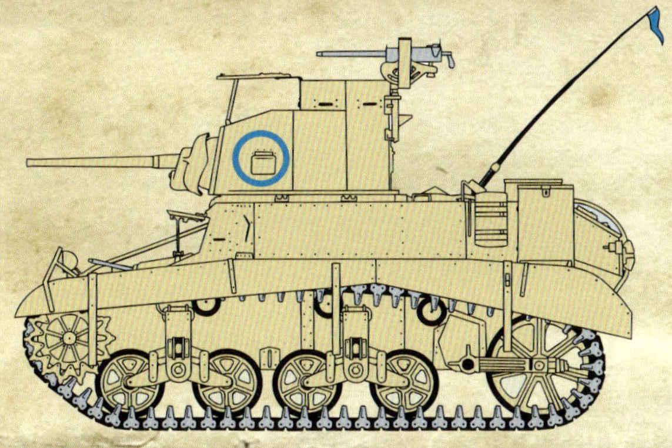

GHQ Middle East ordered all Crusader tanks painted to the standard pattern of Light Stone with Black camouflage (which quickly faded to Dark Grey in the harsh desert sun). Despite this, many other patterns were used by troops in the field.

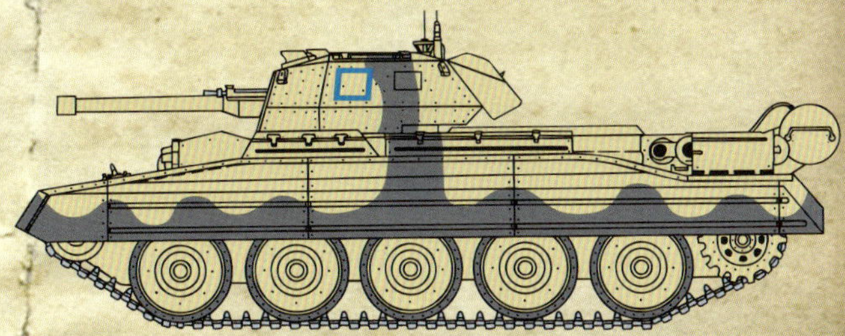

3RTR used an interesting scheme for its Grant tanks. The original US Olive Drab was over painted in Light Stone leaving the top surfaces in the original colour.

The Royal Gloucetershire Hussars used Dark Green, White and Black cement colouring to camouflage their Grant tanks when they couldn't get hold of the regulation paint!

Courageous, a Sherman III tank from the 3rd Hussars shows a typical desert camouflage at the time of the Alamein battles. The Desert Pink tank is over painted with Dark Green swatches.

Sheik is a Sherman III tank of the Royal Scots Greys originally painted in the Alamein period has since had Black spots painted over the Desert Pink to make it more suitable for Italy.

Most tanks fighting in Sicily and Italy were painted Light Mud with Black blotches to better match the hilly terrain. The red-white-red flash on the side of Sheik was often used with this style of camouflage as well.

The Valentine and Crusader tanks of the 6th Armoured Division in Tunisia were painted in the UK-pattern camouflage of Service Colour with Very Dark Brown patches. The yellow triangle shows that this tank is from A squadron of the 16th/5th Lancers.

PAINTING STARS AND STRIPES

	Vallejo Acrylic	Games Workshop
Infantry		
Helmet, bazookas, mortars	Brown Violet (887)	Catachan Green
Jacket	Khaki (988)	Kommando Khaki
Trousers	US Field Drab (873)	Snakebite Leather
Boots	Saddle Brown (940)	Graveyard Earth
Belts, webbing, leggings	Green Grey (886)	Camo Green
Faces and hands	Flat Flesh (955)	Dwarf Flesh
Rifle butt, entrenching tool	Beige Brown (875)	Bestial Brown
Machine-guns, barrels	Gunmetal Grey (863)	Boltgun Metal
Vehicles		
Vehicles	Brown Violet (887)	Catachan Green
Earth yellow camouflage	Dark Sand (847)	Desert Yellow
Earth brown camouflage	USA Tan Earth (874)	Graveyard Earth
Earth red camouflage	Beige Brown (875)	Bestial Brown
Black camouflage	Black (950)	Chaos Black
Tool handles	Beige Brown (875)	Bestial Brown
Machine-guns	Gunmetal Grey (863)	Boltgun Metal
White markings	White (951)	Skull White
Yellow markings	Deep Yellow (915)	Sunburst Yellow

Paint your US infantry and vehicles following the guide for Afrikakorps, substituting the colours in the above lists.

WEATHERING VEHICLES

Flames Of War miniatures benefit greatly if you put a little more time and effort into weathering and making them look like they've been through the wars. Here are a few simple techniques that will make your tanks really stand out on the battlefield.

On the battlefield vehicles were not cleaned often, this gives vehicles a dirty streaky appearance. To recreate this take your lightened Brown Violet and dry brush vertical streaks downward from the top edges of your vehicle.

Once you have applied your decals don't be scared to paint mud splashes or dust over them. This will break up any clean lines, blending the decal into the finished battle-worn effect.

To complete your model, apply a thin coat of matte varnish. This will protect the model from chips and take away any unnaturally glossy surfaces.

To create muddy patches on your vehicle apply small amounts of ready-mixed filler in splash patterns on the front and side of the vehicle.

Once the filler is dry, paint the patches with a suitable mud or dust colour. Dry-brush the area around the filler with the mud or dust colour to blend the mud into the rest of the vehicle. Complete the effect with a drybrush of the lighter colour.

TANK MARKINGS IN NORTH AFRICA, SICILY AND ITALY

1st Armored Division Company Insignia.

Old Ironsides used a system of geometric symbols to distinguish each company and battalion as shown below.

1st ARMORED REGIMENT

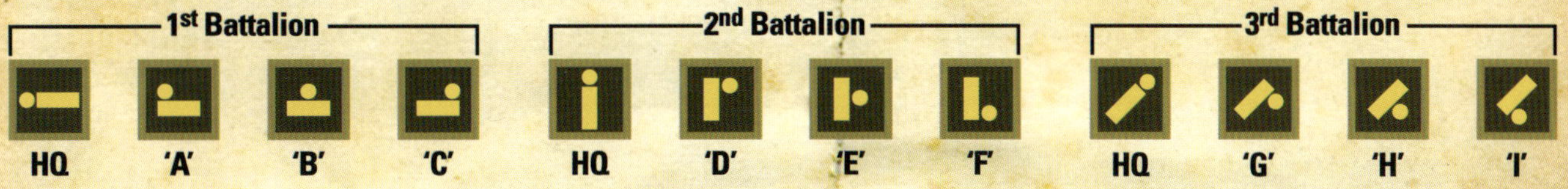

13th ARMORED REGIMENT

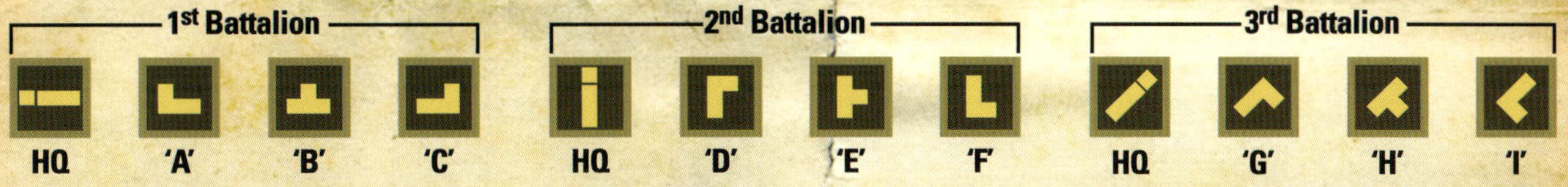

Pre-December 1942, North Africa.

The geometric marking in the front turret stripe designates this tank as from 'D' Company, 2nd Battalion, 1st Armored Regiment. The single dot at the rear of the turret indicates the 1st platoon with the number in the star indicating the 3rd vehicle in the platoon.

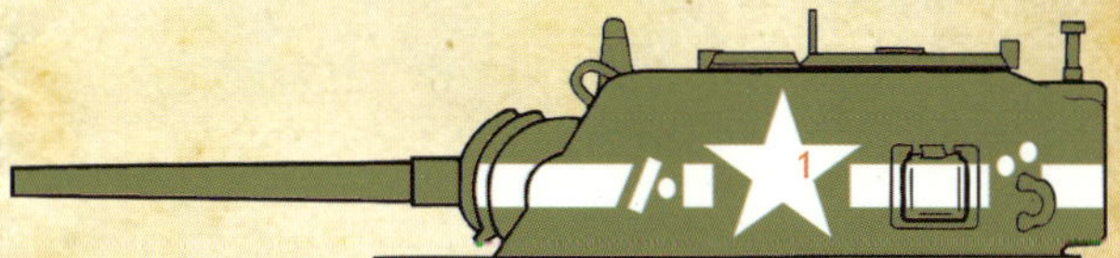

Post-December 1942, North Africa.

The change to white markings was introduced as the yellow was often hidden by the desert dust. This tank is from 'H' Company, 3rd Battalion, 1st Armored regiment. It is the 1st vehicle of the 2nd platoon.

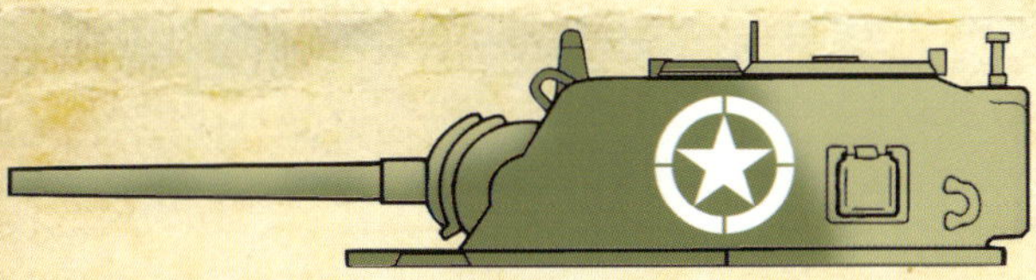

1943, Sicily, Operation 'Husky'.

Prior to the invasion of Sicily, units were instructed to camouflage their tanks with earth yellow (seen here) or earth brown over the standard olive drab. At this time the 'Allied Star', with a circle around the star, was introduced after it was found that the US Star used in the desert could be mistaken for a German cross at a distance. The Allied Star was usually applied to the front transmission housing, turret roof and engine deck as well as the turret sides.

1944, Anzio, Italy.

In Italy platoons were distinguished by barrel bands, the example shows 3rd platoon. The bands were colour coded for each company, red for 'A', white for 'B' yellow for 'C' and blue for 'D' company. Sometimes bands were repeated on the rear of the turret but often a number was used instead. Note the white counter-shading under the barrel, it was also applied to the bottom of the transmission housing. The counter-shading reduced the shadows under the vehicle making it harder to see. Camouflage was earth yellow or in this case red earth over olive drab.

Common tank markings.

The M4 to the right is from 13th Armored Regiment, 1st Armored Division (stenciled on the left transmission housing), 'D' Company, 1st tank (stenciled on the right transmission housing). This series of identification markings were often repeated on the rear of the hull.

Individual companies were distinguished by the names on the sides, 'A' Company had names starting with an A, 'B' Company with a B etc.

The turret top and engine deck had air-recognition stars in the form of the US Star of the period, painted in yellow (pre-December 1942) or white (post-December 1942).

Crews sometimes painted over or obscured the US Stars with engine grease or mud as it was an easy aiming point for the enemy forces.

CRETE INVADED

Vol. 1 Issue 1 31 May, 1941 Free to troops

Our gallant Diving Eagles have done it again! Last week the paratroopers of *7. Fliegerdivision* landed on the British-held island of Crete.

Balkan Blitzkrieg

The southern campaign started on October 28, 1940 when our Italian allies invaded Greece. British forces from Egypt rushed to Crete, freeing up Greek troops to fight in the north. In an arduous winter campaign, the Greeks pushed the Italians back into Albania. The unbeatable German army had little choice but to come to the rescue, and on April 6, 1941, the army invaded Yugoslavia and Greece in Operation Marita.

'W' Force, a mixed force of Australian, British and New Zealand troops under General 'Jumbo' Wilson had been sent to help the Greeks in March, but proved unable to halt the German army thrusting southward. On 24 April the Greeks surrendered. The battle was all but over. 'W' Force was in retreat.

The Eagle Pounces

As the German army approached Athens, the British evacuation was forced westward, across the Corinth canal. The opportunity to cut off the British retreat was irresistible. On April 26, I and II battalions of *2. Fallschirmjägerregiment* captured the bridge over the canal, blocking the retreat. Only the heroic efforts of the British Royal Navy rescued 40,000 soldiers from Greece, without their arms or equipment. By April 30 the last tired survivors were in Egypt and Crete.

Operation Merkur

Although Greece was in German hands, the victory was not yet complete. The island of Crete threatened the vital Romanian oil fields and the convoy routes to North Africa. General Freyberg was placed in command of a motley collection of evacuees from Greece. A seaborne invasion was impossible, the Royal Navy was too strong. Even though the paratroopers would be desperately outnumbered, the only option was an airborne assault!

Code-named Operation *Merkur*, the assault would use the entire *7. Fliegerdivision* for the assault, and fly a mountain division, *5. Gebirgsdivision* in as reinforcements. *Merkur* was scheduled for May 20, 1941.

Maleme

The *Luftlandesturmregiment* landed first at 7:10 am when the gliders of *Sturmbataillon Koch* captured the bridge over the dry bed of the Tavrontis River and the anti-aircraft guns protecting the Maleme airfield beside it. Within minutes they were followed by the rest of the regiment parachuting on both sides of the river—right on top of the New Zealand defenders.

Sturmbataillon Scherber was almost wiped out as it landed to the east of the riverbed, while *Sturmbataillon Gericke* to the east of the river took heavy casualties. Only *Sturmbataillon Stentzler* landing further south escaped relatively unscathed. The situation was desperate. The paratroopers only held half of the airfield. Any counterattack at all would have spelled the end. Fortunately poor communications led the defenders to withdraw instead.

Galatas

More gliders of *Sturmbataillon Koch* attacked the anti-aircraft guns protecting Canea and the port of Suda Bay. A determined defence prevented their capture, leaving *3. Fallschirmjägerregiment* unprotected as they dropped around the town of Galatas to the south. As at Maleme, casualties from the Greek and New Zealand defenders' fire were heavy, leaving the Diving Eagles in possession of the town's prison, but little else. The morning's operations had been disastrous. Losses had been heavy, yet none of the objectives had been taken.

Rethymno And Heraklion

The second wave scheduled for the afternoon was delayed as the surviving Ju52 tri-motor transport aircraft straggled back to the airfields. *2. Fallschirmjägerregiment* finally jumped over the town of Rethymno between 3:00 and 4:30 pm, straight into the waiting fire of the Australian defenders. Once more the result was a slaughter. A similar fate met *1. Fallschirm-jägerregiment* landing several hours later at Heraklion. The afternoon had proved no more successful than the morning. The Diving Eagles faced disaster.

Canea

As is often the case, dawn brought new hope to the paratroops around Maleme airfield. The British counterattack launched during the night had petered out, and during the day reinforcements arrived in another assault landing east of Maleme. By nightfall the airfield was secure.

Over the next few days a continuous stream of Junkers tri-motor transports landed the paratroops' heavy weapons and transport and the mountain division on Maleme airfield, often under heavy fire. While the paratroopers around Rethymno and Heraklion pinned the Australians in place, the reinforcements pushed eastward to Galatas.

Sphakia

A detachment of tired and hungry survivors of *3.Fallschirmjägerregiment* led by Hauptmann Von der Heydte finally took Canea on May 27. The same day General Freyberg ordered the remaining defenders to retreat to Sphakia where the Royal Navy would evacuate them once again.

The last British troops to leave the island went on May 30, leaving thousands behind. The victorious German paratroopers had achieved the impossible, they took the island of Crete from the air!

Airborne Assaults

The planning is over, the drop zones selected, timings finalised, parachutes packed, and the transports loaded. Everything is ready. The drop is on. In a few minutes your company will be spearheading a new airborne assault!

Airborne assault missions are totally different from any other mission you've tried. Plan as you might, the fickle wind and the vagaries of a parachute drop means that there will always be plenty of chaos and confusion for both sides. Your troops will be scattered across the table. Under armed, they must gather their weapons and regroup before the defenders muster the strength to destroy the enemy in their midst.

The special rules for Airborne Assaults presented here cover Parachute Landings and Glider Assaults, allowing you to bring your German and American paratroops into battle from the air as a unique option in addition to ground-based attacks.

CONDUCTING AN AIRBORNE ASSAULT

Airborne assaults require a little more preparation and work than a normal battle, but you wouldn't have passed jump school if you were afraid of hard work! The steps to follow are:

1. **Select your flight line**
2. **Determine the wind direction**
3. **Select your glider landing points**
4. **Select your parachute drop points**
5. **Deploy parachute platoons**
6. **Roll for casualties on landing**
7. **Roll for glider landings**
8. **Shoot with glider machine-guns**
9. **Assault with glider passengers**

After that, it's on to the first turn of the game!

Select Your Flight Line

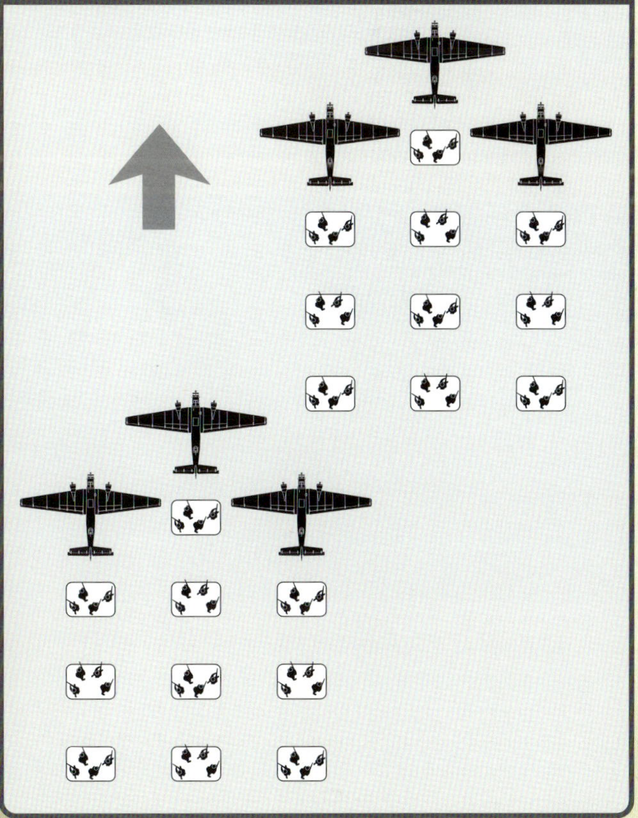

Select Your Flight Line

With so many aircraft trying to drop troops in the same area, they must all follow the same route to avoid collisions.

You must choose a line running across the table as your flight line. All of your aircraft will fly parallel to the flight line. Place an arrow or a pencil on the table to mark the flight line.

Wind Direction

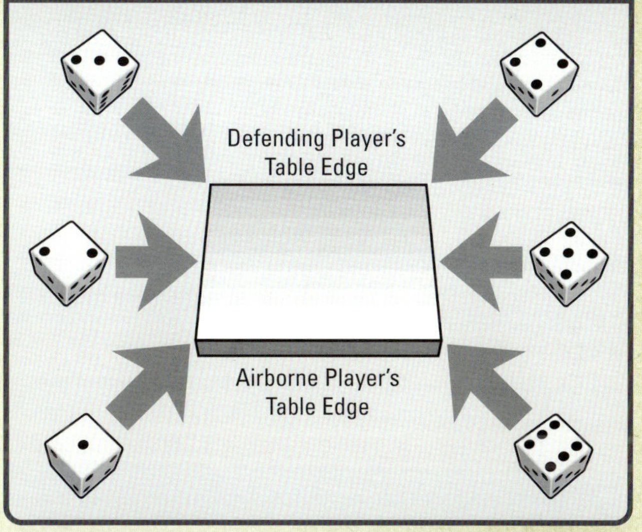

Wind Direction

Although you can plan your flight line before takeoff, you can't control the wind. The strength and direction of the wind is one of the least predictable aspects of an airborne assault. However, since your parachutists will drift down wind while descending, the way the wind is blowing has a major impact on your airdrop.

To determine the wind direction, the airborne player chooses either long table edge as their own, then rolls a die and checks the Wind Direction diagram to determine where the wind is blowing from.

PARACHUTE LANDINGS

While assault gliders are great for pinpoint attacks on important targets, they are too expensive for the bulk of your force. Instead, most airborne troops land by parachute.

The *Fallschirmjäger* use three Junkers Ju52 tri-motor transports (nicknamed *Tante Ju* or Aunty Ju) to carry each platoon. Flown by experienced pilots, they fly in a tight 'V' formation low over the drop zone to ensure that the paratroops land close together.

US paratroopers use a pair of Douglas C-47 transport aircraft per platoon. Each platoon is split into two 'sticks' each containing an officer. Unlike the *Fallschirmjäger*, US paratroopers jump high, but with more equipment. This means that they are more spread out and drift further when they land, but retain their rifles.

Paratroopers jump from their aircraft in rapid succession as it flies along the flight path. When they land, they will be spread out along the aircraft's flight line.

Since they are only over the battlefield very briefly, you don't need to model your transport aircraft.

Select Parachute Drop Points

The first step in a parachute drop is deciding where you want each platoon to land. Despite the skill of your transport pilots, this isn't a precise art. The strength of the wind and the effects of enemy anti-aircraft fire or poor navigation can easily result in your platoon landing well off target.

Place a Command team on the table to mark each platoon's drop point. A platoon drop point may not be within 8"/20cm of another platoon's drop point (otherwise the transport aircraft will collide in mid air!)

Deploy German Parachute Platoons

As the aircraft reaches the drop point, the *Absetzer* or dispatcher releases the containers, then the command team and the rest of the paratroopers jump in rapid succession.

Place Container

Roll a die and multiply the result by 4"/10cm, and place the platoon's container that far down wind of the drop point. This represents the container drifting down wind before coming to earth.

Drift Down Wind

To find out how far the paratroops drifted before landing, roll another die and multiply the result by 4"/10 cm, and move the Command team that far down wind of the drop point.

Place Parachute Platoon

A German parachute platoon deploys in three columns along the flight paths of its transport aircraft.

First Squad

The first squad or section flies in the left-hand aircraft. Place the first team of the squad 4"/10cm to the left of the Command team. Place any remaining teams in the squad 4"/10cm apart in a column parallel to the flight line.

Second Squad

The second squad or section flies in the right-hand transport aircraft. Place the first team from the second section or squad 4"/10cm to the right of the Command team and place the rest of the teams in a column at 4"/10cm intervals parallel to the flight line.

Third Squad

If the platoon has a third or fourth squad or section, these land in the centre after the Command team. Place these teams in a column 4"/10cm apart parallel to the flight path with the Command team forming the head of the column.

Deploying A German Parachute Platoon

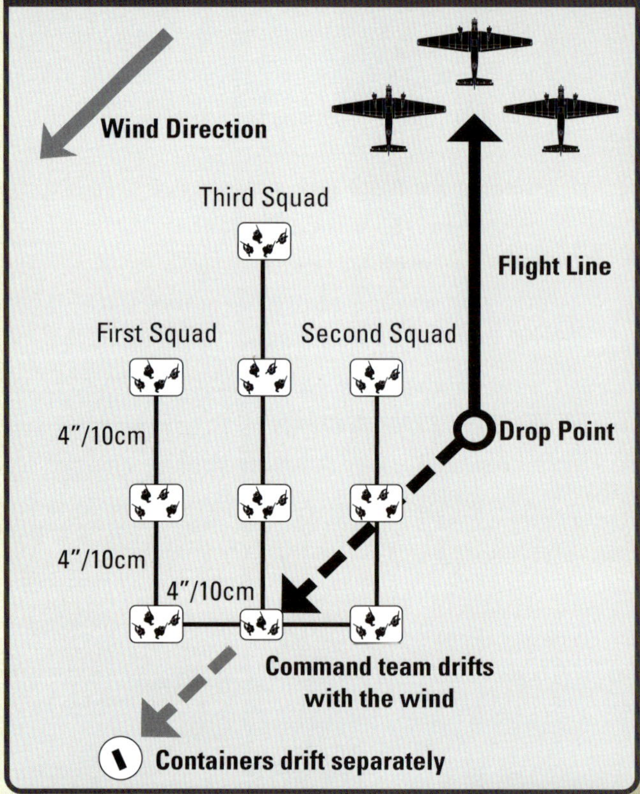

Deploy US Parachute Platoons

As the aircraft reaches the drop point the dispatcher releases the containers, then the command team and the rest of the paratroopers jump in rapid succession.

Organise Sticks

To fit in a pair of Douglas C-47 Dakota transport aircraft, each platoon is split into two 'sticks', each containing an officer.

Normally a parachute platoon operates as a single entity with the second Command team operating as a normal Rifle/MG or Carbine team unless the first is destroyed. However, if the sticks are widely separated on landing, they operate independently until they join up again.

At the start of an airborne attack, divide each platoon into two evenly-sized sticks, each containing a Command team. Treat each stick as a separate platoon until they are landed and in Command Distance of one another at the start of a turn. At this point the two sticks reunite into a single platoon and fight on as normal.

If your platoon has only one Command team, the entire platoon jumps from one aircraft as a single stick.

First Stick

The first stick flies in the left-hand transport aircraft. Place the Command team of the stick 4"/10cm to the left of the drop point.

Second Stick

The second stick flies in the right-hand transport aircraft. Move the Command team of the stick 4"/10cm to the right of the drop point.

Deploying A US Parachute Platoon

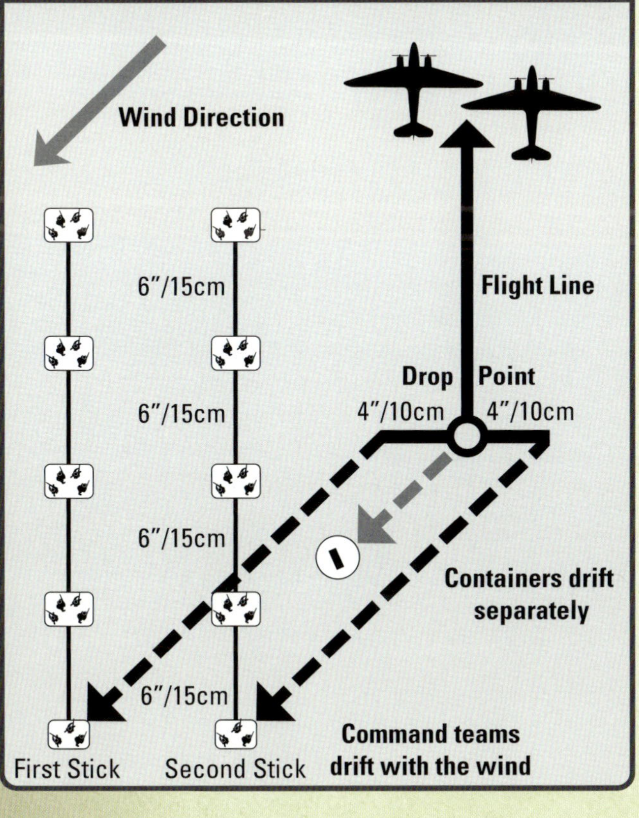

Finding The Landing Zone

Unlike Germans, US transport pilots were not given specific training for parachute operations and frequently had difficulty delivering the paratroops to the right place, especially at night.

After all of your parachute drop points have been selected, roll a die for each platoon.

- On a roll of 3+, the pilots have found the right drop zone and the command teams and their sticks will land as normal.
- On a roll of 1 or 2, the pilots drop the platoon far from the drop zone. Remove the command teams and container from the table. You still need to roll for casualties on landing.

If a platoon missed the drop zone roll a die at the start of each turn. On a roll of 6, the platoon finds their way back to the table having found the correct drop zone having recovered their container.

When the platoon finds its way back to the table, roll another die as if determining the wind direction to decide from which table edge or corner they will arrive. If they arrive from a corner, they must enter the table within 16"/40cm of the corner, otherwise they may arrive anywhere on the table edge. Place the command team at the edge of the table to indicate their arrival point and move the platoon onto the table from this point in the Movement Step.

Place Container

If the pilots found the landing zone, roll a die and multiply the result by 6"/15cm and place the platoon's container that far down wind of the drop point. Since the US Airborne make their jump from higher altitudes, they and their containers drift further before landing.

Drift Down Wind

To find out how far the US paratroops drifted before landing, roll another die and multiply the result by 6"/15cm, and move the Command team that far down wind of the drop point.

Place Parachute Platoon

A US parachute platoon deploys in two columns along the the flight paths of its aircraft.

First Stick

Place the teams of the first stick in a column at 6"/15cm intervals parallel to the flight line.

Second Stick

Place the teams of the second stick in a column at 6"/15cm intervals parallel to the flight line.

Roll For Casualties on landing

They say its not jumping out of the aircraft that hurts you, it's stopping at the bottom! Unfortunately, landing injuries of up to 25% are not out of the ordinary in airborne landings.

Roll a die for each team landing by parachute requiring a score of 2+ to land safely in open terrain or 4+ to land safely in rough terrain. Any teams that land off the table need to roll 3+ to survive their landing.

Any roll less than these results in the loss of the team and its removal from the game. Teams and platoons lost this way do not count as Destroyed for Platoon and Company Morale Checks, so keep them separate from later casualties.

Being seriously tough, Independent teams and containers are never casualties on landing, so you do not need to roll for them.

Landing Off The Table

Sometimes, either through misjudgement or particularly strong winds some or all of a platoon's teams or its container will land off the table. In this case, the airborne player has two options. Either count the surviving teams landing off table as lost (but not Destroyed) and out of the game as those on table fight on without them, or remove the whole platoon (but not its container) as they search for the missing teams.

If you remove the platoon (which you must if its container lands off table), the surviving teams will all return to the game together using the Reserves mission special rules. The platoon will return from the table edge that they straddled on landing. If they landed in a corner, they will return from the table edge over which they lost the most teams. If the container landed off the table, the platoon has recovered it when they return, otherwise, they still must do so.

Landing On The Enemy

Any teams landing within 2"/5cm of an enemy team must move further away from the enemy team at the first possible opportunity. A team that lands directly on top of an enemy team is immediately Destroyed.

WEAPONS CONTAINERS

German paratroopers drop from very low altitudes to ensure a tight drop with little scatter. To do this they use fast-opening parachutes. The down side is that they cannot carry their weapons with them when they jump because the shock of the parachute opening will rip them from their grasp. Instead, the paratroops drop their weapons in containers and collect them when they land. To offset this vulnerable situation, a few *Fallschirmjäger* jumped into battle with their submachine-guns strapped to their bodies.

Until the platoon recovers its own container, they only have their pistols for armament. Consequently they shoot as Pistol teams, regardless of their usual type, except that SMG teams in a platoon are considered to have dropped with their weapons and therefore operate with their normal weapon ratings.

Like their German counterparts, US paratroopers drop all of their machine-guns, mortars and heavy weapons in containers and collect them when they land. Since the US paratroopers drop from higher altitudes, they are able to jump with their personal weapons (usually an M1 Garand), consequently they shoot as a Rifle team if they are a Rifle or Rifle/MG team, or as a Carbine team in other cases.

Each parachute platoon has one container marker dropped with it. This container should be marked with coloured stripes to identify which platoon it belongs to. Red, blue, yellow, and green are common colours.

No team in the platoon, including SMG teams, can observe for artillery bombardments or launch assaults until the platoon has recovered its equipment. The only exception to this is the platoon can assault an enemy platoon that is preventing them from retrieving their container.

Recovering Containers

To recover the platoon's container, a team from the platoon must start a turn adjacent to the container. At that point all teams in the platoon are armed and immediately revert to their normal type of team. Remove the container once it has been recovered.

Moving Containers

Any infantry team starting adjacent to a container may drag it up to 4"/10cm in the Movement Step. The container cannot be moved in the Shooting or Assault steps (no, you cannot move a container in Stormtrooper movement!) This allows a team that has recovered its own weapons to drag another platoon's containers back to it. It also allows enemy platoons to steal your containers and make off with them!

GLIDER ASSAULTS

Only a Fallschirmjägerkompanie may make Glider Assaults.

The German DFS 230 assault glider allows small assault parties to land and assault vital positions before the enemy is even aware that they are under attack. Gliders approach the target in a very steep dive at speeds of up to 125 mph (200 km/h) before pulling up for a short landing run slowed by a braking parachute. The resulting attack was swift and deadly.

Only glider-equipped Parachute Pioneer Platoons and Light Artillery Batteries may land by glider. Each platoon or battery is assigned three DFS 230 gliders. Each glider carries two Infantry teams or one Gun team, with the lead glider having the Platoon Command team as well.

Select Glider Landing Points

The first step in a glider-borne assault is to place your gliders at the start of their landing runs facing into the wind. Pick a landing point with plenty of clear space ahead of the glider so it doesn't crash before it stops its landing run.

Roll For Glider Landings

Once down, each glider pilot attempts to brake his glider as soon as possible, as a long landing run increases the risk of a crash.

To find the length of a glider's landing run, roll a die. Move the glider forward 2"/5cm for each point on the die roll.

On a landing run roll of 1, the glider crash-lands due to pilot error or enemy fire.

If the glider's body runs into rough terrain, an enemy gun or vehicle, or the body of another glider, the glider crashes and stops immediately. However, if a glider's wings hit an obstacle, they just snap off and the wingless fuselage carries on unharmed. The glider only crashes if the fuselage itself hits an obstacle.

If a glider crashes, the passengers may be killed or injured. Roll a die for each team carried in a crashed glider. On a roll of 5+ they survive, but on a lesser roll, they are Destroyed. Due to the grisly nature of glider crashes, any teams destroyed in a crash count as casualties for Platoon Morale Checks.

If the glider's body passes through or ends its run on the position of an enemy Infantry team, the defending player moves the team aside just far enough to avoid the body of the glider as they dive out of its path.

Shooting From Gliders

Each DFS 230 glider has a machine-gun mount above the wing allowing an Infantry team carried as passengers to fire their machine-gun.

As long as the glider hasn't crashed, one Infantry team in each glider can fire their machine-gun as a vehicle-mounted AA MG immediately on landing, even though the game hasn't properly begun yet.

Gliders carrying guns from a Light Artillery Battery are too full of guns and ammunition to spare any space for a machine-gun and cannot shoot.

Glider Passengers Assault

The biggest advantage of landing by glider, aside from landing fully armed in a tight group, is the surprise element. Glider troops can launch an assault before the defenders are even aware that an attack is under way.

After landing, a glider-equipped Parachute Pioneer Platoon can either launch an assault or attempt to move using the Stormtrooper special rule. Even though the game hasn't started, the assault is fought like a normal Assault Step. The troops dismount from the doors of the glider just beneath the wings, so measure their movement from that point.

Light Artillery Batteries carried in gliders remain as passengers until their normal Movement Step.

Shooting At Teams In Gliders

The gliders are only markers showing where the troops land and cannot be shot. Teams inside gliders do not benefit from Concealment as the troops are so tightly packed in. However, teams behind a glider body are Concealed.

Airborne Assault Mission

The nature of air assaults requires a number of special rules to recreate the most important elements of this style of battle in the Death From Above mission.

SPECIAL RULES

Against The Odds

Airborne assaults are always gambles. Even in a good landing the attacking force will lose many of their men and lots of essential equipment.

To allow for the inevitable losses suffered on landing, the airborne attacking force has 25% more points than the defender. In a 1500 point game, the airborne force would be 1875 points, while in a 2000 point game, the airborne force would be 2500 points.

Night Attack

Unlike the German airborne forces, the US paratroopers elected to make their combat jumps at night to minimise casualties.

When a US Parachute Rifle Company attacks in Death From Above, the game starts at night with the Night Fighting rules in effect.

Total Air Superiority

There is no doubt in the minds of the air force as to where the main effort will be once an airborne assault is under way. The air force makes every effort to protect their transport aircraft and support the paratroops on the ground.

If the attacking player has air support they may make one free Ground-attack by a flight of one to three aircraft after the defender deploys but before the attacker deploys.

Surprise

Although they may be expecting an airborne assault, the speed with which the attack begins always catches the defenders by surprise. Many of the troops will be away from their positions, eating, sleeping, or otherwise unprepared.

To simulate the time taken to get the defending force fully ready to fight, all defending platoons on the table start the game Pinned Down and all defending armoured vehicles on the table start the game Bailed Out.

Defending teams may not start the game mounted in their transport vehicles or on tanks, and as normal, may not mount Bailed Out transport vehicles or tanks until the crew have remounted.

Scattered Reserves

One of the biggest problems with defending against an airborne assault is that the assault could happen almost anywhere, or worse still everywhere at once! In order to cover all of the likely landing zones, the defending reserves are scattered across the countryside.

The Scattered Reserves special rule operates in the same way as the Reserves special rule with the following exceptions.

To reflect the way the reserves are scattered and the chaotic nature of airborne operations, the defender's reserves could arrive from almost anywhere. When each platoon arrives from the reserves, the defender rolls a die to decide from which table edge or corner it will arrive (the mission map shows the edge or corner for each roll). If the reserves arrive from a corner, they must enter the table within 16"/40cm of the corner.

Units containing armoured vehicles will always arrive from reserve after units without armoured vehicles. Units containing Tank teams will always be the last platoons to arrive from reserve.

DEATH FROM ABOVE MISSIONS IN TOURNAMENTS

As it is only possible for certain armies, the Death From Above mission won't normally appear as one of the assigned missions in a tournament. However, it makes for such an interesting game that it would be a shame not to play it at tournaments. To make this possible, a player commanding a German Fallschirmjägerkompanie or Fallschirmpionierkompanie, or a US Parachute Rifle Company may submit an alternative force for Death From Above missions, as well as their normal force. If they do this, they may use this force to play the Death From Above mission any time they would normally play the Free-For-All mission.

The alternative force must include the same Headquarters, Combat, and Weapons platoons as the player's main force, but may add extra options or squads to them, and may have different Support platoons and air support. Remember the Against The Odds special rule applies, so this alternative force will have 25% more points than the main force.

The Diving Eagles player must have a copy of this Intelligence Handbook with them, and before the game begins, the Diving Eagles player must allow their opponent to read the Airborne Assault rules, the Death From Above mission, and the special rules.

Death from Above

Death From Above missions use the Airborne Assaults rules on pages 191 to 195, and the **Against The Odds**, **Night Attack**, **Total Air Superiority**, **Surprise**, and **Scattered Reserves** special rules on page 196.

The Death From Above mission reflects the daring airborne assaults conducted by the Diving Eagles and the US Airborne.

YOUR ORDERS

Attacker

Once again your army is on the move. To ensure a speedy victory for the ground forces, your parachute force must first capture vital positions deep in the enemy rear.

Your goal is to take an objective point and hold it against the expected enemy counterattack.

Defender

The enemy has launched a major offensive and your task is to protect key facilities in the rear areas. While you are far from enemy ground troops, attack from the air is always possible.

Your mission is to hold both objectives by driving the attacking force back to a safe distance.

PREPARING FOR BATTLE

1. The player with the airborne force is always the attacker. If both players have airborne forces, both players roll a die. The highest scoring player is the attacker.
2. The defender places one objective anywhere on the table at least 16"/40cm from the table edges.
3. The attacking player places two objectives anywhere on the table at least 16"/40cm from the table edges.
4. The defender must hold at least half of their platoons in reserve at the start of the game. The remaining platoons deploy anywhere on the table.
5. The attacking player now removes one of the objective markers that they placed (not the objective that the defender placed).

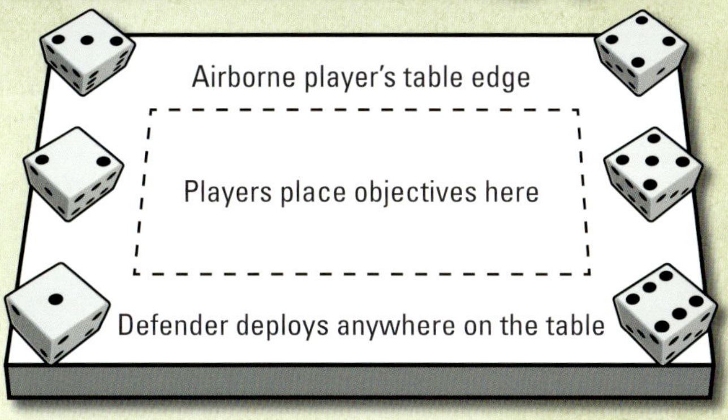

6. The attacker selects their table edge and flight line, and rolls for wind direction.
7. The attacking player deploys their troops using the Airborne Assaults rules.

Beginning The Battle

1. The defending player has the first turn.
2. The defending forces suffer the effects of the Surprise special rule at the start of the game.
3. All teams are moving at the start of the battle, so infantry in the open are not concealed and have not gone to ground.

ENDING THE BATTLE

The battle ends when:

- the attacker starts any turn from turn 6 holding any objective, or
- the defender starts any turn after turn 6 with no attacking teams within 16"/40cm of either objective.

DECIDING WHO WON

The airborne player wins if they hold any objective. The attack has gained a foothold and reinforcements are on the way.

Otherwise the defender wins. The airborne assault has failed.

Use the Victory Points table below to look up your victory points based on the number of platoons that the winner lost during the battle.

Victory Points			
Winner's Losses	*Result*	*Winner's Points*	*Loser's Points*
0 platoons	Stunning victory	6	1
1 platoon	Major victory	5	2
2 or more platoons	Minor victory	4	3

German Arsenal

TANK TEAMS

Name *Weapon*	Mobility *Range*	Armour Front *ROF*	 Side *Anti-tank*	 Top *Firepower*	Equipment and Notes
Tanks					
Panzer II	Fully-tracked	3	1	1	Co-ax MG, Protected ammo.
2cm KwK38 gun	*16"/40cm*	*3*	*5*	*5+*	
Captured 'Honey' Stuart	Fully-tracked	3	2	1	Co-ax MG, Hull MG, Light tank.
M5 37mm gun	*24"/60cm*	*2*	*7*	*4+*	*No HE.*
Panzer III G, H, or J	Fully-tracked	5	3	1	Co-ax MG, Hull MG, Protected ammo.
5cm KwK38 gun	*24"/60cm*	*3*	*7*	*4+*	
Panzer III J (late)	Fully-tracked	5	3	1	Co-ax MG, Hull MG, Protected ammo.
5cm KwK39 gun	*24"/60cm*	*3*	*9*	*4+*	
Panzer III L or M	Fully-tracked	6	3	1	Co-ax MG, Hull MG, Protected ammo.
5cm KwK39 gun	*24"/60cm*	*3*	*9*	*4+*	
Panzer III N	Fully-tracked	6	3	1	Co-ax MG, Hull MG, Protected ammo.
7.5cm KwK37 gun	*24"/60cm*	*2*	*9*	*3+*	
Panzer IV E or F_1	Fully-tracked	5	3	1	Co-ax MG, Hull MG, Protected ammo.
7.5cm KwK37 gun	*24"/60cm*	*2*	*9*	*3+*	*Smoke.*
Firing bombardments	*48"/120cm*	-	*2*	*6*	
Panzer IV F_2 or G	Fully-tracked	5	3	1	Co-ax MG, Hull MG, Protected ammo.
7.5cm KwK40 gun	*32"/80cm*	*2*	*11*	*3+*	
Panzer IV G (late) or H	Fully-tracked	6	3	1	Co-ax MG, Hull MG, Protected ammo.
7.5cm KwK40 gun	*32"/80cm*	*2*	*11*	*3+*	
Tiger I E (early)	Fully-tracked	9	8	2	Co-ax MG, Hull MG, Protected ammo, Slow tank, Wide tracks, Unreliable.
8.8cm KwK36 gun	*40"/100cm*	*2*	*13*	*3+*	*Slow traverse.*
Flammpanzer III	Fully-tracked	6	3	1	Co-ax MG, Hull MG.
1.4cm Flammenwerfer	*4"/10cm*	*4*	-	*5+*	*Flame-thrower*
Assault Guns					
StuG D or E	Fully-tracked	5	3	1	AA MG, Protected ammo.
7.5cm StuK36 gun	*24"/60cm*	*2*	*9*	*3+*	*Hull mounted.*
StuG F/8	Fully-tracked	7	3	1	AA MG, Protected ammo.
7.5cm StuK40 gun	*32"/80cm*	*2*	*11*	*3+*	*Hull mounted.*
Infantry Guns (SP)					
Sd Kfz 250/7 (8cm)	Half-tracked	1	0	0	Rear AA MG.
8cm GW34 mortar	*40"/100cm*	-	*2*	*6*	*Hull mounted, Portee, Smoke bombardment.*
Sd Kfz 251/2C (8cm)	Half-tracked	1	0	0	Rear AA MG.
8cm GW34 mortar	*40"/100cm*	-	*2*	*6*	*Hull mounted, Portee, Smoke bombardment.*
Grille (15cm sIG) H or K	Fully-tracked	2	1	0	Hull MG.
15cm sIG33 gun	*16"/40cm*	*1*	*13*	*1+*	*Bunker buster, Hull mounted.*
Firing bombardments	*56"/140cm*	-	*4*	*2+*	
Bison (15cm sIG)	Fully-tracked	2	1	0	Hull MG, Slow, Overloaded, Unreliable.
15cm sIG33 gun	*16"/40cm*	*1*	*13*	*1+*	*Bunker buster, Hull mounted.*
Firing bombardments	*56"/140cm*	-	*4*	*2+*	
Sd Kfz 251/16C (Flamm)	Half-tracked	1	0	0	Hull MG.
Two 1.4cm Flammenwerfer	*4"/10cm*	*3 (each)*	-	*6*	*Side mounted, Flame-thrower.*
Artillery (SP)					
15cm (Sf) Lorraine Schlepper	Fully-tracked	0	0	0	AA MG, Slow, Overloaded.
15cm sFH13 howitzer	*24"/60cm*	*1*	*10*	*1+*	*Bunker buster, Hull mounted, Smoke.*
Firing bombardments	*64"/160cm*	-	*5*	*2+*	*Smoke bombardment.*

Name *Weapon*	Mobility *Range*	Front *ROF*	Armour Side *Anti-tank*	Top *Firepower*	Equipment and Notes
Tank-hunters					
Panzerjäger I	Half-tracked	0	0	0	AA MG.
4.7cm PaK36(t) gun	*24"/60cm*	*2*	*7*	*4+*	*Hull mounted.*
Diana	Half-tracked	0	0	0	AA MG.
7.62cm FK36(r) gun	*32"/80cm*	*2*	*10*	*3+*	*Hull mounted.*
Marder I	Fully-tracked	0	0	0	AA MG, Overloaded, Slow tank.
7.5cm PaK40 gun	*32"/80cm*	*2*	*12*	*3+*	*Hull mounted.*
Marder II	Fully-tracked	1	0	0	AA MG.
7.5cm PaK40 gun	*32"/80cm*	*2*	*12*	*3+*	*Hull mounted.*
Marder III (7.62cm)	Fully-tracked	1	0	0	Hull MG.
7.62cm PaK36(r) gun	*32"/80cm*	*2*	*11*	*3+*	*Hull mounted.*
Anti-aircraft (SP)					
Sd Kfz 10/5 (2cm)	Half-tracked	-	-	-	
2cm FlaK38 gun	*16"/40cm*	*4*	*5*	*5+*	*Anti-aircraft.*
Sd Kfz 7/1 (Quad 2cm)	Half-tracked	-	-	-	
2cm FlaK38 (V) gun	*16"/40cm*	*6*	*5*	*5+*	*Anti-aircraft.*
Armoured Cars					
Sd Kfz 221 (2.8cm)	Wheeled	0	0	0	
2.8cm sPzB41 anti-tank rifle	*16"/40cm*	*2*	*7*	*5+*	*Hull mounted, No HE.*
Sd Kfz 222 (2cm)	Wheeled	1	0	0	Co-ax MG.
2cm KwK38 gun	*16"/40cm*	*3*	*5*	*5+*	*Self-defence anti-aircraft.*
Sd Kfz 223 (radio)	Wheeled	1	0	0	AA MG.
Sd Kfz 231 (8-rad)	Jeep	2	0	0	Co-ax MG.
2cm KwK38 gun	*16"/40cm*	*3*	*5*	*5+*	
Sd Kfz 233 (7.5cm)	Jeep	2	0	0	Hull MG.
7.5cm KwK37 gun	*24"/60cm*	*2*	*9*	*3+*	*Hull mounted.*

GUN TEAMS

Weapon	Mobility	Range	ROF	Anti-tank	Firepower	Notes
MG34 HMG	Man-packed	24"/60cm	6	2	6	ROF 2 when pinned down.
2.8cm sPzB41 anti-tank rifle	Man-packed	16"/40cm	3	7	5+	No HE.
7.5cm LG40 recoilless gun	Man-packed	16"/40cm	2	9	3+	Recoilless.
8.8cm RW43 (Püppchen) launcher	Man-packed	16"/40cm	1	11	5+	
8cm GW42 (Stummelwerfer) mortar	Man-packed	32"/80cm	-	2	6	Smoke bombardment.
8cm GW34 mortar	Man-packed	40"/100cm	-	2	6	Smoke bombardment.
10.5cm NbW35 mortar	Man-packed	40"/100cm	-	3	4+	Smoke bombardment.
7.5cm leIG18 gun	Light	16"/40cm	2	9	3+	Gun shield, Smoke.
Firing bombardments		48"/120cm	-	3	6	
15cm sIG33 gun	Heavy	16"/40cm	1	13	1+	Bunker buster, Gun shield.
Firing bombardments		56"/140cm	-	4	2+	
2cm FlaK38 gun	Light	16"/40cm	4	5	5+	Anti-aircraft, Gun shield, Turntable.
3.7cm PaK36 gun	Light	24"/60cm	3	6	4+	Gun shield.
Firing Stielgranate		8"/20cm	1	12	5+	
4.2cm PJK41 gun	Light	24"/60cm	3	9	5+	Gun shield.
5cm PaK38 gun	Medium	24"/60cm	3	9	4+	Gun shield.
Captured 6 pdr gun	Medium	24"/60cm	3	10	4+	Gun shield, No HE.
7.5cm PaK40 gun	Medium	32"/80cm	2	12	3+	Gun shield.
7.62cm PaK36(r) gun	Heavy	32"/80cm	2	11	3+	Gun shield.
8.8cm FlaK36 gun	Immobile	40"/100cm	2	13	3+	Gun shield, Heavy anti-aircraft, Turntable.
7.5cm GebG36 gun	Heavy	16"/40cm	2	9	3+	Gun shield, Smoke.
Firing bombardments		72"/180cm	-	3	6	Smoke bombardment.
7.62cm FK36(r) gun	Heavy	32"/80cm	2	10	3+	Gun shield.
Firing bombardments		80"/200cm	-	3	6	
Captured 25 pdr gun	Heavy	24"/60cm	2	9	3+	Gun shield, Smoke, Turntable.
Firing bombardments		80"/200cm	-	4	5+	Smoke bombardment.
10.5cm LG40 recoilless gun	Light	24"/60cm	1	10	2+	Gun shield, Recoilless, Smoke.
Firing bombardments		64"/160cm	-	4	4+	
10.5cm leFH18 howitzer	Immobile	24"/60cm	1	10	2+	Gun shield, Smoke.
Firing bombardments		72"/180cm	-	4	4+	Smoke bombardment.
15cm NW41 rocket launcher	Light	64"/160cm	-	3	4+	Smoke bombardment.

INFANTRY TEAMS

Team	Range	ROF	Anti-tank	Firepower	Notes
Pistol team	4"/10cm	1	1	6	
Rifle team	16"/40cm	1	2	6	
Rifle/MG team	16"/40cm	2	2	6	
MG team	16"/40cm	3	2	6	
SMG team	4"/10cm	3	1	6	Full ROF when moving.
Light Mortar team	16"/40cm	1	1	4+	Can fire over friendly teams.
Anti-tank Rifle team	16"/40cm	2	4	6	
Flame-thrower team	4"/10cm	2	-	6	Flame-thrower.
Staff team			cannot shoot		Moves as a Heavy Gun team.

Additional Training and Equipment

Panzerknacker teams are rated as Tank Assault 5. Pioneer teams are rated as Tank Assault 4.

TRANSPORT TEAMS

Vehicle *Weapon*	Mobility *Range*	Armour Front *ROF*	 Side *Anti-tank*	 Top *Firepower*	Equipment and Notes
Trucks					
BMW & Sidecar or Kübelwagen	Jeep	-	-	-	Optional Passenger-fired hull MG
Kettenkrad, or Kfz 15 car	Jeep	-	-	-	
Horch, Krupp, or Steyr Kfz 70 truck	Wheeled	-	-	-	
Opel Blitz 3-ton truck	Wheeled	-	-	-	
Opel Kfz 68 radio truck	Wheeled	-	-	-	
Tows					
Sd Kfz 10 (1t), Sd Kfz 11 (3t), or Sd Kfz 7 (8t) half-track	Half-tracked	-	-	-	
Armoured Personnel Carriers					
Sd Kfz 250, Sd Kfz 250/5 or Sd Kfz 251/1C half-track	Half-tracked	1	0	0	Hull MG, HMG Carrier, Passenger-fired AA MG.
Sd Kfz 250/10 or Sd Kfz 251/10C (3.7cm) half-track *3.7cm PaK36*	Half-tracked *16"/40cm*	1 *2*	0 *6*	0 *4+*	Passenger-fired AA MG. *Hull mounted*
Sd Kfz 250/11 (2.8cm) half-track *2.8cm sPzB41*	Half-tracked *16"/40cm*	1 *2*	0 *7*	0 *5+*	Passenger-fired AA MG. *Hull mounted, No HE.*
Sd Kfz 251/7C (Pioneer) half-track	Half-tracked	1	0	0	Hull MG, Passenger-fired AA MG. Assault bridge.
Sd Kfz 253 (StuG) or Sd Kfz 254 half-track	Half-tracked	1	0	1	AA MG.
Recovery Vehicles					
Sd Kfz 9 (18t) half-track	Half-tracked	-	-	-	Recovery vehicle.

AIRCRAFT

Aircraft	Weapon	To Hit	Anti-tank	Firepower	Notes
Ju 87D Stuka	Bombs	4+	5	1+	
Ju 87G Stuka	Cannon	3+	11	4+	
Hs 129B	Cannon	2+	9	4+	Flying Tank
Bf 109E or FW 190F	Cannon	3+	7	5+	
	Bombs	4+	5	2+	

ITALIAN ARSENAL

TANK TEAMS

Name Weapon	Mobility Range	Armour Front ROF	Armour Side Anti-tank	Armour Top Firepower	Equipment and Notes
L6/40 *20/65 gun*	Half-tracked *16"/40cm*	2 *2*	1 *5*	1 *5+*	Co-ax MG.
R.35 *37/21 gun*	Fully-tracked *24"/60cm*	3 *2*	2 *4*	1 *4+*	Co-ax MG, Slow tank. *One-man turret.*
M14/41 *47/32 gun*	Fully-tracked *24"/60cm*	3 *2*	2 *7*	1 *4+*	Co-ax MG, Twin hull MG.
Lancia da 90/53 *90/53 gun*	Wheeled *40"/100cm*	- *3*	- *13*	- *3+*	Awkward layout, Overloaded, Slow, Stabiliser jacks. *Heavy Anti-aircraft.*
Carro Comando *13.2mm machine-gun*	Fully-tracked *16"/40cm*	4 *3*	2 *3*	1 *5+*	
Semovente 47/32 *47/32 gun*	Half-tracked *24"/60cm*	3 *2*	1 *7*	0 *4+*	
Semovente 75/18 *75/18 gun*	Fully-tracked *24"/60cm*	4 *2*	2 *9*	1 *3+*	
Semovente 90/53 *90/53 gun*	Fully-tracked *40"/100cm*	2 *2*	0 *13*	0 *3+*	Ammo carriers, Awkward layout, Slow.
AB41 *20/65 gun*	Wheeled *16"/40cm*	1 *2*	0 *5*	0 *5+*	Co-ax MG, Hull rear MG.
Anti-aircraft (SP)					
20/65 on 3-ton truck *20/65 gun*	Wheeled *16"/40cm*	- *4*	- *5*	- *5+*	*Anti-aircraft, Portee.*

GUN TEAMS

Weapon	Mobility	Range	ROF	Anti-tank	Firepower	Notes
Brixia 45mm mortar	Man-packed	16"/40cm	2	1	5+	Can fire over friendly troops.
Firing bombardments		24"/60cm	-	0	6	
Mod 37 HMG	Man-packed	24"/60cm	6	2	6	ROF 2 when pinned down.
Solothurn anti-tank rifle	Man-packed	16"/40cm	3	5	5+	
47/32 gun	Man-packed	24"/60cm	3	7	4+	
65/17 gun	Light	16"/40cm	2	8	3+	
Firing bombardments		64"/160cm	-	2	6	
81/14 mortar	Man-packed	48"/120cm	-	2	6	Smoke bombardment.
20/65 gun	Light	16"/40cm	4	5	5+	Anti-aircraft, Turntable.
88/56 gun	Immobile	40"/100cm	2	13	3+	Heavy anti-aircraft, Turntable.
90/53 gun	Immobile	40"/100cm	2	13	3+	Heavy anti-aircraft, Turntable.
37/45 (German 3.7cm PaK 36) gun	Light	24"/60cm	3	6	4+	Gun shield.
75/39 (German 7.5cm PaK97/38) gun	Medium	24"/60cm	2	10	3+	Gun shield.
75/27 gun	Heavy	24"/60cm	2	9	3+	Gun shield, Smoke.
Firing bombardments		64"/160cm	-	3	6	Smoke bombardment.
Captured 25 pdr gun	Heavy	24"/60cm	2	9	3+	Gun shield, Smoke, Turntable.
Firing bombardments		80"/200cm	-	4	5+	Smoke bombardment.
100/17 howitzer	Immobile	24"/60cm	1	10	2+	Gun shield.
Firing bombardments		72"/180cm	-	4	4+	

INFANTRY TEAMS

Team	Range	ROF	Anti-tank	Firepower	Notes
Rifle team	16"/40cm	1	2	6	
Rifle/MG team	16"/40cm	2	2	6	
SMG team	4"/10cm	3	1	6	Full ROF when moving.
Flame-thrower team	4"/10cm	2	-	6	Flame-thrower.
Staff team			cannot shoot		Moves as a Heavy Gun team.

Additional Training and Equipment

Passaglia Bombs are rated as Improvised Tank Assault 3. Pioneer teams are rated as Tank Assault 4.

TRANSPORT TEAMS

Vehicle	Mobility	Armour Front	Armour Side	Armour Top	Equipment and Notes
SPA TL-37, Dovunque 3-ton, or lancia 3 RO 6-ton truck	Wheeled	-	-	-	
L6/40 ammo carrier	Half-tracked	2	1	1	Ammo carrier.

AIRCRAFT

Aircraft	Weapon	To Hit	Anti-tank	Firepower	Notes
FIAT CR.42 Falco	MG	3+	5	5+	
	Bombs	4+	5	2+	
Macchi C.200 Saetta	MG	3+	5	5+	
	Bombs	4+	5	2+	
Ju.87 Picchiatello	Bombs	4+	5	1+	

ITALIAN VEHICLE SPECIAL RULES

Ammo Carriers

The Semovente 90/53 self-propelled gun is an amazing piece of engineering. They managed to squeeze a 90mm gun on to a 14-ton tank chassis! The price though was high. The Semovente doesn't have much space for ammunition and the loaders stand on the ground behind it in action.

In order to keep up a high rate of fire, the Semovente 90/53 needs another vehicle to bring up its ammunition—the L6/40 ammo carrier.

A Semovente 90/53 has its basic ROF increased to 3 if it has an L6/40 ammo carrier adjacent to it. Unlike the loaders standing behind the gun, the L6/40 ammo carrier is a separate team and can be hit and destroyed separately. Each L6/40 ammo carrier can only supply one Semovente 90/53 per turn.

One Man Turret

Captured french tanks like the R.35 had cramped one-man turrets making it almost impossible for the tank commander to guide the driver, locate targets, load the gun, and still fire!

A tank with a one-man turret may not fire its main gun while moving and may not fire both the main gun and the machine-gun in the same turn.

Stabiliser Jacks

The Autocannone Lancia da 90/53 mounts a huge 90mm anti-aircraft gun with a huge gun shield and all-round traverse on a heavy truck. To stop the vehicle tipping over when it fires it has six large stabiliser jacks that must be lowered before firing.

Once the jacks are lowered, it is much harder to put the gun out of action as most hits to the truck have little effect on the gun's ability to keep shooting and the extremely large gun shield protects the gun and its crew.

If a Lancia da 90/53 did not move in its previous turn it is protected by its gun shield and counts as having Bullet proof Cover against all shots coming from in front of the line of the gun shield in the enemy turn.

BRITISH ARSENAL

TANK TEAMS

Name Weapon	Mobility Range	Armour Front ROF	Armour Side Anti-tank	Armour Top Firepower	Equipment and Notes
Light Tank					
'Honey' Stuart	Fully-tracked	3	2	1	Co-ax MG, Hull MG, Light tank.
M5 37mm gun	*24"/60cm*	*2*	*7*	*4+*	*No HE.*
Cruiser Tanks					
Crusader II	Fully-tracked	4	2	1	Co-ax MG, Fast tank, Unreliable.
OQF 2 pdr gun	*24"/60cm*	*2*	*7*	*4+*	*No HE, Tally Ho.*
Crusader II CS	Fully-tracked	4	2	1	Co-ax MG, Fast tank, Unreliable.
OQF 3" howitzer	*24"/60cm*	*2*	*5*	*3+*	*Smoke.*
Firing bombardments	*40"/100cm*	*-*	*3*	*6*	*Smoke bombardment.*
Crusader III	Fully-tracked	4	2	1	Co-ax MG, Fast tank, Unreliable.
OQF 6 pdr gun	*24"/60cm*	*2*	*10*	*4+*	*No HE.*
Valentine III	Fully-tracked	6	5	1	Co-ax MG, Slow tank.
OQF 2 pdr gun	*24"/60cm*	*3*	*7*	*4+*	*No HE.*
Heavy Tanks					
Grant	Fully-tracked	5	3	1	Co-ax MG.
M5 37mm gun	*24"/60cm*	*3*	*7*	*4+*	*No HE.*
M2 75mm gun	*32"/80cm*	*2*	*9*	*3+*	*Hull-mounted, Smoke, Semi-indirect fire.*
Grant (Lee turret)	Fully-tracked	5	3	1	Co-ax MG, Cupola MG.
M5 37mm gun	*24"/60cm*	*3*	*7*	*4+*	*No HE.*
M2 75mm gun	*32"/80cm*	*2*	*9*	*3+*	*Hull-mounted, Smoke, Semi-indirect fire.*
Sherman II, III, or V	Fully-tracked	6	4	1	Co-ax MG, Hull MG.
M3 75mm gun	*32"/80cm*	*2*	*10*	*3+*	*Smoke, Semi-indirect fire.*
Infantry Tanks					
Matilda II	Fully-tracked	7	6	2	Co-ax MG, Slow tank, Unreliable.
OQF 2 pdr	*24"/60cm*	*3*	*7*	*4+*	*No HE.*
Matilda II CS	Fully-tracked	7	6	2	Co-ax MG, Slow tank, Unreliable.
OQF 3"	*24"/60cm*	*2*	*5*	*3+*	*Smoke.*
Firing bombardments	*40"/100cm*	*-*	*3*	*6*	*Smoke bombardment.*
Valentine II	Fully-tracked	6	5	1	Co-ax MG, Slow tank, Tow hook.
OQF 2 pdr	*24"/60cm*	*2*	*7*	*4+*	*No HE.*
Valentine VIII	Fully-tracked	6	4	1	Protected Ammo, Slow tank, Tow hook.
OQF 6 pdr	*24"/60cm*	*2*	*10*	*4+*	*No HE.*
Churchill I	Fully-tracked	8	7	2	Co-ax MG, Hull MG, Protected ammo, Slow tank, Wide tracks.
OQF 2 pdr	*24"/60cm*	*3*	*7*	*4+*	*No HE.*
OQF 3"	*24"/60cm*	*2*	*5*	*3+*	*Hull-mounted, Smoke.*
Firing bombardments	*40"/100cm*	*-*	*3*	*6*	*Smoke bombardment.*
Churchill III	Fully-tracked	8	7	2	Co-ax MG, Hull MG, Protected ammo, Slow tank, Wide tracks.
OQF 6 pdr	*24"/60cm*	*3*	*10*	*4+*	
Self-propelled Anti-tank Guns					
2 pdr portee	Wheeled	-	-	-	AA MG, Tip and Run.
OQF 2 pdr gun	*24"/60cm*	*3*	*7*	*4+*	*No HE, Portee.*
6 pdr portee	Wheeled	-	-	-	AA MG, Tip and Run.
OQF 6 pdr gun	*24"/60cm*	*3*	*10*	*4+*	*Hull-mounted, No HE, Portee.*
Deacon	Wheeled	1	2	0	AA MG, Overloaded, Slow, Tip and Run.
OQF 6 pdr gun	*24"/60cm*	*3*	*10*	*4+*	*No HE.*

Name Weapon	Mobility Range	Armour Front ROF	 Side Anti-tank	 Top Firepower	Equipment and Notes
Self-propelled Guns					
Bishop	Fully-tracked	1	0	0	AA MG, Slow tank.
OQF 25 pdr	*24"/60cm*	*2*	*9*	*3+*	*Hull mounted, Smoke.*
Firing bombardments	*64"/160cm*	*-*	*4*	*5+*	*Smoke bombardment.*
Priest	Fully-tracked	1	0	0	.50 cal AA MG.
M2A1 105mm howitzer	*24"/60cm*	*1*	*9*	*2+*	*Hull mounted, Smoke.*
Firing bombardments	*72"/180cm*	*-*	*4*	*4+*	*Smoke bombardment.*
Autocar 75mm SP	Half-tracked	1	0	0	
M1897 75mm gun	*24"/60cm*	*2*	*9*	*3+*	*Hull mounted, Smoke.*
Firing bombardments	*64"/160cm*	*-*	*2*	*6*	*Smoke bombardment.*
Self-propelled Anti-aircraft Guns					
Breda 20mm SP	Wheeled	-	-	-	
Breda 20mm gun	*16"/40cm*	*4*	*5*	*5+*	*Anti-aircraft.*
Oerlikon 20mm SP	Wheeled	-	-	-	
Oerlikon 20mm gun	*16"/40cm*	*4*	*5*	*5+*	*Anti-aircraft.*
Engineer Tanks					
Matilda Scorpion	Fully-tracked	7	6	1	Co-ax MG, Mine flail, Slow tank, Overloaded, Unreliable.
OQF 2 pdr gun	*24"/60cm*	*2*	*7*	*4+*	*No HE.*
Reconnaissance					
Universal Carrier	Half-tracked	0	0	0	Hull MG.
with Boys anti-tank rifle	*16"/40cm*	*2*	*4*	*5+*	*Hull-mounted*
with .5" MG	*16"/40cm*	*3*	*4*	*5+*	*Hull-mounted*
Indian Pattern Carrier	Half-tracked	0	0	0	Hull MG.
with Boys anti-tank rifle	*16"/40cm*	*2*	*4*	*5+*	*Hull-mounted*
with .5" MG	*16"/40cm*	*3*	*4*	*5+*	*Hull-mounted*
Daimler Dingo	Jeep	1	0	0	AA MG.
Humber LRC III	Jeep	0	0	0	Turret Front MG.
Boys anti-tank rifle	*16"/40cm*	*2*	*4*	*5+*	
Otter LRC I	Jeep	0	0	0	Turret Front MG.
Boys anti-tank rifle	*16"/40cm*	*2*	*4*	*5+*	
Armoured Cars					
Marmon Herrington III	Wheeled	1	0	0	Turret Front MG.
Boys anti-tank rifle	*16"/40cm*	*2*	*4*	*5+*	
with Captured weapon	*16"/40cm*	*2*	*6*	*4+*	*Hull-mounted*
Humber II or III	Wheeled	1	0	0	Co-ax MG.
Besa 15mm gun	*16"/40cm*	*3*	*5*	*5+*	
Daimler I	Wheeled	1	0	0	Co-ax MG.
OQF 2 pdr gun	*24"/60cm*	*2*	*7*	*4+*	*No HE.*
AEC I	Wheeled	4	2	0	Co-ax MG, Overloaded, Slow.
OQF 2 pdr gun	*24"/60cm*	*2*	*7*	*4+*	*No HE.*

GUN TEAMS

Weapon	Mobility	Range	ROF	Anti-tank	Firepower	Notes
Vickers HMG	Man-packed	24"/60cm	6	2	6	ROF 2 when pinned down.
Firing bombardments		40"/100cm	-	-	-	
Blacker Bombard	Man-packed	16"40cm	1	8	1+	Turntable.
ML 3" mortar	Man-packed	32"/80cm	-	2	6	Smoke bombardment.
ML 4.2" mortar	Light	48"/120cm	-	3	4+	Smoke bombardment.
Bofors 40mm gun	Immobile	24"/60cm	4	6	4+	Anti-aircraft, Turntable.
OQF 2 pdr gun	Medium	24"/60cm	3	7	4+	Gun shield, No HE, Turntable.
OQF 6 pdr gun	Medium	24"/60cm	3	10	4+	Gun shield, No HE.
OQF 17/25 pdr gun	Immobile	32"/80cm	2	13	3+	Gun shield, No HE.
OQF 25 pdr gun	Heavy	24"/60cm	2	9	3+	Gun shield, Smoke, Turntable.
Firing bombardments		80"/200cm	-	4	5+	Smoke bombardment.

INFANTRY TEAMS

Team	Range	ROF	Anti-tank	Firepower	Notes
Rifle team	16"/40cm	1	2	6	
Rifle/MG team	16"/40cm	2	2	6	
MG team	16"/40cm	3	2	6	
Light Mortar team	16"/40cm	1	1	4+	Can fire over friendly teams.
Anti-tank Rifle team	16"/40cm	1	4	5+	Tank Assault 4.
PIAT team	8"/20cm	1	10	5+	
Staff team			cannot shoot		Moves as a Heavy Gun team.

Additional Training and Equipment

Sticky bombs are rated as Improvised Tank Assault 3. Pioneer teams are rated as Tank Assault 4.

TRANSPORT TEAMS

Vehicle	Mobility	Armour Front	Armour Side	Armour Top	Equipment and Notes
Jeep	Jeep	-	-	-	
CMP 15 cwt or 3-ton truck	Wheeled	-	-	-	
Quad or Morris AA tractor	Wheeled	-	-	-	
White scout car	Jeep	1	0	0	
OP or Mortar Carrier	Half-tracked	0	0	0	
MMG Carrier	Half-tracked	0	0	0	HMG Carrier, Passenger-fired hull MG.

AIRCRAFT

Aircraft	Weapon	To Hit	Anti-tank	Firepower	Notes
Hurricane IIC	Cannon	3+	8	5+	
	Bombs	4+	5	2+	
Hurricane IID	Cannon	3+	11	4+	
Kittyhawk	MG	3+	6	5+	
	Bombs	4+	5	2+	

US ARSENAL

TANK TEAMS

Name *Weapon*	Mobility *Range*	Armour: Front *ROF*	Armour: Side *Anti-tank*	Armour: Top *Firepower*	Equipment and Notes
Tanks					
M3 or M3A1 Stuart	Fully-tracked	3	2	1	Co-ax MG, Hull MG, AA MG, Light tank.
M5 37mm gun	*24"/60cm*	*2*	*7*	*4+*	
M5A1 Stuart	Fully-tracked	4	2	1	Co-ax MG, Hull MG, AA MG, Light tank.
M6 37mm gun	*24"/60cm*	*2*	*7*	*4+*	*Stabiliser.*
M3 Lee	Fully-tracked	5	3	1	Co-ax MG, Cupola MG.
M5 37mm gun	*24"/60cm*	*3*	*7*	*4+*	*Stabiliser.*
M2 75mm gun	*32"/80cm*	*2*	*9*	*3+*	*Hull-mounted, Smoke, Stabiliser.*
with long M3 75mm gun	*32"/80cm*	*2*	*10*	*3+*	*Hull-mounted, Smoke, Stabiliser.*
M4 or M4A1 Sherman	Fully-tracked	6	4	1	Co-ax MG, Hull MG, .50 cal AA MG.
M3 75mm gun	*32"/80cm*	*2*	*10*	*3+*	*Smoke, Stabiliser.*
Support Weapons					
M4 81mm MMC	Half-tracked	1	0	0	
M1 81mm mortar	*40"/100cm*	*-*	*2*	*6*	*Hull mounted, Portee, Smoke bombardment.*
T30 75mm HMC	Half-tracked	1	0	0	
M1A1 75mm howitzer	*24"/60cm*	*2*	*6*	*3+*	*Hull mounted, Smoke.*
Firing bombardments	*64"/160cm*	*-*	*3*	*6*	*Smoke bombardment.*
M8 Scott HMC	Fully-tracked	3	2	0	.50 cal AA MG, Light tank.
M1A1 75mm howitzer	*24"/60cm*	*2*	*6*	*3+*	*Smoke.*
Firing bombardments	*64"/160cm*	*-*	*3*	*6*	*Smoke bombardment.*
Tank Destroyers					
M6 37mm GMC	Wheeled	-	-	-	
M3 37mm gun	*24"/60cm*	*3*	*7*	*4+*	
M3 75mm GMC	Half-tracked	1	0	0	
M1897 75mm gun	*32"/80cm*	*2*	*9*	*3+*	*Hull mounted, Smoke.*
M10 3in GMC	Fully-tracked	4	2	0	.50 cal AA MG.
M7 3in gun	*32"/80cm*	*2*	*12*	*3+*	*Slow traverse.*
Artillery					
T19 105mm HMC	Half-tracked	1	0	0	Awkward layout.
M2 105mm howitzer	*24"/60cm*	*1*	*9*	*2+*	*Hull mounted, Smoke.*
Firing bombardments	*72"/180cm*	*-*	*4*	*4+*	*Smoke bombardment.*
M7 Priest HMC	Fully-tracked	1	0	0	.50 cal AA MG.
M2A1 105mm howitzer	*24"/60cm*	*1*	*9*	*2+*	*Hull mounted, Smoke.*
Firing bombardments	*72"/180cm*	*-*	*4*	*4+*	*Smoke bombardment.*
Anti-aircraft					
M13 MGMC (twin .50 cal)	Half-tracked	1	0	0	Awkward layout.
M33 twin .50 cal machine-gun	*16"/40cm*	*5*	*4*	*5+*	*Anti-aircraft.*
T28E1 CGMC (37mm)	Half-tracked	0	0	0	Awkward layout.
T28E1 37mm combination mount	*24"/60cm*	*4*	*5*	*4+*	*Anti-aircraft.*
M15 CGMC (37mm)	Wheeled	1	0	0	Awkward layout.
M15 37mm combination mount	*24"/60cm*	*4*	*5*	*4+*	*Anti-aircraft.*

INFANTRY TEAMS

Team	Range	ROF	Anti-tank	Firepower	Notes
Carbine team	8"/20cm	1	1	6	Automatic rifles.
Rifle team	16"/40cm	1	2	6	Automatic rifles.
Rifle/MG team	16"/40cm	2	2	6	
SMG team	4"/10cm	3	1	6	Full ROF when moving.
Bazooka team	8"/20cm	1	10	5+	Tank assault 4.
Staff team			cannot shoot		Moves as a Heavy Gun team.

Additional Training and Equipment

Pioneer teams are rated as Tank Assault 3.

GUN TEAMS

Weapon	Mobility	Range	ROF	Anti-tank	Firepower	Notes
M2 .50 cal MG	Man-packed	16"/40cm	3	4	5+	
M1919 LMG team	Man-packed	16"/40cm	5	2	6	ROF 2 when pinned down.
M1917 HMG team	Man-packed	24"/60cm	6	2	6	ROF 2 when pinned down.
M2 60mm mortar	Man-packed	24"/60cm	2	1	3+	Can fire over friendly troops.
Firing bombardments		32"/80cm	-	1	6	
M1 81mm mortar	Man-packed	40"/100cm	-	2	6	Smoke bombardment.
4.2in Chemical mortar	Light	48"/120cm	-	3	4+	Smoke bombardment.
M2 .50 cal AA gun	Heavy	16"/40cm	4	4	5+	Anti-aircraft, Turntable.
M1 Bofors gun	Immobile	24"/60cm	4	6	4+	Anti-aircraft, Turntable.
M3 37mm gun	Light	24"/60cm	3	7	4+	Gun shield.
M1 57mm gun	Medium	24"/60cm	3	10	4+	Gun shield, No HE.
M1A1 75mm pack howitzer	Light	24"/60cm	2	6	3+	Smoke.
Firing bombardments		48"/120cm	-	3	6	
M2A1 105mm howitzer	Immobile	24"/60cm	1	9	2+	Gun shield, Smoke.
Firing bombardments		72"/180cm	-	4	4+	Smoke bombardment.

TRANSPORT TEAMS

Vehicle	Mobility	Armour Front	Armour Side	Armour Top	Equipment and Notes
Trucks					
Jeep	Jeep	-	-	-	Optional Passenger-fired AA MG or .50 cal AA MG
Dodge 3/4-ton or GMC 2 1/2-ton truck	Wheeled	-	-	-	
Armoured Personnel Carrier					
M2 or M3 half-track	Half-tracked	1	0	0	Optional Passenger-fired AA MG or .50 cal AA MG.
M3A1 armored car	Jeep	1	0	0	.50 cal AA MG, two Passenger-fired AA MG.
Recovery and Engineer Vehicles					
M31 TRV recovery vehicle	Fully-tracked	5	3	0	Recovery vehicle.
Bulldozer	Fully-tracked	-	-	-	Bulldozer, Very Slow.
Turretless M4 Sherman dozer	Fully-tracked	6	4	0	Bulldozer.

AIRCRAFT

Aircraft	Weapon	To Hit	Anti-tank	Firepower	Notes
P38 Lightning	Cannon	3+	7	5+	
	Bombs	4+	5	2+	
P40 Warhawk	MG	2+	6	5+	
	Bombs	4+	5	2+	

GE042 Panzer IV F_2

US030 M3 Lee

US002 M3A1 Stuart

GE104 Marder III (7.62cm)

US570 M2A1 105mm howitzer

GE885 Feldmarschall Erwin Rommel

GE160 Sd Kfz 10/5 (2cm)

US201 M3 half-track

AFRIKAKORPS

GEAB02 Afrikakorps 1500pt Army
GPS02 Afrikakorps Paint set
GBX02 Panzer III J Platoon
GBX03 Panzer IV F_1/F_2 Platoon
GBX04 Motorised Panzergrenadierkompanie
GBX05 8.8cm Flak36 Platoon
GBX08 Fallschirmjägerkompanie
GE011 Panzer II F
GE031 Panzer III G
GE032 Panzer III H
GE033 Panzer III J
GE034 Panzer III L, N
GE035 Panzer III M
GE041 Panzer IV E
GE042 Panzer IV F_1, F_2
GE044 Panzer IV G
GE070 Tiger I E (Tunisia)
GE104 Marder III (7.62cm)
GE113 Diana
GE148 Bison (15cm sIG)
GE149 15cm (Sf) Lorraine Schlepper
GE160 Sd Kfz 10/5 (2cm)
GE166 SdKfz 7/1 (Quad 2cm)
GE200 Sd Kfz 250/1, /10 (3.7cm) (early)
GE205 Sd Kfz 250/7 (early, 8cm)
GE207 Sd Kfz 250/8 (early, 7.5cm)
GE216 Sd Kfz 253 (StuG)
GE217 Sd Kfz 254 (Saurer)
GE240 Sd Kfz 251/1C, /10C (3.7cm)
GE244 Sd Kfz 251/2C (8cm)
GE252 Sd Kfz 251/9C (7.5cm)
GE270 Sd Kfz 7 (8t) tractor
GE272 Sd Kfz 11 (3t) tractor (x2 resin)
GE273 Sdkfz10 (1t) Tractor (x2 resin)
GE300 Sd Kfz 221 (MG/2.8cm)
GE301 Sd Kfz 222 (2cm)
GE302 Sd Kfz 223 (Command)
GE340 Sd Kfz 231 (8-Rad)
GE341 Sd Kfz 233 (7.5cm)
GE401 BMW & sidecar (Afrika) (x4)
GE409 Kübelwagen (x3 resin)
GE413 Kfz 15 (x2 resin)
GE426 Steyr Kfz 70 truck (x2 resin)
GE431 Opel Blitz 3-ton truck (x2 resin)
GE490 Opel Blitz radio truck
GE501 3.7cm PaK36 gun (x2)
GE502 3.7cm PaK36 gun (FJ x2)
GE510 5cm PaK38 gun (x2)
GE520 7.5cm PaK40 gun (x2)
GE525 7.62cm PaK36(r) gun (x2)
GE542 2cm FlaK38 gun (x2)
GE543 2cm FlaK38 gun (FJ x2)
GE550 8.8cm FlaK36 gun
GE560 7.5cm leIG18 gun (x2)
GE561 7.5cm LG40 (x2)
GE563 7.5cm GebG36 or 10.5cm LG40
GE571 10.5cm leFH18 how (x2)
GE590 15cm Nebelwerfer 41 (x3)
GE670 German Stowage
GE726 Pioneer Platoon
GE741 Company HQ (Afrika)
GE743 Panzergrenadier Platoon (Afrika)
GE744 Machine-gun Platoon (Afrika)
GE745 Mortar Platoon (Afrika)
GE749 Artillery HQ (Afrika)
GE762 Fallschirmjäger or Pionier Platoon
GE763 Fallschirmjäger Platoon (Battle worn)
GE764 Fallschirmjäger Machine-gun Platoon
GE765 Fallschirmjäger Mortar Platoon
GE885 Feldmarschall Erwin Rommel
GE886 Oberst Josef-Wilhelm Rettemeier
GE942 DAK Decals
DD004 DAK Dice
AT521 DAK Token Set

UNITED STATES

USAB01 US 1500pt Rifle Company
UPS01 US Paint Set
UBX01 Armored Rifle Platoon
UBX02 M4A1 Sherman Platoon
UBX03 Rifle Company
UBX04 M10 Tank Destroyer Platoon
US002 M3A1 Stuart
US005 M5A1 Stuart
US030 M3 Lee
US040 M4 Sherman
US042 M4A1 Sherman
US049 M4 Sherman Dozer
US101 M3 75mm GMC
US102 M10 3in GMC
US140 T30 75mm HMC
US141 T19 105mm HMC
US142 M8 Scott HMC
US143 M7 Priest HMC
US160 M13 MGMC
US161 T28E1 CGMC
US200 M2 half-track
US201 M3 half-track
US202 M4 81mm MMC
US300 M3A1 armored car
US409 Jeep and Trailer (x2 resin)
US411 Jeep (x3 resin)
US413 Dodge 3/4-ton truck (x2 resin)
US431 GMC 21/2-ton truck (x2 resin)
US500 M3 37mm gun (x2)
US501 M1 57mm gun (x2)
US541 M1 Bofors gun (x2)
US560 M8 75mm howitzer (Para x2)
US570 M2A1 105mm howitzer (x2)
US670 US Stowage
US701 Company HQ
US702 Rifle Platoon
US703 Armored Rifle Platoon
US704 Machine-gun Platoon
US705 Mortar Platoon
US706 Engineer Combat Platoon
US707 Armored Recon Platoon
US709 Artillery HQ
US710 Weapons Platoon
US711 Chemical Mortar Platoon
US716 Bazooka pack (x10)
US718 Armored Rifle Plt Dismounted MG's
US723 Parachute Rifle Platoon & HQ
US724 Parachute Machine-gun Platoon
US725 Parachute Mortar Platoon
US880 Major General Ernest N Harmon
US881 Staff Sergeant Cole 'Reb' Jackson
US883 Darby's Rangers
US940 US Decals
DD001 American Dice
AT525 American Token Set